All the

Countries

the

Americans

have ever

Invaded

ALL THE COUNTRIES THE AMERICANS HAVE EVER INVADED

MAKING FRIENDS AND INFLUENCING PEOPLE?

CHRISTOPHER KELLY
& STUART LAYCOCK

AMBERLEY

First published 2015

Amberley Publishing
The Hill, Stroud
Gloucestershire, GL5 4EP

www.amberley-books.com

British Library Cataloguing in Publication Data.
A catalogue record for this book is available from the British Library.

ISBN 978 1 4456 5176 7 (paperback)
ISBN 978 1 4456 5177 4 (ebook)

Typeset in 10pt on 12.5pt Sabon.
Typesetting and Origination by Amberley Publishing.
Printed in the UK.

Contents

Acknowledgments

Thanks to many institutions that have helped, particularly the IWM Duxford, the RAF Museum Hendon, the Cambridge-American Cemetery, the American Embassy in London, the Battleship *Texas*, the USS *Pampanito*, the West Point Museum, the Maryhill Museum of Art, Visit Spokane and the Whitehaven Archive in Cumbria.

Introduction

In the second half of the twentieth century simply no other country on earth had the kind of global military reach as that of the United States of America. And even in the twenty-first century, as China becomes increasingly self-confident, as Russia once again expands its ambitions and as countries like India start to become new global forces, the US is still unique.

The question of exactly how many countries America has invaded is something that is frequently discussed, often heatedly. This book sets out to answer this question and also answer the question of how Americans have interacted militarily with almost every country on earth. It's an amazing story that starts even before 1776 and is ongoing today.

To some, America is the great champion of freedom and democracy in the world. To others it is the enemy of freedom, an empire in all but name, prepared to use military force to extend the reach of American capitalism. To most, it has seemed a country that has done both good and bad. In that sense it is like most countries, but because of its global reach, where it has done good it has often done so on an epic scale (like the key role it played in defeating Hitler), but where it has done bad, its failings too have often been on a larger scale than those of many less-powerful countries.

Whether you love America or whether you loathe it, an option few people have is to ignore it entirely. And in that sense the story of its global military activity, of how it has interacted with just about every country, is of relevance to just about every person in the world.

The core of this book is American invasions and places where America has fought in conflict. However, because America has over the years run an extensive network of US military bases in independent countries and has also conducted an extensive programme of military assistance to other nations, this book will also look at those areas as a secondary focus.

Obviously at times the OSS, CIA and other US intelligence agencies have been involved in organising activities that would clearly fall into a military category. These organisations are not the prime focus of this book and espionage itself is not within its remit. We have, however, included some instances where these organisations have been involved in organising significant military activity.

The US has a long history of conducting secret operations and in recent years, as US forces have increasingly focused on fighting organisations like al-Qaeda, Al Shabaab and ISIS, the importance and prevalence of such operations has only grown. Particularly with more recent secret operations, it is often hard to say precisely what's going on without ending up in the realm of speculation and controversy. A broad, general book like this cannot adequately deal with such controversies where hard facts can be few and far between, and so we have restricted ourselves to mentioning such operations only when the evidence for them is most extensive and most generally agreed, and where they are also significant in the broad picture.

It is also beyond the remit of this book to speculate on the motivation behind some current US military activity. For instance, some may see US involvement in training troops from assorted African countries as peacekeepers as an innocent attempt to send African troops who know their continent better than Americans and Europeans to solve African problems. Others may interpret such US efforts as attempts to get Africans to fight wars as US proxies. It is another area of speculation and controversy with which a broad, general book like this cannot adequately deal.

We've used modern boundaries as the basis of the book because they are the most readily recognisable and easily accessible for many people.

A book this size can't possibly deal with every American military action and activity, and we've focused less on the widely known aspects of US military activity and more on the less-widely known aspects, we have also avoided studying US military history within the current boundaries of the United States (it's pretty obvious that the US has been fairly heavily militarily involved with that, and a lot of people are already broadly aware of bits of history like the American Revolution, the expansion of US power westwards to the Pacific, and the American Civil War) but we do hope the examples we've chosen to include do give a useful outline of US military history around the world.

Finally, a book like this obviously takes a long time to research and write and many significant events have happened during that period. We have tried to make sure, where major events happened after the relevant country chapter had already been written, that the relevant chapter has been updated, but if we have missed anything that should definitely have been included, then we can only apologise and say that we'll try to make sure that it is included when and if another edition of the book is published.

This book is a revised, re-edited and reworked version of the book published in the United States as *America Invades*.

Afghanistan

Quite a country to start with. But then Afghanistan is first alphabetically in the list of the world's countries and, frankly, the first country a lot of people would list if you asked them to name a country America has invaded.

Despite flirting with Imperial Germany and the Axis powers, Afghanistan ultimately remained neutral in both world wars. It was in the post-war decades that America started to have some involvement in Afghanistan. For instance, from 1949 until 1979 the US built the Helmand Valley Authority, which was modelled on the Tennessee Valley Authority. In 1963, King Zahir Shah of Afghanistan visited the United States, meeting President Kennedy and even touring Disneyland, and in 1964 the king introduced a new constitution that included a number of liberal measures.

The king, however, was toppled by a coup in 1973, orchestrated by his cousin Daoud, and Afghanistan was declared a republic. Then in 1978 Afghan Communists seized power in another coup and introduced a secular and Marxist-Leninist programme of action. This, in a strongly Muslim country, led to a spreading insurrection against the government.

Amidst increasing rebellion and Afghan Communist disarray, in December of 1979 the Soviets then launched their invasion. An army of over 120,000 was deployed to occupy the country. If the Soviets thought this would stabilise the country, they were very wrong. Very, very wrong. Instead, the presence of foreign invaders increased support for the insurrection, which led to increasingly brutal Soviet counter-measures, which obviously didn't win them many local friends either.

President Carter reacted to the Soviet invasion with a boycott of the 1980 Moscow Olympics, and after Ronald Reagan was elected in the autumn of 1980, US support for the Afghan resistance increased substantially. Amidst other measures, the CIA began shipping Stinger missiles to the mujahedeen to help counter Soviet air superiority that had caused the resistance so much trouble.

Rather than providing direct assistance to the mujahedeen, the United States chose generally to use Pakistan's intelligence service, ISI, as a proxy intermediary with them. While this may have saved some American lives, it also meant that few firm links between Americans and the mujahedeen were formed. Saudi Arabia also provided financial support and volunteers to the mujahedeen. One of the mujahedeen who emerged from obscurity in this conflict was a young Saudi called Osama bin Laden.

The ten-year-long war would cost the Soviets over 14,000 lives. However, it would cost Afghanistan much, much more. Over one million Afghans (mostly civilians) were killed, and the economy and infrastructure of the country were devastated.

By the end of it, however, the Afghan tribesmen, with outside help, had humbled a superpower. It was not the last time a superpower would find itself in major difficulties in Afghanistan.

When the Soviet occupation came to an end in 1989, Najibullah, the pro-Soviet ruler, managed to remain in power until 1992. In January 1992, all Russian aid to Afghanistan was cut off and mujahedeen warlords captured Kabul in April 1992. They were, however, soon fighting amongst themselves. The United States took little interest. With the Soviet withdrawal and the end of the Cold War, Afghanistan seemed to lack importance to American policymakers.

Later a new force arose to challenge the warring warlords. The Taliban, a fundamentalist Islamic movement which had links to the ISI, started taking ground from often fragmented and ineffective opposition. In 1996, they took Kabul. Najibullah, who had been sheltering with the UN, hoping for safe passage out of the country, was castrated, dragged through the streets behind a truck and then hung from a lamp post.

The Taliban instituted a harsh regime that denied many basic human rights and dealt brutally with opposition. Education for females was suspended. Singing, dancing and even kite-flying were banned. In March 2001, the Taliban destroyed two monumental, 1,500-year-old Bamiyan Buddhas.

Two days before the 9/11 attacks, the leader of the Northern Alliance, Ahmad Shah Massoud, was assassinated by al-Qaeda operatives posing as cameramen. And soon after 9/11, President George W. Bush visited the smoking ruins of Ground Zero in New York. He seized a bullhorn and gave an impromptu speech, 'I can hear you. The rest of the world hears you. And the people who knocked down these buildings will hear all of us soon.' To this day, the 9/11 memorial site remains a popular venue for enlistment and re-enlistment ceremonies for American serving military. Many of the first bombs that fell on Afghanistan were inscribed with 'FDNY' to commemorate those firemen killed on 9/11.

The Taliban had won themselves very few friends in the international community. This and the sympathy generated by the 9/11 attacks helped the United States gain considerable support from its traditional allies for the invasion of Afghanistan. Over twenty-five different nations would contribute troops, equipment or services to Operation Enduring Freedom.

The first covert team inside Afghanistan, code-named Jawbreaker, arrived on 27 September 2001. The CIA operatives in Jawbreaker carried $3 million in $100 bills to distribute to Afghan warlords. Nearly £1.7 million of supplies were also airdropped to the tribal leaders of the Northern Alliance.

On 7 October 2001, the air campaign against Taliban-controlled Afghanistan began. F-14 and F/A-18 strike fighters were launched from the decks of two American supercarriers, *Carl Vinson* and *Enterprise*. A combination of massive air power and special forces from the US (and other nations), meant the Northern Alliance soon looked set to eradicate the Taliban as a military force. Rapidly, US Marines would join the battle as well.

Kabul was captured on 13 November 2001. The first American casualty in Afghanistan was Johnny Michael Spann, a CIA operative and former Marine, who was killed in a Taliban prisoner-of-war uprising on 25 November 2001.

From 12 to 17 December 2001, the battle of Tora Bora raged. The United States deployed fewer than 100 US Special Forces (Delta) along with about 1,000 Afghan militia. Air strikes were called in, and Gator cluster mines were dropped on the snowy passes of Tora Bora. Around 16 December, Bin Laden managed to escape from Tora Bora across the mountains with hundreds of al-Qaeda followers. At the end of the year, Hamid Karzai was sworn in as the president of the Afghan Transitional Administration and the UN Security Council established ISAF, the International Security Assistance Force.

The Taliban had not, however, been eliminated. After the initial shock of the invasion, they regrouped and switched from fighting as the army of a government to fighting as a guerrilla army, in particular making devastating use of roadside bombs (IEDs).

The war in Afghanistan is far too big a subject for just one chapter of this book. The war has been long, tough and complex, and it is impossible to cover the campaigns, battles and combat in the detail they deserve here, so we will mention just a few points in this continuing story.

In 2003, the invasion of Iraq (Operation Iraqi Freedom) diverted US military strength and resources and political attention from the campaign in Afghanistan. On 11 August 2003, NATO assumed peacekeeping duties in Afghanistan.

The next year in April, Pat Tillman, a former NFL player with the Arizona Cardinals, was killed in a friendly fire incident in Afghanistan.

In 2005, Hamid Karzai became the first democratically elected president in Afghanistan's history. That same year, on a mission in Afghanistan, Marcus Lutrell became the lone survivor of the worst debacle in the history of the US Navy SEALs. The same code of Pashtunwali that harboured Osama bin Laden in Afghanistan helped to save Lutrell's life. In some ways, Lutrell's fate paralleled that of Dr Brydon, except the Englishman never got a movie deal.

President George W. Bush ordered a 'silent surge' in the autumn of 2006, raising US troop levels from 21,000 to 31,000 to counter a deteriorating security situation on the ground.

In 2007, Bush's Secretary of Defense Robert Gates increased the length of military tours in Afghanistan from twelve months to fifteen. Suicide bombings continued. In the autumn of 2008, President-elect Obama interviewed Gates. Gates asked if Obama would go after violent extremists wherever they lived. Obama replied, 'Yes, I'm no peacenik.' Obama had campaigned on the pledge to raise the US commitment in Afghanistan – a conflict that his party approved of in distinction to the war in Iraq.

The following year, Obama appointed General Stanley McChrystal to head up the US forces in Afghanistan. McChrystal was an expert in counter-insurgency who had successfully implemented the surge in Iraq and was credited with helping to track down and kill al-Qaeda's leader in Iraq – al-Zarqawi. In December 2009, Obama announced an additional 30,000 troop surge into Afghanistan, raising American total strength to just over 100,000.

Obama's presidency also saw a massive expansion of drone attacks on the other side of the Afghan border in Pakistan (*see* Pakistan).

In 2011, a drawdown of US forces committed to Afghanistan began. On 2 May 2011, the raid that killed Osama bin Laden in Abbottabad (Operation Neptune Spear) was launched from a US airbase in Jalalabad, Afghanistan. 6 August of that same year, however, proved to be the deadliest day for the United States in Afghanistan when Taliban forces managed to shoot down a CH-47 Chinook helicopter, killing thirty Americans.

At the time of this writing, more than 2,000 Americans have been killed while serving in Afghanistan and over 19,000 have been wounded. Many soldiers from other countries and many thousands of Afghans have also been killed or wounded. The war in Afghanistan, spanning two administrations and over twelve years, is now the longest war in American history. The difficult terrain, Afghan society's cultural and ethnic complexity, its reaction to foreigners, the role of drugs in subsidizing the Taliban and spreading corruption in official circles, and Taliban links inside Pakistan have all played a major role in making America's experience so frustrating.

The ISAF mission was declared completed at the end of 2014. At the beginning of 2015 a smaller non-combat mission called Resolute Support started work assisting Afghan government forces. The future of Afghanistan currently looks uncertain.

Albania

America and Albania are both very big on eagles as national symbols, but the Albanian eagle does have one more head than the American one.

After the Second World War, Albania was largely closed off to the outside world by its somewhat eccentric Communist ruler, Enver Hoxha. Obviously the Cold War didn't do much to encourage Western tourists to visit Communist countries, but Albania under Hoxha was a bit in a league of its own, which is a shame because it's an interesting place with an interesting history, and America played a part in it.

In 1912, after the Ottomans were defeated in the Balkan Wars, Albania became independent. What euphoria there was, however, wore off pretty fast, as Europe collapsed into the chaos of the First World War and Albania ended up fragmented and fought over. The United States got involved with the fighting in Albanian waters, with American subchasers (small boats aimed, not surprisingly, at chasing submarines) playing a brave role in the 1918 Battle of Durazzo (named after the Albanian port city of Durrës – Durazzo in Italian). By the end of the war, Albania had assorted victorious Allied troops controlling big chunks of it.

Between the two world wars, the key figure in Albanian politics was King Zog. King Zog was purported to have survived no less than fifty-five assassination attempts, including one in Vienna where he saved himself by returning fire with the revolver he habitually carried.

Zog's days, however, were numbered. In April 1939, even before the actual start of the Second World War, the Italian army seized control of Albania. The Second World War was almost as chaotic in Albania as the First World War had been, and into the middle of it all boldly strode the Americans of the OSS (Office of Strategic Services, the forerunner to the CIA).

In 1943, after the Allied invasion of Italy, OSS agents, following in the footsteps of the British Strategic Operations Executive, or SOE (who were tasked by Winston Churchill to 'set Nazi-occupied Europe ablaze' and about whom you will read more in this volume), were dispatched to Albania. At the time, Enver Hoxha was leading a partisan band of Communists. The Albanian Balli Kombëtar (National Front), on the other hand, was anti-Communist but was also accused of collaborating with the Nazis. A third Albanian group, the Legalitetei (Legality Party), sought the return of King Zog but weren't as interested in fighting.

The main goal of the American OSS and the British SOE allies was the defeat of Hitler and his allies, so this left them with little choice but to assist the Hoxha-led partisans and to hope for the best. The idea was, of course, that 'the enemy of my enemy is my friend' which as anybody who's studied history at all, or indeed, experienced life will tell you, does sometimes produce the hoped for results – other times it all gets a bit complicated.

The OSS supplied food, ammunition and advisors to the Albanian partisans, and they called in air strikes from the USAAF to help Hoxha's forces. Captain Tom Stefan was an

Albanian-American from Laconia, New Hampshire. Fluent in Albanian, he was recruited by the OSS and served as a direct liaison with Enver Hoxha.

Two famous actors were involved in helping the Albanians fight the Nazis. The British actor, Anthony Quayle, was with the SOE. Quayle would later star in *Guns of Navarone* and *Lawrence of Arabia*. The American actor, Sterling Hayden, gave up a Hollywood career to become a US Marine captain and member of the maritime division of the OSS. A skilled captain, Hayden piloted boats laden with American supplies from Italy to Albania. In the movie *The Godfather*, Hayden played the role of Captain McCluskey – the crooked cop who gets an extra dollop of marinara in the forehead from Michael Corleone.

After southern Italy was occupied by the Allies in 1943 and the Italian government surrendered (leaving many desperate Italian solders trapped between the Germans and the partisans), airbases in Italy were used to bomb southern Axis targets, such as the vital Ploesti oil fields in Romania. Inevitably, therefore, Allied planes sometimes went down in Albania and Yugoslavia. On 8 November 1943, a Dakota C-53 transport plane carrying thirty Americans, including thirteen army flight nurses, crash-landed in Albanian territory. Albanian Communist partisans helped them make their way back to Allied territory.

On 17 November 1944, after heavy fighting, Tirana, the capital of Albania, was liberated from German occupation by Albanian partisans with the assistance of Allied air support. Also, several German divisions, which could otherwise have fought the Allies in Italy or France, were pinned down in Albania. That night, OSS forces raised the flag at the American legation in Tirana for the first time in years.

But this wasn't to be the end of America's secret war in Albania. Although, in the next round of it, the US was on the opposite side to Hoxha and his Communists. Things hadn't quite turned out how America had hoped, and after the war in 1949, the CIA tried to foment a resistance movement in Albania with a ragtag army of exiled royalists and anti-Communists.

Over a period of about three and a half years, the exiles were sent into Albania by land, sea and air. In one operation, a ship was launched from Malta with nine Albanians in a commando-type raid. Three were killed immediately and the rest were rounded up. At the end, there was little to show for the effort, apart from hundreds dead or in prison. How much success the operation could have had is uncertain, but information given to the Russians by the notorious British mole Kim Philby, and perhaps information from others, meant that too often Hoxha's forces had been tipped off before the infiltrators arrived in Albania.

After remaining a fan of Stalin, even when the Soviet Union denounced the moustachioed Uncle Joe, and after a flirtation with Maoist China, Enver Hoxha died of natural causes in 1985. Communism officially collapsed in 1992, seven years after his death.

In 1997, as chaos and unrest swept across Albania in the wake of a collapsed savings scheme, US Marines were sent into Albania to secure American property and rescue US citizens.

Two years later, in 1999, American forces were in Albania again. With the Kosovo crisis erupting just next door, Albania became a key area of American and NATO interest with American troops, aircraft and helicopters arriving in large quantities. Kosovar refugees who had fled across the border needed help, and there was the possibility of a ground offensive into Kosovo if the Serbs did not give in. Indeed, before a peace deal was signed, US General Wesley Clark already had troops repairing the main road from the Albanian capital Tirana to Kukës, near the Yugoslav border, to ease the passage of invasion troops and US heavy tanks. Other Americans were also there on a rather different basis – members of the Atlantic Brigade of the Kosovo Liberation Army went to fight the Serbian forces in Kosovo.

More recently, Albania has sent troops to Afghanistan, and today Albania is a NATO member. Among other military links, the New Jersey National Guard is partnered with Albania.

Algeria

Algeria is a big country. In fact, it's huge – the tenth largest country in the world. Algeria's capital is, not surprisingly, Algiers. Algeria is an ancient land with a long and culturally rich history. Among its early glories are the amazing Tassili n'Ajjer rock paintings, the product of a prehistoric culture that emerged when the Sahara was green. Yep, surprising but true.

Somehow Algeria is not a country many people would associate with American attacks, but it's definitely seen a couple.

During part of its long history, Algeria, like much of North Africa, became a home for the Barbary pirates. And it was big, big business. From the sixteenth to the nineteenth century, these raiders are said to have captured and enslaved over one million Europeans. That's a lot of Europeans.

And it wasn't just Europeans suffering. Algerian pirates captured their first American ship in 1785. And America wasn't happy about it. Not happy at all.

American independence from Britain obviously had its advantages, but one of its disadvantages was that merchant ships from the United States would no longer be under the protection of the powerful Royal Navy. In May 1794, War Secretary Henry Knox decided it was time to do something about the Barbary pirates, and he appointed Philadelphian Joshua Humphreys as 'Constructor of the Navy of the United States'. Humphreys was a gifted naval architect who designed the 44-gun frigates (which could, in fact, carry over fifty guns), such as the USS *Constitution*. These were faster and more powerful than their European counterparts. By contrast, a typical British frigate had just thirty-two to thirty-six guns. Amazingly, considering how old it is, the USS *Constitution* is still afloat today.

Despite having ships under construction, however, the US government was still cautious at that stage about picking a fight with the then fairly formidable Barbary pirates, preferring instead to pay ransoms and tribute. In 1795, to ransom 115 sailors, America paid $1 million in cash, supplies and a frigate to the Dey of Algiers alone, a staggering amount at the time. Assorted treaties with Algiers and the other Barbary pirates followed, but the problem never seemed to go away permanently.

Thomas Jefferson, understandably in this situation, eventually got fed up with paying tribute, and when in 1801 the pasha of Tripoli (*see* Libya) rather unwisely declared war on the United States, Jefferson sent ships and troops against the pasha's forces in the First Barbary War. America won that war, while Algiers wisely kept out of it. Despite that, the US was still in a position where the Treaty of Peace and Amity of 1805 obliged the US to a pay a ransom of $60,000 to the Dey of Algiers for each sailor. That's a lot of money.

In 1815, however, having dealt with the rather urgent matter of the War of 1812, America was determined that things were going to change between Algiers and the United States. Stephen Decatur of the US Navy commanded a squadron in the Second Barbary War, also known, reasonably enough, as the Algerian War since it was basically America versus Algiers. It wasn't much of a war, really. Decatur managed to capture the Algerian flagship *Mashuda* with 406 sailors aboard. Soon after that, the American ships turned up off Algiers and, after assorted threats, pretty much dictated terms to Algiers. There was to be no tribute ever again; there were to be no American slaves ever again. Oh ... and Decatur wanted an immediate $10,000 compensation payment.

During the First World War, Americans were operating in the waters off Algeria again. In 1918, the USS *Lydonia*, which was basically a converted yacht, was helping escort a convoy from Bizerte in Tunisia to Gibraltar. Off the Algerian coast, she and a British warship got into a battle with the German submarine UB-70, which seems to have been sunk.

In November of 1942, the US returned to Algeria. In the period after the Barbary Wars, France had become the colonial power in Algeria (or Algérie, as they put it), which meant that, after the German invasion of France, it was under the control of the pro-Nazi Vichy regime.

Operation Torch was launched with the British to invade Vichy-controlled parts of north-west Africa, so that, with the British advancing from the east, the Axis troops in the region would be squeezed between two Allied forces. The operation posed many risks as there were nearly 120,000 French troops in North Africa and US commanders weren't at all sure what kind of fight they might put up.

Major General Fredendall led US forces that landed near Oran and Algiers. Their mission was to push on into Tunisia as rapidly as possible into the rear of Rommel's forces that had been threatening British-held Egypt and the Suez Canal.

On 7 November 1942, US paratroopers in thirty-nine C-47s flew 1,100 miles from airfields in Cornwall to two airfields near Oran. It was the first American airborne operation of the war, and it wasn't a great start. In fact, it was a near total disaster. Many of the planes got lost. Others were hit by anti-aircraft fire. Some landed in Spanish Morocco where the men would be interned for three months.

The next day, on 8 November 1942, American troops landed near Algiers. They had hoped the French would surrender immediately to troops from America's oldest ally. In fact, the battle with the French lasted just over three days. Resistance was strongest near Oran where the Big Red One (the 1st Infantry Division of the US Army) suffered more than 300 casualties. After the battle, though, Oran, a deep-water port, was rapidly transformed into a vast Allied supply depot. By 12 November, thanks to a deal with Admiral Darlan, all Algeria, as well as Morocco, was under Allied control. Allied forces would soon be making a push eastwards into Tunisia.

Brigadier General Theodore Roosevelt Jr was among those leading forces in this invasion of Algeria. The filmmaker Darryl Zanuck, who would later make *The Longest Day*, also landed in Algeria with American troops, serving as a colonel in the Signal Corps.

The Allies' deal with French Admiral Darlan meant putting him in charge of civil administration throughout North Africa. This then inevitably ignited a political firestorm of criticism in the United States over the question of working with a Vichy representative and collaborator. The problem, however, was removed finally (very finally) by Darlan's assassination at his headquarters in Algiers by a young monarchist on 24 December 1942.

After a bloody seven-year civil war, Algeria gained its independence from France in 1962.

In October 1980, after a devastating earthquake in the country, US Air Force planes rushed in hundreds of tons of humanitarian aid. US Navy ships now call on ports in Algeria on a regular basis, and the United States has developed a number of other military links with Algeria, including bilateral exercises.

Andorra

A tiny country with some beautiful mountains and places to ski, located in the Pyrenees between Spain and France, Andorra has only a tiny army, basically used for ceremonial duties. It did, however, declare war on Germany in 1914. What's more, because it was so small, nobody bothered to include it in any peace deal at the end of the First World War, so technically it went on fighting the First World War decades longer than anybody else.

Clearly, if they wanted to, the mighty US armed forces could swallow little Andorra in an afternoon (or less) but they never have. Having said all that, strange as it seems, there are stories of an American connection in two attempts to take control of Andorra, both in 1934.

1933 had been a bad year for Andorra. The two princes of Andorra – who, because of Andorra's vulnerable position squeezed between Spain and France, are always the Bishop of Urgell and the President of France – had, unusually, intervened in Andorra's internal affairs over an election dispute. French gendarmes had ultimately been sent in as well. There had been resentment among some Andorrans.

Perhaps because of this, someone may have thought 1934 would be a good year to offer the Andorrans a new ruler. In March 1934, it was reported that the Council of Andorra had received a letter from an unidentified American, originally from Chicago, offering to buy Andorra. There was wild speculation (well, some speculation) in the press about the identity of the mystery American and some suggested Samuel Insull, a former utilities operator from Chicago who had fled to Greece after the collapse of his utilities empire and some questions over the possibility of things like fraud. If the offer was real, the Andorrans seem to have rejected it.

Meanwhile in late 1933, one Boris Skossyreff, a man with a very varied past, turned up in Andorra, and at his side was an American divorcee with whom he'd been living, one Florence Marmon, ex-wife of an automobile magnate from Indiana. In December 1993, Boris acquired Andorran citizenship, and in May 1934, he presented his plans for reform of the government of Andorra. Then at some stage, he declared himself King of Andorra, allegedly with some local support but apparently definitely not with the support of the Bishop of Urgell, who sent the Spanish police to get him and end his brief reign. It seemed unlikely that American Florence was ever going to be Queen of Andorra.

During the Second World War, Andorra stayed neutral and it became a major destination for escaping Allied airmen who had been shot down, including some Americans. Not all, though, made it to Andorra. Some sadly died of cold and exhaustion in the Pyrenees.

Angola

There's a little extra bit of Angola in the north, the Cabinda enclave, which is separated from the rest of Angola by a strip of the Democratic Republic of the Congo. Apparently Angola gets its name from the *ngola*, the ruler of the Kingdom of Ndongo.

Some of Angola used to be major slave-trading territory, so not surprisingly, the first American military involvement with Angola was when the US Navy's Africa squadron was sent to the area in the nineteenth century to try to suppress slavery. In fact, US ships even had a base at the time in Angola. In 1859, their depot was moved from Cape Verde to St Paul de Loando. Two areas of particular concern for the US Navy in Angola were Cabinda itself, situated at the mouth of the Congo, and Ambriz. For instance, in 1850, the USS *John Adams* and the USS *Perry* between them seized three ships at Ambriz. Two ships were seized at Cabinda in 1845, another two in 1846, one in 1859, and another in 1861. It wouldn't be right to claim that the navy's efforts did huge damage to the slave trade, but they did some.

But the US Navy didn't just concern itself with slavery. In March 1860, Commander Thomas W. Brent sent marines and seamen ashore from the USS *Marion*, in traditional fashion, to protect American property at Kissembo in Angola.

Angola was for a long time a Portuguese colony. In the second half of the twentieth century, oil extraction became a major industry, and by 1973 it had replaced coffee as Angola's biggest export. Then in 1974, a leftist military coup in Portugal signalled the beginning of the end of the Portuguese Empire, and in 1975 Angola became independent. Tragically, what followed was twenty-seven years of civil war as different factions, with the support of assorted outside countries, fought for control of the country. The US played its own secret and semi-secret role in supporting first the FNLA (National Front for the Liberation of Angola) and then UNITA (National Union for the Total Independence of Angola) against the MPLA (Popular Movement for the Liberation of Angola) that was supported by Cuba and the Soviet Union. The Clark Amendment to the US Arms Export Control Act of 1976 was supposed to restrict aid from America to warring factions in Angola, but the amendment was repealed in 1985, much to UNITA's delight.

The 1990s saw occasional periods of peace and others of renewed fighting. In 1992, the US Air Force, as part of Operation Provide Transition, flew demobilised soldiers home in Angola. However, it was only in 2002, after Jonas Savimbi, UNITA's long-time leader, was killed that the civil war finally came to an end.

In recent years, relations have become friendlier between Angola and the United States. In 2009, Hillary Clinton declared Angola a 'strategic partner' of the United States.

Antigua and Barbuda

Antigua's highest peak used to be called Boggy Peak (elevation 1,319 feet). Not anymore. In 2009, the highest peak on this popular Caribbean island was renamed Mount Obama.

In 1798, the US ship, the *Retaliation* under Lieutenant William Bainbridge was cruising off Antigua when it came across two French warships. Unfortunately for Bainbridge and the *Retaliation*, America was then in a sort of quasi-war with France, and the ship was captured thus demonstrating that sometimes you have to be just as careful about quasi-wars as the non-quasi type.

However, for most of the colonial period, Antigua and Barbuda were controlled by the British, and therefore much of US military involvement with the islands and islanders has involved them as well. During war between Britain and the US, assorted ships from Antigua and Barbuda were a target for American warships. In 1814, the American privateer *Frolic* captured the schooner *Encouragement* carrying sugar, molasses and rum from Antigua to Nova Scotia. And in October 1814, US Marines assisted in the capture of the British ship *Mary* by the US sloop *Peacock* off Barbuda.

Since then, of course, US warships have visited the islands on a more friendly basis, and during the Second World War, Antigua featured in the 1940 destroyers-for-bases deal in which, in return for the right to establish military bases in assorted territories then controlled by Britain, America gave destroyers to the British to help fight the Germans.

In Antigua, the US built a naval air station at Crabbs Peninsula and built Coolidge Air Force Base on the other side of Parham Harbour. During the war, air transport and anti-submarine patrols were flown from Coolidge. The closure of wartime bases, however, was not the end of US forces in Antigua. For instance, America kept a missile-tracking facility there.

Antigua and Barbuda became an independent state in 1981. In 1983, Antigua and Barbuda offered military and political support to the invasion of Grenada. Since then, the US has developed assorted military links with the islands, including exercises.

Argentina

The United States and Argentina are two great American nations, but with a long geographic distance between them and, on occasions, quite a big political distance as well.

Argentina wasn't exactly the area of most major interest to the United States in the nineteenth century, but that didn't stop them sending in the marines when things looked dodgy for US interests ashore.

In October 1833, marines and seamen from Commodore Woolley's squadron landed in the capital, Buenos Aires, on a mission to protect US citizens and property. Not for the last time. In February 1852 more US Marines arrived in the same location and on the same mission, though this lot were from Commodore McKeever's squadron.

No big break this time because just a few months later, in September of the same year, the US sloop *Jamestown* was offloading marines into Buenos Aires to protect American property. Then again in 1890, as political unrest hit again, the schooner USS *Tallapoosa* turned up in Buenos Aires to protect American diplomats.

It was during the twentieth century, however, that the US was to take a closer interest in Argentina. The US had attempted to encourage Argentina into the First World War, but in the Second World War, tensions between Argentina and the US really rose.

Argentina had a large German population, and because of that and other reasons, it just wouldn't declare war on Germany and Japan. Argentine neutrality angered President Roosevelt who had expected more support after his introduction of a so-called Good Neighbour Policy towards Latin America. Argentina's distant but very powerful and rather insistent neighbour put huge pressure on the country, and finally, in March 1945, Argentina declared war. However, the dispute left a sour taste on both sides, and stories of Nazis in Argentina after the war didn't exactly improve the American opinion of the country.

However, after the war, links between the United States and Argentinian military did develop as Argentina eventually began to be seen in US government circles as a bulwark against Communism. A coup put a military junta in power in Argentina in 1976, and what followed was the so-called Dirty War involving appalling human rights abuses as the junta's forces sought to crush left-wing opposition. America did eventually impose restrictions on its military co-operation with the junta, but the question of how much was known by some members of US intelligence and the US government remains.

The 1982 conflict involving the UK and Argentina in the Falkland Islands (or the Malvinas, as Argentina calls them) posed a bit of a dilemma for the United States as it was aligned to both the UK via NATO and Argentina via the OAS (Organisation of American States). Jeane Kirkpatrick, US ambassador to the United Nations, declared that Latin America had become 'the most important place in the world for us.' However, President Ronald Reagan clearly tilted towards Britain, which was led at the time by the 'Iron Lady', Margaret Thatcher. In spite of American neutrality, the United States provided surveillance, satellite intelligence and significant supplies that helped Britain win back the islands.

In 1991, Argentina did send ships to help free Kuwait, and Argentine forces have taken part alongside US forces in assorted exercises. But in recent years, some tensions have arisen again between the Argentinian and US governments.

Armenia

A nation with a long and fascinating Christian tradition, Armenia is a land of the Caucasus. It is also famous these days as a land with a Kardashian connection.

During the period after the First World War, the American Military Mission in Armenia toured the area, including Yerevan, the capital of Armenia, before returning and reporting to the US government. America also put significant effort into relieving the suffering of the Armenians in the post-war years.

Armenia eventually became part of the Soviet Union and consequently received some attention from America during the Cold War. On 20 November 1956, a U-2 plane piloted by Francis Gary Powers flew over Armenia observing targets there.

In 1988, though, USAF personnel flew into Armenia for a very different reason, helping rush in aid after a devastating earthquake hit the area.

Armenia became independent again in 1991. In 1992, America opened an embassy in Yerevan and in recent years, the US has started to develop military links with Armenia. Armenians served alongside US troops in Iraq and Afghanistan and the US has given millions of dollars of communications equipment to Armenia's Peacekeeping Battalion.

The Kansas National Guard is partnered with Armenia.

Australia

So what have Americans been up to down under? More than you might think, as it happens.

Americans played a significant role in the Eureka Blockade Revolution of 1854 when miners rebelled against the authorities. Among the best-trained and best-equipped of the rebels were the so-called First Rifles, or Californian Rifles, and the Independent California Rangers Revolver Brigade. The American rebels included experienced veterans of the Mexican-American War.

During the Second World War, almost a million US service personnel passed through Australia. That's a lot of military personnel. The first American forces arrived in Australia as early as December 1941 and were there, among several other reasons, to help the Australians defend themselves against any attempt by the advancing Japanese to invade Australia.

But Australia rapidly became a major base for training US troops before they were sent to the battlefront and a major destination for US troops' rest and recuperation. It was also a major base for the US Army Air Forces (USAAF) conducting combat missions against the Japanese forces. The Fifth Air Force established its headquarters in Australia in 1942, and large numbers of US aircraft operated out of Australian bases. For example, on 5 April 1942, B-26 Marauders took off from bases in Queensland, Australia, refuelled at Port Moresby, and hit Japanese targets at Rabaul. In May 1942 a B-17 flying out from an Australian base spotted a Japanese invasion fleet at the start of the Battle of the Coral Sea.

Maintaining the shipping lifeline between the US West Coast, Hawaii and Australia was vital for Allied continuation of the war in the Pacific. When Douglas MacArthur withdrew from the Philippines, he retreated to Australia and set up his headquarters in Melbourne. After the decisive battle of Midway, the Allies began to advance in the Pacific using Australia as their launch pad and supply depot.

Generally, Americans and Australians got along well. Sometimes, very, very well. Over 12,000 Australian women became American war brides. But tensions arose occasionally as well. On 26 November 1942, the so-called Battle of Brisbane erupted as US and Australian troops brawled.

In the period after the Second World War, military links between Australia and the United States remained strong. Both countries became members of SEATO (South East Asia Treaty Organisation) and ANZUS (Australia, New Zealand, United States Security Treaty), and the US conducts regular exercises, training and visits with the Australians. Australia sent troops to fight in Vietnam, and more recently, it has sent troops to both Iraq and Afghanistan.

The US has had facilities in Australia after the war, in particular the Nurrungar (now closed) and Pine Gap bases. Both bases have been linked to tracking missiles, but some people have also suspected involvement with a range of other military and intelligence roles. The Pacific is becoming an area of increasing strategic interest for the United States, and in 2011, President Obama announced he eventually wants 2,500 US Marines to be located in Australia. Hundreds have already been sent, and the Australia government is building new facilities at Robertson Barracks and the Royal Australian Air Force base in Darwin to cope with the increasing numbers rotating through.

Austria

Ah, Austria, land of (among many other things) Mozart, mountains, Viennese waltzes and assorted other items which have Viennese in the name. Austria is still known to many around the world because of the classic American movie *The Sound of Music*.

America did fight Austria-Hungary during the First World War, however, most of this fighting took place in the mountains of northern Italy. In 1938, as featured in, yes, *The Sound of Music*, Adolf Hitler (himself born in Austria) sent troops into Austria to join it to Germany. Inevitably, therefore, as the Second World War raged, targets inside Austria were to receive a lot of attention from the USAAF. Oil refineries and aircraft factories in the vicinity of Vienna were regular targets for US bombers.

Soon, Americans would be operating on the ground inside Austria as well. For instance, Lieutenant Colonel Franklin Lindsay of the OSS had parachuted in to work with the Slovene partisans in 1944, and along with them, he had attempted to advance into southern Austria. Other OSS teams were dropped into Austria itself.

In the last weeks of the war, as General Dwight Eisenhower ordered American troops to halt their advance into Czechoslovakia (*see* Czech Republic), US troops pushed south into Austria. At the same time, US troops were also pushing towards Austria from the south, from Italy, and on 4 May 1945, the two thrusts met.

By the end of the war, in addition to the corridor in Western Austria linking with Italy, US forces held a big chunk of north-west Austria, including Linz and (yes, it's Mozart and *The Sound of Music* again) the beautiful city of Salzburg (liberated on the same day as the link-up with troops from the Italian front).

Austria's capital, Vienna, was, and remains, the home of the famous white Lipizzaner stallions. Colonel Alois Podhajsky was the head of the Lipizzaner School and a former Olympic equestrian. He removed the horses from the capital and brought them to the attention of the US Army and General George S. Patton Jr, begging for their protection. Patton, a fellow Olympian (modern pentathlon, Stockholm 1912) and cavalryman, responded and enthusiastically offered to make the horses 'wards of the US Army'.

Austria was divided into four Allied occupying zones after the war, and Americans held Salzburg and Upper Austria. Vienna itself was also divided amongst the four powers. Austria regained its independence in 1955 and was declared a permanently neutral country.

During the Cold War, this neutrality and Austria's strategic location between east and west made it a popular destination for espionage agents from both sides.

Austria today remains neutral but has granted overflight rights for Operation Enduring Freedom and Operation New Dawn. Austrian troops have trained alongside US troops, and have served alongside each other in Kosovo.

Azerbaijan

With a coast on the Caspian Sea, Azerbaijan is an oil-rich nation in the Caucasus.

After the Russian Revolution in 1917, like people of other nations in the area, the Azeris wanted to break away from Russian control and form their own country. However, President Wilson wasn't keen on this (though he did say nice things about the Azeri delegation he met), preferring instead that the Azeris form part of a confederation with other peoples in the area.

Ultimately, considerable fighting took place in the area in the period around the end of the First World War. Of the Allies, the British were more involved in the fighting than the Americans, though the American Military Mission to Armenia did, during its investigations, travel to Baku, the capital of Azerbaijan.

Eventually Azerbaijan became part of the Soviet Union.

During the Second World War, Baku played a key role in US efforts to aid the Soviets against the Nazis. America sent supplies and aircraft up through Iran and through Baku, which at that stage was part of the Soviet Union.

During the Cold War, American-made aircraft were in the sky over Baku once again. For instance, on 20 November 1956, a U-2 flown by Francis Gary Powers flew over Baku.

In 1991, Azerbaijan became independent again.

Military links between the Azeris and the United States increased after 2001. Azerbaijan became a vital route for US military aircraft and supplies being taken in and out of Afghanistan. Azerbaijan has taken part in operations alongside America in Afghanistan and in Kosovo and Iraq as well. US and Azeri military personnel have shared co-operative training. The Oklahoma National Guard is partnered with Azerbaijan.

The Bahamas

Ah, the Bahamas. Where Christopher Columbus made his first landfall in the New World all those centuries ago. Widely known as a holiday destination. Not quite so widely known, admittedly, as a destination for American military activity, but actually the country still has an interesting past in that respect.

For a start, in the early eighteenth century, Anglo-American pirates operated out of the Bahamas, and both British and American ships set out to hunt them. Colonel William Rhett, a plantation owner in the Province of Carolina, fitted out and led ships in an attempt to stop pirates operating. By 1730, a concerted campaign by the authorities had largely forced the pirates out.

But the Revolutionary War was to see plenty of American military activity in the area. On 3 March 1776, Commodore Esek Hopkins, in the first amphibious assault in US military history, landed marines and sailors on New Providence Island and managed to seize Fort Nassau. The American forces occupied this for two weeks and, during that time, loaded on board badly needed gunpowder and many artillery pieces.

And in 1778, they cheekily did it again. On 27 January of that year, Captain John Rathbun arrived at New Providence Island with the appropriately named US ship, *Providence*. Rathbun landed his men and captured Fort Nassau, this time freeing American prisoners held there and capturing more weapons and vessels as well.

American military involvement with the Bahamas during the Revolutionary War wasn't finished yet. Not at all. Both American supporters of the revolution and opponents were about to get even more deeply involved. In May 1782, a Spanish and American fleet, including twelve American ships, arrived off New Providence Island and demanded its surrender, and on 7 May, the British governor of the islands did indeed surrender. But the islands were not to remain out of the control of the Crown for long because, in May 1783, American Major Andrew Deveaux, fighting on the Crown's side, successfully led an expedition to recapture the islands.

During the American Civil War, the Bahamas became a key location for Confederate blockade-runners. In early 1862, the sloop of war USS *Adirondack* was sent to attack blockade-runners off the Bahamas, which it did until it hit a reef which rather ended its blockade-running career. And in August 1862, the Confederate commerce-raider CSS *Florida*, having been built in Liverpool in the UK, was commissioned at Green Cay in the Bahamas.

Eventually, the United States and the United Kingdom became friends, and at times since then, America has had assorted bases on the islands. During the Second World War, the US Navy had a base in the Exuma area. America has also had rocket-tracking facilities on the islands, and after the Second World War, the US Navy established an underwater research facility on Andros Island.

The US and the Bahamas co-operate on a number of security issues these days, including on the fight against illegal narcotics. The Rhode Island National Guard is partnered with the Bahamas.

Bahrain

Bahrain is home (among many other things, of course) to the United States Fifth Fleet.

From 1861 until 1971, Bahrain was closely aligned with Britain, which managed its foreign affairs and maintained a naval presence. Oil was discovered in the 1930s.

Bahrain joined the Allied side alongside Britain with the start of the Second World War in 1939. After Mussolini joined the Axis cause, in one of the more extraordinary but little-known episodes of the war, Bahrain's oil refineries were bombed in 1940 by Italian aircraft flying from the distant Mediterranean island of Rhodes.

Britain still has connections with Bahrain, but from the 1970s onwards, American influence in the Gulf, including Bahrain, expanded.

America has assisted Bahrain's armed forces with military training, exercises and sales of huge quantities of military equipment. In 1991, Bahraini planes flew missions during the Gulf War, and Bahrain has sent troops to both Iraq and Afghanistan.

US aircraft were based in Bahrain during both Operation Enduring Freedom and Operation Iraqi Freedom.

Bahrain has been a base for US Navy activity in the Persian Gulf since 1947. In 1971, when the British withdrew, the United States took over the naval base from them. And American ships operated from Bahrain against the Iranians during the Tanker War of the 1980s (*see* Kuwait).

In 1996, Bahrain became the headquarters for the United States Fifth Fleet, and it is today one of the most important US Navy bases in the world, home to thousands of US personnel.

In 2011, the Arab Spring spread to Bahrain with demonstrators demanding greater political rights.

Recently the American navy has dramatically increased its footprint in Bahrain with an expansion in progress that will almost double the size of the US Navy base there.

Bangladesh

During the Second World War, with Burma so close, extensive fighting against the Japanese took place nearby.

US forces and supplies moved through the area and they had a number of important airbases there. US transport planes based at Tejgaon Airport near the capital of Bangladesh, Dhaka, and at Kurmitola Airfield, now Shahjalal International Airport, moved supplies into southern China. The airfield at Chittagong, now Shah Amanat International Airport, being close to the fighting was also used for combat and reconnaissance missions. Among US aircraft based there were P-38 Lightnings and C-46s that could drop supplies to Allied troops in the field. The US Navy also made use of port facilities in what is now Bangladesh, including those at Chittagong.

Between 1947 and 1971, the area was part of Pakistan and became known as East Pakistan. The US did have military links with Pakistan, but these were suspended in 1965 during the war between India and Pakistan and were not resumed until 1975. In 1971, after the Bangladesh Liberation War, however, the country separated from Pakistan and became independent as Bangladesh.

Since Bangladeshi independence, America has developed some links with the country's forces. Bangladesh sent troops to join the 1991 Gulf War coalition and the US has been involved with training and developing the country's peacekeeping and anti-terrorist procedures. In addition, US military forces have played a role in helping Bangladesh deal with some of the disasters that have hit it over the years and providing expertise in dealing with emergencies.

The Oregon National Guard is partnered with Bangladesh.

Barbados

Huge numbers of Americans have enjoyed visiting Barbados over the years. Some of them before the United States even existed. In 1751 even George Washington himself visited. He wasn't a man who spent much time outside the United States, so that's got to be pretty special.

But not all Americans have been interested in Barbados just for its lovely scenery. During the Revolutionary War and the War of 1812, US warships targeted assorted ships bound for Barbados and ships departing Barbados. In January 1814, the US frigate *President* with marines on board captured a number of British ships off Barbados.

Things didn't always go to plan, though, from the American point of view that is. In 1779, the sixteen-gun privateer *Cumberland*, under the command of John Manley, was captured by a British frigate, and ship and crew were taken to Barbados where they were imprisoned. In the end, though, Manley and his men managed to bribe a jailer, seize a British government tender, place the crew in irons, and escape to the United States.

During the Second World War, Barbados wasn't part of the destroyers-for-bases deal, but US forces did make some use of the island.

And there was more US military activity after the war. For instance, in the 1950s, America commissioned the United States Naval Facility Barbados at Harrison's Point in Saint Lucy. That operated there for twenty-two years.

In 1983, Barbados played a major role in Operation Urgent Fury, the invasion of Grenada, offering political and military support, and with Barbados being used as a staging post for the invasion.

In recent years, the US has been involved militarily with Barbados through assorted training, exercises, ship visits and humanitarian operations.

Belarus

A large country, but this really isn't going to be a large chapter.

Belarus is next to Russia, often in more senses than one. Belarus is close to Russia geographically (with a long, shared border) and has often been close politically as well, so it's perhaps not surprising that the US hasn't had vast amounts of military involvement with it.

In the period just after the Second World War, the CIA and other Western intelligence agencies, which envisaged using nationalists within Belarus to oppose the Soviet regime, re-established in the area after the wartime Nazi occupation. The CIA's controversial efforts with assorted exiles and exile groups had little effect in the end, however.

Among other Cold War operations linked to Belarus were U-2 spy flights over it. For instance, on 9 July 1956, a U-2 set off to fly over targets in Ukraine and Belarus.

In the uncertain period following the break-up of the Soviet Union, the US Department of Defense and military, along with various charities, commenced assorted humanitarian efforts in Belarus under Operation Provide Hope.

Belgium

Ah, Belgium. A land with great chocolate, great beer and great chips (as well as lots of other great and less calorific attractions); Belgium deserves to be better known.

Belgium seems as if it's been around forever but isn't even as old as the United States. In fact, at least one American was fighting on what is now Belgian soil before Belgium, as we now know it, even existed.

In June 1815 Sir William Howe De Lancey and his new bride, Magdalene Hall, were invited to, but did not attend, the famous Duchess of Richmond's ball in Brussels that preceded the Battle of Waterloo. De Lancey, born in New York City, served as the British Duke of Wellington's deputy quartermaster-general in the Waterloo campaign. His father, Stephen De Lancey, had also served as an officer in the 1st New Jersey Loyal Volunteers in the American Revolution. Sadly, while accompanying the Duke of Wellington at the Battle of Waterloo on 18 June 1815,

De Lancey encountered a ball of a rather less fun type than the one planned by the Duchess of Richmond – he was struck by a bouncing cannon ball and fatally wounded.

In August 1914, with the outbreak of the First World War, Belgium was invaded, and mostly occupied, by the Kaiser's army. After President Woodrow Wilson led the United States into war on the side of the Allies in 1917, in part due to the violation of Belgian neutrality, many Americans would fight in and over Belgium.

Robert Lovett, a Yale graduate who would become Secretary of Defense in the Korean War, served as a pioneering naval aviator in the First World War. One of his missions was to bomb German submarine pens based in Bruges, Belgium. Americans also played a vital role in campaigns that liberated large chunks of Belgium in the last months of the war. In August and September 1918, the American II Corps helped the British wipe out the German-held Lys salient, and in October, the 37th and 91th Divisions joined in an attempt to cross the Scheldt. Finally, on 2 November 1918, just a few days before the Armistice, the 37th managed to get across the Scheldt at Heurne.

Over 100,000 Americans were involved in the fighting in Belgium then, and many of them would never return home. Hundreds of American soldiers from the American Expeditionary Forces (AEF) are buried at the Flanders Field American Cemetery in Belgium at Waregem, only a few miles from the scene of the crossing of the Scheldt by the 37th.

In May 1940 Belgium was once again invaded by the Germans who occupied the country until September 1944. On 3 September the US First Army crossed the Belgian border and liberated the city of Mons and the surrounding area. Advancing American troops reported being greeted by bottles of cognac and champagne and by pretty girls. 25,000 Germans would soon be captured in the Mons pocket.

However, anyone expecting a quick end to the fighting was in for a surprise. One of the largest battles in American military history was fought primarily on the soil of Belgium – yes, it's the Battle of the Bulge.

Hitler had begun planning operation *Wacht am Rhein* (Watch on the Rhine) shortly after the D-Day landings in June. In spite of the Ultra decrypts, the Germans managed to achieve strategic surprise with a massive counter-attack through the Ardennes.

At 5:30 a.m. on 16 December 1944, a huge German artillery barrage broke out near the Ardennes forest.

The Germans advanced against inexperienced US divisions or the remnants of shattered units that had been put into a quiet part of the front in order to recuperate, and the attackers were helped by bad weather, which countered Allied air superiority. The 101st Airborne Division had been rushed to the front by truck, but was soon completely surrounded at Bastogne.

On 22 December 1944, Von Lüttwitz, commander of the German forces besieging Bastogne, sent two officers to request the surrender of the American garrison. Brigadier General McAuliffe, in temporary command of the 101st, laughed and famously exclaimed 'Nuts' in response.

It was near the Belgian town of Malmedy that the most notorious massacre of unarmed American soldiers in US history took place. Sixty-seven men of Battery B of the 285th Field Artillery Observation Battalion who had surrendered were killed by machine gun fire from SS Panzers. At least 400, including over 100 Belgian civilians, were killed by Joachim Peiper's 1st SS-Panzer Division. After the war, he was tried and sentenced to death, but Peiper managed to cheat the hangman's noose, and he was released from prison in 1956.

The German offensive had already caused considerable chaos in the American rear, and Skorzeny's English-speaking German commandos disguised as Americans just added to it. David Niven, an actor who moved to Hollywood seeking fame and fortune, served in the British Army during the Second World War and found himself caught up in it. When suspicious GIs demanded he tell them who had won the World Series in 1940, he had to confess he had no idea, but he was able to point out to the GIs that he had made a picture with Ginger Rogers in 1938. They let him pass.

In an Allied strategy conference held on 19 December, General George S. Patton Jr assured Eisenhower that he would be ready to counter-attack in forty-eight hours. Eisenhower expressed scepticism. Patton, however, was not going to be put off. His view was that the Germans had put their heads in a mincer, and he wasn't going to miss the opportunity to mince them.

Patton kept his word, attacking two days later with the US 4th Armored Division and relieving the 'Battling Bastards of Bastogne' on 26 December. With the weather now improved, allowing Allied air superiority to reassert itself, as German supplies ran out and Allied support began to arrive in force, the German offensive stalled.

The Ardennes Offensive was Hitler's last in the west. With its collapse, the Germans were once again forced into retreat and by February 1945 Belgium was finally free from the Nazis. But it had come at a heavy price. Thousands of American soldiers from both world wars are buried in three American battle monument cemeteries in Belgium.

Since the war, very close military ties have developed between the United States and Belgium. The country became a founding member of NATO in 1949. The headquarters of the NATO alliance is now located just outside Mons in Belgium, and assorted US military units have been based in Belgium since the war. For instance, today, the US Air Force's 309th Airlift Squadron operates at Chièvres Air Base in Belgium.

Belize

It's not exactly the country that the US has had the most military involvement with, but it has had a just a little bit.

For most of the nineteenth and twentieth centuries, Belize was a British colony, and British influence remained strong after independence, so that limited US involvement somewhat. Plus America focused more on neighbouring Guatemala, and since Guatemala and Belize have had a long-running border dispute, that probably didn't exactly help spread American influence in Belize either.

Obviously, however, the United States hasn't always been friends with Britain. During the War of 1812 (though actually this was in January 1813), the US Navy brig *Viper* was in waters off Belize when it was captured by HMS *Narcissus* under Captain Lumley, and a force sent by William Walker, American adventurer (*see* Nicaragua), didn't exactly enjoy their time in Belizean waters either. Their schooner, the *Susan*, hit a reef and their mission had to be abandoned.

However, some Americans who had been involved in war received more of a welcome in Belize. A number of Confederates fleeing after the American Civil War ended up in Belize and founded New Richmond there.

During the 1960s, Guatemala and Belize turned to America to try to mediate the border dispute between them, and President Lyndon B. Johnson appointed a US lawyer to consider the matter. However, the Belizeans rejected the resulting proposal, and despite a lack of US enthusiasm, Belize became independent in 1981.

Since independence, however, things between the United States and Belize have become more friendly, and the US military has developed a number of links with the country.

America opened a military assistance office in Belize in 1983 and has helped provide the Belize Defence Force (BDF) with some training and equipment. The US and Belizean governments co-operate in fighting illegal narcotics.

The Louisiana National Guard is partnered with Belize.

Benin

Situated on the African coast, with Togo to its west and Nigeria to its east, Benin was the home of the great African kingdom of Dahomey.

The port of Ouidah in Benin used to be a major slave port, so not surprisingly the town appears a lot in descriptions of what the United States' Africa Squadron did in its attempts to stop slaving ships from operating. In July 1854, Commodore Mayo, on board the USS *Constitution*, dropped anchor at Ouidah. In three days, he then proceeded to send boarding parties aboard at least eight ships. All were then subsequently released (so not exactly huge amounts has been achieved), but at least he was looking.

What is now Benin eventually became the French colony of Dahomey. In 1960, Dahomey became independent, and in the 1970s, Dahomey acquired a Marxist-Leninist government under Major Mathieu Kérékou and became Benin. Perhaps not surprisingly, considering the Marxist-Leninist bit, the US didn't have major military involvement with Benin at that time. Kérékou was president from 1972 to 1991 and then again from 1996 to 2006.

In recent years, America has had some links with the Beninese military. For instance, US Marines and Beninese soldiers carried out an exercise in silent scouting and observation in Benin in Shared Accord 2009. More broadly, the US has been involved with Benin's efforts to build up multinational peace-keeping expertise. Benin has supplied hundreds of troops to the French-led effort in Mali, to which the US has also given political and logistical support.

Bhutan

Militarily, Bhutan has a strong tradition of archery, which is not surprising since that's its national sport. But it also now has an army trained by India. Bhutan is a kingdom situated at the eastern end of the Himalayas with China to the north and India surrounding it to the south.

Mao once described Bhutan as one of the five fingers of Tibet that he aimed to take control of, so it has been a potentially strategic location. However, perhaps because of its close foreign policy and defence ties to its regional superpower, India, America doesn't seem to have ever had much planned military involvement with the country.

Unfortunately, however, American servicemen have died in Bhutan. The time when America had its highest military presence in the region (though not in Bhutan itself) was during the Second World War, particularly with its programme of flying supplies over the Hump from India to China.

During this period, American planes entered Bhutanese airspace on a number of occasions, and some of them crashed there. On 3 November 1945, just over a month after the war ended, an American C-45 took off from Chabua in northern India, which was a major airbase for flying the Hump, taking men to Karachi in what is now Pakistan, so they could return home. They never made it. The plane crashed in Bhutan near Chhukha killing all on board.

Bolivia

Bolivia derives its name from Simón Bolivár. Officially, it is known as the Plurinational State of Bolivia because of the different peoples it contains. Plurinational. Interesting word.

The US has played a significant role in various periods of

Bolivia's history. For instance, in the 1920s the United States was given control over Bolivian taxation services in return for lending the Bolivians $33 million. And at times, the US has had very close links with the Bolivian military. In the 1960s, significant numbers of Bolivian troops, including most of the senior army officers, had received US training either in America or in the Panama Canal Zone. And America had supported the general, René Barrientos, who was in power in Bolivia in 1967.

In this context, we need to take a look at probably America's most famous military involvement in Bolivia, which is surely the capture and killing of Che Guevara.

Two little-known facts about Che are that 'Che' just means 'pal', and that Che's father, Ernesto Guevara Lynch, had Basque and Irish ancestors.

By the time of his encounter in Bolivia, former Argentinian medical student Che had already had a couple of brushes with the CIA. Che had fled a CIA-supported coup that took power in Guatemala in 1954, and he had subsequently played a hugely significant part in the Cuban revolution. But Che was a dedicated Marxist and, perhaps even more, a dedicated revolutionary. Not content with revolution merely in Cuba, he was determined to export revolution across the globe. After Cuba, he ended up fighting alongside guerrillas in the Congo (*see* Democratic Republic of the Congo) against CIA-supported forces. And he ended up losing.

Bolivia was to be his next attempt at revolution, his next conflict with the CIA, his next defeat and indeed his last. When in early 1967 the CIA became aware that Che was operating with a band of guerrillas in Bolivia's southern mountains, they sent weapons, equipment and special forces trainers to help the Bolivian army against the rebels. It worked. After a few initial successes by Che's forces, Bolivian Special Forces managed to surround his encampment, and Che was captured and wounded but very much alive on 8 October 1967. He was interrogated but the Bolivian high command ordered his execution, and he was killed the next day. His body was then photographed and put on public display to prove he was really dead.

US involvement in Bolivia, however, did not end with Che Guevara's death. For instance, some suspect that the Nixon administration gave significant support to right-wing General Hugo Bánzer Suárez who launched a failed coup attempt in

1970 and a successful coup attempt in 1971 that toppled a left-leaning president.

Today, once again, the US government has its differences with a left-leaning Bolivian president, this time Evo Morales, and in 2008, the US Drug Enforcement Agency was expelled from that country.

Bosnia and Herzegovina

Sarajevo, the capital of Bosnia and Herzegovina, was the site in 1914 of the assassination of the Archduke Franz Ferdinand that eventually led to the First World War and the scene, a lot less bloodily, of the 1984 Winter Olympics.

On 2 June 1995, Captain Scott O'Grady was shot down over Bosnia, and in 2001, the movie *Behind Enemy Lines* came out. The O'Grady incident was one of the reasons for the development of the unmanned drone programme America has today. But the 1990s weren't the first time US military personnel had been active over Bosnia.

In 1941, the Germans invaded Yugoslavia, which at that time included Bosnia and Herzegovina (among others). America sent aircraft to target the German war machine in Bosnia and to help those resistance groups on the ground that were fighting it. Bombing missions would hit targets, such as rail facilities and airfields. In one such mission, in January 1944, B-24s bombed the airfield at Mostar. Meanwhile, other aircraft would fly supplies and OSS teams in to assist the resistance fighters and to evacuate the wounded and allied aircrew who had been shot down.

Winston Churchill had formed the SOE and commanded them to set Nazi-occupied Europe ablaze with support for local resistance movements. 'Wild Bill' Donovan, the leader of the OSS, wanted to use American resources to accomplish the same mission. Soon, nearly sixty OSS agents were serving directly with Tito, and arms shipments were pouring into Yugoslavia to the partisans and to other resistance fighters.

The first army air force aircraft to land in the Balkans were two C-47s that landed on a rough airstrip at Medeno Polje near Tito's headquarters at Drvar in Bosnia on the night of 2 April 1944. They airlifted out thirty-six partisans that night. In the next few weeks, hundreds more were airlifted out. After a German attack on Tito's headquarters almost captured him, American aircraft airlifted out members of his staff. And the amount of supplies being taken in was impressive as well. US aircrews made a huge contribution to the defeat in Bosnia of German forces and their allies.

During the Second World War, the internal politics of which group of locals was fighting whom in Bosnia were complex, and in the 1990s, they were to be complex again. In 1992, Bosnia and Herzegovina declared independence from Yugoslavia. Civil war was already raging in neighbouring Croatia between those who wanted independence and local Serbs who didn't, and soon it would be in Bosnia as well. In addition, though, in the middle of that civil war, Croats and Bosniaks who had previously been fighting the Serbs side by side turned on each other. That was sorted out only with the help of a US government keen to prevent the Croat/Bosniak war from further destabilising Bosnia. And a mini-civil war took place inside the Bihac pocket.

Early in the war, the UN agreed on an arms embargo on Bosnia, and NATO helped enforce that by sea and by air. Then in April 1993, NATO began Operation Deny Flight, an operation to impose a no-fly zone over Bosnia. This was not without incident. In one mission, on 28 February 1994 US F-16s shot down a number of Serb jets that had violated the no-fly zone during a bombing attack on an arms factory at Novi Travnik. And soon NATO's role extended to assisting UN ground forces; for instance, hitting Serb targets when the Gorazde safe area was threatened.

In June 1995, Scott O'Grady was shot down and rescued after days spent evading capture. And then in August 1996, NATO began Operation Deliberate Force, again unambiguously named, which involved widespread bombing of Serb targets in Bosnia. Meanwhile, since the start of the war, Croat and Bosniak forces had improved considerably both in terms of training and weapons, and some have speculated about a US role in that. The bombing, advances on the ground by Croat and Bosniak forces, and changes in Slobodan Milosevic's attitude eventually led to the Dayton peace conference and the end of fighting in Bosnia.

This did not, however, mean the end of a US military role in Bosnia. Not at all. After the Dayton Peace agreement, NATO ground forces, including US ground forces, moved into Bosnia to help secure the peace. The US-led Multinational Division North took control of the north-east part of Bosnia. The initial force IFOR (Implementation Force) handed over in 1996 to SFOR (Stabilisation Force), which in turn handed over in 2004 to EUFOR (European Union Force).

Bosnia has assorted military agreements with the US and participates in exercises with US forces. Bosnia has sent troops to Iraq and Afghanistan, and the Maryland National Guard is partnered with Bosnia.

Botswana

A big chunk of Botswana is the Kalahari, but it also has places like the Okavango Delta.

Botswana is one of those African countries in which the US has recently shown some interest in military matters. A significant percentage of the officer corps of Botswana, for instance, has received training from the United States.

Much US involvement in Botswana has been focused on Thebephatshwa Airbase and facilities there. Large parts of Southern Accord, a major bilateral US and Botswana exercise in 2012, took place there.

Brazil

A big country with a big future, Brazil is one with which the US has had quite a lot of military involvement over the years.

It wasn't long after American independence that US ships were involved in military operations in the waters off Brazil. In December 1812, the USS *Constitution* faced HMS *Java* in a three-hour engagement off the Brazilian coast and defeated the British ship.

And in 1813, the USS *Hornet* was blockading a British sloop with a not very British name, *Bonne Citoyenne*, in Salvador, Brazil. However, fortunately for *Bonne Citoyenne* and unfortunately for *Hornet*, the arrival of British reinforcements forced it to abandon the blockade and head for the Caribbean instead.

In the nineteenth century, the US Navy had its own Brazil Squadron, originally formed in 1826 to protect American commercial interests, but later also used in the fight against slavery. It seized six ships between 1845 and 1849. Not exactly on its own a death blow to slavery, but better than nothing.

The waters off Brazil were to see more action by American warships during the American Civil War. In October 1864, the Confederate cruiser *Florida* was captured by Commander Napoleon Collins (great name) of the USS *Wachusett* while it was anchored in Bahia.

In 1894, however, the US was more worried about events ashore in Brazil, and with conflict raging, it sent US ships as a display of force to Rio de Janeiro in an attempt (a rather heavily armed and not hugely subtle attempt) to protect its property and interests in that city.

During the First World War, Brazil declared war on Germany in 1917 and took part in some operations. The Brazilian navy also conducted patrols off West Africa.

Links between the US and Brazilian navies continued after the war, with a US naval mission being sent to Brazil.

In the Second World War, Brazil was again neutral at first but increasingly looked to the Allied side. In 1942, Brazil allowed America to establish airbases in Brazil for air-ferrying and transport purposes. Two particularly important airfields were at Belém and Natal.

Brazilian ships were torpedoed, and in August 1942, Brazil declared war on Germany and Italy.

At sea, once again, the Brazilian navy fought to keep merchant ships safe from the U-boats. On land, the Brazilian Expeditionary Force fought alongside US troops and, with US assistance, in Italy. In the air, Brazilian pilots flew P-47 Thunderbolts as part of the 350th Fighter Group of the USAAF.

In the period after the war, too, America had assorted links with the Brazilian military, including the US Military Assistance Program. US involvement with the military coup in Brazil in 1964 and in the repression that followed it is another matter.

Recent links between the US military and the Brazilian military include participating in multinational exercises.

Brunei

Surrounded on its land side by Malaysia, Brunei is a small sultanate that's big in oil and natural gas. Brunei also has a long history, and America has played a small role in it.

As early as 1845, the USS *Constitution* dropped in hoping to acquire rights to coal deposits. And in 1850, as Brunei began to get a little concerned about British intentions, they signed a Treaty of Peace, Friendship, Commerce and Navigation with the United States, which apparently is still in force.

In 1865, the US consul general to Brunei, Claude Lee Moses, even managed to get from the sultan of Brunei a ten-year lease over a big chunk of northern Borneo, but since this area is now part of Malaysia, we'll cover the story in that chapter.

Eventually, as the nineteenth century wore on, Brunei became an area of British influence, and when in 1945 the Allies arrived to liberate Brunei from Japanese occupation, it was mainly Australian troops that did so. However, American ships and aircraft were a vital part of the invasion forces, being involved in extensive operations against targets in the Brunei area.

More recently, since Brunei gained full independence from Britain, America has conducted joint exercises and assorted other forms of military cooperation with Brunei. In 1994, the United States signed a memorandum of understanding on military defence cooperation with Brunei.

Bulgaria

Ah, Bulgaria on the Black Sea. Well the coast of Bulgaria, that is.

The Bulgars have a fascinating history. Already by the seventh century, they had built an empire that was scaring the mighty Byzantines, and the Bulgars even laid siege to Constantinople itself. Yep. Pretty impressive. Well, unless you were a besieged Byzantine and then it was probably mostly just depressing and annoying.

American missionaries first began visiting Bulgaria in the nineteenth century when the area was still part of the Ottoman Empire, and actually Americans built up quite a lot of influence in nineteenth-century Bulgaria. For instance, they opened schools in Bulgaria, and Robert College opened a campus in Istanbul. Soon, over half of its students were Bulgarian, and three future prime ministers of Bulgaria attended.

In 1876, a rebellion broke out in Bulgaria against Ottoman rule. The Ottoman authorities crushed the rebellion, and massacres ensued. The American consul general in Istanbul and an American journalist with the (unusual and rather interesting) name of Januarius MacGahan played key roles in telling the world about the massacres.

Eventually, Russia demanded the Ottomans enact measures to ensure the protection of, among others, the Bulgarians. When the Ottomans refused, Russia went to war and, after fierce fighting, defeated it, leading to Bulgarian independence under nominal Ottoman rule.

Bulgaria declared itself fully independent in 1908, and because of its close links to Russia, it might have seemed likely that, with the arrival of the First World War, Bulgaria would have joined the Allied side. However, territorial disputes with Serbia, Romania and Greece eventually meant Bulgaria joined the war in 1915 on the side of Germany and Austria-Hungary instead. Not a good choice, as it turned out.

The United States, however, had no particular quarrel with Bulgaria, and the influence of American missionaries was still significant there, and when the US declared war on Germany and subsequently on Austria-Hungary in 1917, it did not declare war on her ally Bulgaria. This led to the slightly improbable situation of the US still being at peace with a country that a short distance beyond its southern borders was fighting bitter battles against America's allies.

Eventually in 1918 as Allied forces broke through Bulgarian defences, the country was forced to ask for peace and lost a lot of territory in the peace deal that followed. The inter-war years were also often not easy ones for Bulgarians. In 1939, another war broke out, and once again, Bulgaria joined the losing side. So a consistent track record, but not a good one.

In January 1941, 'Wild Bill' Donovan went on a whirlwind tour of the Balkans that was paid for by MI6. Donovan met Tsar Boris III of Bulgaria who thought the American naive and ignorant of Balkan politics and history. Donovan, for his part, thought Boris an extremely frightened man. He would not be deterred from joining the Axis, which seemed supremely victorious at the time.

During his trip, Donovan accompanied George Earle, the US ambassador to Bulgaria, to a Sofia nightclub. Meanwhile, Abwehr agents broke into his room at the Bulgarie Hotel and stole his travelling bag. When the bag was later recovered by Bulgarian police, a list of questions posed by the US Navy was the only missing item.

Later in the Second World War, although Bulgaria joined the Axis, it refused to send its troops to fight in Operation Barbarossa. On 13 December 1941, Bulgaria, less than a week after the Pearl Harbor attack, declared war on the United States, and the United States would soon be targeting Bulgaria. In 1943 and 1944, the USAAF conducted multiple bombing raids on Sofia. Hundreds of Allied airmen, including many Americans, were shot down and became POWs in Bulgaria.

While the British SOE focused its Balkan efforts on Yugoslavia, it encouraged the OSS to penetrate Bulgaria and Romania where it did not operate. The Cereus network was designed to encourage widespread sabotage in Bulgaria.

In August 1943, Tsar Boris III died under suspicious circumstances after paying a visit to Adolf Hitler who had berated him for not assisting in the invasion of the Soviet Union. Perhaps Boris was the naive one about the threats to himself and his country.

In September of 1944, the Red Army invaded Bulgaria, and Bulgaria abandoned Germany and joined the Allies. However, Soviet influence was strong, and a pro-Soviet government soon took control in Bulgaria.

An American Military Mission with General Crane initially in command formed part of the Allied Control Commission for Bulgaria. By mid-1945, fifty American officers and enlisted men were stationed in Bulgaria, mainly living at the American college near Simeonovo, a few miles from the capital. The ground section under Lieutenant Colonel John Bakeless continued intelligence activities, including gathering information about Soviet forces. Bulgaria soon came under firm Soviet domination.

One of the better-known Bulgarians of the Cold War period was Georgi Markov. He was a Bulgarian writer who defected to the West in 1969. He later worked for Radio Free Europe out of London before being poisoned by a ricin pellet that had been injected into his thigh with an umbrella while crossing Waterloo Bridge. He is buried in a small country churchyard in Dorset.

Since the collapse of Communism in Bulgaria, close links have been established between the US and Bulgarian militaries; Bulgaria sent a contingent to fight in Iraq in 2003, joined the NATO alliance in 2004, and a Bulgarian contingent has served alongside US forces in Afghanistan.

Currently, about 2,500 US military personnel are serving at

a number of bases within Bulgaria. The US Navy pays regular visits to Bulgarian ports. The Tennessee National Guard is partnered with Bulgaria.

Burkina Faso

A landlocked country in West Africa, Burkina Faso is about the size of Colorado. It used to be called Upper Volta (Burkina Faso that is, not Colorado). Its football team is named 'Les Étalons', the Stallions, after a legendary twelfth-century warrior, horsewoman and mother of the Mossi Empire, Princess Yennenga. Basically, the US (unlike Princess Yennenga) hasn't had a lot to do with this country militarily.

In recent years America has, however, trained troops from Burkina Faso for peacekeeping operations in Darfur. Also, Burkinabé troops took part alongside US forces in Flintlock 10, an AFRICOM-sponsored exercise, centred on Ouagadougou (capital of Burkina Faso) and designed to boost Special Operations Forces' capabilities in the region.

Burkina Faso is strategically located close to areas where the United States is concerned about the activities of Islamist jihadists. Burkina Faso has recently become a member of the Trans-Sahara Counter-Terrorism Partnership (TSCTP), and Ouagadougou has become a focus of some US counter-terrorism interest and activity.

Burma

One famous name that will be forever linked to US military involvement with the land of Burma is, of course, Merrill's Marauders. Great name, incidentally.

The story of Merrill's Marauders in the Second World War is an epic of endurance, daring and courage. Fighting behind enemy lines in Japanese-occupied Burma against larger numbers of Japanese, they had to cope with the challenges of warfare in very difficult conditions and very far from base. The Marauders caused large numbers of casualties to the Japanese and extensive disruption to their communications, and the culmination of their efforts was the capture, with the assistance of Nationalist Chinese troops, of Myitkyina in the summer of 1944.

However, the brave efforts of Merrill's Marauders were certainly not the only US military involvement in Burma during the Second World War. For instance, 'Vinegar Joe' Stilwell led Nationalist Chinese troops in Burma, the USAAF flew large numbers of missions in the area in support of Allied ground troops, and OSS Detachment 101 helped train and organise and fight alongside Kachin resistance groups.

The end of the war wasn't to be the end of American military involvement with Burma either. Though it was to be the end of major US military successes in Burma as it happens.

The CIA has been involved in Burma as well. In 1951, during the Korean War, the CIA began helping train and arm Nationalist Chinese troops in the part of Burma near the Chinese border, encouraging them to infiltrate China. The operation was not, however, a success. Their infiltration attempts were ruthlessly countered by the Communist Chinese, and some of the Nationalist Chinese switched to harvesting opium poppies in Burma's Golden Triangle instead.

In 1962, General Ne Win took power in Burma in a coup and instituted policies that left Burma isolated from the international community in many senses for decades. Now, though much less isolated, the country still faces many challenges.

After the devastating Tropical Cyclone Nargis hit Burma in 2008, the US military rushed to send humanitarian help. The first US military relief flight flew to Rangoon in May. Opposition from the Burmese authorities has, however, impeded some assistance from US forces.

Recent attempts at rapprochement between the US and Burma have had occasional problems.

Burundi

It's not the largest country in the world. And this isn't going to be the longest entry either.

Like its rather better-known neighbour, Rwanda, Burundi has had at times a turbulent history, involving coups and ethnic conflict between Hutus and Tutsi.

In April 1994, President Bill Clinton sent troops to Burundi in order to be ready to evacuate American and other civilians from Rwanda. And in September 1996, a US Air Force C-141 flew into Bujumbura, the capital of Burundi to evacuate civilians threatened by the situation in the country.

In recent years, America has had some involvement in training the Burundian military. Burundi has contributed peacekeepers to Somalia, and much of US military involvement with Burundi has focused on peacekeeping expertise.

In March 2013, US troops were giving Burundian soldiers deployment logistics training at Gakumbu Camp in Burundi. In December 2013, as the French moved into the Central African Republic (CAR) to try to stop the fighting, the United States offered to help by sending planes to airlift Burundian troops to the CAR in support.

Cambodia

It's not exactly going to come as a surprise to that many people that America has been militarily involved with Cambodia. Though what may surprise a few is just how far back in its history that the US first attacked targets in Cambodia.

Cambodia was a French protectorate from 1867 to 1953 when it gained its independence. However, it was occupied by the Japanese during the Second World War, which brought about America's first military involvement with the country. On 7 February 1945 US B-29s bombed targets in and around Phnom Penh. Obviously, it wasn't to be the last time US heavy bombers would pound targets inside Cambodia.

On 7 April 1954, President Dwight Eisenhower articulated the domino theory: 'You have a row of dominoes set up, you knock over the first one, and what will happen to the last one is the certainty that it will go over very quickly.' Cambodia was, perhaps, the domino that fell the hardest of all.

Cambodia was to see appalling tragedy as competing forces battled for control in a complex and sometimes confusing (and confused) pattern of changing alliances.

In 1965, during the Vietnam War, Prince Sihanouk allied Cambodia with North Vietnam and China. Sihanouk allowed Communists from North Vietnam to use the Ho Chi Minh trail that wound through his country to resupply the Viet Cong (VC) in South Vietnam. The VC also found sanctuary from American air attacks in neighbouring Cambodia.

However, battling to balance forces within the country, Sihanouk also allowed his pro-American defence minister Lon Nol to crack down on Cambodian leftists. The result was the rise of the Khmer Rouge and the beginning of the Cambodian Civil War as the central government battled increasingly bitter and effective Communist guerrillas.

In March 1970, a coup deposed Prince Sihanouk from power while he was out of the country. Lon Nol, the premier and defence minister who led the coup, immediately asked for American support.

Sihanouk was soon in Beijing and renewed his Communist alliance, teaming up with the Khmer Rouge to fight the new government. If ever a chance had existed of keeping Cambodia out of the carnage that had engulfed Vietnam, it was now almost gone.

In April 1970 President Richard Nixon launched an 'incursion' into Cambodia aimed at smashing the infrastructure that helped enable the Viet Cong to operate within South Vietnam. Direct US ground forces involvement lasted about three months; about 30,000 US troops and 50,000 Vietnamese army troops took part. Most US forces were withdrawn from Cambodia by 30 June 1970, but the US bombing of targets inside Cambodia continued.

At almost the same time, though, the Communists were also starting to advance inside Cambodia, and US air power was used to try to support government troops against them. The United States dropped more than 540,000 tons of explosives in Cambodia, claiming at least 30,000 lives, until Congress cut off funds in August 1973.

Well before 1975, signs of strain had been showing in the Khmer Rouge, primarily supported by Beijing and the North Vietnamese who were looking more to Moscow, but the Cambodian government and its forces were in total disarray and unable to stop the Khmer Rouge's advance on Phnom Penh.

Lon Nol resigned on 1 April to give negotiations a chance, but on 12 April, with the city about to fall, Operation Eagle Pull evacuated US diplomats from Phnom Penh.

In May 1975 a US-flagged merchant ship, *Mayaguez*, was seized by a Khmer Rouge gunboat. Thirty-nine crew members were held hostage. President Gerald Ford, determined to avoid a second *Pueblo* incident (*see* North Korea), ordered F-4 Phantom fighters based in Thailand to attack Koh Tang Island. On 14 May, an assault force of about 175 US Marines assaulted dug-in Khmer Rouge positions. The *Mayaguez* crew were later rescued from a fishing boat. Forty American servicemen were killed in the operation.

Pol Pot took over in Cambodia and launched a vast genocide. Pol Pot's Khmer Rouge were responsible for approximately two million deaths as Cambodia was transformed into a 'killing field' from 1976 to 1979.

Many different groups, including various religions, were targeted for destruction. Only 1,000 out of approximately 60,000 Cambodian monks survived the terror. The Muslim Cham were slaughtered, and their mosques were converted or razed to the ground. The Catholic cathedral in Phnom Penh was destroyed along with nearly half of Cambodia's Catholics.

Pol Pot also persecuted ethnic minorities, such as Vietnamese. Vietnam eventually decided it had had enough of Pol Pot and launched a full-scale invasion of Cambodia on Christmas Day 1978. Phnom Penh was captured in 1979, and Pol Pot was driven into exile in Thailand.

The US government wasn't too enthusiastic about a new status quo in Cambodia dictated by Vietnam, but in recent years, ties between the US military and the Cambodian government have restarted in a limited sense. For example, in 2002 the US Navy deployed a medical research unit to Phnom Penh. Since 2006, the US Navy has resumed port visits to Phnom Penh and assisted the Cambodian navy in training exercises.

Cameroon

Cameroon is located to the south and east of Nigeria. It's a fairly big country by world standards, about the size of California, but this is going to be quite a short chapter, since the US just hasn't had that much military involvement with Cameroon. Cameroon also still has military links with France, one of its former colonial powers.

However, US Navy ships were in the area in the nineteenth century during anti-slaving operations, and US Navy ships have been in the area occasionally since. Cameroon has taken part in maritime exercises and training alongside US forces.

On land, over the years, the US has also supplied training, for instance, recently training Cameroonian peacekeepers. The USAF has also flown humanitarian relief missions there. In 2014, the US Army Africa led multinational Exercise Central Accord in Cameroon.

Canada

Oh, Canada, land of the Maple Leaf. Canada is now one of America's oldest and closest allies (it couldn't get that much closer geographically either). The Peace Arch marks the border between Washington State and British Columbia. America fought alongside them in two world wars. They are founding members of NATO. So surely America has never invaded its ice hockey-loving friends to the north?

But of course it has. Even before America was a country, Americans were invading Canada. Americans, along with the British, invaded French Canada during the Seven Years War (or French and Indian War, 1754–1763). In fact, George Washington gained his first military experience fighting in the Ohio Valley in this conflict.

At the Battle of Quebec, which took place on 13 September 1759, British General Wolfe defeated French General Montcalm, with six companies of American rangers participating alongside British forces in the battle. The French lost Canada to the British.

Voltaire's cynical verdict on the Seven Years War was that the two countries were fighting over a few acres of snow and that the war was costing more than Canada was really worth. This fight over a few acres of snow in Canada was, however, to have rather far-reaching consequences. The cost of paying for this war compelled the British to raise taxes on their American colonies. Not a great move by Britain, as it turned out.

And even before the actual Declaration of Independence, the American colonials were invading Canada. In 1775, General Philip Schuyler (an ancestor of author Chris Kelly) led the Continental Army on an invasion of Canada. The patriot forces hoped to rally the French-speaking Canadians to their cause. It wasn't a great success for the Americans. In fact, it was a bit of a disaster. The American forces took Montreal and besieged

Quebec, but failed to take it, and British reinforcements launched a counter-offensive that drove the invaders out.

After the American Revolution was won, many American Tories fled to Canada. Other Americans, however, were casting covetous glances on their northern neighbours. Benjamin Franklin, a revolutionary with pacifist leanings, suggested that America should purchase Canada from the British. Thomas Jefferson, more bellicose and a believer in a so-called 'Empire of Liberty', wrote in a letter dated 4 August 1812, 'The acquisition of Canada, this year, as far as the neighbourhood of Quebec, will be a mere matter of marching; & will give us experience for the attack of Halifax the next, & the final expulsion of England from the American continent.' The Anglophobic Jefferson encouraged his protégé and fellow Democrat James Madison to declare war on Britain, which he did in 1812.

During the War of 1812, the hapless Stephen Van Rensselaer III (another ancestor of Chris's!), led the New York militia in an invasion of Canada at the Battle of Queenston in October 1812.

Many know that the British burned the White House in 1814 during the 1812 war (Tony Blair offered a belated apology to George W. Bush not long ago). Fewer, however, are aware that the burning was a reprisal for the American burning of York (now Toronto) that followed the American victory at the Battle of York on 27 April 1813. And it wasn't just burning. A fair bit of plundering took place as well. The parliamentary mace of Upper Canada disappeared off to Washington, and the Canadians got hold of it again only in 1934, courtesy of President Franklin D. Roosevelt.

During the war, Master Commandant Oliver Hazard Perry led the fledgling US Navy to victory over the mighty Royal Navy in the Battle of Lake Erie on 10 September 1813. After the battle, Perry wrote to his commanding officer, 'We have met the enemy and they are ours.'

The War of 1812 was a war of choice, which was divisive and tremendously unpopular in Federalist strongholds, such as New England. Support or opposition to the war ran very closely along partisan political lines. Many farmers in New England even sold cattle and supplies to the British during the war. A secessionist movement even convened at the Hartford Convention of 1814 in opposition to 'Mr Madison's war.' The Federalist governor of Massachusetts, Caleb Strong, actually wrote a letter to his counterpart, the governor of Nova Scotia, offering a separate peace in exchange for settling the border with what later became the state of Maine.

Ultimately, the war was essentially a draw for America and Britain. It was, however, a decisive victory for Canada, which was never really invaded again by the United States. But it was also a decisive defeat for the First Peoples of Canada, who lost their great leader Tecumseh and any real hope of halting the American westward expansion. Native Americans who had fought loyally alongside the British in North America were not even invited to attend the peace conference at Ghent, which concluded the war.

That did not, however, mean the end of border disputes between the United States and Canada. For example, they had the Aroostook War of 1838–1839. This actually ended without violence, in a compromise, though militias had been called out.

In 1844, the Democratic presidential candidate and eventual winner, James K. Polk, ran on a platform of taking control over the entire Oregon Territory and adopted the famous campaign slogan, 'Fifty-four Forty or Fight!' after the line of latitude serving as the northern boundary of Oregon at 54°40'. Polk's plan was to claim, and go to war over, the entire territory for the United States. Under Polk's scheme, virtually all present-day British Columbia would have formed part of the United States. After he was elected president, however, Polk instead turned his attention south fighting the Mexican-American War (*see* Mexico) from 1846 to 1848.

And then we come to the famous, or possibly infamous, Pig War of 1859. The San Juan Islands lying between Vancouver Island and the North American mainland were the subject of dispute between the United States and Britain. In 1859, things got serious, particularly for a certain pig, after an American farmer on the island found it in his garden and shot it. Unfortunately for the situation between the United States and Britain, the pig had belonged to an employee of the Hudson's Bay Company. The conflict began to escalate. US troops landed on the island, and soon after that, British warships turned up. A tense stand-off began. In the end, however, the dispute did go to arbitration, and the United States got the islands. The only casualty of this 'war' was porcine.

As absurd as the Pig War may seem to us now, it raises some fascinating historical conjectures. What if President James

Buchanan had led the United States into a shooting war with Great Britain in 1859? Would the American Civil War have been postponed or deferred as all states, slave and free, rallied against a common enemy ... over bacon?

From 1866 to 1870, the Fenian Brotherhood (Americans of Irish descent who supported independence for Ireland) mounted five unsuccessful raids into British Canada. The Fenians, most of them veterans of the American Civil War, sought to influence events in Ireland by attacking British-held Canada.

The Fenians were led by Union Army veteran officers like John O'Neil, who had a distinguished record in the Seventh Michigan Cavalry. The Fenian raiders were the first forces to serve under the banner of the Irish Republican Army. The Fenians even tried out a submarine in New York's East River!

Some have speculated that the American government may have turned a blind eye to these activities in part due to British support for the Confederacy during the American Civil War. In any event, the decisive Canadian defeat of these raiding parties at the Battle of Ridgeway in 1866 helped to bind the Canadian confederacy and form a stronger Canadian national identity.

A border dispute between Alaska and Canada was solved by compromise and without violence after arbitration in 1903.

An interesting point is that, though America is such good friends with Britain and Canada today, even as late as the 1920s and 1930s it had a secret war plan for what might happen if it ended up fighting a war against the British Empire. This is War Plan Red, and a key part of it was, yep, an American invasion of Canada.

Cape Verde

Not one of the biggest countries in the world, but interestingly enough, hundreds of thousands of Americans have ancestors from Cape Verde, with a particularly big community located in New England.

In that context, it's not that surprising to find that America has a long history of links, including some military ones, with the islands. Already by the eighteenth century, American whalers were recruiting crew from the islands, and the United States had a consul there by 1818.

In addition, for much of the time, it was conducting anti-slavery operations off the African coast. In the nineteenth century, the US Navy's African Squadron was based at Porto Praya in the Cape Verde Islands. And they even captured a number of slavers in and around Porto Praya. In 1846, the schooner *Robert Wilson* had been forced into Porto Praya by bad weather. When Captain Skinner of the USS *Jamestown* investigated the ship, he found evidence on board that it was indeed a slaving vessel. The vessel was confiscated and in the United States its master was given a fine of $1,000 and a three year jail sentence, to be later pardoned in April 1847.

U-boats operating off Cape Verde were a concern during the Second World War, and US ships were accordingly dispatched to patrol the waters.

At one stage, General Marshall apparently authorised spending $500,000 to draw up a plan to have US commandos invade the Cape Verde Islands, but it never happened.

Cape Verde became independent in 1975, and in recent years, the US has had assorted links with the country. The US Navy and US Coast Guard have worked with the Cape Verde Coast Guard and police.

Central African Republic

The Central African Republic is located, not surprisingly, in Central Africa. It has faced some very difficult times over the last decades, including its brief transformation into the Central African Empire under Emperor Bokassa the First (who was almost certainly also Bokassa the Last), and it is still facing difficult times.

The US hasn't exactly had a huge military involvement with the country, but has had some. There were three mutinies against the government in 1996 and 1997, and in May 1996, President Bill Clinton deployed US military personnel to the capital of the Central African Republic to help evacuate US citizens and boost the security of the US Embassy there.

In 2002, Operation Shepherd Sentry again saw US troops on a mission to evacuate people from the Central African Republic.

In recent years, the US military offered some assistance to the Central African Republic's military in attempts to counter the activities of the notorious militia, the Lord's Resistance Army, with American teams based in Obo and Djema.

Sadly, in 2013, the fighting between different militias in the Central African Republic started to get much worse, and large numbers have been killed there. In December 2013, as the French moved into the Central African Republic to try to stop the fighting, the United States, among other actions, sent three C-17s and air force personnel to airlift Burundian troops and supplies into the country to provide further assistance.

Chad

Yep, it's a guy's name, and what about those 'hanging chads' from the 2000 US election? But Chad is also the name of a huge landlocked African country that has long sat astride important and often valuable trans-Saharan trade routes and is now an oil producer as well.

It was a French colony from 1920, and during the Second World War, unlike some other French colonies, which stayed under the control of the pro-German Vichy regime, Chad rapidly (and wisely) joined the free French side. That meant it was open for use by the Allied war effort and open for use by America's own trans-Saharan efforts. The French airbase at what was then Fort Lamy (now Ndjamena, the capital) was a vital transit base for Allied planes crossing from African ports on the Atlantic coast to the Middle East, which meant visits from American aircraft and aircrew.

But it was some time after Chad gained its independence in 1960 that the US really started taking an interest in Chad militarily.

The independent nation faced plenty of challenges, including conflict between southerners and northerners, but that wasn't primarily why America was interested in Chad. In fact, the person who made America interested in Chad wasn't even from Chad – but was instead the infamous Colonel Gaddafi.

Libya shares Chad's northern border, and in the repeated conflicts that spread across Chad, Gaddafi grabbed the opportunity and launched repeated Libyan interventions, both military and diplomatic, in its southern neighbour.

In 1981, after the Gulf of Sidra incident where US planes

were fired on by the Libyan air force and two Libyan planes were subsequently shot down (*see* Libya), the US government was desperately looking for greater leverage in its dealing with Gaddafi.

So the CIA began funnelling arms and support to Hissène Habré and helped him take power in Chad and fight Gaddafi. It has been estimated that a massive half billion dollars' worth of support went to Chad in the 1980s, and in August 1983, President Ronald Reagan even reported the deployment of eight F-15s, two AWACS planes, and ground support staff to help fight the Libyans.

The story has more plot twists and turns than many Hollywood thrillers, but by 1987 after thousands of Libyans had been killed and they had finally fallen out with their main local allies at the time, the Libyans were pushed out of Chad. It was a massive defeat for Gaddafi, but Habré's success came at a high price for Chad as well.

Habré turned out to be not exactly an ideal leader, and he was deposed in 1990. Further periods of conflict followed, including cross-border tension with Sudan.

More recently, the US government has been taking a renewed interest in the area, for instance, offering counter-terrorism training to Chadian troops.

Chile

Ever heard of the Chilean-American War? No? Fair enough. Well that's probably because it never actually happened, but it almost did.

As US horizons began to expand in the early nineteenth century, it was inevitable that pretty soon the United States would come into close contact with the new, young state of Chile. And indeed as early as 1811, with the Chilean struggle for independence from Spain still in progress, one Joel Roberts Poinsett appeared in Chile. He was appointed by President James Madison as Consul General in the area, but this was a man who didn't limit his diplomacy to that of the more conventional type. Instead, in his mission to protect American ships from seizure, he ended up fighting as part of the Chilean army. Very forceful diplomacy.

By the late nineteenth century Chile, with a certain amount of support from Britain, was making itself something of a regional power. The Chilean navy, modelled after the British Royal Navy, became a formidable force, with access to ships like the *Almirante Cochrane*, a 3,560-ton ironclad frigate built in Hull in 1874. In the War of the Pacific from 1879 to 1883, Chile took on both Peru and Bolivia and won. As a consequence of that war, Bolivia lost her entire coastline and remains a landlocked nation to this day. And Chile even began a modest overseas territorial expansion of its own, annexing the Easter Islands in 1888.

With Chile's links to Britain and with the United States having its own ambitions in South America, Chile's expanding power wasn't entirely to American liking. The United States had lent some support to Peru during the War of the Pacific. And things between the Chileans and the US didn't get any friendlier when the Chileans rejected American attempts to bring an earlier end to the War of the Pacific.

In 1891, civil war broke out in Chile, and America supported one side, while Britain supported the other. The US seized an arms shipment bound for the other side, and when its side lost, it gave asylum in the US mission to some of the leaders. So, when in October 1891 sailors from the USS *Baltimore* came ashore on leave in Valparaiso, things were already tense, and they were about to get a lot more so as fighting broke out, leading to the deaths of two US sailors. The United States demanded immediate reparations; the Chileans refused until a judicial investigation was complete. War was a strong possibility for some time, but in the end, it never happened.

During the 1891 crisis, some in the US military actually feared that Chilean ships might start shelling American coastal cities. However, in the end, Chilean fears that the United States would attack it eventually led it to agree to US terms.

Chile was the last nation to join the Allies in the Second World War, declaring war on Japan in 1945 near the war's end. Still, as the saying goes, better late than never.

During the Cold War, many Americans feared Communist expansion into central and Latin America. The Monroe Doctrine provided American foreign policymakers with a rationale for intervening to prevent the spread of Soviet and Cuban influence in this region.

In Chile's 1964 presidential election, the CIA secretly helped to fund the successful candidacy of Eduardo Frei Montalva against his Socialist rival Salvador Allende.

The election of Salvador Allende as president in a three-way election by a 1.5 per cent margin in 1970, therefore, represented a dilemma for American policymakers who were already facing severe problems in Vietnam. Henry Kissinger called Chile 'a dagger pointed at the heart of America.' The CIA received orders to plan for a coup, and identified General Camilo Valenzuela as 'a general with balls' who could lead a successful coup. Chilean General Schneider was assassinated among rumours of CIA involvement.

The Chilean coup occurred on 11 September 1973. Allende had accepted the support of Fidel Castro and alienated the Chilean military. Surrounded in his own presidential palace, he ended up shooting himself with an AK-47 that had been a gift from Castro. Ironically, and in spite of repeated allegations of CIA involvement, there is little evidence for its direct meddling in the coup that toppled Allende. At most, the CIA was aware of the plot and may have lent encouragement.

Augusto Pinochet, the chief plotter against Allende who received US government support after the coup, was accused of murdering more than 3,200 people over his seventeen-year reign.

In recent years, the US military has worked with Chile on assorted security matters, including the development of a joint Chilean and US base for peacekeeping training at Fort Aguayo in Chile. Also, the USAF sent teams to Chile to help after an earthquake in 2010.

The Texas National Guard is partnered with Chile.

China

China is a huge land with an amazing history and culture and such resources and potential that it seems certain to become even more powerful as the twenty-first century proceeds. In fact, China is now such a major military power that it seems almost surprising that US forces have ever been in action on Chinese soil. But, they have. In fact, American troops were regularly in action in China for about an entire century from the 1840s to the 1940s.

In the nineteenth century, America was one of the Western powers eager to open up China to Western trade and influence. It was far from always a peaceful process, and from 1843 onwards, the United States regularly sent in troops to protect its citizens and its interests in China, particularly in the so-called treaty ports in which Western traders held a privileged position. A particular focus of American concern was the American part of the Shanghai International Settlement.

Most of these incidents were small, short-term operations, like brief US involvement in bombarding Chinese forts in the Second Opium War, the 1855 Battle of Ty-Ho Bay against Chinese pirates, or the punitive Formosan Expedition of 1867. But as the nineteenth century turned into the twentieth century, that was all about to change.

The Society of the Harmonious Fist (Boxers) was a Chinese secret society that led an anti-foreign and anti-Christian uprising in China from 1899 to 1901. In the summer of 1900, there was a famous siege of the international legations area in Beijing, including the American legation, in which American soldiers under the command of Captain John T. Myers played a heroic role in holding out against huge numbers of attackers. Eventually in August, after a battle at Yangcun in which troops of the US 14th Infantry Regiment played a key role, an international force broke through to Beijing and lifted the siege of the legations. Looting and reprisals followed.

China managed pretty much to stay out of the First World War, though Germany lost her colonial foothold in Tsingtao. Throughout the First World War, America's 15th Infantry Regiment remained stationed in China, and although a lot of Americans today don't know it, the regiment actually was based there until 1938, which is why its regimental crest is a dragon.

Another element of US activity in China was the Yangtze Patrol, a fascinating part of US naval history that deserves to be much better known, in which US ships cruised along China's mighty river.

In the period between the wars, China saw plenty of major political turmoil, and the US continued regular deployments in China. For instance, in 1925, America sent in troops to protect civilians in the Shanghai International Settlement from rioting and fighting. In 1926, with fighting going on in Hankow and Kiukiang, the United States sent in troops again. And in 1927, with more fighting going on in Shanghai and Nanking, the US again deployed troops and warships. Then in 1932, in a sign of things to come, the United States sent in troops to protect Americans in Shanghai as the Japanese entered the city.

In the 1930s, Imperial Japan took advantage of a weakened China to invade and occupy Manchuria and much of coastal China. Ahead lay a bitter and brutal war that lasted until the defeat of Japan in 1945 and saw the deaths of vast numbers of Chinese, often in appalling and horrifying circumstances, like the Rape of Nanking.

Increasingly, individual Americans and America itself were sucked into the war. Arthur Chin, a Chinese-American (Chinese father, Peruvian mother) from Portland, Oregon, volunteered for service in the Nationalist Air Force and became the first American fighter ace (five confirmed Japanese planes shot down) of the Second World War.

America, in spite of isolationism, had strong pro-Chinese leanings fed by a pro-China lobby. President Franklin D. Roosevelt saw a valuable ally in Chiang Kai-shek and the Nationalists against the rising power of Japan. Claire Chennault, an LSU Tiger, had become an American air adviser to Chiang Kai-shek in 1937. In April 1941, months before the Pearl Harbor attack, FDR authorised, formally or informally, the creation of the American Volunteer Group of pilots that made up the Flying Tigers. These pilots were drawn from the US Navy, Marines (including 'Pappy' Boyington, later of the Black Sheep Squadron), and the Army Air Corps. Twelve days after Pearl Harbor, Flying Tigers forces were already engaged with Japanese forces in China shooting down three Japanese bombers near Kunming. With the snarling teeth painted on their aircraft that became such a legendary sight, the Flying Tigers fought heroically against far larger numbers of Japanese planes and did significant damage to the enemy.

After Pearl Harbor, any hesitancy about helping the Chinese against the Japanese was a thing of the past, and from late 1941 until victory in 1945, America made great efforts to help the Chinese war effort. In the air, the China Air Task Force of the USAAF inherited the mantle of the Flying Tigers (and some of their pilots) but with huge additions of American manpower, planes and supplies. In August 1942 Chennault became commander of the 14th Air Force.

Most of the Doolittle Raiders of April 1942 landed in China where the Japanese authorities pursued them, killing hundreds of thousands of Chinese in the process.

Eventually US aircraft achieved air superiority over the Japanese and launched a vast strategic bombing campaign, Operation Matterhorn, with B-29s partly based in China. In addition, American transport planes airlifted invaluable supplies to the Chinese forces over what became known as the Hump, the eastern end of the Himalayas. Later in the war, Allied advances on the ground also allowed the opening of a land route for supplying Chinese forces, the Ledo Road. American generals, including General Albert C. Wedermeyer, worked with Chiang Kai-shek in trying to modernise and improve the Nationalist Chinese forces.

The OSS operated in China long before Pearl Harbor and continued to do so throughout the war.

In August 1945, shortly after atomic bombs were dropped on Hiroshima and Nagasaki, the Japanese surrendered. Peace did not, however, come to China. With Japan out of the picture, the stage was set for a long-awaited final showdown between Chiang's Nationalists and the Communists led by Mao Zedong and supported by Stalin's Soviet Union.

On 25 August 1945, Captain John Birch, an intelligence officer attached to Chennault's 14th Air Force, was shot and killed by Chinese Communists at a roadblock.

As well as the Nationalists, the US had worked alongside the Chinese Communists in fighting the Japanese during the war, but now, with the Cold War making the situation icy between the Soviets and Americans, America took the side of the Nationalists in China. It didn't turn out well. Despite the supplies, training and occasional deployment of US forces to help them, the Nationalists were hampered by too-often corrupt and ineffective leadership, and gradually gave way to the advancing Communists. Eventually, the US withdrew its forces from China, and in 1949 Chiang Kai-shek retreated to the island of Taiwan, starting the separation of Taiwan from the rest of China that is still in operation today. In 1950, the Chinese Communists took control of Tibet.

Ahead lay decades of animosity between the United States and Communist China, which saw plenty of Cold War and occasional 'Hot War'. America started training and supplying

Chinese Nationalist forces in Burma, stuck there after the war, and Tibetan rebels as well.

Then came the Korean War (*see* North Korea *and* South Korea). Mao, believing the United States was a 'paper tiger', was willing to roll the dice on the Korean peninsula. In August 1950 over 200,000 troops of the People's Liberation Army moved south to support the North Korean war effort. They conducted costly human-wave mass attacks. The war eventually evolved into a stalemate around the thirty-eighth parallel, dividing the country into two equal but unequal parts. This remains pretty much the situation to this day.

Taiwan became a source of long-term tension between Communist China and America. In 1955, the US Navy helped evacuate the Dachen Islands before the Communists took control there. Chairman Mao believed that international tension could help mobilise the population. On 23 August 1958, the People's Liberation Army rained 30,000 artillery shells in just one hour on the Nationalist-controlled island of Quemoy, killing 600 of Chiang's soldiers. The United States, obligated by a 1954 defence treaty, responded immediately with a massive naval deployment to the straits of Taiwan and the dispatch of 200 aircraft. From 1958 to 1979, the USAF maintained a presence at Ching Chuan Kang airbase in Taiwan. It remains a Republic of China airbase today.

Mao sought to export the socialist revolution by supporting the North Vietnamese during the Vietnamese war (*see* Vietnam).

In February 1972, though, President Nixon went to China and shook Chou Enlai's hand. The era of Ping-Pong diplomacy was born, and the Sino–Soviet Communist monolith was, thereby, broken up.

In 2010, China passed Japan to become the second-largest economy in the world, and currently, China is America's largest trading partner and debt holder. However, recent tensions over islands in the Pacific have shown how easily problems can occur.

Colombia

Even before the United States had been founded, Colombia was the site of the very first large-scale American invasion of a foreign country. During the War of Jenkins' Ear in 1741, the

Royal Navy Admiral Edward Vernon, known as 'Old Grog', landed a party of British and about 3,600 American colonial troops in an assault on Cartagena, Colombia. It wasn't a huge success. They failed to take the city and suffered heavy losses from disease. Lawrence Washington, George's older half-brother, participated in the Colombia expedition. George Washington's Virginia home, Mount Vernon, was later named after the British admiral.

For many years Colombia formed part of the Spanish Empire which possessed many precious metals. Colombia gained her independence from Spain in 1811 and soon was known as New Grenada. In 1846, the United States signed a treaty with New Grenada to uphold their sovereignty over the Isthmus of Panama. America would later have second thoughts about that policy.

President Teddy Roosevelt recognised Panamanian independence on 6 November 1903. The United States acted as midwife at the birth of Panama through which Roosevelt planned to build a canal. In 1921, seven years after the canal was built, the US government agreed to compensate Colombia $25 million for the loss of Panama.

During the Second World War, the US sent naval and military aviation missions to Colombia to assist Colombia's defences. The Panama Canal was obviously an area of particular strategic concern for the US. America also supplied Colombia with military equipment under Lend-Lease. After U-boats attacked a number of Colombian ships, Colombia entered the war on the Allied side in 1943.

In November of 1950, Colombia dispatched an infantry battalion to fight alongside American and UN forces in Korea. In fact, Colombia was the only Latin American nation to fight in the Korean War.

But in Colombia itself, civil war had broken out. In 1948, the assassination of presidential candidate Gaitá marked the beginning of a period known as La Violencia. It was a period of often intense political and military conflict, and out of it grew a variety of guerrilla groups. In the late 1950s and early 1960s, US advisors offered recommendations on developing a Colombian counter-insurgency strategy. The Special Survey Team issued its final report in May 1960, and in 1962, the Yarborough Team headed for Colombia. In 1962, the

Colombian security forces began to implement Plan Lazo. A key element of this plan was targeting leftist guerrilla groups in assorted enclaves. In 1964, Operation Marquetalia attacked one of these guerrilla enclaves, the so-called Republic of Marquetalia. Many of the guerrillas escaped, but the increased threat from security forces led a number of guerrilla groups to amalgamate and create the Revolutionary Armed Forces of Colombia – FARC.

Along with FARC, more urban-based guerrilla movements were also to emerge, first the ELN (National Liberation Army) and, then in the 1970s, the 19th of April Movement, or M-19. Also, in the 1970s, the Medellin Cartel, led by drug lord Pablo Escobar, headquartered its drug production and trafficking operations in Colombia. The growing illegal drug trade would add another source of huge instability in Colombia.

In the early 1980s, things seemed to be calming down a bit on the political front, but in November 1985, M-19 launched an attack on the Palace of Justice in Bogotá. What followed in the late 1980s and early 1990s were more ceasefires and more progress towards peace but also more violence on some fronts. M-19 eventually ceased their guerrilla war and became a political party. Meanwhile, drug gangs had killed three presidential candidates. However, Pablo Escobar himself was killed in late 1993. .

Despite this, drug gang violence continued during the 1990s and on into the twenty-first century, and so did the activities of FARC and ELN. It has been a brutal war.

The United States has provided extensive military aid and training to Colombian government forces. In 1999, Plan Colombia was launched, and over the years, support worth billions of dollars from the US government has been delivered. And US military personnel have been significantly involved.

US Special Forces have played a significant role in Colombia. For instance, in 2003, the United States expanded its involvement with the country by deploying special forces in Colombia to train Colombian soldiers in anti-terrorism. US personnel have operated out of a number of bases in Colombia. A 2009 agreement to give US personnel access to more bases in Colombia caused huge controversy.

The South Carolina National Guard is partnered with Colombia.

Comoros

The archipelago of the Comoros is located in the Indian Ocean between Mozambique and Madagascar. And yes, Americans have attacked them, or at least, one of them.

In 1850, the American whaler *Maria* and its captain and crew were seized by locals on the Island of Johanna, also known as Anjouan Island.

In 1851, the USS *Dale*, a 16-gun sloop under Captain William Pearson turned up at Mutsamadu to find out what was happening and demand from the sultan the release of the American ship, plus a hefty compensation fee of $20,000. The sultan instead offered $500 cash, plus bullocks and trinkets to the same value. That's probably quite a lot of bullocks and trinkets in 1851 terms. But Pearson was playing hardball. He refused the offer and pulled his ship up not far from the beach, with eight guns trained on the port's fortifications. The offer from the sultan went up to $5,000, leaving Pearson unsure how to proceed next. However, when he saw local military reinforcements arriving in the town, Pearson decided it was time to act and opened fire. After six shots, a white flag went up on the fort, and Pearson ceased fire, while sending a launch with marines and Lieutenant Fairfax to find out what was going on. When, however, negotiations could still not be satisfactorily accomplished, *Dale* opened fire again, and after about another hour of firing, Lieutenant Fairfax returned to the town. This time, he was given the whaler's captain, $1,000, an offer of a $5,000 bond, a plea from the sultan to stop the bombardment, and an offer to surrender the town. With the addition of a treaty giving America favoured trading status, Pearson accepted the deal on offer, and the war was finished.

In 1887, the USS *Alliance*, investigating the allegedly fraudulent sale of an American schooner on Anjouan Island, turned up and seized parts of the outfit of the ship.

In recent years, US military personnel have returned to the Comoros on a much friendlier basis. In 2007, the USS *Forrest Sherman* became the first US Navy ship to visit the Comoros in thirty-three years.

Costa Rica

Ah, Costa Rica, sandwiched between Panama to its south and Nicaragua to the north. Costa Rica means 'rich coast'.

Costa Rica played a leading role in the alliance of Central American nations against William Walker's filibuster movement in Nicaragua (*see* Nicaragua). It was Costa Rica's General Joaquin Mora, the brother of President Mora, who led his allied troops against the Yankees in 1856. Many of the Costa Rican officers were the European-educated sons of coffee barons and were themselves excellent horsemen. Their conscripted troops wore white trousers and shirts with straw hats circled with red bands. Very dashing.

General Walker's force of mostly American filibusters invaded Costa Rica from Nicaragua. On 20 March 1856, the Battle of Santa Rosa was fought, which resulted in the deaths of nineteen Costa Ricans and fifty-nine of Walker's men. Great result for the Costa Ricans (except those who died obviously) but terrible result for Walker and even worse (obviously) for the fifty-nine. The filibusters had been driven from the field by a peasant army.

After Walker's subsequent defeat in Nicaragua, US Navy ships, such as the *Decatur* and *St Mary's*, helped to evacuate Walker filibusters from Costa Rica. Lieutenant David McCorkle was assigned the duty of marching 300 filibusters from Nicaragua to Punta Arenas in Costa Rica.

Costa Rica joined the allies along with other Central American nations on 8 December 1941, and German business interests were seized by the government. Costa Rica wasn't exactly a major focus of US military interest during the war, but at one stage the US considered building an airbase on Cocos Island to protect the Panama Canal. In the end it was never built, but they did put early warning radar on the island.

In 1948, Costa Rica experienced a month-long civil war, which claimed around 2,000 lives. The US did not intervene directly in the conflict, but they did have a clear preference in the outcome. The existing Picado regime was supported by the Popular Vanguard Party – a Communist party. The Truman administration, concerned about the spread of Communism in North America, mobilised forces in the neighbouring Panama zone and sought to cut off supplies to the Picado regime.

José Figueres eventually became the victorious rebel leader

who toppled Picado in Costa Rica. Figueres had initial CIA support for his activities. He served three times as president of Costa Rica between 1948 and 1974. In 1959, however, Figueres would send arms to Fidel Castro in Cuba, and there have been alleged CIA operations against him. In the 1980s, the Contras also had a presence in Costa Rica.

Since 1949, Costa Rica's constitution has banned a standing army and in 2010, a decision by Costa Rica to allow US military access to it caused some local controversy. In recent years, the US has been heavily involved with helping Costa Rica fight illegal drug smuggling, and it has also been involved in a number of emergency relief operations as well.

The New Mexico National Guard is partnered with Costa Rica.

Croatia

Croatia is a land with some superbly beautiful Adriatic coastline. And it's a coastline the US military has seen quite a lot of over the years, in fact. Maybe they love the scenery too.

If so, they haven't been the only ones. Croatia had been part of the Austro-Hungarian Empire, and at the end of the First World War, American troops were sent to occupy parts of what is now southern Croatia until it was established exactly who would rule the area after the war. A certain amount of friction developed with the Italians, who were keen to take over the area, and at Trogir, the USS *Cowell* moved in to prevent the Italians taking control. Meanwhile a rather similar situation was also developing in northern parts of the country, in the Croatian port of Rijeka (then frequently known by its Italian name, Fiume). Here, Italian moves prompted the withdrawal of an Allied force, including some US forces and the USS *Pittsburgh*.

American forces were prepared to take action, but probably not enough to actually fight a war with their allies over the area – however beautiful the scenery. In the end, the Italians got Rijeka and Istria in the north (until they lost it again in the Second World War), and the new country of Yugoslavia got most of Croatia.

In 1941, during the Second World War, the Germans invaded Yugoslavia. Some Croatians resisted them, obviously including

Croat partisans, but other Croatians formed an independent state allied to the Nazis. As such, Croatia, both the part that had been occupied by the Italians and the part allied to the Germans, became a major target for American military activity. Rijeka was, for instance, heavily bombed. US aircraft flew missions specifically to support partisan operations in Croatia, and OSS personnel on the ground in Croatia also assisted. The Allies even had a base on Croatian soil, on the island of Vis in the Adriatic. It was fortunate for one George McGovern that they did. In December 1944, McGovern's B-24, based in Italy, was badly damaged on a mission to bomb a factory at Pilsen. Unable to make it to Italy, McGovern managed to land the plane on a challenging airstrip on Vis and save his crew.

The end of the Second World War produced in some sense a similar situation to the end of the First World War, and once again, American forces were sent in to try to help sort things out. The main area of contention was in the north of Yugoslavia, in the area that had been held between the wars by the Italians. Consequently, the beautiful Croatian city of Pula on the tip of the Istrian peninsula was put under Allied Military Control, with US troops, among others, stationed there for a couple of years until it could be decided who would administer it permanently. In the end, it became part of Yugoslavia.

But that was not truly the end. In 1991, as a desire for independence grew among the different peoples making up the Federal Republic of Yugoslavia, Croatia declared independence. A bitter civil war followed in which Serbs living in parts of Croatia bordering Bosnia and Serbia, with the help of Milosevic's Yugoslav Army, seized control of big chunks of Croatian territory and continued to hold them while the civil war in Bosnia-Herzegovina raged next door.

Bosnia, of course, was the main focus of American military activity during this period, but the US did get involved in Croatia again as well. Planes from the Serb-held area of Croatia were being used against targets inside Bosnia, in contravention of NATO's Operation Deny Flight. In response, US aircraft were involved in attacking Serb-held Udbina airbase inside Croatia's border.

In 1991, the new Croatian army, short of weapons and training, had not been able to prevent the secession of much Croatian-Serb territory. In 1995, however, it swiftly retook all the areas held by the Serbs. Partly this was due to the changed attitude of Milosevic to the Croatian Serbs, but some people have also speculated about the role of American advisers from private companies in the rebuilding of the Croatian army during this period.

Since the end of the war, the US has developed assorted links with the Croatian military, supplying equipment and training, and Croatian forces regularly take part alongside US forces in exercises. America has a variety of military agreements in force with Croatia, and the Croatian Army has sent troops to Afghanistan.

Cuba

The beautiful island of Cuba is just ninety miles from Florida, so it's not entirely surprising that over the years America has taken a close interest in the island. A very close interest. Repeatedly.

Already by the early nineteenth century, American forces were in action there. At this stage, America's main concern was combating piracy, and in the 1820s they made a number of landings, including one in July 1823 when three American vessels attacked a pirate schooner off Matanzas, Cuba. When some of the pirates managed to make it ashore, an American landing party went after them. It was a small start to US involvement in Cuba, but plenty more was to come.

In the same year that the pirate schooner off Matanzas was being put out of business, John Quincy Adams, then Secretary of State, was having thoughts about gravity and falling apples but Newtonian physics wasn't exactly his main interest. That was Cuba. He wrote, 'If an apple, severed by the tempest from its native tree, cannot choose but fall to the ground, Cuba, forcibly disjoined from its unnatural connexion [sic] with Spain, and incapable of self-support, can only gravitate towards the North American Union.'

1823 was quite a big year in US foreign policy, because in December President Monroe produced the Monroe Doctrine. The Monroe Doctrine (nothing to do with Marilyn, obviously) basically stated that America could just about accept existing European colonies in the Americas, but from then on, they were going to regard outside interference in North and South

America as interference with US interests. To be fair, having chucked Britain out of America, some Americans felt a natural fellowship for any other locals wanting to join them in chucking out European powers. But over the decades, as US power grew, the Monroe Doctrine also began to be interpreted as a concept that the United States, as the biggest power in the Americas, had a special responsibility for what goes on around it. Both of these attitudes, coupled with the idea of Manifest Destiny as well, were to provide the backing for American involvement with Cuba.

In 1858, in the Ostend Manifesto, a bunch of American diplomats in Europe recommended that the United States buy Cuba and suggested that if, by any chance, it wasn't for sale, the United States would be justified in seizing the island from Spain. The manifesto is somewhat surprisingly named after a port and popular cross-channel ferry destination in Belgium because that's where the diplomats ended up meeting. Nothing came of it in the end partly because some Northerners saw in it a Southern attempt to add another slave-owning Southern state to the Union. Still at least maybe they got to enjoy some nice Belgian beer and chocolate.

Spain had long-term ties to the island of Cuba, with Columbus having reached it on his first voyage on 28 October 1492, but by the 400th anniversary of his arrival, things were beginning to look a bit problematic on the island for Spain. In 1868, a local insurrection burst out and dragged on for about ten years, from which, not surprisingly, it got the name of the Ten Years War. Then again in 1895, another rebellion was launched. Harsh measures taken by the Spanish in their attempts to smash the rebellion boosted fellow feeling in America for those fighting for freedom from a European power. But the US still wasn't about to go to war. Not quite yet anyway.

The newspaper publisher William Randolph Hearst (of *Citizen Kane* fame) wanted a war in order to help sell newspapers. Hearst had a famous exchange of telegrams with his photo-journalist Frederic Remington who was in Cuba prior to the Spanish-American war. Hearst received a telegram from Remington that said, 'Everything is quiet. There is no trouble here. There will be no war. I wish to return. Remington.' Hearst sent the answer, 'Please remain. You furnish the pictures, and I'll furnish the war.'

On 25 January 1898, the USS *Maine*, an armoured cruiser, arrived in Havana harbour. The largest island in the Caribbean had been experiencing an insurrection by local Cuban rebels against their Spanish overlords for the past three years. On 15 February 1898, at 9:40 p.m., one or perhaps two explosions rocked the battleship. About three-quarters of her crew (266 lives) were lost.

What really happened that night remains a mystery that will, perhaps, never be solved. The US Navy's Sampson Board of Inquiry ruled unanimously that a foreign device or mine triggered the explosion and sinking. A variety of suggestions and counter-suggestions have since been put forward for what really happened that night.

If the *Maine* was, in fact, destroyed by a mine, it is by no means even certain that the Spanish government placed it there, although they did have motivation. It could be that the Cuban rebels themselves might have used a mine in order to get the Americans more deeply involved in Cuba.

Many in Cuba today are convinced that a false-flag conspiracy (the US Navy sank its own ship) was to blame. There is no evidence to suggest such a thing. What we do know for certain is that President William McKinley, who had only the US Navy Sampson report to go by, pressed for war with Spain.

The US Congress debated and passed resolutions calling for Cuban independence. Spain responded by declaring war. President McKinley's opening move was to impose a naval blockade of Cuba.

In late June 1898, American troops landed in Cuba. On 1 July, Teddy Roosevelt, with the assistance of the African-American Buffalo Soldiers, led his Rough Riders to victory over the Spanish in the Battle of San Juan Hill. The Americans and their Cuban allies had won the war in just over three months at a cost of just under 3,000 killed – most of these attributable to disease. Nearby Puerto Rico was annexed as part of the peace settlement.

At the time, America also got another bit of real estate that you've heard of. The United States began construction of its oldest overseas naval base, Guantanamo Bay, in 1898. A long-term lease was negotiated with the Cuban government in 1903.

Having helped free Cuba from a European colonial power,

the US wasn't about to turn Cuba into an American colony – not officially anyway – but it did now regard it as very much part of its sphere of influence, and it was determined to protect its growing interests there. By force if the US thought it necessary. And regularly if thought necessary.

From 1906 to 1909, Teddy Roosevelt (now president) dispatched US forces to occupy Cuba again. The Cuban rebels laid down their arms at the sight of US troops, and there was no bloodshed. The US Army built fifty-seven miles of roads and supervised the free election before their withdrawal.

In 1912, President William Taft sent the navy and US Marines to support the Cuban government in suppressing another rebellion. And in 1917, during the First World War, US forces, with the excuse of being invited to practice drilling in a warm climate, helped to combat political unrest that was causing damage to the sugar industry and sugar harvest. This became known, not entirely unreasonably, as the Sugar Intervention.

By the end of 1941, of course, Americans had quite a lot else on their minds apart from Cuba, like the need to win a world war. Cuba wasn't exactly on the frontlines during the Second World War, and for one resident, it was all just too quiet. Ernest Hemingway, a resident of Cuba and avid fisherman, could not stand the idea of missing a war. From the summer of 1942 to the end of 1943, Hemingway, based on Cuba, took *Pilar*, his wooden fishing yacht, armed with machine guns and hand grenades, out into the Caribbean hunting for German U-boats. He did allegedly finally sight one, only for it to submerge before he could reach it.

After the war, Cuba became a fleshpot with casino gambling and the US mafia. Batista, realizing that he could not win electoral victory, seized power in a coup in 1952. Organised crime leaders such as 'Lucky' Luciano, Meyer Lansky and Santo Trafficante helped turn Havana into a Latin Las Vegas.

Fidel Castro was the illegitimate son of a wealthy Galician immigrant to Cuba. Six foot three and powerfully built, he became an accomplished athlete. In 1949, he was offered a contract to pitch for the New York Giants baseball team, but he turned them down. History might have been so different, and so might the Giants.

Instead of playing ball with the US, Castro began launching attacks on the Moncada army barracks in 1953 to start the

Cuban revolution, which lasted until the collapse of the Batista regime in 1958. Batista fled the country on New Year's Day 1959.

Fidel Castro, who had not started as a Communist, had become America's worst Cold War nightmare – a revolutionary Communist government on America's doorstep that was allied with the Soviet Union. The US hadn't been too keen about Spain ruling Cuba, and it was even less keen about Russia moving in next door.

On 4 March 1960, another ship explosion in Havana harbour influenced the course of Cuban-American links and history. This time it was the Belgian *La Coubre*. Loaded with ammunition, it blew up, causing widespread devastation. This explosion was probably the result of negligence, though Fidel used it as an excuse to accuse the United States of sabotage and to request more arms from the Soviet Union.

The Bay of Pigs Fiasco must rank among the more disastrous interventions in US military history. On 15 April 1961, eight American B-26s bombed Cuban airfields as the CIA's brigade of Cuban exile volunteers approached the Bay of Pigs. President John F. Kennedy, however, refused to provide additional air support for the doomed invasion and the bitter fighting that followed.

After the Bay of Pigs fiasco, the US government tried other ways of getting at Castro. The Kennedy brothers initiated Operation Mongoose, which attempted many times to assassinate Fidel Castro. They tried exploding cigars and poisoned ice cream, among other ridiculous attempts.

JFK retaliated against Cuba in February 1962 by banning the importation of Cuban cigars. A devoted smoker, Kennedy had stocked up on his personal supply in advance.

During the Cuban Missile Crisis in October 1962, the world came closer to thermonuclear war than at any other time in its history. After a US reconnaissance flight over the island took photos of a missile site under construction, many options were explored on how to deal with the introduction of Soviet medium-range nuclear missiles on Fidel's Cuba, some of them involving a US invasion of the island. Ultimately, cooler heads prevailed, and America opted for a naval blockade of Cuba.

Soviet ships that were delivering more missile parts turned around, but the Soviets gained their original strategic objective by forcing the United States to withdraw its own medium-range missiles from Turkey, and Cuba gained a pledge that the United States would never again invade Cuba.

And since then, the US has remained in Guantanamo, and the Communist government has remained in power in Havana. But just recently a rapprochement finally has started between the US and Cuba.

Cyprus

Cyprus was famous for copper mining in the ancient world. One of those little-known facts is that the word 'copper' is derived from the Greek name for this island, Kupros.

Cyprus has not exactly been the scene of vast amounts of US military activity and much of what there has been has been linked to America's alliance with the British. Although, on one occasion, it was rather aimed at them. In October 1956, in defiance of American wishes, Britain and France invaded Egypt over the Suez Crisis. In the run-up to that invasion, in September 1956, two U-2 spy flights were sent over Cyprus and Malta and the Eastern Mediterranean in an attempt to photograph any British military build-up there. Even friends can fall out sometimes.

This, however, was the exception. Due to Cyprus's key strategic location, close to the conflicts of the Middle East, the US has a history of sharing communications and intelligence facilities with Britain on the island.

American planes have also used British air facilities on the island on a number of occasions. During the 1970s, American U-2s flying from RAF Akrotiri in Cyprus were used to monitor the Arab-Israeli situation in the Middle East, and American casualties were evacuated to RAF Akrotiri after the 1983 Beirut bombing. Technically, however, British bases on Cyprus have not actually been in the nation state of Cyprus since independence in 1960. They are situated in legally British sovereign territory.

In the 1960s and 1970s, America played a significant, but still controversial, role in the crisis between Cyprus, Greece and Turkey that led to the Turkish invasion in 1974. And in July, after the Turkish army landed on the island, US Navy ships were deployed to evacuate US civilians.

Czech Republic

The Czechs have a long and proud history, but for a lot of the time the modern Czech Republic tends to be known, potentially confusingly in the history books, as places like Bohemia and Moravia. In 1918, that all changed. As the Austro-Hungarian Empire fell apart, new nations were born, among them Czechoslovakia, the land of the Czechs, and to the east, the land of the Slovaks, united in one state. And even before the new state existed, the US was involved with it.

During the First World War, Czechs and Slovaks hoped that an Allied victory would lead to independence for their peoples, and formed Czechoslovak Legions to fight for the Allies, but ultimately to fight for their own freedom as well. Czech and Slovak volunteers fought alongside the Russian army, but various Czechoslovakian units were also formed in France, and among those fighting in these units were several thousand Americans of Czech and Slovak ancestry. Men from the Czechoslovak Legions would go on to form a key part of the armed forces of the new country.

America had quite a lot to do with the formation of the country politically as well. The tenth point of President Woodrow Wilson's Fourteen Points demanded, 'The peoples of Austria-Hungary, whose place among the nations we wish to see safeguarded and assured, should be accorded the freest opportunity to autonomous development.' The new state of Czechoslovakia actually declared its independence in October 1918, even before the First World War was finished. However, its borders were to be discussed in the Paris Peace Conference in 1919. Among the considerations was the future of German-speaking parts of the new country. In the end, it was decided that German-speakers should not be separated, and international acceptance of the new state was formalized in the Treaty of St Germain in 1919. German speakers within Czechoslovakia were, in less than two decades, to be at the heart of the Sudetenland Crisis, a key point on the road to the Second World War.

In October 1938, after Munich and the failure of Chamberlain's attempts for 'peace in our time' German troops entered the Sudetenland. But that was not enough for Hitler, and in March 1939, German forces occupied Bohemia and Moravia as well. In addition to territory, Hitler also acquired some very useful heavy industry, including that in advanced armaments. Many of the German tanks that participated in the invasion of France and the low countries in 1940 had actually been produced by the Czech company Škoda. And that was one reason, when America started its bombing campaign in Europe, some of the targets were in what is now the Czech Republic. Not surprisingly, the Škoda armaments plant at Pilsen came in for particular attention.

In 1945, though, as German resistance began to crumble away, the crucial question for America became not what to bomb in the country but what to do about a land invasion.

Near the end of the Second World War in Europe, there was a certain amount of turmoil in the Allied ranks over how best to proceed in Czechoslovakia. On 12 April 1945, Franklin D. Roosevelt, America's wartime president, died. In late April 1945 Patton's Third Army crossed the Czech border.

Winston Churchill wanted the Allied forces to liberate Prague before the Soviets arrived. Dwight Eisenhower, however, was more concerned with minimizing US casualties and adhering to the Yalta agreements in order not to upset the Soviets. Patton, predictably, was all for pressing on and liberating more of Czech territory and heading for Prague. The situation led to some tension among the US military leadership. On 6 May, Omar Bradley found himself phoning Patton to try to get Patton to obey Eisenhower's orders and shouting at him, ordering him to halt.

The situation was made even more difficult by the return of an OSS team from Prague, which reported that news of the American advance into Czech territory had set off a rising against the Germans in Prague and that the SS were ruthlessly crushing the rebels, even as the American advance had, because of Eisenhower's wishes, ground to a halt just forty miles away. Patton again pleaded for permission to advance and liberate Prague, and again he was denied. Unsure who was going to liberate them, some Czech villagers erected signs saying 'Welcome Americans' on one side of their village and 'Welcome Russians' on the other side. In the end, Eisenhower managed to halt the advance along a line between Pilsen and Karlsbad in Bohemia.

The Red Army would take Prague instead, and post-war Czechoslovakia would become part of the Soviet sphere of influence. And in 1968, Soviet tanks would once again advance into Prague, this time to crush the Prague Spring.

It was not until the Velvet Revolution of 1989 that the Czechoslovakians would once again be free of Soviet influence. In 1993, Czechoslovakia separated peacefully into the separate nations of the Czech Republic and Slovakia.

The Czech Republic has been a NATO member since 1999. Czech units have participated alongside American forces in recent campaigns in Afghanistan and Iraq. However, President Obama did scrap a missile defence programme in the Czech Republic in 2009.

The Texas and Nebraska National Guards are partnered with the Czech Republic.

Democratic Republic of the Congo

A lot of people tend to get this country confused with the Republic of the Congo, which is also on the list (*see* Republic of the Congo). Basically, this Congo is the former Belgian colony straddling much of the mighty Congo River (Joseph Conrad, author of *Heart of Darkness*, served here as captain on a steamship) and has a capital at Kinshasa, while the Republic of the Congo is the former French colony on the north bank of a bit of the Congo River with a capital at Brazzaville. Between 1971 and 1997, the Democratic Republic of the Congo was called Zaire, and it tends to be in the news more than the other Congo, often for not very positive reasons.

The mouth of the Congo was a major slaving area and received a lot of attention from the United States Africa Squadron in its anti-slaving activities. In fact, it seized more vessels in the Congo area than in any other one location. Between 1853 and 1861, it captured twelve vessels here, not including those taken at nearby Cabinda (*see* Angola).

In May 1879, the US Navy returned (not all of it, obviously) as the USS *Ticonderoga* ventured a short distance into the Congo River on a mission to promote American trade with the area.

One American (or Anglo-American) who played a major though controversial part in the history of the area is the controversial (very controversial) figure of Henry Morton Stanley. He was born John Rowlands in Wales, and by 1859, he had reached the United States, where he managed to get himself adopted by a rich merchant, Henry Hope Stanley, and changed his name. During the Civil War, he first joined the Confederate Army and fought at the Battle of Shiloh. Then after being taken prisoner, he briefly joined the Union Army and eventually ended up in the Union Navy. Interesting CV already. By the 1870s, he was in Africa, sent by a New York newspaper magnate to locate the well-known missionary Dr David Livingstone. This he did, and later in the decade, in an expedition that only saw about a third of those who set out on it complete the trip, he traced the Congo River to the sea. This and subsequent exploration work in the area on behalf of King Leopold II of the Belgians eventually led to the creation of a Belgian-controlled territory in the area, the Congo Free State, that would eventually become the Democratic Republic of the Congo. The Congo Free State, however, saw some particularly brutal and nasty atrocities perpetrated by some of those in authority. These abuses eventually led to a major international human rights movement, one that received support from, among many others, Mark Twain and Sir Arthur Conan Doyle.

During the Second World War, the USAAF used the airports at Léopoldville and Elisabethville for transport aircraft on one of its trans-Africa routes.

The Democratic Republic of the Congo became independent in 1960. Soon after independence, the mineral-rich province of Katanga tried to secede, and the Prime Minister Patrice Lumumba was killed.

A UN mission was sent in to help sort out the Katanga problem, and America was involved with that, with the USAF helping airlift UN troops into the Congo and the US Navy transporting troops and supplies as well. To what extent America was or was not involved with the actual death of Lumumba remains controversial. His death would eventually lead to the seizure of long-term power in the country by Mobutu, with whom America developed a lot of friendly links, seeing him as an ally against Communism in the Cold War. When a few years later Che Guevara turned up in the Congo to assist rebels there, America assisted Congolese forces to defeat him. And in 1978, the US flew in Belgian and French forces to help tackle rebels.

However, with the early 1990s seeing the end of the Cold War, Mobutu began to lose his value as an ally, and America was less inclined to ignore the shortcomings of his dictatorial rule. Inside the country, Mobutu's authority was starting to crumble as well. In 1991, when unpaid troops started looting the capital Kinshasa, the US again flew in Belgian and French paratroopers to evacuate civilians. Mobutu was forced out of the country in 1997.

By 1996, the country was about to enter a horrific period of civil wars. Even after the main war, sometimes known as Africa's World War because of the involvement of nine African countries, ended in 2003, instability and conflict have lasted in some parts of the country until very recently. It has been a period in which violence, disease and hunger have killed millions, and other atrocities, like rape, have become appallingly frequent.

In 1996, President Bill Clinton sent US planes to assist in surveying part of the east of the country for humanitarian relief efforts; some of these aircraft were shot at. In 1997, Clinton sent an evacuation force to nearby Gabon, ready if it was needed to evacuate civilians from the Democratic Republic of the Congo.

The United States has helped train some of the peacekeepers from other African countries who have been operating in the Congo and has trained some Congolese troops in military medical operations and in demining techniques. US troops have also been in the Democratic Republic of the Congo to train a battalion as part of efforts to defeat the notorious Lord's Resistance Army.

Denmark

1,100 years ago, the word 'Danes' struck terror into the hearts of people across Europe. These days, though, we might instead think of the Little Mermaid who doesn't scare anybody and is not known for raiding and pillaging.

The country was invaded and occupied by Germany on 9 April 1940, during the German campaign to control Denmark and Norway. The Danes didn't stand much of a chance. They had tiny military forces compared to Germany, and unfortunately (for the Danes, not the *Wehrmacht*) they were situated right next door to Germany, with the Jutland peninsula giving the invaders direct access by land to much of Denmark. The Danish government surrendered within hours.

However, there were two bits of land that were part of the Kingdom of Denmark that the Germans were never to get their hands on. One was Iceland (though that became independent during the Second World War), and the other was Greenland, which still today remains part of the Kingdom of Denmark.

As the war progressed and the Atlantic convoy routes and air-ferry routes from the United States to Britain became ever more important, control of Greenland and Iceland also become vital. The Danish government and king remained in Denmark under German occupation and were clearly not really in a position to authorise occupation of Greenland or Iceland by the Allies.

The British had invaded Iceland in 1940 (before handing it over to the US in 1941), and on 9 April 1941, a year after the German invasion of Denmark, President Franklin D.Roosevelt announced that the United States had concluded an agreement with the Danish envoy to the United States and with the support of the Greenlanders themselves to occupy Greenland and set up bases there. Subsequently, thousands of US troops were sent to garrison Greenland, and airbases and a naval base were established.

Soon the war came even to Greenland. A bit. It was a war over weather but rather more serious than two forecasters disagreeing. The Germans attempted to establish clandestine weather stations on the eastern side of Greenland in order to support their sea and air operations. And it was the job of US forces working with the Northeast Greenland Sledge Patrol to stop them. Greenland's army consisted of only a few people and was the smallest in the Second World War. Nevertheless, this tiny battle had important implications for the wider war, and people did die. One corporal in the Sledge Patrol was killed fighting in Greenland.

Sabine Island saw a number of incidents on this distant front of the Second World War. In the spring of 1943, a German post there was detected but then withdrawn before it could be attacked. Later, another German station was detected on the island, and this time, it was attacked by American bombers based in Iceland, and then the Coast Guard went in.

In 1946, there was apparently discussion in US government circles about the possibility of purchasing Greenland from Denmark for $100 million in gold, but when the offer was made, no deal was agreed.

Despite that, however, America kept bases on Greenland after the war. For instance, Bluie West One became Narsarsuaq Air Base until 1952, and Bluie West Eight became Sondrestrom Air Base, and the US stayed there until 1992.

In the post-war period, though, it is the airbase at Thule that has become the main focus of America's military activities in Greenland. Thule Air Base in Qaasuitsap Greenland lies within 800 miles of the Arctic Circle. The 12th Space Warning Squadron located there is in charge of monitoring arctic air space for missile attack. Outside temperatures there are almost constantly below freezing.

During the Second World War, US forces weren't in action in just Greenland; they were also involved with Denmark itself. The USAAF conducted a variety of operations over Denmark during the war, including bombing missions against a major Luftwaffe base at Aalborg. But other mission types took place as well. On 12 May 1944, five B-17s dropped 1.74 million propaganda leaflets over Denmark. Even such non-bombing missions, however, carried risks. On that mission, two airmen were killed and three wounded. And in Operation Carpetbagger, the so-called Carpetbaggers of the 492nd Bombardment Group dropped supplies to resistance groups in assorted countries, including Denmark and Norway.

America had military personnel based in Denmark also in the post-war period with, for instance, US Air Force planes based at Kastrup Airport Copenhagen.

Denmark became a founding member of NATO in 1949 and remains a key member today. US military links with Denmark are strong, and in recent years Danish contingents have served alongside the US military in Bosnia, Iraq and Afghanistan and in air operations over Libya.

Djibouti

Yes, Djibouti. Even though a lot of people couldn't quickly locate it on a globe, Djibouti is currently of big importance to the United States.

Djibouti, a tiny nation on the Horn of Africa, was a French colony from the late nineteenth century until it gained its independence in 1977.

The French Foreign Legion used to have a base in Djibouti, called Camp Lemonnier. The base was named after Emile Lemonnier – a French general beheaded by the Japanese for refusing to sign a surrender document while serving in Indochina in the last months of the Second World War. Camp Lemonnier is conveniently located next to Djibouti-Ambouli International Airport and is close to the Djibouti port as well.

Djibouti itself is in a strategic location, especially because of its vital sea routes (about 10 per cent of the world's petroleum passes near Djibouti's waters every year), particularly those affected by Somali pirates. It is handy for Somalia (next door), Yemen (less than fifty miles distant, across the sea), and other areas of conflict where extreme Islamists are active. And it is handy for Sudan, South Sudan, and areas where the Lord's Resistance Army has been active. Djibouti, worried about Islamic extremism, has kept friendly relations with the United States. Thousands of French troops, including some from the Foreign Legion are still stationed there. A great location then for a US base, particularly after a civil war was brought to a final end in 2001.

In 2002, the USS *Whitney* arrived at Djibouti and landed a party of US Marines. The marines began cleaning up Camp Lemonnier, which had been abandoned and fallen into extreme disrepair.

In recent years, many have speculated about the extent of US involvement in Africa and the number of bases it might have there, but the existence of Camp Lemonnier, AFRICOM's main African facility, is not in dispute. It is a United States Naval Expeditionary Base and home to the Combined Joint Task Force Horn of Africa. Thousands of Americans, including Special Forces, have been based in Camp Lemonnier with access to large amounts of equipment, including both manned and unmanned aircraft type (drones). However, it has been suggested recently that drone operations will be moved from Camp Lemonnier and Djibouti airport to Chabelley Airfield, some ten kilometres distant.

As AFRICOM's premier African facility and with a long history of drone and Special Forces activity in counter-terrorism and anti-piracy operations in the surrounding region, Camp Lemonnier has been involved in a wide variety of actions, many of them secret.

One action reported in 2012 involved a mission to rescue an American and a Danish worker held hostage for ransom for months in Somalia. Navy SEALs from Camp Lemonnier parachuted in, hiked to where the hostages were held, killed nine of the hostage-takers, and flew out with no losses of their own and the hostages safe.

Dominica

Not to be confused with the Dominican Republic, Dominica is not an island that Americans had much to do with militarily, although the US does have a small connection with the area.

In December 1800, during the Quasi-War against the French, the US frigate *Philadelphia* captured French privateer *La Levrette* off Dominica. 'Levrette' means 'female greyhound' but, unfortunately for the French, obviously in this instance the greyhound didn't run fast enough.

Dominica seems to have been an area of some interest to US warships during this conflict because the USS *Constitution*, also on the trail of French privateers, is recorded as joining up with Commodore John Barry's squadron at Dominica during this period.

Dominica lent its support to the invasion of Grenada in 1983, and in recent years, personnel from Dominica have taken part in assorted exercises alongside US personnel, including training for the fight against illegal narcotics and organised crime. In 2012, the United States gave Dominica two patrol boats to help with law enforcement and maritime security.

Dominican Republic

Not to be confused with Dominica, the Dominican Republic is situated on the eastern side of the Caribbean island of Hispaniola, with Haiti on the western portion. It has long had strong and close ties with the United States, and today more than a million people of Dominican origin live in the United States. The US has taken an interest in the Dominican Republic pretty much from the beginning of US history, and has sent in the marines a few times. Well, quite a lot of times, actually.

The Dominican Republic was first colonised by the Spanish and then the French. Some of America's first military engagements in the area were against them. During the Undeclared War against the French in 1800, marines from the USS *Constitution* under Captain Daniel Carmick captured the French ship *Sandwich* before spiking guns at Puerto Plata.

African slaves were imported to work the sugar-cane plantations. Toussaint L'Ouverture's Revolution in the first decade of the nineteenth century (*see* Haiti) meant that Haiti ruled the Dominican Republic until it gained its independence in 1844.

During the American Civil War, the Dominican Republic reverted to Spanish rule. American distraction with fighting the Civil War made it difficult to enforce the Monroe Doctrine.

In April 1903, marines from the USS *Atlanta* landed to guard US diplomats in Santo Domingo City during conflict there.

Things got even busier in 1904 as the USS *Detroit* was dispatched to try to bring peace between the different factions in the country and 'protect US interests'. In January, the USS *Detroit* landed marines at Puerto Plata. A few days later, the ship landed marines at Sosua. After a few more days, the USS *Detroit* and this time the USS *Hartford* were landing more US Marines and sailors in the country. In February, it was the turn of USS *Newark* and *Columbia* to land marines and sailors, this time at Santo Domingo. The Clyde Line steamer *New York* had been fired upon by revolutionaries, and the revolutionaries had also opened fire on the American landing party. With the assistance of naval gunfire, the American force drove the revolutionaries out of the city.

Things were a little more peaceful in 1905 and 1906. America kept a floating battalion in Dominican waters on board the USS *Yankee*, but in the end, they were withdrawn. Something similar happened with the USS *Prairie* in 1912.

In 1914, US ships intervened with gunfire to prevent the bombardment of Puerto Plata, and in 1916 American forces went in again. President Woodrow Wilson intervened on behalf of Jimenes, who was the fifth Dominican president since 1911. Jimenes was engaged in a civil war with the anti-American Secretary of War, Desiderio Arias. Admiral Caperton of the US Navy landed a party of 600 bluejackets and marines at Santo Domingo on 12 May 1916, and on 13 May, he delivered an ultimatum to Arias to get himself and his forces out of the city.

US occupation of the country followed with assorted operations. The US Navy gunboat *Sacramento* landed 130 marines at Puerto Plata on 1 June 1916. That day, H. J. Hirshinger became the first US Marine to be killed in the Dominican Republic. Colonel 'Uncle Joe' Pendleton led an assault that captured Santiago. He declared, 'We are not in an enemy's country though many of the inhabitants may be inimical to us.' Nicely put.

The US Marines would occupy the country from 1916 to 1924. They brought a sort of peace to the country. And also helped to bring baseball.

During the Second World War, the Dominican Republic joined the Allied side, and accordingly, America sent Lend-Lease military aid, including aircraft to the Dominican Republic. To some extent, military links continued after the Second World War. In 1947, the US Navy helped the Trujillo government intercept craft carrying rebels who were supported by Cuba. And throughout the 1950s, the United States sent military aid to the Dominican Republic, along with a variety of training missions.

Gradually, however, the United States began to distance itself from the repressive Trujillo regime. Military assistance was cut off in 1960, and in 1961, Trujillo was assassinated. And following the re-emergence of two of Trujillo's brothers in the Dominican Republic, the US Navy put on a show of force to demonstrate US disapproval.

A few years later, America sent in the troops yet again. After another civil war broke out, President Lyndon B. Johnson intervened in the Dominican Republic in 1965. The US Marines and two brigades of the 82nd Airborne were deployed alongside the forces of other OAS nations.

US military links with the Dominican Republic were strong in the period after the intervention. President Balaguer was in power from 1966 to 1978, and the United States increased its military aid during his first term. During the rule of President Guzmán after that, President Jimmy Carter's administration sent hundreds of US military personnel to help after the devastation caused by Hurricane David.

Recent years have also seen extensive links between the US military and the Dominican Republic. The Dominican Republic sent troops to fight alongside US forces in Iraq, and the United States and Dominican Republic have co-operated in the fight against the traffic in illegal substances, US forces have shared training exercises with Dominican military personnel and the US government has financed the construction of a $1.5 million naval base in Saona Island, just off the Dominican coast.

The Puerto Rico National Guard is partnered with the Dominican Republic.

Ecuador

Ecuador means 'equator' in Spanish, and – you guessed it – it's on the equator.

Actually, America hasn't had as much to do militarily with Ecuador as it has with some other South American countries. But of course it's had some involvement.

And some of it was quite early. During the War of 1812, the USS *Essex* under Captain David Porter captured a number of British ships off the Galapagos Islands before heading across the Pacific to the Marquesas (*see* France).

Also, during the Second World War, the US had a naval and airbase (Seymour Island Airfield) on Isla Baltra (Galapagos Islands), and from 1942 to 1943, America had an airbase at Salinas on the mainland. A major aim of both was to combat any threat from Japanese submarines and any threat to the Panama Canal.

At times America has also assisted the Ecuadorian military with training and equipment. What links the CIA may have had with the Ecuadorian military is a different question.

Things between the United States and Ecuador haven't always been friendly, however. Starting in the 1960s, we've had Ecuador versus the United States in the great 'tuna war.' Okay, not actually a war, but it does involve tuna. Ecuador decided it needed a 200-mile territorial limit off its coast. The US decided it didn't. In 1963, a US fishing boat was seized and fined, and many more vessels were seized after that. The US responded with various measures, including intermittently suspending military aid. In 1971, tensions increased when an Ecuadorian warship fired warning shots at a US ship hundreds of miles off the coast of Ecuador. Later, however, an apology was given.

In recent years, the United States and Ecuadorian governments have seen matters very differently on a number of other subjects. The two countries have co-operated on anti-narcotics measures, but in 2009, the Ecuadorean government refused to renew the ten-year lease on a base at Manta Airport, from which American E-3 AWACS and P-3 Orion surveillance planes had carried out drug control work.

However, this did not put an end to all links between the US military and Ecuador, and the Kentucky National Guard is partnered with Ecuador.

Egypt

The land of the pharaohs and pyramids, Egypt is also, of course, the land of the Nile. Although it won't surprise you to know the Battle of the Nile against Napoleon was not fought by the US fleet, some Americans actually were present at it.

In 1798, Ralph Willet Miller served under Admiral Nelson as captain of HMS *Theseus*. Miller had been born in New York in 1762 to a Tory father. This American was one of Nelson's hardy forces that destroyed the French fleet on 12 August 1798.

But American state forces have operated on Egyptian soil. During the Urabi Revolt in July 1882, the British seized control of Alexandria, and US troops landed in the city to protect US interests and help the British keep order. So it's not exactly an Egyptian military operation on the scale of what Rameses II, or even 1920s Hollywood might have dreamt up, but it is something.

Interestingly enough though, at roughly the same time, a number of American military men were themselves also serving in the Egyptian army of the Khedive of Egypt. American soldier and explorer Charles Chaillé-Long was second-in-command to General Gordon in the 1870s, and Charles Pomeroy Stone, who'd had, to put it mildly, a controversial career during the American Civil War, was basically head of the Egyptian Army in the early 1880s.

During the Second World War, even before the Pearl Harbor attack, the United States supplied Lend-Lease equipment and support to Britain. President Franklin D. Roosevelt recognised that arms and war material would do more good in British hands than in American storage facilities. Winston Churchill told Parliament the Lend-Lease Act was 'the most unsordid act in the history of any nation.' American Sherman tanks and other equipment were sent directly to Egypt where they played an important part in the fight against Rommel.

But Egypt was also an important base for US air crew and US air operations during the Second World War. US 9th Air Force bombers and fighters operated out of Egypt in support of the British Eighth Army's drive westwards along the North African coast against Rommel, and America actually built its own airbase in Egypt at Payne Field near Cairo.

After the removal of King Farouk in 1952, Gamal Abdel Nasser came to power. During the Cold War, Nasser at first attempted to steer a neutral course but also bought weapons from Soviet and Warsaw-Pact sources. On 26 July 1956, Nasser ordered the nationalisation of the Suez Canal, which had been built by the British and the French in the nineteenth century. The British and the French weren't happy about it. They weren't happy about it at all. Both were still imperial powers, despite a battering during the Second World War, and neither had entirely come to terms with their newly reduced role in a post-war world dominated by the two superpowers of the United States and the USSR. They thought that invading Egypt, even against US wishes, was a good idea. It wasn't.

In 1956, the United States played an enormous role in the Suez crisis by not intervening militarily in Egypt and by opposing the intervention of her closest Second World War allies and Israel. This is particularly remarkable, given how close President Dwight Eisenhower was to the British on account of his role in planning Operation Overlord (*see* France). Early on, Eisenhower wrote to Prime Minister Anthony Eden saying that American opinion was totally against the use of force, particularly because it did not seem that every peaceful means of protecting vital interests had been tried. And when subtle hints didn't work, Eisenhower began to put on the pressure, including heavy financial pressure. At the same time that British amphibious forces were landing in Egypt in Operation Musketeer, Eisenhower ordered an American-fuelled run on British currency while America also prevented Britain accessing funding from the International Monetary Fund.

Eventually Britain and France succumbed to US and international pressure and withdrew their forces. Israeli forces were successful in invading the Sinai but were compelled to withdraw under American pressure.

During all this chaos, however, US forces did play one active role in Egypt. Eisenhower ordered the deployment of a US Marine Corps battalion in Egypt to help evacuate US nationals and others from Alexandria during the Suez Crisis.

In 1957, fearing that Egypt might interfere with the movement of US merchant ships headed for Israel and Jordan, the US Navy instituted a destroyer patrol in the Straits of Tiran and the Gulf of Aqaba.

During the 1973 Yom Kippur War, Soviet naval and armed forces were deployed towards the Middle East in support of Egypt, and US security was raised to DEFCON 3 (Defence Readiness Condition Three; USAF's alert state requiring readiness to mobilise in fifteen minutes).

Egypt's major initial successes in this war were followed by devastating Israeli counter-attacks, and after the war, Egypt turned sharply away from the Soviets. Eventually Egyptian President Anwar Sadat chose to make a historic visit and speech to Israel's Knesset in 1977 and to barter land for peace.

The Camp David accords returning the Sinai to Egypt as part of a peace deal were signed in 1978. Billions of dollars of American military and economic support began flowing towards Egypt and has continued in every subsequent American administration to the present.

Another consequence of the peace deal was the return of US forces to Egyptian soil and their long-term stationing there. It's definitely one of America's lesser-known international postings, but first in the Sinai Field Mission and subsequently as part of the Multinational Force and Observers (not a UN mission because the UN Security Council couldn't agree on it), Americans have been deployed in Sinai helping keep the peace between Egypt and Israel.

Anwar Sadat was assassinated on 16 October 1981, by Islamic extremists who opposed peace with Israel. And that wasn't the only challenge Egypt was facing by any means. In 1983, Airborne Warning and Control aircraft (AWACS) were sent because of fears of a threat from Libya after a Libyan plane had bombed a city in Sudan, Egypt's southern neighbour.

Since 1980, America had been conducting joint exercises with the Egyptian military deploying troops and aircraft into Egypt, in particular in the series of Bright Star exercises. However, in 2011, Sadat's successor, Hosni Mubarak, was swept out of power in the Arab Spring, and the military toppled President Morsi in 2013. The Bright Star series of exercises was consequently suspended until the US government could work out exactly what's happening and what is likely to happen in Egypt.

El Salvador

In 1906, El Salvador invaded its neighbour Guatemala and the USS *Marblehead* was used to arrange a truce between combatants by American officials. Otherwise, El Salvador wasn't an area of huge concern for the United States. That is, until the civil war in El Salvador.

In 1979, after a period of instability characterised by increasing radicalisation among both left and right-wing factions, a junta toppled President Carlos Humberto Romero. The junta's failure to deliver all the improvements it promised and the revolution in nearby Nicaragua gave a boost to the left-wing guerrilla groups of the FMLN (Farabundo Marti para la Liberacion Nacional).

On 24 March, the Roman Catholic archbishop and human rights campaigner Oscar Romero, who opposed US support for the Salvadoran government, was assassinated, and in the aftermath of the murder, El Salvador descended into civil war. Right-wing death squads killed thousands.

The Cold War was in full swing at this time after the Soviet invasion of Afghanistan in 1979, and El Salvador's Sandinista-controlled neighbour, Nicaragua, had aligned itself openly with Cuba. Determined to prevent left-wingers from coming to power in El Salvador as well, the Reagan administration gave extensive military support to the Salvadoran government – a massive $6 billion from 1981 to 1992.

A bitter struggle ensued. In the end, an estimated 75,000 people were killed.

In 1981 hundreds died in what has become known as the El Mozote Massacre. In 2011, Salvadorian Foreign Minister Hugo

Martinez asked forgiveness for what he called the 'blindness of state violence'. The guerrillas took control of parts of north and east El Salvador and launched a campaign aimed at sabotaging the economy.

The guerrilla campaign would also claim some American victims. On 19 June 1985, the FMLN rebels attacked a restaurant in San Salvador, which killed four US Marines and three US businessmen. The war dragged on through the 1980s and into the 1990s. Finally, in January 1992, a ceasefire was signed.

In the 2004 election in El Salvador, the George W. Bush administration openly supported Antonio Saca, the winning candidate, over his opponent, who was a former Communist guerrilla. In 2009, though, former rebel Mauricio Funes of the FMLN was elected president, and subsequently in 2014, Salvador Sanchez Ceren, another FMLN candidate was voted in as president.

El Salvador has sent troops to both Iraq and Afghanistan, and strong security links exist on a number of other levels, including counter-terrorism and the fight against the illegal drug trade, plus ship visits, military exercises and humanitarian missions. The United States operates a facility at Comalapa in El Salvador, which exists for the purpose of, among other things, supporting US aviation units assigned to counter illicit trafficking operations.

The New Hampshire National Guard is partnered with El Salvador.

Equatorial Guinea

As the name suggests, Equatorial Guinea straddles the equator. Well, sort of. Its mainland chunk, by far the biggest part of the country, is actually north of the equator, but Equatorial Guinea also has some islands to the south of the equator. As the Guinea part of its name suggests, it is not far from the Gulf of Guinea; although somewhat confusingly, it's a long, long distance from two other African countries with similar names, Guinea and Guinea-Bissau, which are respectively further north and much further west.

One of the islands that are situated south of the equator

is now called Bioko, but Western seamen used to know it as Fernando Po, after the Portuguese explorer who landed on it in 1472. Britain's anti-slaving patrol had a base on Fernando Po, and it was also a regular stop for American anti-slaving naval operations in the nineteenth century.

For much of the nineteenth and twentieth centuries, what is now Equatorial Guinea was a Spanish colony, and a sort of mini-Spanish Civil War even took place in the colony while the main Spanish Civil War was being fought far to the north. Equatorial Guinea became independent from Spain in 1968.

The country has faced some very challenging situations and some major human rights issues at times, and the United States and Equatoguinean (yes, that's the adjective) governments haven't always been that close. The US suspended diplomatic relations with Equatorial Guinea in 1976, and they didn't resume until 1979. And then again in 1995, America closed its embassy in Equatorial Guinea and transferred its functions to the embassy in neighbouring Cameroon. In recent decades, Equatorial Guinea has become a significant oil producer, and the American Embassy in Equatorial Guinea reopened in 2006 as a result of growing US interests in the country.

The US has had some minor military involvement with Equatorial Guinea in the past decades as well. In 1988, for example, America gave the navy of Equatorial Guinea a patrol boat and provided some training of Equatoguinean forces in the 1980s and 1990s.

Eritrea

The name Eritrea is derived from the Greek word for 'red' and yes, it's located on the Red Sea.

In the early twentieth century, Eritrea was an Italian colony. In 1941, as part of the war between Britain and Italy, Britain occupied Eritrea. Then after the war in 1952, under a UN resolution that America supported, Eritrea was joined to Ethiopia. This marriage didn't entirely work out and, after a very, very long war, Eritrea got its independence in 1993.

After Britain took Eritrea from the Italians, America had a wartime airbase and a Technical Services Command depot at Asmara, the capital of Eritrea. And after the war it continued to have a major presence in the area. This was Kagnew Station, near Asmara, an old British base that the US took over and turned into one of its major communications centres in the region. At its peak in the 1960s, it was home to thousands of Americans.

Supplies either were flown in from Saudi Arabia or came in by ship to the main Eritrean port of Massawa. America even had 'R & R' centres for the staff on the coast at Massawa and in the mountains at Keren. In the end, however, increasing use of satellite communications, a growing rift with the Ethiopian government after Emperor Haile Selassie had been toppled, and the growing war between Ethiopia and Eritrean guerrillas led to Kagnew's closure in 1977.

The US did play a significant role in the negotiations that led to the independence of Eritrea from Ethiopia, but hasn't had much to do politically or militarily with the current regime in Eritrea. In 2008, the United States condemned Eritrea for aggression against its friends in Djibouti and called on both sides to resolve the border dispute peacefully.

Estonia

Estonia is the most northern of the three Baltic countries, which means that it's just along the coast from St Petersburg in Russia.

Historically, it's been at a junction where competing spheres of influence from great powers have met, particularly those of Sweden and Germany to the west and Russia to the east. This has not made for the smoothest of rides. To put it mildly.

By contrast, the US came quite late to the area. Plus, it's a long distance across the Atlantic, so America hasn't really played a huge military role in Estonia's history, but it has played a small one.

In 1918, in the chaos after the end of the Russian Revolution, Estonia declared independence from Russia, and after fighting off both Bolshevik and German forces, the Estonians managed to establish the freedom of their country.

America had naval forces in the area at the time, protecting US interests and assisting with US relief efforts. For instance, the USS *Pittsburgh* operated in Estonian waters. On one occasion in 1920 when the USS *Pittsburgh* sighted Soviet submarines off Estonia, it enthusiastically asked to be allowed to regard them as hostile. Washington, however, was less keen on the whole idea and refused.

A number of Americans also played a role in helping Estonia during its war of independence. Some US military officers became advisors to the Estonian army.

In the aftermath of the failure of the Allied intervention in newly communist Russia, Estonia became a friendly base from which the US could observe the USSR. American officers conducted intelligence operations there, and American foreign-policy luminaries, such as Chuck Bohlen and George Kennan, worked in Estonia while studying Russia and the Russian language. But evidently it wasn't all work. Bohlen commented that he could never entirely stop being surprised by the sight of nudism on Estonian beaches. He served as an advisor to every American president from FDR to Nixon and became the American ambassador to the Soviet Union under Eisenhower.

Estonian independence, however, was short-lived. In June 1940, with the eyes of the world on the German occupation of France on the other side of Europe, Stalin ordered the blockade of Estonia. On 14 June 1940, Harry Anthiel, a twenty-seven-year-old American State Department employee and courier, was among those killed when a commercial aircraft, the Kaleva, was shot down by Soviet planes after taking off from Tallinn. A few days later, Soviet forces invaded and occupied Estonia, and Stalin annexed it to the Soviet Union, a move the United States refused to recognise.

The chaos and the carnage of the Second World War was to come, and then decades under Soviet rule. Assorted US intelligence efforts inside Estonia followed, including those to help the anti-Soviet Baltic resistance at the end of the Second World War and also during the post-war period.

Finally with the end of the Cold War, the US government once again recognised a free Estonia on 4 September 1991, and military links between Estonia and the United States have been re-established. Estonian forces operated alongside US forces in Baghdad, and Estonia has contributed a small force to the conflict in Afghanistan. Estonia joined NATO in 2004, and today, NATO's Cooperative Cyber Defence Centre of Excellence is headquartered in Tallinn.

After Russia's occupation of the Crimea in 2014 and in the light of ongoing conflict in eastern Ukraine, the US has played a major role in Operation Atlantic Resolve, a programme of multinational exercises and other military activity designed in particular to show commitment to the security of the Baltic States and Poland. In 2015, US troops who had been training in Estonia took part in Dragoon Ride, driving along a route through Eastern Europe to further demonstrate US commitment to the region.

The Maryland National Guard is partnered with Estonia.

Ethiopia

Early American involvement with Ethiopia involves fascinating stories of some individual Americans. A significant number of American Civil War veterans joined the army of the Khedive in Egypt, and many of them, including William Wing Loring, Charles Chaillé-Long and William Dye, were involved in the Ethiopian wars. It didn't turn out too well for some of them. The British General Gordon, also fighting for the Khedive, records an unnamed American killed during the fighting in 1875, and Surgeon Major Thomas D. Johnson, a Confederate veteran, was wounded and captured by the Ethiopians.

Then, when Mussolini's Italian army attacked Ethiopia in 1935, the head of the small Ethiopian air force at the time was an African American pilot and colonel, John C. Robinson, who would later find fame in the United States as the Father of the Tuskegee Airmen. As the Ethiopians struggled to resist the overwhelming might of the Italian army, many other African Americans volunteered to fight for Ethiopia but were prevented from doing so at the time by America's Neutrality Act.

America, however, refused to recognise Italy's occupation of Ethiopia, and it wasn't to last long. In 1941, British Commonwealth and Ethiopian troops defeated the Italians and on 5 May, Emperor Haile Selassie returned to Addis Ababa. In 1945, President Franklin D. Roosevelt met Haile Selassie on board the USS *Quincy* to strengthen links, and in the post-war years, America co-operated closely with the Ethiopians. In 1953, the US signed a mutual defence assistance agreement with Ethiopia under which it would supply military equipment and training, and America was Ethiopia's main arms supplier from 1945 to 1977.

However, in 1974, Haile Selassie was toppled, and in the ensuing years, the Ethiopian revolutionary government got steadily closer to the Soviet Union and Cuba.

During the 1990s though, the US began to get a little friendlier again with the Ethiopians, and although some political differences between the United States and Ethiopia remained, some military links resumed as America became involved in sponsoring assorted training programs.

In recent years, American troops have been located in a number of places in Ethiopia. For instance, in 2006, at Camp Hurso in Ethiopia, US soldiers from the 294th Infantry Regiment in Guam spent a year training members of the Ethiopian Army. America has also been on the same side as Ethiopian troops against Islamist militiamen in Somalia, and Ethiopia is strategically located in an area of importance for the United States.

In 2011, it was reported that the US Seventeenth Air Force had started flying drones out of Arba Minch in southern Ethiopia, near Somalia, though the drones were apparently unarmed due to the sensitivities of the Ethiopian government.

Fiji

For a country that, in the late nineteenth century, was firmly within the British sphere of influence, the US has actually had a surprising amount of military involvement with Fiji prior to that. Mostly this was concerned with the US Navy making attempts, sometimes rather heavily armed and forceful attempts, to secure recompense on behalf of Americans who'd had their property on the islands damaged in some of the conflicts that occurred during that period.

Already by 1840, the United States Exploring Expedition was doing a bit more than just exploring Fiji. Somehow, two US Navy personnel were killed by locals, and in a response, the US landed a force of sailors on Fiji. Two villages were burned, and a number of Fijians were killed.

Then we come to a certain John Brown Williams. John Brown Williams owned a store in Fiji, and he also happened to be the US consul. His store suffered assorted damage, and by

1855, the US Navy was returning to the island again demanding tens of thousands of dollars in compensation for damage to US property. Now tens of thousands of dollars is a lot of money these days but it was a lot, lot more then. Marines and sailors from the USS *John Adams* went ashore in an attempt to capture the local ruler Cakobau. The landing party defeated local resistance, but one sailor was killed and two marines wounded, and Cakobau escaped.

In 1858, the US Navy was once again in Fiji, with USS *Vandalia*, demanding compensation. And in 1867, USS *Tuscarora* arrived at Levuka and threatened to open fire unless compensation was paid.

Eventually Cakobau decided that forming a government with assorted settlers and eventually having the islands taken over by Britain was his best option for dealing with his problems, so that's what he did.

The US military returned to Fiji during the Second World War, though this time it was on a much friendlier basis. Forces from New Zealand had previously been assisting the local defenders of the islands, but in 1942, American forces took over. Bomber squadrons were based at Nadi. The US assisted with 155mm coastal defence artillery and anti-aircraft defence, and the 37th Division, which had originally intended to go to Northern Ireland, arrived in Fiji and Tonga instead. Assorted US facilities were built, including the Martintar Naval Air Station. Some US troops trained on a Fijian island prior to the attack on Guadalcanal, and while the situation on Guadalcanal remained uncertain, Fiji remained at risk from a Japanese invasion.

Fiji became independent from Britain in 1970. After the coup in Fiji in 1987, the United States suspended defence co-operation. Another government was toppled in 2000, and another coup took place in 2006, which the United States condemned.

Finland

The Finns love their saunas so much that apparently Finnish peacekeepers have built saunas around the world. Something to look forward to after a bit of peacekeeping.

Finland had spent a long time under Russian control when in

1917 it declared independence, or perhaps Finndependence. But was Russian control finished? (Or indeed, Finnished?)

The early years of Finnish independence included intervention by the Germans (who were America's enemies at the time) and a civil war between White Finns and Red Finns. It sounds a bit like a battle in an aquarium but was, in fact, between nationalist (White) Finns and Bolshevik (Red) Finns.

The US delayed recognising Finland until it had managed to work out exactly what was going on. The White Finns eventually won the war, and between the world wars, America got quite friendly with the country. But by 1939 things weren't looking great for Finland.

A secret protocol of the Nazi-Soviet non-aggression pact that preceded the start of the Second World War in Europe provided for an assault on Finland. On 30 November 1939, Stalin's Soviet Union attacked Finland, but the outnumbered Finns, trained skiers and skilful in using their home territory to their military advantage, fought the Soviets almost to a standstill in the Winter War.

Americans, including many Finnish-Americans, had great sympathy for the gallant Finns who defended their homeland from Stalin. An American-Finnish legion made up of about 350 Americans, primarily of Finnish descent, volunteered to serve in the Winter War and finally arrived on the front line just as the war was finishing. Kermit Roosevelt (great name), the son of former President Teddy Roosevelt, led a group of British volunteers who fought in the Russo–Finnish war. Sheer Soviet might did, however, hold in the end, and the treaty of Moscow finished the Russo–Finnish war in March 1940.

In spite of the fact that Finland allied herself with the Nazis in their 1941 invasion of the Soviet Union, the United States remained at peace with the Finns, even after Pearl Harbor. In 1942, the OSS recruited Thérèse Bonney, a war correspondent and photographer, for a mission to Finland. She had a clandestine meeting with Marshal Carl Mannerheim in Helsinki where she attempted to persuade him to abandon Hitler. She failed but returned to Washington with detailed information on Finland's military and political status. Additionally, despite their alliance with Hitler, the Finns sent a steady stream of information to the OSS office in Stockholm. Wilho Tikander, a Finnish-American, worked for the OSS in Scandinavia. The Finns offered Russian army communication codes to Tikander for sale to the Americans. In spite of America's wartime alliance with the Soviets, 'Wild Bill' Donovan approved the $62,500 payment.

Eventually, however, in September 1944, the Finns did sign an armistice with the Soviets and the British (but understandably not with America since it wasn't officially at war with them).

Finland was heavily influenced by the Soviets during the Cold War period, though Finland escaped Soviet occupation. With the might of the Red Army just next door and with a previous history of Russian control and Russian invasion, it's hardly surprising that the Finns wanted to avoid antagonising the Soviet Union. The term 'Finlandisation' was coined to describe nations whose foreign policy had to toe the Soviet line.

Having said that, some links did exist during this period, for example, intelligence links, between the Finns and Western forces, which included the Americans. In addition, America flew occasional spy flights that went over Finnish territory.

Since the end of the Cold War, more open links have developed between the United States and Finnish militaries. Finland has sent troops to Afghanistan, and US and Finnish military personnel have co-operated in exercises.

France

Ah, the beautiful land of France, *la belle France*. And, of course, the site of, perhaps, the most famous invasion involving American forces of all time.

When the American Revolution broke out, Louis XVI wasn't that worried. His own slight problems with revolutionaries (losing his throne, losing his head, etc.) were still in the future and instead he increasingly saw an opportunity to stick it to the old enemy across the Channel. Nevertheless he was reluctant to commit to the American cause until gentleman Johnny Burgoyne surrendered his force after the Battle of Saratoga in October 1777. The Marquis de Lafayette arrived in America that same year serving as a Major General in the Continental Army and French Commander-in-Chief Rochambeau landed a force of about 6,000 French soldiers in Providence, Rhode Island. These forces, and critically the French navy led by the Comte de Grasse, helped secure the surrender of Lord Cornwallis's army at Yorktown.

Louis, no doubt hugely enjoyed Britain's suffering at the hands of revolutionaries, that is until he was on the receiving end of it himself.

Even the US alliance with France soon came under pressure. Well, in fact, a bit more than just 'under pressure'. The so-called Quasi-War with revolutionary France was fought by the US Navy on the high seas between June 1798 and March 1801. On 9 February 1799, Captain Thomas Truxton of the *Constellation* fought and captured the French frigate *L'Insurgente*. The war was settled by the Treaty of Mortefontaine after Napoleon Bonaparte assumed control as First Consul.

France and the United States also very nearly came to blows over the French invasion of Mexico, which was launched by Napoleon III during the American Civil War. The United States supplied Mexico with arms and support to drive the French out of North America (*see* Mexico), not exactly a gesture designed to delight *la belle France*.

However such tensions were not to last and the twentieth century would see Americans fighting and dying for France's freedom in huge numbers.

Even before America's entry into the Great War, Americans were in combat in France. Young American pilots volunteered to serve in the French air force forming the Lafayette Escadrille hoping to repay America's debt to France. Ten out of the 'Valiant 38' American men who served in the Lafayette Escadrille were killed in action. Americans had also volunteered for the French Foreign Legion.

And after President Woodrow Wilson led the nation into war on the Allied side, American doughboys were shipped to France and the trenches of the Western Front in large numbers. They were called 'doughboys' because they tended to be larger and better fed than their French comrades-in-arms.

The earliest units of the American Expeditionary Forces to see action were engineering units rushed into the British line in November 1917. But it was in 1918 that American troops were really to have an impact on the Western Front. Eddie Rickenbacker, flying French-built aircraft, such as the SPAD S.XIII, became the leading American fighter ace of the First World War scoring twenty-six air combat victories. A few American land and air units and even America's First Gas Regiment were committed to action in April 1918 to stem the

German Spring Offensive, which used German troops released from the Eastern Front by peace with Russia in an attempt to deal a knockout blow before American troops could be deployed in large numbers.

In late May and June, the Germans tried to push forward at the Chemin des Dames along the Aisne River. Aisne bridges were captured, Soissons fell, and the Germans reached Château-Thierry on the Marne with Paris less than forty miles distant. American troops battled fiercely to prevent the Germans from crossing the Marne and then, on 6 June, a date that would later become famous for other reasons, successfully counter-attacked at Belleau Wood, where the US Marines earned the nickname '*Teufel Hunden*', or 'devil dogs'. Further German attacks on the Marne followed and were fought off by American troops, earning the 38th Infantry of the Third Division its name 'Rock of the Marne'.

The Germans were now exhausted, and it was the turn of the Allies to attack. American troops played a key role in July in helping destroy the German-held Marne salient. From then on, American units assisted major campaigns by the British and the French, but General Pershing had also got his wish for an independent American operation, and in September, about half a million Americans of the US First Army went into action against the German-held St Mihiel salient. The operation was a significant success. Finally, from September to November 1918, the First Army ground through the Meuse-Argonne offensive. The fighting was bitter, and casualties were at times heavy, but major progress was made, and by the Armistice, the First Army had dealt a huge blow to the German divisions.

The American Expeditionary Forces had played a vital role in liberating France and in winning the war against Germany, but it had come at a high cost in American blood. The beautiful Aisne-Marne American Cemetery, for instance, next to Belleau Wood and just six and a half miles from Château-Thierry, contains almost 2,300 war dead, most of whom fought in the area and in the Marne valley in summer 1918.

But the 'war to end all wars' didn't end all wars and soon American forces would be fighting on French soil again.

Even before D-Day, Americans began the liberation of France with the invasion of Corsica in autumn 1943.

D-Day, 6 June 1944, marked the start of perhaps the most

famous invasion in all history. With a terse, 'Okay, let's go', Eisenhower had resolved all doubts in the Allied deliberations over weather conditions prior to the invasion. The time had finally arrived. Eisenhower later compared the invasion force to a coiled spring ready to 'vault the English Channel'.

On the night of 5 June Private John Steele, a paratrooper with the 82nd Airborne, got his parachute caught on the tower of the church at Ste-Mère-Église. He survived the conflagration and firefight that shook the sleepy Norman town that night by playing dead. A visitor to Ste-Mère-Église today will find a stained-glass window in the church has the Virgin Mary surrounded by American paratroopers. The American paratroopers of the 82nd and 101st Divisions would secure the western flank of the Normandy invasion.

On Utah Beach, fifty-six-year-old Brigadier General Theodore Roosevelt Jr (oldest son of President Teddy Roosevelt) was landed about a mile away from his intended target and, when asked whether to re-embark the 4th Infantry Division, said simply, 'We'll start the war from right here!' Bloody Omaha had received an abbreviated naval bombardment from ships such as the battleship *Texas* lasting only thirty-five minutes. Its bare beaches offered no cover for the American invaders as German machine guns, concealed in fortified gun emplacements, swept the beaches. The US Rangers, who had trained earlier on the cliffs of Dorset, scaled the sheer cliffs of Pointe Du Hoc while being shot at by German soldiers; their mission was to destroy artillery pieces that threatened to sweep the landing zones. Their commander that day was Lieutenant Colonel James Rudder. Unknown to Rudder's Rangers, most of the artillery had already been moved by the Germans. They held the position for two days in the face of fierce counter-attacks by the 916th Grenadiers of the *Wehrmacht*. At the Ranger Memorial at Pointe du Hoc, one can still see massive craters created by Allied naval bombardment on D-Day.

As commander of the US Third Army after D-Day, General Patton led an army that advanced further and faster than just about any army in military history, crossing twenty-four major rivers and capturing 81,500 square miles of territory, including more than 12,000 towns and villages. Patton loved to quote Danton who said, '*De l'audace, et encore de l'audace, toujours de l'audace!*' ('Audacity, more audacity, always audacity!')

In August 1944, American troops participated in a much less widely known invasion, Operation Dragoon that landed in the south of France. Everyone knows about 6 June 1944, but how many know about 15 August 1944? Yet the parachute drop by the 1st Airborne Task Force, landings by American troops, primarily the 3rd, 36th and 45th Infantry Divisions, and a French armoured division were highly successful. Allied casualties were light, and most German resistance crumbled fairly fast. By mid-September, they had pushed their way up the Rhone Valley near the German border. Some of the invasion targets, like the beach of St Tropez, famous for film stars in the post-war period, sound rather fun, but people were still fighting and dying.

Meanwhile to the north, on 25 August 1944, the French 2nd Armoured Division, led by General Leclerc, was allowed the honour of being the first Allied force to liberate Paris. General Charles de Gaulle spoke from a balcony at the Hotel de Ville, 'Paris outraged! Paris broken! Paris martyred! But Paris liberated! Liberated by itself, liberated by its people, with the help of the whole of France!' De Gaulle seems to have temporarily ignored the contribution of the Americans, British, Polish, Canadian and other Allied troops that fought so hard to liberate France.

Robert Capa, the famous war photographer, rode into Paris on an American-built tank that day. Ernest Hemingway personally led a group of irregulars that liberated the Ritz Hotel drinking numerous martinis that night in its bar.

And there was still much fighting remaining before all of France was liberated. It wasn't until 22 November 1944, after American troops had captured the vital, strategic pass at Saverne, that French troops liberated Strasbourg, the most easterly major city in France. And at about the same time, after bitter fighting to the north-west, the US Third Army was finally taking Metz, a heavily fortified French city, close to the border with Germany.

The liberation of France would claim 134,000 American casualties. Thousands of Americans would be buried in French cemeteries, such as the beautiful one that overlooks Omaha Beach.

France became a founding member of NATO in 1949. Though strained by its Indochina and African commitments, France also contributed an infantry battalion that served alongside Americans in the Korean War. (Author Chris Kelly's father, Robert E. Kelly, served as a clerk typist in the US Army based in Verdun, France, during the Korean War. He liked to say that he 'kept the North Koreans out of France'.)

Fifty-six French troops would be killed alongside American marines in the Beirut bombing in October 1983. French forces would also serve in the Gulf War of 1991 that liberated Kuwait. And French forces have served alongside Americans in Afghanistan.

France still has assorted territories around the world, which used to be part of its empire. So we need to deal with American military involvement there in this chapter.

One example is where the US Navy built an advance base on Nuku Hiva Island in the Marquesas Islands, now part of French Polynesia, in 1813. Captain Porter briefly claimed Nukuhiva for the United States and named it Madison Island. The village built there was known as Madison's Ville, and the water next to it, Massachusetts Bay. Yep.

It's also worth mentioning Nouméa, in the French territory of New Caledonia, which is situated east of Australia. This became an important US base during the Second World War. In fact, it became the US headquarters for the whole of the South Pacific with tens of thousands of US personnel stationed there.

The most fun of the French territories from the point of view of American invasions is Clipperton Island. Few people have heard of it, and even fewer know how America invaded it. It doesn't sound very French (unless you call it Île de Clipperton or its other name, Île de la Passion, when it does sound a lot more French).

It's an uninhabited coral atoll lying in the Pacific Ocean west of Costa Rica and north-west of the Galapagos Islands. The French were the first Europeans to find it, and it's French today, and, even though it's not the most attractive bit of real estate in the world, it's been invaded by others over the years, including, yes, Americans.

The Guano Islands Act of 1856 was supposed to promote American use of islands that had plenty of guano on them, and this being one of the few things Clipperton did have on it, the American Guano Mining Company claimed it. Guano mining caused a minor diplomatic incident in 1897 when the French found that three American guano miners had raised the Stars and Stripes. The US State Department eventually gave in to the French. However, during the Second World War, the US returned because President Franklin D. Roosevelt thought the place might be useful as a flying base. In December 1944, the US occupied the island and raised the American flag again, not admittedly against much, or indeed any, resistance, sending in a meteorological team protected by troops. However, the mission didn't last long and was eventually withdrawn, leaving Clipperton and its seabirds to the French.

Gabon

The name Gabon apparently comes from the Portuguese word '*gabão*', which is a type of cloak. Located on Africa's Atlantic coast, America's first military contact with it was due to anti-slaving operations as the US government finally turned against the slave trade.

The US Africa Squadron seized a number of vessels in the area, even if they didn't always achieve very much by doing so. They seized the ketch *Brothers* at Mayumba on 8 September 1858, believing the vessel to be equipped for slaving, but the charges were later dismissed in the United States. And they seized the *Emily* at Loango on 21 September 1859, again because they believed it was equipped for slaving, and once again, the charges were dismissed in the United States.

In the later twentieth century and into the twenty-first century, Gabon became a significant oil producer. In recent years, the US has had some military involvement, though France is the former colonial power and quite a lot of French influence remains.

In 1997, US military personnel were deployed to Gabon as part of an evacuation force ready to rescue Americans and others from problems in nearby Zaire (now Democratic Republic of Congo). The US has also been involved with the Gabonese military in peacekeeping training.

The Gambia

The smallest country on the African mainland, The Gambia is another of those African countries where slaving posts on the

Atlantic coast brought early attention from the US Navy's Africa Squadron.

As The Gambia was a British colony, during the Second World War, the US military unsurprisingly made some use of facilities there. The navy used the port at what was then Bathurst (now Banjul, the capital). The USS *Memphis* was sent to Bathurst, so that on the night of 13 January 1943 President Franklin D. Roosevelt could sleep there before going on to the conference at Casablanca. The USAAF also used the airport at Bathurst during the Second World War to ferry aircraft north to Morocco.

The Gambia became independent in 1965. A coup in 1994 interrupted American military links with The Gambia, but they have resumed to some extent since then. In 2009, the High Speed Vessel (HSV) *Swift* paid a visit to Banjul in the most important US naval visit since the coup and the US ran exercise Africa Endeavor in 2011 in The Gambia.

Georgia

No, this Georgia is not the US state, and has not so much to do with Jimmy Carter either. This is the nation in the Caucasus, which has Russia to its north and Turkey, Armenia and Azerbaijan to its south.

After the Russian Revolution of 1917 brought the Russian Empire to an end, Georgia became independent for a few years, along with other nations in the Caucasus. America had a bit of military involvement in the area at this point. The American Military Mission in Armenia visited the Georgian capital Tbilisi during its investigations in the area.

In 1921, Georgia became part of the Soviet Union. Stalin was Georgian, and if you've ever wondered about the name Operation Bagration, the epic Soviet offensive that almost entirely destroyed German Army Group Centre in 1944, its name (whatever anyone might think) has nothing to do with bags or rations. It's the name of a Georgian royal family and also of the famous Georgian general in the Russian army, Pyotr Bagration, who (among many other things obviously) led Russian troops against the Revolutionary French in Italy (another fascinating story).

During the Cold War, Georgia was occasionally the target of US surveillance efforts, but since the end of the Cold War, the US has developed close military links with Georgia (which also involves Americans from states other than Georgia).

Georgia has sent large contingents of troops, many of them trained by the United States, to fight in Iraq and Afghanistan. In 2008, with the war between Russia and Georgia, President George W. Bush announced that US Air Force and naval personnel would deliver humanitarian and medical aid to Georgia, and the US government sided with the Georgian government, offering air transport for Georgian troops to return home from where they were serving in Iraq.

Close links between the US and Georgian military continue today. For instance, in May 2015, US and Georgian troops teamed up in Exercise Noble Partner in Georgia. And, neatly enough, the US state of Georgia has had a partnership programme with the country of Georgia since 1995. So, American guardsmen from the Georgia National Guard have trained alongside Georgians (from Georgia the country) in the Georgian military. Georgia the country, though, also has a Georgian National Guard, so frankly, it could all get pretty confusing at some stage.

Germany

At first it wasn't so much Americans invading Germany as Germans invading America.

The British, in fact, used Hessian troops to help fight the colonists in the American Revolution and a certain 'Baron' von Steuben from Magdeburg, Prussia, became a Major General in the Continental Army and literally wrote the book on drill in the Revolutionary War (imaginatively called the *Revolutionary War Drill Manual*).

However, in the twentieth century that would eventually change – big time.

In the First World War, the violation of Belgian neutrality, unrestricted submarine warfare, and fears of a German conspiracy to bring Mexico over to the German side, eventually helped propel America into the war on the Allied side. It's also worth pointing out that, as the largest bondholder to assorted Allied governments, the United States had an enormous financial stake in an Allied victory. American forces fought the Germans in the trenches on the Western Front, engaged in dog-fighting in the skies, and sailed on the high seas against the Kaiser's U-boats, but US forces would never actually fight on German soil in the First World War.

American troops did, though, march into Germany as victors after the Armistice. American troops of the Third Army were given the job of occupying the Koblenz bridgehead, and even though much of the army gradually returned to the United States, it wasn't until 1923 that President Warren Harding ordered the last US forces home from Germany.

The First World War stirred up strong anti-German sentiment in the United States. For a time, frankfurters were renamed 'victory dogs', sauerkraut became 'victory cabbage', and Beethoven and Bach were banned from repertoires. Some have even partly blamed the passage of Prohibition on the backlash against German-American brewers that followed the war.

In 1933, Hitler came to power in Germany. By September 1939, Europe was at war once more.

At first, as with the First World War, America kept out of it, but ultimately, as Hitler's tanks crushed France and the Luftwaffe bombed Londoners, the sympathies of a lot of Americans increasingly lay with Britain in its lonely struggle against the Germans. In Brest, France, a monument had been erected to commemorate the US Navy's efforts in the First World War. On 4 July 1941, prior to Pearl Harbor, the Germans destroyed this monument and replaced it with a naval command bunker. Meanwhile, an undeclared naval war was raging in the waters of the Atlantic with the US Navy and Merchant Marine fighting German U-boats. On 31 October 1941, German submarines torpedoed and sank the USS *Ruben James* while it was escorting merchant ships to Britain.

Shortly after the Pearl Harbor attack, Hitler declared war on the United States, thus fulfilling his treaty obligations to Imperial Japan. The United States would now fight a two-front war.

America's first chance to strike at German soil directly was from the air. German cities faced an increasingly relentless bombing campaign from the USAAF. The RAF and USAAF flew missions day and night. Eventually, P-51 Mustang escort fighters would be deployed that could reach Berlin and provide vital air protection for the bombers.

American aircrews showed enormous bravery, did extensive damage to the German war effort, and often suffered appalling casualties, particularly in the early days of limited fighter cover. In an August 1943 raid against factories working on German aircraft components in Regensburg and Schweinfurt, sixty bombers were lost and many more heavily damaged. In a follow-up raid on Schweinfurt, even more bombers were lost and even more damaged.

German civilians also, however, suffered terribly. Bombing left 400,000 Germans dead and 7.5 million homeless. After the fire-bombing of Dresden, which claimed about 25,000 lives, an American Private First Class of German descent, one Kurt Vonnegut, who had been captured earlier in the war, was pressed into service by the SS gathering bodies and carrying them to pyres.

But soon the chance to strike at German soil on land would also present itself.

On D-Day, 6 June 1944, American forces landed alongside British and Canadian troops in Normandy. The liberation of Paris in August 1944 and Brussels shortly afterwards fuelled Allied optimism that the war could be brought to a swift conclusion by Christmas of 1944. This optimism was misplaced. American strategy, somewhat cautious, called for advance on a broad front. The Allies also faced fuel and logistical difficulties due to scarce port facilities as most had been destroyed by the retreating Germans.

Nevertheless, in October of 1944 Aachen, the burial place of the emperor Charlemagne, was the first major German city to fall to the Allies when American troops took it after fierce fighting. German forces towards the end of the war would include children and men of retirement age, but there were still plenty of men ready to fight the advancing US forces. A series of bloody battles took place in the Hürtgen Forest in the last months of 1944, and then the Germans launched a massive counter-attack with the Battle of the Bulge (*see* Belgium *and* Luxembourg).

However, as the German counter-attack faltered and then stalled in the face of Allied reinforcements and Allied airpower, the advance eastwards resumed. The Americans and their allies raced on to the Rhine. On 6 March 1945, units of the US 9th Armored Division managed to cross the bridge at Remagen, which allowed forces to cross over the Rhine into the heart of Germany.

On 17 March 1945, US troops captured the German city of Koblenz, which other US troops had occupied after the First World War. Suitably enough, just as the US Third Army had occupied it then, General George Patton's Third Army took it this time.

As Western armies firmly established themselves on the eastern side of the Rhine, some Western leaders like Churchill and Patton were tempted to ignore the agreement reached at Yalta on zones of influence between the Allies and to push on, to try to take Berlin before the Russians could. Operation Eclipse was the plan drawn up to drop American and British paratroopers on key airfields in the Berlin area, but eventually fears of high casualties and conflict with the Russians led to the abandonment of the idea.

As the worst war in human history drew to a close, the Americans discovered the horrors of the Nazi concentration camps. After Eisenhower visited Ohrdruf Concentration Camp that had been liberated by American troops on 4 April, he declared, 'We are told that the American soldier does not know what he is fighting for. Now at least he will know what he is fighting against.'

On 18 April, Magdeburg, birthplace of 'Baron' von Steuben who wrote the US Revolutionary War drill book all those decades ago, fell to troops of the 30th Infantry Division, and on the same day, resistance in the Ruhr pocket finally collapsed. When it was all finished there, hundreds of Germans had been taken prisoner.

On 20 April, the Seventh Army took Nuremberg, the backdrop to Nazi rallies, and two days later, they crossed the Danube. Then on 25 April, elements of the American First Army met up with Russian forces advancing from the east, splitting Hitler's Reich in two, and on the next day, an official link-up ceremony was held at Torgau.

On 30 April, units of the Seventh Army captured Munich, scene of Hitler's Beer Hall Putsch in 1923, and on the same day, far to the north, in Berlin, Hitler committed suicide. A few days later, American troops reached Berchtesgaden, the site of Hitler's mountain residence, the Berghof.

The much feared Alpine Redoubt where Nazis were alleged to be planning a ferocious last stand in fact fell quickly and easily to US troops.

On 8 May 1945, VE Day finally came, marking the end of the European part of the most destructive war in history. In July 1945, the same month that President Harry Truman headed for the Potsdam Conference, just outside Berlin, the first US army unit, troops of the 2nd Armored Division, entered the former Nazi capital of Berlin.

After the war, Germany was divided into British, French, Soviet and American zones of occupation. With the onset of the Cold War, the situation between Western allies and the Soviets became increasingly tense. In June 1948, the tensions between the Western allies and the Soviets over plans for the future of Germany erupted as the Russians instituted the Berlin Blockade. In reply, America and the other Allied powers in Berlin instituted the Berlin Airlift.

Just a few years previously, the Luftwaffe had failed to supply the Sixth Army, surrounded in Stalingrad, from the air. Admittedly, by 1948, it was no longer wartime, but the Berlin Airlift had to supply not just an army but also a big chunk of one of the world's major cities.

Despite the enormous difficulties faced, a combination of Allied determination, wartime experience of airlifts, and the hard work of the Berliners eventually saw the targets of necessary daily supplies achieved. In fewer than ninety days, German civilians under French direction even built a new airport, often using their bare hands. And a French general took the risk of blowing up a radio tower controlled by the Soviets that was causing problems on the approach to the new airport.

By April 1949, the Russians had to admit that the blockade was not working, and they called it off. Seventeen American aircraft had been lost, and thirty-one Americans killed in the race to supply Berlin.

The NATO alliance was formed in April 1949, and West Germany was declared an independent state in the following month. It became a key US ally during the Cold War, joining NATO in 1955. But the other German state, the German Democratic Republic, declared independent in October 1949, became a major opponent during the same period, and the United States conducted assorted espionage operations on their soil during the period, the details of which are outside the remit of this book.

In November 1989, free passage through the Berlin Wall

was allowed, and its demolition began almost immediately. Less than a year later, West Germany and East Germany were reunited into a single nation once more.

In recent years, German troops have served alongside Americans in Kosovo and in Afghanistan, and the United States maintains a significant military establishment in Germany to this day.

Ghana

Some major slave-trading ports were located in what is now Ghana, so the area received quite a lot of attention from America's Africa Squadron during its anti-slaving operations. Though the fleet spent much of their time cruising up and down the coast, the ability of comparatively few navy ships to do much about the slave trade was limited. On 28 December 1858, the USS *Vincennes* did seize the barque *Julia Dean* at Cape Coast Castle in what is now Ghana and sent the vessel to the United States, where the case was dismissed by the courts.

What is now Ghana became the British Gold Coast colony, and in the Second World War, American forces were back. Although Ghana is a long way from where the main Second World War action took place, US operations there became vital in winning the war. With North Africa and the Mediterranean a battleground, the area became a key site on the route that enabled aircraft from the United States to be shipped safely across the Atlantic, across Africa, and up to the Middle East and beyond.

In fact, the entire operation is sometimes called the Takoradi Route, named after Takoradi in what is now Ghana. There, planes that had been shipped unassembled across the Atlantic were assembled for flight onwards across Africa. America also had another airbase at Accra, now the capital of Ghana. The route became less important after the Allied conquest of North Africa in 1942 and 1943.

After the war, as Britain began to give up its empire, Ghana again became something of a focus for America. Kwame Nkrumah had arrived in America from the Gold Coast in 1935. He studied hard, picking up a number of degrees and associating with a number of leading left-wing thinkers and intellectuals. On his return to Ghana in 1947, he started campaigning for self-governance. The British authorities eventually jailed him, but when they held an election in 1951, Nkrumah's party, even though he was still in prison, won by a landslide. The British set Nkrumah free, and in 1952, he became prime minister. By 1957, he was leader of an independent and free Ghana.

Not everybody, however, liked Nkrumah's left-leaning and sometimes authoritarian politics, and in 1964, he was toppled in a coup. There has been huge speculation and controversy over what America and the CIA did or did not know about the coup and did or did not do to support it. Nkrumah died in exile in 1972.

In recent years, the US military has had extensive links with Ghana's military, including many joint training exercises and assistance in assorted construction projects.

The United States also has a history of getting involved with Ghana's troops on peacekeeping missions. The USAF flew Ghanaian troops to Liberia to aid in the peacekeeping operations of ECOMOG (Economic Community of West African States Monitoring Group), and more recently AFRICOM has included Ghana in its programme of helping a number of African countries further develop their peacekeeping expertise.

The North Dakota National Guard is partnered with Ghana.

Greece

This (often) sun-dappled land in the Eastern Mediterranean Sea was the cradle of democracy. And, although as we watch politicians in action and see how democracy can have its problems, we must remember Churchill's famous words, 'It's the worst form of government, except for all those other forms that have been tried from time to time.'

For all these reasons and more, when in 1821 the Greeks rose against their Ottoman rulers, philhellenes across Europe and America urged them on. And some of them did more than urge – they went to fight. From Britain, for instance, came the famous – or infamous – or perhaps famous *and* infamous Lord Byron. And from America came assorted volunteers like George Jarvis, a New Yorker who arrived in Greece in 1822 and became a guerrilla fighter. He wore the foustanella, the traditional skirt of warriors, and served as adjutant to the aforementioned

Lord Byron. Jarvis died in 1828 and is buried in Argos. Other Americans, too, would head for Greece to fight for its freedom, including Captain Jonathan P. Miller and James Williams, a former slave who died fighting there.

Having said all that, not all military links between Americans and Greeks in this period were to be of the friendly type. Between 1825 and 1828, America had warships in the Aegean to protect its merchant ships against attack by those Greeks who happened to be more keen on piracy than Plato. Sometimes the action was at sea, as when Lieutenant Goldsborough of the USS *Porpoise* and his men freed a British ship taken by pirates, killing or wounding something like ninety of them in the process. But sometimes the action involved landings, as when US sailors and marines landed on Mykonos, now a popular holiday destination. They were led by Lieutenant Kearny who commanded a USN sloop – the *Warren*. However, on that occasion the American forces didn't take their towels and head for the beach. They were there to recapture stolen goods and, in the fighting that followed, one pirate boat was burned and the town was shelled. Rather more than even the most badly behaved tourists get up to on Mykonos these days.

In the First World War, Greece, like the United States, declared war on the Central Powers in 1917. American submarine chasers were based on the Greek island of Corfu to help enforce a mobile barrage of ships across the Adriatic, placed there to prevent enemy submarines escaping from their Adriatic bases through the Strait of Otranto into the Mediterranean. Some of these Corfu submarine chasers ended up being involved in one of the biggest sea battles of the war, the Battle of Durazzo (*see* Albania).

In 1940, Greece was invaded from Albania by Mussolini's Italian forces, but the Greeks not only managed to repel the invasion but even pushed into Albania as well. The Germans, however, launched an attack on Greece in the spring of 1941 forcing Greek's British and Commonwealth allies to evacuate after a second Battle of Thermopylae. Crete was captured by an airborne invasion, and Allied forces were compelled to withdraw from that as well, though resistance by locals there to the German invaders started pretty much as soon as the first German paratroopers landed in Crete and lasted until the last Germans left or surrendered.

The British SOE, based in Cairo, began guerrilla operations in Crete and in the Greek mountains, and subsequently the OSS, including many Greek-Americans, also began carrying out commando attacks on railroads, bridges and telephone exchanges. The OSS parachuted Special Forces into Greece and used caiques (light skiffs used for fishing) to take personnel in and out and to send in supplies. The OSS tended to be a bit more pragmatic than the SOE in their support for Greek resistance forces, being more ready to support the left-wing Communist ELAS (Greek People's Liberation Army) as well as the right-wing nationalist EDES (National Republican Greek League). In light of US policy in Greece after the war, this seems, as we shall see, somewhat ironic.

During the war, also, the USAAF conducted raids against a variety of targets in Greece and on the Greek islands. In 1943, USAAF bombers based in Cyprus provided air support for the brief and ultimately disastrous British invasion of the island of Leros which, because of the large Italian coastal guns on Leros may have partly inspired Alistair Maclean's *Guns of Navarone*. On 28 July 1944, American bombers attacked a marshalling yard at Florina, and on 4 October 1944, P-51s strafed the airfields at Tatoi, Kalamaki and Eleusis.

By the autumn of 1944, however, German forces were retreating throughout Europe. British forces landed in Greece, and Athens was liberated on 14 October 1944. That same month, Churchill and Stalin held a conference in Moscow where they allegedly agreed that Britain would have prime influence over post-war Greece whereas Russia would have more influence in assorted parts of the Balkans.

Friction between Communists and nationalists first led to fighting in late 1944 and early 1945. But a ceasefire was patched up (it has been suggested that Stalin may have been trying to keep his side of the bargain with Churchill) and held until just about November 1946. From there, it was bitter civil war until 1949. This conflict marked the commencement of the global Cold War and claimed the lives of about 80,000 Greeks, and while it was the British who had taken the lead over America in Greece during the Second World War, in the period after the Greek Civil War the US came to play a very major role.

The Truman Doctrine, announced on 12 March 1947, declared that the United States would 'support free peoples who are resisting attempted subjugation by armed minorities or by outside pressures.' The US Military Advisory and Planning Group Greece, launched in 1948, was one of the first Cold War organisations that helped to assure the Greek government's victory over the Communists. The US sent huge amounts of military equipment for the Greek government's armed forces and hundreds of US military personnel to help them win. In the end, the Communists gave in and announced a ceasefire in October 1949.

Greece joined the NATO alliance in 1952, and US military influence remained strong in Greece after its civil war.

In 1967, days before the start of an election campaign that could have brought to power a politician keen on improving links with the Soviet Union and not hugely keen on NATO, a Greek junta, dubbed 'the Colonels', seized power in Athens. The junta had strong links to the United States. Its rule was brutal and authoritarian and came to an end in 1974 after its attempt to topple Archbishop Makarios in Cyprus had helped lead to the Turkish invasion of the island. The American ambassador in Cyprus and the CIA station chief in Athens were killed in a wave of anti-American fervour.

Democratic elections were held in November 1974, and in 1981, Greece joined the European Union. Greece was still a part of NATO, and America retained some close military connections with the country. In 1990, it had 3,700 US military personnel in Greece, mainly at the Nea Makri Communications Station at Marathon, at the Hellenikon Air Base in Athens, and on Crete at the Souda Bay base and the Iraklion Communications Station.

American personnel and facilities in Greece have been the target of some terrorist attacks. On 12 January 2007 a rocket-propelled grenade hit the US Embassy.

Today the US still has access to some key facilities in Greece, most importantly Naval Support Activity Souda Bay with its deep-water port and airfield. Greece is still a significant member of NATO, for instance, sending troops to Afghanistan and taking part in NATO's Ocean Shield counter-piracy operation.

Grenada

A beautiful small island in the Caribbean with a population of about 100,000, Grenada is also known as the 'Island of Spice'

– it produces cinnamon, cloves, and about 20 per cent of the world's nutmeg. And yes, of course, America has invaded it.

Grenada was a French colony but came into British hands from 1763. So inevitably there was a certain amount of French and British invading that went on then. During the British period, America first got involved militarily with Grenada. Nothing major but still perhaps worth mentioning.

During the Revolutionary War, American privateers targeted ships leaving Grenada's ports. Mind you, the United States didn't have it all its own way. There were also privateers operating out of Grenada that preyed upon American shipping.

During the Second World War, US forces occasionally visited the island, on one occasion allegedly attempting to set up an artillery post on Richmond Hill, but finding no suitable site.

Grenada gained its independence from Britain in 1974 but remains part of the Commonwealth.

In 1983, Grenada was the site of America's largest military intervention since the Vietnam War. Ronald Reagan had defeated Jimmy Carter in the election of 1980 to become America's fortieth president. Reagan took a more aggressive view about confronting Communism than his Cold War predecessors. Political upheaval on the island of Grenada gave Reagan an opportunity to reverse militarily what he saw as a dangerous expansion of Cuban and Soviet influence.

On 19 October 1983, Bernard Coard, the hard-line Communist deputy prime minister of Grenada, led a coup against Prime Minister Maurice Bishop, a Marxist who had assumed power after a coup in 1979. A few days later, Bishop and two other members of his cabinet were assassinated.

There were intelligence reports indicating that Russia and Cuba had been building military infrastructure, in particular a 10,000-foot airstrip.

With the Organisation of East Caribbean States calling for a military response from the United States and despite being warned that there would be 'a harsh political reaction' to a US invasion, on October 22, just a few days after the coup, Reagan decided the invasion should go ahead.

Operation Urgent Fury was launched on 25 October 1983. The US Army Rapid Deployment Force, which included Ranger battalions, the 82nd Airborne Division, marines, and Navy SEALs, was augmented by a few hundred troops from Jamaica and other countries. These forces engaged about 1,500 troops from the Grenadian Army and about a few hundred Cuban military Special Forces. The fighting was short (just three days) and sometimes sharp, costing nineteen American lives and over 100 total fatalities, including some civilians.

The UN General Assembly condemned the US invasion calling it 'a flagrant violation of international law' and voting 108 to 9 against it. Reagan's ideological soulmate, Prime Minister Margaret Thatcher, was thrust into an awkward position by the US invasion as Grenada was still a member of the Commonwealth. Thatcher was disappointed by the American lack of consultation prior to taking action in Grenada.

However, there was also widespread American support for the invasion, particularly after the ABC broadcast *Nightline* featured an interview with American medical students from St George's University School of Medicine who expressed their gratitude for the invasion and towards the US Army Rangers.

US troops were withdrawn in December of 1983, and Grenada held elections in December of 1984. The operation can be seen as marking an end to some of the reluctance for overseas military interventions evident in the period after the end of the Vietnam War. 25 October, the day American forces arrived, is celebrated in Grenada as a national holiday known as 'Thanksgiving Day'. The airport has been renamed Maurice Bishop International Airport in honour of the assassinated prime minister.

Guatemala

Guatemala is located just to the south of Mexico in Central America and has a fascinating history, including, of course, the history of its amazing Mayan culture.

Guatemala gained its independence from Spain in 1821 and later joined forces with other Central American republics to fight General William Walker's American-led invasion of Nicaragua in the 1850s (*see* Nicaragua).

In 1920, US forces were ordered to protect American diplomats and American interests during turmoil in the country.

Guatemala, home to a substantial German overseas population, remained neutral at the start of the Second World

War. However, after the Pearl Harbor attack on 7 December, Guatemala declared war on Japan, and shortly after that it declared war on Germany too. Guatemala wasn't exactly going to play a vast role in the Second World War, but it did play some.

America occasionally had forces based in Guatemala. It made use of assorted airbases in the country during the Second World War. In particular, it had aircraft based at Guatemala City Air Base, some of them conducting anti-U-boat operations.

By the 1950s, the United Fruit Company owned 42 per cent of the arable land in Guatemala. In 1953, a government led by Jacobo Arbenz, inspired by the New Deal, began expropriating land. The Eisenhower administration feared the spread of Communism in Central America. Arbenz's wife publicly declared that the triumph of Communism was inevitable in the world. The United States imposed an arms embargo on Guatemala and airlifted arms to neighbouring Honduras. A US naval force was sent to the area for potential evacuation duties.

Told by CIA director Allen Dulles that the chances of success were somewhere between 40 and 50 per cent, President Eisenhower gave the green light for a coup attempt, code named PBSUCCESS. Mercenaries were trained in Florida and in neighbouring Honduras. The CIA helped to provide air support and jammed the government airwaves. The 1954 coup removed Arbenz and replaced him with Colonel Carlos Castillo Armas, who would be assassinated by a security guard in 1957.

In the summer of 1960, anti-Castro Cubans began training in Guatemala to prepare for a CIA-sponsored invasion of Cuba, and in 1961, the Kennedy administration used airbases in Guatemala to support its failed Bay of Pigs invasion.

A long bloody civil war raged in Guatemala from 1960 until 1996, in which left-wing guerrillas fought the army and the government. Fearing the growth of Communism, the United States gave extensive support to the army and the government. Huge numbers were killed during the war, very many of them unarmed civilians, and very many of them killed by government forces. In particular, Mayan suffering was enormous. In 1999, President Bill Clinton visited Guatemala after an independent report on the war and expressed regret, 'It is important that I state clearly that support for military forces or intelligence units which engaged in violent and widespread repression of the kind described in the report was wrong, and the United States must not repeat that mistake. We must, and we will, instead continue to support the peace and reconciliation process in Guatemala.'

In recent years, links between the US military and Guatemala have focused on fighting drug traffickers, ship visits, humanitarian efforts, and exercises such as Medical Readiness Training Exercises.

In 2012, 200 US Marines flew into Guatemala City and proceeded to patrol the coastline looking for drug smugglers.

The Arkansas National Guard is partnered with Guatemala.

Guinea

Located on West Africa's Atlantic coast, what is now Guinea at one stage formed part of some of the great West African empires, like the Mali and the Songhai empires.

Rio Pongo, in what is now Guinea, was a major slaving area and therefore of great interest to American anti-slaving patrols as the US government eventually turned against the slave trade. On 24 March 1845, at Rio Pongo, the USS *Truxtun*, acting on intelligence about an American slaving ship in the area, seized the New Orleans ship *Spitfire*. The USS *Truxtun* was operating alongside a British ship, and when the anti-slaving vessels approached, the *Spitfire* ran up the Stars and Stripes to try to deter the British vessel, only to find that it was facing a US vessel as well. There were no slaves yet on board, but 300 were waiting to be loaded, and one of the officers of the *Truxtun* noted the appalling conditions in which hundreds of slaves would be packed into the comparatively small ship. In June 1845, the captain Peter Flowery was sentenced in Massachusetts for the slaving expedition, but because he had not actually loaded the slaves yet and because the jury recommended mercy, he was sentenced to only five years' imprisonment and a fine of $2,000. In the end, after only twenty-one months, he was released on grounds of ill health.

Guinea became a French colony and eventually gained independence in 1958. It has had a difficult history involving many coups, extensive human rights abuses, and much authoritarian rule.

Ahmed Sékou Touré became president of the newly independent country and stayed president until his death in 1984. Touré had links to a variety of nations at different stages of his career, including the United States and Soviet Union. In 1960, US Air Force planes flew into the capital Conakry to airlift Guinean troops to take part in the UN operation in the Congo.

Touré's death, unfortunately, didn't bring Guinea's problems to an end, and the country has seen periods of instability in the years since. American military involvement with the country has been limited, but US military personnel have visited the country to supply training. Recently, Guinea was one of the countries participating in Western Accord 2012 in Senegal, an AFRICOM-sponsored multi-lateral exercise led by US Marine Corps Forces Africa.

Guinea-Bissau

Located on Africa's Atlantic coast, Guinea-Bissau lies to the north of Guinea and its capital is, perhaps not surprisingly, Bissau.

Slave trading posts were located in Guinea-Bissau, so its coast and the waters off them were of interest to the US Navy's anti-slaving patrols in the nineteenth century.

Guinea-Bissau became independent after a long guerrilla war against Portuguese colonial authorities. The country has had, at times, a fairly turbulent history.

The US has had some minor military involvement there. America signed an international military training agreement with Guinea-Bissau in 1986, and prior to 1998, the US was helping the Guinea-Bissau navy with training and some communications and navigation equipment.

In 1998, the Guinea-Bissau Civil War broke out. In June of that year, US military personnel and aircraft were sent to Dakar in neighbouring Senegal to be ready to help evacuate US citizens. In fact, by then forty-four Americans had already left Bissau on a Portuguese boat and a Senegalese ship.

African peacekeepers trained under a US programme have served in Guinea-Bissau.

Guyana

Situated on South America's northern coast, Guyana used to be British Guiana, although in the colonial period the French and Dutch also controlled different bits of it at various times. And, in fact, Guyana still has its own New Amsterdam, unlike America which lost its own New Amsterdam some time ago and now has a little place called New York instead.

Because of the British influence, America didn't have much military and political involvement there until after Guyana's independence, but even before, it did have a little. For instance, during the War of 1812, in February 1813, the USS *Hornet* under Captain James Lawrence defeated HMS *Peacock* after the *Hornet* chased a British merchant ship into the mouth of the Demerara River in British Guiana.

In the late nineteenth century, after Venezuela appealed to the United States for help over a border dispute with British Guiana, President Grover Cleveland got involved and persuaded Britain to agree to international arbitration.

Under the destroyers-for-bases deal during the Second World War, America got two bases in what was then British Guiana, a USAAF base at Atkinson Field, and a seaplane base at Makouria. Atkinson had a mission to combat U-boats in the area and protect other US interests, including bauxite deposits, but it also rapidly developed into a vital link in the South Atlantic air-ferry and transport route connecting to Africa and beyond to the Middle East.

Guyana became independent in 1966, but in the years prior to that, the US government had become worried about a possible spread of Communism in British Guiana. Cheddi Jagan was a dentist who had been educated in the United States and was married to a woman from Chicago. He was also, however, a left-winger and, despite British opposition, had been elected into power three times in British Guiana. In 1961, he visited President Kennedy in the Oval Office. However, US government concern about Jagan's politics continued, and it has been alleged that Kennedy and the CIA launched an extensive campaign against him. Jagan lost power in 1964. He eventually returned as President of Guyana from 1992 and remained in control until his death in 1997, when his wife, Janet, would be elected president shortly after.

From 1964 to 1985, one man, Forbes Burnham was basically in control of Guyana. Finally, in 1982, because of its dislike of the Burnham government, the US government suspended aid to Guyana. However, links began to improve after Burnham's death in 1985, and in the 1990s, the US military was occasionally training alongside the Guyana Defence Force and was involved in humanitarian projects in the country. Such links continue today. In 2012, in Exercise Fused Response, members of the US military and of the Guyana Defence Forces teamed up to improve co-operation.

Haiti

Haiti may be known for the extreme poverty of many of its inhabitants today, but in the eighteenth century, it was the richest jewel in the French overseas empire.

Haiti produced 60 per cent of the world's coffee supply and 40 per cent of the world's sugar supply. Labour was supplied in brutal working conditions by African slaves whose life expectancy was extremely short. The slave population outnumbered the white planter population by a factor of ten to one.

The French Revolution broke out in 1789 proclaiming the rights of man. Toussaint L'Ouverture, a former slave who had been born on the island, asserted that human rights belonged to *all* men, and the Haitian Revolution followed in 1791.

While some Americans in the South were terrified by the prospect of a slave revolt on Haiti, other Americans saw the uprising as an opportunity for profit. American merchants, mainly from New England, sold 30,000 muskets to Toussaint and his rebels. And America was even, to a certain extent, attacking the French in and around Haiti. During the so-called Quasi-War against the French, the US attacked many French ships in the area. In 1800, marines from the USS *Constitution* assisted in the capture of the French schooner *Esther* off Cap François.

And some of the French reckoned that the whole 'human rights for all' bit had gone rather too far on Haiti. In 1801, Napoleon dispatched his brother-in-law, General Leclerc, to invade Haiti and restore French rule, the property rights of the planters, and slavery. The French had some success against the rebels and captured Toussaint, who was sent back to prison in France.

However, news of his death and concern over other French actions reignited the rebellion, and thousands of French troops were killed by yellow fever, including Leclerc who died in 1802. So not a massive success for the French in the end.

Leclerc had not been able to fulfil the second part of his orders, which was to proceed to New Orleans to strengthen the French presence in the New World. As a direct result of this Haitian debacle, Napoleon chose simply to sell the Louisiana Territory to the Jefferson administration. The Louisiana Purchase, negotiated in 1803, accounts for about 23 per cent of the total area of the current United States.

Meanwhile in Haiti, in what had become an increasingly bitter fight, the rebels finally defeated the French, and on 1 January 1804, Jean-Jacques Dessalines, known as Emperor Jacques I of Haiti, declared independence.

The road that lay ahead for independent Haiti was not an easy or a smooth one, featuring extensive political instability and turmoil, and an embargo aimed at securing payments to France for the loss of Haiti did its share of damage.

In the nineteenth century, America started a pattern of regularly getting involved in Haiti. Marines landed in 1817 to protect American interests and property. And again in 1818. And in 1821.

America put on a show of force in 1888 and compelled the Haitian government to release an American steamer they'd seized.

In the late nineteenth century, Germans began migrating to Haiti setting off alarm bells in Washington. Two German ships threatened to shell Port-au-Prince in 1897. Did the Kaiser want a colony in the Caribbean?

In 1914, US Marines landed in Haiti yet again. A number of times, in fact. At Port-au-Prince, which was convulsed by a civil war at the time, Captain Smedley Butler led the marines in numerous firefights against the Cacos, or peasant guerrillas. A squad of eight US Marines removed $500,000 in gold from the Banque Nationale in Port-au-Prince for safekeeping; the funds were shipped to New York via the USS *Machias*.

In 1915, President Woodrow Wilson sent in the US Marines yet again amid political and economic turmoil over concerns that the Germans might exploit the Haitians. And this time, perhaps tired of all the coming and going, the marines were going to stay there a long, long time. In fact, the United States would basically run Haiti for almost the next twenty years. The United States took control of Haiti's customs receipts, and the US naval commander there dissolved Haiti's congress and introduced a new constitution. US Marines were to be garrisoned on the island until 1934.

However, the US occupation would not come without resistance. US Marine aviators in De Havilland DH-4 and Curtiss Jenny biplanes were used to dive-bomb Haitian guerrillas. The US Marines would fight no fewer than 200 firefights in Haiti in one year alone. In 1919, Captain Herman H. Hanneken managed to infiltrate the rebel camp and shoot rebel leader Charlemagne Péralte dead with a pistol.

Due to the large role played by the US Navy and the US Marine Corps, Wilson's Secretary of the Navy, Josephus Daniels, was greeted by other Cabinet members as 'Josephus the First, King of Haiti.' (Incidentally, also, the term 'cup of Joe' was coined due to Daniels's enthusiasm for encouraging coffee-drinking in the American navy.) Later, President Franklin D. Roosevelt's Good Neighbour Policy shifted the United States away from direct control over Haiti.

After the attack on Pearl Harbor, Haiti declared war on Japan and then on Germany and Italy. America supplied extensive amounts of Lend-Lease equipment to Haiti, including aircraft, artillery and tanks. It helped train and equip a Haitian air force, and the US Coast Guard stationed a detachment at Bizoton to help the fight against U-boats.

The end of the war meant the end of much of this activity, but America did have various military links with Haiti in the post-war period as well. For instance, the USAF used the airbase at Bowen Field. And from 1959 to 1963, in response to a request from President Duvalier for help in reorganising the armed forces, a US Naval Mission was present in Haiti.

The Kennedy administration had had its doubts about the Duvalier regime for some time and had taken some measures against it, but things got rapidly worse in April 1963 when the regime announced it had exposed a plot against it. The thirty-strong US Marine Corps training force was withdrawn, and US Navy vessels, including USS *Boxer*, evacuated over 2,000 civilians.

Duvalier died in 1971 and was succeeded by his son Jean-Claude Duvalier. Eventually, in 1986, the Haitian army forced him out. In 1990, elections put into power Jean-Bertrand Aristide, but in September 1991, a coup toppled him and installed a military regime.

In July 1994, President Clinton ordered 20,000 troops to Haiti in Operation Uphold/Support Democracy to restore Aristide to power. Ten Haitians were killed in a brief firefight with US Marines.

A disputed parliamentary election and a presidential election boycotted by the opposition in 2000 created another political crisis in Haiti, and Aristide finally resigned in disputed circumstances in 2004. After Aristide's departure, President George W. Bush quickly dispatched 1,000 marines to Haiti who, along with forces from other nations, helped restore order. Subsequently, MINUSTAH, the United Nations Stabilisation Mission, arrived in Haiti with US support.

But it hasn't been just conflict that has taken US forces to Haiti. On 12 January 2010, a massive earthquake measuring 7.0 on the Richter scale hit Haiti. Over 100,000 people were killed, and millions made homeless. The United States intervened with military assets, including the supercarrier *Carl Vinson* and a brigade of the 82nd Airborne Division to provide emergency relief assistance.

The Louisiana National Guard is partnered with Haiti.

Honduras

In 1821, Honduras gained its freedom from Spain. It has had a pretty eventful history at times since then, and America has played a pretty significant part in that.

General William Walker, a native of Nashville, Tennessee, who managed to get elected president of Nicaragua after leading a group of filibusters (the word is derived from the Dutch *vrijbuiter*, or 'freebooter') arrived in 1860 in Honduras. At the age of thirty-six, he was leading his third attempt to invade Nicaragua by first landing in neighbouring Honduras. It was to be his last attempt to do that and pretty much his last attempt to do anything, in fact. He was captured by Honduran troops who were aided by Royal Navy warships and Royal Marines. Captain Norvell Salmon of the Royal Navy handed Walker over to the Hondurans, who then carried out an execution on the beach at Trujillo on 12 September 1860.

But soon American armed involvement with the country was to become a lot more official. By the end of the nineteenth century, the Honduran banana industry was becoming a major industry, and US financial and strategic interest in the country was increasing. One result would be an increase in US military involvement there.

In 1903, America sent warships to the seas off Honduras after a revolution there, and marines were sent ashore to protect American diplomats, and again, in 1907, America sent marines ashore to protect US interests. Later that same year, it got involved with sorting out a war between Honduras and Nicaragua.

On 11 February 1911, the US Navy cruiser *Tacoma* landed men again to protect US banana interests in Puerto Cortez, Honduras, and the US got involved with arranging a deal to end a civil conflict that had hit Honduras.

In 1912, troops landed once again, this time to prevent the Honduran government from taking over an American-owned railroad. (Though, in this instance, official disapproval from within the United States eventually forced withdrawal of the troops.)

Another US landing force was sent in again in 1919, and the US helped install an interim government after internal disputes once more hit Honduras.

Three major fruit companies, Standard, United and Cuyamel ran much of the economy. Standard was organised by the Vaccaro brothers – a Sicilian family out of New Orleans. A civil war broke out in Honduras in 1924 where different political factions sought the support and patronage of the banana magnates. US warships were sent in, and detachments of US Marines were landed in Honduras, one setting up its headquarters in the Vaccaro brothers' warehouse. In April 1924 the American Secretary of State, Sumner Welles, arrived in Honduras to settle the conflict.

And in 1925, once more, US troops were sent in to protect foreign civilians.

After that, things finally quietened down a bit, though America did retain significant military links with the country. For instance, in 1934 the Military Aviation School of Honduras was founded with, perhaps inevitably, a US colonel as its commandant. From 1932 to 1949, Tiburcio Carías Andino was in power, despite seeing a number of challenges to his rule.

On 8 December 1941, the day after the Pearl Harbor attack, Honduras joined the Allied cause in the Second World War.

In 1954, the US government feared the growth of Communism in neighbouring Guatemala. Part of America's response to this was to rush weapons to Honduras to counter any attempt to invade it. The crisis, however, passed (from a US government point of view) when a military coup toppled the Guatemalan government.

Plenty of sports fans feel passionate about their teams, but usually that passion stops short of actual war. Not so in Central America. In 1969, Honduras and El Salvador fought the famous, or indeed, infamous, Football War. The catalyst for the four-day-long war was violence at a series of qualifying matches between El Salvador and Honduras for the 1970 World Cup. Basically, the only direct US involvement in this conflict, was the use of US equipment, including vintage fighters from the Second World War, such as P-51s and Corsairs, by both sides in the fighting, but it's worth including as a fascinating bit of both sporting and military history.

In the 1980s, as it became concerned about events in both neighbouring El Salvador and Nicaragua, the United States began to concentrate on building up the Honduran military. Questions arise about the human rights records of some Honduran personnel during these years and how much the US government and CIA knew about, for instance, Battalion 316's alleged operations in Honduras.

Honduras also became the base for a massive secret war fought with huge US support. The United States helped established Contra ('Counter-revolutionary') bases in Honduras with the intention of subverting the Sandinista regime in neighbouring Nicaragua. The 1980s generally saw a peak in the involvement of the US military in Nicaragua, which included major construction projects, particularly on airfields.

In 1983, the US government, fearing that neighbouring Nicaragua might invade Honduras, sent 100 Green Beret military advisors to the country and a powerful naval task force to the seas off Nicaragua.

In 1988, President Reagan authorised Operation Golden Pheasant, which deployed 3,000 US troops to Honduras. Sandinista forces, which had invaded Honduras, were compelled to withdraw to their own country.

Joint Task Force Bravo has been operational in Honduras since the 1980s and is now stationed at the Soto Cano Air Base.

In recent years, US security concerns in Honduras have focused increasingly on efforts to counter the smuggling of narcotics. The drug war has seen the United States set up a series of bases in Honduras, including Forward Operating Base Mocoron.

The Puerto Rico National Guard is partnered with Honduras.

Hungary

Sitting astride the mighty Danube River, Hungary is a land (among many other things obviously) of gorgeous salami and spicy paprika.

Hungary includes places like Székesfehérvár, which looks as if it ought to be pronounced 'sexy-forever' but somewhat disappointingly probably isn't pronounced quite like that.

Some have claimed that the first king of Hungary was Attila the Hun, one of those characters in history that can at best be described as controversial. The first definite king of Hungary, though, was St Stephen I. He is said to have been crowned either on 25 December 1000, or on 1 January 1001 (and a long time before anyone was worrying about the millennium bug anyway). St Stephen I is linked to the famous and beautiful Holy Crown of Hungary, which today appears on the coat of arms of Hungary. (America, interestingly, has quite a role to play in the history of this amazing crown because at the end of the Second World War it ended up in the hands of the US Army. It was then kept safe in Fort Knox until 1978 when Jimmy Carter sent it home to Hungary where it belonged.)

By 1867, Hungary was a key part of the Austro-Hungarian Empire, which, of course, found itself on the losing side in the First World War. The US Navy clashed with Austro-Hungarian forces in the Adriatic, and the US army fought Austro-Hungarian units in Italy.

During the Second World War, Hungary, despite being landlocked, was ruled by Admiral Horthy, who had served in the Austro-Hungarian navy. Under some duress, he allied his country with Adolf Hitler during the Second World War, and Hungarian units participated in Operation Barbarossa, the invasion of the Soviet Union, which began in June 1941.

Just as in the First World War, Hungary was a bit too far into

Eastern Europe for American armies to reach, but this time, the US Air Force did pay a few visits. On 2 June 1944, as part of Operation Frantic, bombers took off from Italy, bombed Debrecen in Hungary, and then landed at Poltava in the Soviet Union. And, as an example of another mission, on 13 September 1944, the Eighth Air Force bombed the steelworks at Diosgyor in Hungary.

However, while American planes were in the air over Hungary, there were also some American feet actually on the ground as well. During the Second World War, 'Wild Bill' Donovan of the OSS plotted to bring Hungary out of its alliance with Hitler's Germany and over to the Allied side – just as the Italian government had a few months earlier. Operation Sparrow went ahead in March 1944 to convey an American peace proposal to Hungary. At that point, it was already clear that the Allies would win the war.

Colonel Florimund Duke (amazing name) and two of his subordinates were parachuted by a British Halifax bomber into Hungary near the border with Croatia. Duke had been an American football star and then worked for *Time* magazine as an advertising manager.

The Sparrow team planned to infiltrate Hungary by becoming prisoners of war of the Hungarian army. They then hoped to make contact with General Stephen Ujszaszi, the army's chief of intelligence. They succeeded in this and were cordially received. Ujszaszi helped to set up meetings with two Hungarian cabinet members to discuss the possibility of a Hungarian defection from the Axis.

On Sunday 19 March the OSS team were roused before dawn for a meeting with Ujszaszi. However, at the same time, three German panzer divisions had just crossed the border from Austria, and 240 Gestapo agents were also on their way to Budapest. German intelligence had learned of the American plans. Colonel Duke and his OSS agents spent the remainder of the war as prisoners in the infamous Colditz Castle, a medieval German castle, originally designed to keep people out, which the Germans had turned into a POW camp designed to keep people in. It was generally reserved for prisoners either of high value or those who were likely to try to escape. In some instances, it harboured both.

After the war, in 1956, the United States once again attempted to shape events inside Hungary. Stalin had died in 1953, and there was uncertainty about Khrushchev's willingness to use force. Spontaneous demonstrations against Soviet power erupted in Hungary in October. A crowd at Budapest City Park tore a statue of Stalin from its pedestal and Imre Nagy, a former prime minister, denounced the crimes and mistakes of the previous decade.

The Eisenhower administration was optimistically hoping for a miraculous unravelling of Soviet control. John Foster Dulles, the Secretary of State, wanted to roll back Communism. His brother Allen Dulles, the CIA director, assumed that 80 per cent of the Hungarian army would defect to the rebel side.

The Soviets responded to the uprising by dispatching 200,000 troops and 2,500 tanks to crush the uprising. About 20,000 Hungarians were killed, and 20,000 more were sent to prison camps in Siberia. Furthermore, about 200,000 Hungarians fled the country. Nagy was secretly tried and hanged.

American military intervention would not be forthcoming because Eisenhower was unwilling to risk a third world war over Hungarian independence.

In recent years, with the Cold War long finished, US forces have spent time based in Hungary. During operations in the former Yugoslavian states, Taszár Air Base in the south of the country became an important base for the US military, and today Papa Air Force Base in Hungary is home to US personnel serving with the international Heavy Airlift Wing. Hungary is a NATO member and has sent troops to Afghanistan.

The Ohio National Guard is partnered with Hungary.

Iceland

Iceland has the northernmost capital in the world, Reykjavik. From Iceland, the Vikings expanded to Greenland and then went in search of Vinland (not Finland; that's in the other direction entirely).

Pretty much everybody has heard of the Vikings, but not many know that America occupied Iceland during the Second World War – and occupied Iceland even before it was officially in the war.

The British launched an unopposed invasion with Operation

Fork in 1940 to prevent any German stab (fork pun) at occupying it and threatening the vital Atlantic convoy routes. In the summer of 1941, prior to Pearl Harbor, American forces relieved and replaced the British garrison after the US government made an agreement with Icelandic and Danish officials (at the time, the Danish king was also King of Iceland) that the US occupation force would be withdrawn after the war.

Task Force 19, including the First Provisional Marine Brigade, and numerous warships, departed Newfoundland on 1 July and arrived off Reykjavik on 7 July, landing there on 8 July. In the end, tens of thousands of Americans were based on Iceland during the war. The island was a crucial transit point for aircraft moving between America and Europe and was also used as a naval and airbase from which to fight the German U-boats hell-bent on menacing merchant shipping through the Atlantic waters.

In 1942, the US started building what would become Keflavik airbase (still around today as Iceland's main airport, Keflavik International). The fighter field, Patterson Field, went into operation first. And that was followed in 1943 by the bomber field, Meeks Field.

On 17 June 1944, while the war was still going on with bitter fighting in Normandy and while America was still occupying Iceland, the island became an independent nation after the Icelanders voted overwhelmingly in a referendum to split from Denmark, which at the time was still occupied by the Germans.

In 1949, amidst some controversy (there were riots), Iceland became a NATO member. But Iceland has no standing army, so the Iceland Defence Force, made up of US Navy, Marines and Air Force was based in the country to protect it from 1951 until its withdrawal in 2006. US naval forces in Iceland during the Cold War played a significant role in countering Soviet submarines in North Atlantic waters.

In October 1986, Presidents Reagan and Gorbachev met in Reykjavik. In a meeting at Hofdi House on a bleak stretch of Icelandic coast, the United States and USSR narrowly missed agreeing on the elimination of their nuclear arsenals. Reagan refused to back down on his Strategic Defense Initiative programme. When George Schulz later asked Gorbachev what was the turning point in the Cold War, he replied immediately, 'Reykjavik.'

A small Icelandic contingent (mainly coast guard forces) was deployed in the Iraq War. And in the years since the US withdrawal from Iceland in 2006, American forces have still taken part in exercises there. For instance, in 2011, the US jointly led planned exercise Northern Viking (those Vikings again) with Iceland.

India

A land with so much fascinating history and culture, and a country that looks to be one of the great powers of the twenty-first century, India is already the world's largest democracy in terms of population.

During the Second World War, America did have large numbers of US military personnel stationed in India and used its facilities. In fact, during the war, something like 350,000 US troops served in India in support of operations in Burma and China.

Merrill's Marauders trained in India before heading into Burma, and Americans even got involved in actual fighting on Indian soil during the bitter battles around Imphal and Kohima after the Japanese invaded India in 1944.

Large numbers of USAAF personnel and planes were based in India during the Second World War. One major mission was flying supplies from India to China. Another major mission was supporting ground troops in action in Burma. Chabua Airfield was one of the most important airbases in north-east Assam. B-24 Liberators flew combat missions from there, but its major significance was as a base for aircraft and air crews flying supplies over the Hump (the Himalayas) to China. The airbase was attacked by Japanese aircraft, but the major danger for the crews was flying in hugely challenging mountainous conditions without many of the modern aids used by pilots today.

Because it's such a major nation, in some senses it's surprising that America hasn't had more military links with India in the post-war period. However, a variety of factors, including India's association with the Non-Aligned Movement during the Cold War, India's development of nuclear weapons in the 1990s, and the long-running tensions between Pakistan and India have all created barriers to closer military links between the United States and India.

Things got a bit tense during the Bangladesh crisis of 1971 when President Nixon deployed the USS *Enterprise* to the Bay of Bengal in a show of support for Pakistan. Prime minister Indira Gandhi, however, directed her Indian navy officers to invite the US Navy officers aboard their ships for tea!

In recent years, more links have developed. For example, India provided intelligence and other aid for the coalition attack on Afghanistan in 2001. And more generally, links like naval visits and joint exercises have expanded. In November 2013, Indian and US naval forces, including the guided-missile destroyer USS *McCampbell* (DDG 85), co-operated in Exercise Malabar, which featured both onshore and at-sea training in the Bay of Bengal.

Indonesia

Indonesia's not exactly a next-door neighbour to the United States, so it's a bit of a surprise to find out how long ago the earliest US military involvement with the area actually was.

Already by 1800, Captain Edward Preble and the USS *Essex* were conducting escort duties for merchant ships in the Sunda Strait, and in 1815, the USS *Peacock* carried out one of the last actions of the War of 1812 in the same area. It came across a small British East India Company ship that tried to point out to Captain Warrington of the *Peacock* that the war had finished months before. Warrington had obviously, however, been out of contact for some time and thought the British were trying to trick him, so he fired a broadside and boarded the British ship anyway, only to find out later that they had been indeed telling him the truth.

And in the 1830s, threats to merchant ships led to two US military expeditions into what is now part of Indonesia. In 1831, a US merchant ship, the *Friendship*, got a rather unfriendly reception in the Aceh town of Kuala Batee. In fact, pirates attacked the ship, killed some of its crew and stole its cargo. In response, Commodore John Downes and the USS *Potomac* were sent to do something about it. In 1832 the something they did was to send an attack party into the harbour, burning shipping and bombarding the town and its forts.

In 1838, another American ship, this time, the *Eclipse*, was attacked in the area, and its crew massacred. This time, the USS *Columbia* and USS *John Adams* were sent in. First, they bombarded Kuala Batee, and then they headed for the village of Muckie. An American landing party went in and destroyed the village.

Eventually, the Dutch became the dominant colonial power in the region, meaning in 1941 their colonial possessions in the region suddenly became a target for the advancing Japanese. American, British, Dutch and Australian forces in the area combined as ABDACOM in a desperate attempt to halt the Japanese onslaught, but the scale and speed of the Japanese attack made that a tough mission. Small numbers of American troops were among the Allied defenders on Java, but within two weeks, the Japanese were in control of the island. On land, Allied forces suffered a series of defeats.

And at sea, things were little better. The Battle of Badung Strait, the Battle of the Java Sea, and the Battle of Sunda Strait (Sunda again!) were all naval defeats for the Allies.

By the time the Japanese advance into what is now Indonesia had been halted, a lot of territory had fallen, and much needed to be recaptured. It would be a long, tough series of campaigns by land, by sea and by air. The New Guinea campaign saw a series of dramatic Allied amphibious assaults on islands, like Morotai and Biak, and on the coast of New Guinea, like the landing at Hollandia. American forces also made a major contribution to the Allied campaign in Borneo in 1945.

Soon after the war, Indonesia became independent, but a rough road lay ahead. In 1958, as fears grew among some in Washington that Indonesian leader Sukarno was getting too close to Communists, rebels attempted to topple him. The coup, however, was crushed.

Over the years, the United States has had assorted military links with the Indonesian military, including shared training and visits amongst other things. But political disputes, particularly in the past over East Timor, caused disruption to some links.

More recently, in 2012, building work began with US funding on barracks for the Indonesian Peace and Security Centre in West Java. In 2013, US and Indonesian naval personnel trained alongside each other in Cooperation Afloat Readiness and Training 2013.

The Hawaii National Guard is partnered with Indonesia.

Iran

It's not exactly going to come as a shock to many that America has long been involved with the country, sometimes in a friendly sense, sometimes quite a lot less so.

To begin with, though inevitably it will come as a surprise to many, the US was definitely involved in a friendly sense. In the late nineteenth and early twentieth centuries, Iran, or Persia as it was then known, found itself squeezed between two empires, the Russian (and after the Revolution, the Soviet) Empire to the north and the British Empire to the south and east. America, by contrast, with much less influence in the region, was seen as something of a safe alternative. Americans like Arthur Millspaugh and Morgan Shuster held high rank in the country offering advice on modernisation. Americans opened schools and colleges. One American at the time even fought and died for constitutional democracy in the country. Howard Baskerville, born in North Platte, Nebraska, became a teacher at the American Memorial School in Tabriz. In 1909, aged twenty-four, with royalist forces besieging the city, Baskerville led a volunteer force against them. He was killed by a sniper, but even today he is honoured in Iran.

During the Second World War, Iran was vital to Allied victory. After the Anglo–Soviet occupation of the country, about $18 billion worth of American Lend-Lease material poured through Iran on its way to the Soviet Union. America's Persian Gulf Command took control of US efforts in the country, organising improvements to infrastructure to help the flow of war supplies and setting up a plant at Abadan near the coast with the 17th Air Depot Group where aircraft could be assembled before onward transmission first to Tehran, and then to the Soviet Union. American influence was seen elsewhere as well. For instance, in 1942, H. Norman Schwarzkopf (not the leader of Operation Desert Storm but his father – *see* Kuwait) was put in charge of organising the Iranian police force.

And, of course, the principal Allied leaders of the war, Roosevelt, Churchill and Stalin all met for a wartime conference in Tehran. Roosevelt mixed martinis for Churchill and Stalin, and asked the Soviet leader how he liked his drink. Stalin answered that it was okay but cold on his stomach.

Stalin pressed the Western allies to commit to opening up a

second front. Roosevelt settled on General Eisenhower to be the supreme commander in Europe, responsible for Operation Overlord. Little discussion was given over to the question of post-war Iran or the Persian Gulf.

After the war, Iran emerged as the fourth-largest oil exporter in the world, supplying 90 per cent of Europe's petroleum. In the early 1950s with the Cold War raging, the UK and US governments and intelligence agencies started to get nervous about what might happen in Iran.

Iran shared a 1,000-mile border with the Soviet Union and had an active Communist (Tudeh) party. The crisis really began, however, when Mohammad Mossadeq, the democratically elected prime minister, in a move to take more of the profits from Iran's oil, started to nationalise the Anglo–Iranian Oil Company, a move deeply unpopular with Britain, who imposed sanctions.

In 1953, President Eisenhower authorised a CIA-led coup against Mossadeq in favour of Shah Mohammad Reza Pahlavi. Kermit Roosevelt (Teddy Roosevelt's son) was put in charge of Operation Ajax, and funds were used by the CIA to recruit Iranian mobs, which eventually helped drive Mossadeq from office. Eisenhower subsequently awarded Kermit Roosevelt the National Security Medal in a closed-door ceremony in December 1953.

In the period after the coup, America helped build up the Shah with military and other aid, and the Shah became a firm partner of the United States in the Cold War. The US Military Assistance Advisory Group in the country had widespread involvement with Iran's military and security structures prior to the 1979 revolution.

In 1979, the Iranian Revolution broke out, and soon the Shah was gone from Iran forever. So much has happened between the United States and Iran since the revolution that this can only be a summary of some of the main events.

In 1979, American hostages were seized in Tehran after the US Embassy was stormed. The CIA working closely with the Canadian ambassador managed to 'exfiltrate' six Americans under the noses of the Iranian militants. Ross Perot also hired a retired ex-Green Beret officer to free two of his Electronic Data Systems employees from Iranian kidnappers. After almost six months, though, fifty-two Americans remained in custody.

President Jimmy Carter authorised Operation Eagle Claw, an attempt to rescue the hostages using navy helicopters and a Delta Force under the command of Colonel Charles Beckwith. Carter's Secretary of State, Cyrus Vance, resigned over the decision. In the early hours of 25 April, a helicopter rotor blade struck a Lockheed C-130 on the ground causing a massive explosion. The bodies of eight Americans were left in the Persian desert. The mission's failure severely weakened the Carter presidency, and the hostages were not released until after he had been defeated in the 1980 presidential election.

The Iran-Contra arms-for-hostages scandal of the Reagan years nearly brought down Carter's successor. Meanwhile, in Lebanon, another hostage crisis was brewing with Iran's ally Hezbollah.

Because of its problems with post-revolution Iran, the United States tended to favour Iraq in the brutal Iran-Iraq War. The war, launched by Saddam Hussein, lasted from 1980 to 1988 and claimed over a million lives. US and Gulf Arab support for Iraq led to huge tensions with Iran in the Persian Gulf and eventually actual violence.

In an attempt to put pressure on Iraq's Gulf allies, Iran commenced attacks on their oil tankers in the Persian Gulf. In response, in Operation Earnest Will, America agreed to offer naval protection to tankers reflagged under the Stars and Stripes and took a number of other actions as well.

In October 1987, after a missile hit the *Sea Isle City*, a Kuwaiti-flagged oil tanker, America launched Operation Nimble Archer against two Iranian oil rigs, which had been used to co-ordinate attacks on merchant shipping. After four warships shelled the platforms, US Special Forces boarded them and planted explosives.

During Operation Earnest Will, in early 1988, the USS *Samuel B. Roberts* hit a mine and was almost sunk. Operation Praying Mantis was launched four days later. US forces again attacked and destroyed two Iranian oil rigs, and when the Iranian navy tried to counter-attack, US forces sank the Iranian frigate *Sahand*, disabled another Iranian frigate, destroyed the missile patrol boat *Joshan*, and sank or damaged a number of other Iranian patrol boats. Iran's fleet was not big, and by the end of the action, half of it was sunk or severely damaged.

On 3 July 1988, the USS *Vincennes* accidentally shot down

an Iranian commercial jet liner with 290 passengers, all of whom were killed. The US government agreed to pay over $130 million in compensation. The Iran-Iraq War came to an end shortly after this tragedy.

In the State of the Union address George W. Bush delivered on 31 January 2002, he accused Iran of forming part of 'an axis of evil' in the world. In August of 2002, evidence emerged that Iran was building a uranium-enrichment facility in Natanz and a secret heavy water production plant in Arak. In June 2005, Mahmoud Ahmadinejad was elected president of Iran. In power, Ahmadinejad used rhetoric against countries such as the United States and Israel. Iran claimed its nuclear programme was for peaceful purposes, but Iran's support for Shi'ite forces opposed to the United States in Iraq, and inevitably raised concerns for Hezbollah and Hamas about whether the Iranian nuclear programme was in reality mainly designed to create nuclear weapons.

Over the years, Iran has been the target of assorted US surveillance and intelligence operations, and it has been speculated that the United States has had contacts with groups mounting cross-border operations into Iran, as well as other activities inside Iran.

In 2010, the malware known as Stuxnet targeted cascades and centrifuges at the Natanz uranium-enrichment plant in Iran and is reputed to have delayed the process by as much as two years. It is widely speculated that United States and Israeli intelligence organised the Stuxnet operation.

Recent negotiations have raised hopes that problems over Iran's nuclear programme might be solved peacefully, but little is certain at this stage.

Iraq

Unless you have just returned from a very long space journey (and one with communications failure at that), you are aware that the United States invaded and occupied Iraq.

But 2003 didn't mark the beginning of US military involvement with the country.

During the Second World War, America had forces in Iraq, though admittedly they weren't there to fight. Instead, they were there to help with air-ferry routes and particularly with the supply of military aid to Russia in its fight against the Nazis. Among various locations in the region, the US had a military presence at the airbase at Basra at this time and also at RAF Habbaniya near Baghdad.

In the post-war era, America had friendly links with the royal government of King Feisal II of Iraq, and in 1952, he came to the United States to meet President Harry Truman. He also met, among others, Deborah Kerr, James Mason and Jackie Robinson. So, quite a visit really. He didn't, however, get to enjoy his holiday photos for long. By 1958, Feisal was dead, murdered along with other members of his family in a military coup.

Immediately after the coup, King Hussein of neighbouring Jordan (who had been at Harrow with Feisal) requested Western support to prevent any threat from the new Iraqi regime. The British led in responding, but America also offered support. And pretty much the same situation occurred in 1961 when the Iraqi regime briefly threatened Kuwait. Not, of course, was that the last time that was going to happen.

In 1963, another coup took place in Iraq, this time putting the Ba'ath party in power.

For much of the 1960s and 1970s, fighting took place between the Iraqi government and the Kurds. The Kurds received much help from Iraq's neighbour (and rival) Iran, at that stage run by the Shah. The Shah was a major US ally, and the United States gave some support to the Kurds in their efforts against the Soviet-linked Baghdad regime. However, in 1975, the Shah did a deal with the Iraqi government.

In some senses, 1979 would change everything in Iraq, as it did in Iran. Saddam Hussein took total control in Iraq, while in Iran the revolution toppled the Shah and brought to power the Ayatollah Khomeini. The change, however, did not end the competition for regional power between Iran and Iraq, nor did it solve the problems faced by the Kurds. In addition, Saddam feared the influence of Khomeini on Iraq's own large Shi'a population. In 1980, Saddam invaded Iran.

With the Shah gone, though, and the United States now a major focus for Khomeini, US priorities in the region had changed somewhat. Despite the USS *Stark* incident in which an Iraqi missile killed thirty-seven US personnel in 1987, the United

States played an active part in defending Arab oil tankers, which were being targeted by the Iranians because of support given by various Arab governments for Saddam. The full extent of US support specifically given to Iraq during this period is still a matter of debate.

In March 1988, Saddam's forces launched their notorious and horrifying chemical weapons attack on the Kurdish town of Halabja. In August 1988 hostilities ceased between Iran and Iraq, with both sides having suffered appalling casualties. Two years later in August 1990, Iraq went much further than it had in 1961, and this time it invaded Kuwait.

Although the story of the liberation of Kuwait mainly belongs in the chapter on Kuwait, it did also, of course, involve much US military activity inside Iraq. Coalition aircraft extensively bombed targets inside Iraq, and coalition Special Forces operated there. Plus when the ground campaign to liberate Iraq actually began, a thrust through Iraqi territory to the west of Kuwait was a major component.

In the aftermath of the war, as President George H. W. Bush called upon Iraqis to topple Saddam in a radio broadcast, rebellions broke out in the south of the country and in the Kurdish north. Saddam unleashed massive force against the rebels and crushed those in the south, though he had less success in the north. In 1991, in Operation Provide Comfort, US troops were sent along with other troops to the Kurdish areas to assist with the crisis there, and in 1992, America helped to impose no-fly zones over areas of both southern and northern Iraq. Massive sanctions that had been imposed on Iraq after the invasion of Kuwait were maintained in order to put pressure on the Iraqi regime and force it, among other things, to pay reparations and eliminate weapons of mass destruction, or WMDs.

On 26 June 1993, after receiving information from the CIA that blamed Iraqi intelligence for an attempted assassination plot against former President George H. W. Bush in Kuwait, President Clinton ordered the launch of twenty-three Tomahawk cruise missiles at targets inside Iraq.

In September 1996, in response to an Iraqi attack on Kurdish areas and Iraqi targeting of US fighters, America launched Operation Desert Strike, a cruise-missile and bombing attack on Iraqi targets, particularly air defence targets.

In December 1998, after Iraq had impeded the work of WMD inspectors, Britain and the United States followed up with Operation Desert Fox, a three-day bombing and cruise-missile campaign aimed at facilities believed to be associated with WMDs, as well as other targets, including some associated with the Iraqi Secret Police and Republican Guard.

In March of 2003, President George W. Bush ordered the execution of Operation Iraqi Freedom, a US-led invasion of Iraq. Bush declared that the purpose of the operation was 'to disarm Iraq of weapons of mass destruction, to end Saddam Hussein's support for terrorism, and to free the Iraqi people.'

Senator Barack Obama, by contrast, in a 2002 speech, characterised the idea of invading Iraq as 'a dumb war'.

The causes of few other wars have been the subject of so much debate and controversy as the invasion of Iraq, but a variety of causes obviously had at least some impact.

Saddam Hussein's regime had a history of appalling brutality and barbarity that had already been responsible for the deaths of hundreds of thousands. He also had a track record of invading other countries, of using poison gas against both defenceless civilians and the Iranian military on a mass scale, and of attempting in the past to acquire nuclear technology. Many genuinely believed at the time of the invasion of Iraq that he possessed WMDs, and even today, questions remain about exactly what happened to some of the stockpile of chemical weapons he had once had. He had supported terrorism against Israel. He had continued to challenge the international community in the decade after his invasion of Kuwait, and the rigorous sanctions aimed at his regime caused the Iraqi population far more suffering than that felt by Saddam and his cronies. Saddam had two sons, Uday and Qusay, who might one day have succeeded Saddam and who were both generally regarded as just as cruel and brutal as their father.

Ironically, well before 9/11, President Bill Clinton made, in some sense, the most cogent case for a regime change in Iraq. In a 1998 televised speech, he said:

The hard fact is that so long as Saddam remains in power, he threatens the well-being of his people, the peace of the region, and the security of the world.

The best way to end that threat once and for all is with a new

Iraqi government – a government ready to live in peace with its neighbours, a government that respects the rights of its people ... Heavy as they are, the costs of action must be weighed against the price of inaction. If Saddam defies the world and we fail to respond, we will face a far greater threat in the future. Saddam will strike again at his neighbours. He will make war on his own people.

And mark my words, he will develop weapons of mass destruction. He will deploy them, and he will use them.

International interventions in Sierra Leone and Kosovo had created an environment in which many politicians had come to believe, wrongly as it turned out, that a military intervention in Iraq could lead to a stable and peaceful situation within a short space of time. And the devastation of 9/11 meant Americans were suddenly aware of the real possibility of an attack on their home soil causing thousands of deaths and overwhelming destruction.

It is also clear that Iraq, with its vast oil resources and its key Middle East location, is a country of obvious strategic interest for the West. And it is clear some might have hoped that if a successful pro-Western democracy could be created in Iraq, it might serve as a valuable example in a region that has suffered so much from dictatorships.

This much is clear. What is less clear, and perhaps may never be entirely clear, is in which order this complex assortment of motivations and aspirations ranked. Which were ultimately less important and which were ultimately more important in leading to war? Inevitably, all the causes that contributed to the Iraq invasion and occupation are now judged through the lens of a conflict that was, as it turned out, very, very far from being the quick, low-casualty, successful intervention those who decided it should go ahead had hoped for.

The war has had tremendous impact on Iraq, on the United States, and on the other countries that fought alongside the United States there, and this one chapter in this book can deal with only a few of its aspects.

That war began on 20 March 2003, with the launch of forty Tomahawk cruise missiles from American ships near the Middle East in an attempt to 'decapitate' Iraqi leadership. The strikes failed to kill Saddam Hussein. By the eighteenth day of the war, over 700 Tomahawks had been fired by the US Navy.

The 'shock and awe' air campaign began the next day. More than 1,500 sorties a day were flown by the USAF and US Navy.

General Tommy Franks led the coalition forces that were made up primarily of about 148,000 US forces. A significant force (about 45,000 troops) from Great Britain fought alongside the US. Ultimately over forty different nations, including Australia, Poland, Italy, Japan, Albania, Mongolia and the Dominican Republic, made up the Coalition of the Willing that contributed troops to this conflict.

The greatest Iraqi resistance was composed of the fedayeen, or 'martyr' battalions, irregular forces that were armed with AK-47s and RPGs.

On 26 March, troops of the 173rd Airborne brigade conducted the first US Army combat jump since the Second World War landing near Bashur Airfield in northern Iraq. By 10 April these troops, along with Kurdish fighters, had liberated Kirkuk – Iraq's largest northern city.

By 3 April US armoured forces were on the outskirts of Baghdad. The Iraqi information minister was proclaiming to the media that no Americans had entered Baghdad, even though a battle could clearly be heard raging and tanks were not far off. Thunder runs made up of Abrams tanks and Bradley fighting vehicles began charging through downtown Baghdad on 5 April. The A-10 Warthog, whose production had been championed by the legendary fighter pilot John Boyd, proved to be effective in destroying Iraqi vehicles with its 30mm cannon.

On 9 April Iraqis pulled down a large statue of Saddam in al-Fardous square in downtown Baghdad.

On 23 July members of the 101st Airborne Division tracked down and killed Saddam Hussein's sons Uday and Qusay. Uday had personally ordered the torture of Iraqi athletes, including those who had performed at the Olympics who did not match up to his expectations. Qusay had conceived the destruction of Iraq's southern marshes (a massive environmental disaster) and ordered the deaths of many political prisoners.

Saddam himself was captured by US forces near Tikrit in December 2003. After his trial and conviction, he was executed on 13 December 2006.

US and allied forces were well prepared and trained to defeat Iraqi forces on the battlefield but not so well prepared to win the peace. In the spring of 2003, the mood of Baghdad swiftly changed from jubilation at the collapse of Saddam's regime to despair at the chaos and looting that ravaged the nation's capital. The regime's police force collapsed, and Allied forces did not manage to fill the void.

Looters stole some 15,000 objects from Baghdad's National Museum. They broke into the Iraq Central Bank. Saddam Hussein was a brutal repressive dictator, but it seemed to many Iraqis that the Americans brought chaos in their wake. Huge problems occurred with restoring basic services, such as power, telephone services and water supplies in many areas. Saddam himself had contributed to the chaos by emptying the prisons prior to the country being overrun.

Many mistakes were made during the occupation. Many Iraqi army ammunition dumps were not secured, which allowed insurgents access to high explosives for IEDs (improvised explosive devices). The greatest error may have been the dismissal of the Iraqi army, which effectively made many armed young and trained Iraqi men unemployed and unhappy.

The upshot of this was an insurgency movement that also received arms, support and some manpower from hostile states, such as Iran and Syria.

In the spring of 2004, US forces were unable to drive the insurgents out of Fallujah. The increasing level of violence and particularly the extensive use of IEDs forced the United States to extend military tours of duty by ninety days. The US Marines spearheaded the second battle of Fallujah in late 2004, which finally drove insurgents from the city. Ninety-five Americans were killed.

In the same year, the Abu Ghraib prison scandal erupted into the open. Donald Rumsfeld has recently expressed his regret over President George W. Bush's rejection of his offer to resign, which followed disclosures about Abu Ghraib.

In January 2005 nationwide elections were held in Iraq. It was the first Iraqi election since 1958. In a third election held that same year in December, nearly 80 per cent of the population voted. The purple-stained fingers of Iraqi voters may have contributed to the Arab Spring, which continues to reverberate throughout the Middle East.

After the bombing of the Shi'a Golden Mosque of Samarra on 22 February 2006, sectarian violence exploded throughout Iraq. Three years after the invasion, over 2,500 Americans had been killed. By 2006, the war had become deeply unpopular with many of the American people.

In November 2006, President Bush accepted the resignation of Donald Rumsfeld as Defense Secretary. To replace him, Bush tapped Robert Gates who had been the president of Texas A&M University but also had an extensive Washington résumé with a focus on defence and intelligence issues. For the new US commander in Iraq, Gates soon settled on General David Petraeus, who literally wrote the book on counter-insurgency (*Field Manual 3–24: Counterinsurgency*). Secretary Gates also championed the introduction of MRAPs (mine-resistant ambush-protected vehicles) that dramatically reduced the vulnerability of American troops to IEDs.

On 10 January 2007 Bush announced a surge of five brigades to Baghdad and two battalions of marines to Anbar. In all, about 30,000 additional troops were eventually sent to Iraq. The surge was hugely controversial, but later Secretary of State Hillary Clinton would simply state, 'The Iraq surge worked.'

Another crucial development was the rise of the Sunni Awakening that, with US and Iraqi government support, began to fight against al-Qaeda.

Suicide bombings and casualties did not suddenly and entirely stop, but the level of violence steadily declined.

Shortly after being inaugurated president, Barack Obama announced on 27 February 2009 the withdrawal of US troops from Iraq. America's combat role in Iraq finally ended on 31 August 2010, about seven and a half years after the invasion. US losses included 4,427 Americans killed and 34,275 injured. Figures for Iraqi casualties in the period have been a subject of much debate, but over 100,000 Iraqis have also been killed.

Currently the Iraqi government is locked in a bitter struggle with Islamic State forces. President Obama in August 2014 authorised US air strikes against Islamic State targets in northern Iraq. American advisers have also been deployed to assist the Iraqi government against Islamic State.

Ireland

About 10 per cent of Americans are of Irish stock, and many more exuberantly celebrate St Patrick's Day every year. Many Irish have served in the US military over the years, including John Barry of County Wexford who is widely acclaimed (along with John Paul Jones, of course) as being the 'Father of the American Navy'.

But has the US ever sent forces to what is now the Republic of Ireland?

Well, for a start, during the Revolutionary War, John Paul Jones and assorted privateers cruised in and operated in Irish waters. And more American privateers operated in Irish waters during the War of 1812. Captain Hailey in the *True Blooded Yankee* went as far as landing on Irish soil and burnt seven ships in one harbour. He even sailed into Dublin harbour and destroyed a schooner there.

During the First World War, the US had substantial military involvement with Ireland. Huge numbers of Americans were shipped through the Irish Sea from 1917 to 1918 to bring the AEF to Europe. It should come as no surprise, therefore, that the American Navy took an active interest in Ireland and its surrounding waters. US naval ships, including six American submarines, were based in Cork, and US submarine chasers were based at Queenstown. The US Navy also built a naval air station in Wexford, to help counter the Kaiser's submarines.

This, of course, was at a time when the whole of Ireland was part of the United Kingdom. That was soon to change after the First World War, and American volunteers went to join the fight on the Irish Republican side. In January 1921, for instance, the Philadelphia correspondent of the *New York Tribune* reported that five companies of Irish volunteers had been raised willing to fight, wearing uniforms similar to the Republicans in Ireland, and that individuals and small groups were headed for Ireland through 'roundabout channels' to avoid interception by the British. Éamon de Valera, a leading Irish Republican, was born in New York City in 1882, but moved to Ireland at the age of two. After his release from prison in 1917, he fled to America where he toured and raised about $6 million for the Irish Republican cause.

During the Second World War, Northern Ireland, as part of the UK, took a major part in the war.

The Republic of Ireland, however, maintained its neutrality. Some Irish Republicans did have contacts with the Nazis, but the Irish government itself and much of the Irish population clearly leaned in the Allied direction. For example, over 350 Allied airmen who went down over Ireland were released during the war while Axis airmen were interned for the duration. American planes refuelled during the war at Shannon Airport, and Allied planes were allowed the use of the Donegal Corridor, a short stretch of airspace linking Northern Ireland to the Atlantic through Irish airspace. Over 70,000 Irish volunteers fought alongside American forces while serving in the British Army. Irish weather stations offered critical reporting on atmospheric conditions prior to D-Day.

During the Cold War, Ireland again remained neutral.

The IRA had not, of course, disappeared after the Anglo–Irish Treaty of December 1921 that partitioned Ireland. Some members of the IRA rejected the treaty and went on to fight and lose a civil war against Irish pro-treaty forces, and subsequently engaged in repeated campaigns of bombings and shootings against Britain in an attempt to unite Northern Ireland with the rest of Ireland. The Provisional IRA Campaign lasted from 1969 until the last ceasefire in 1997 and was mainly fought in Northern Ireland, with occasional campaigns on the UK mainland. It did involve some Irish living south of the border as well. As before, support, particularly financial, from some Americans was a significant factor in assisting Irish Republican activity during this period.

In recent years, Shannon Airport has been used as a staging area for American troops and supplies headed for Iraq and Afghanistan. In addition, Ireland has long held a significant role in international peacekeeping forces, including in Kosovo.

Israel

Due to religious, cultural and ethnic links, America has long had a strong, deep and lasting commitment to Israel.

But it was during the Second World War that American forces first arrived in the territory of what is now the modern state of Israel. US air crews used the RAF based at Lydda (which later became Lod Airport and eventually Ben Gurion International Airport) for air transport and air-ferrying missions. During the fighting between Rommel and the British and Commonwealth troops in nearby Egypt to the west, American bombers were based at a number of locations in the Palestine Mandate with B-17s at Lydda and B-24s at Ramat David.

After the Second World War, Britain eventually announced its withdrawal from a fractious Palestine Mandate, and on 14 May 1948, the modern state of Israel was launched. The US government recognised the state of Israel only eleven minutes after the first Israeli Prime Minister Ben Gurion declared its independence. Fighting intensified between Arabs and Jews, and neighbouring Arab countries invaded.

Foreign volunteers, or Machal, came from a wide range of countries to help Israel, America included. Most were veterans of the Second World War, including the famous Micky Marcus, a colonel in the US Army who went to Israel, became a brigadier general, and helped break the Siege of Jerusalem in 1948. In May 1948 a handful of Jewish-American aviation veterans fought in German Messerschmitt BF-109s that had been purchased from Czechoslovakia. They would form the foundation of the Israeli Air Force.

There was some official US involvement as well. In June 1948 when the US Consul General was killed by sniper fire, a marine force from the USS *Kearsarge* was ordered to Jerusalem. And on 23 July, flying a UN flag, the USS *Putnam* evacuated UN team members from the Israeli port of Haifa.

By 1949, Israel had joined the United Nations.

The Holocaust had created massive American sympathy for the concept of a Jewish homeland. American arms and financial support began flowing to Israel during the Truman administration. A tradition of shared training and military exchange between the United States and Israel was established.

US government support for Israel, however, was not automatic (or unconditional). For example, in 1956, President Dwight Eisenhower refused to endorse the invasion of the Suez Canal and Sinai by forces from Britain, France and Israel. U-2 intelligence gave the president vital information on what was happening on the ground at the time. In the end, Israel withdrew its forces from the Sinai.

During the Six Day War of 1967, Israel delivered a pre-emptive strike on the Egyptian air force destroying most of its Soviet-made aircraft while they were still on the ground. The conflict more than doubled the amount of territory under Israel's direct control with the addition of the Sinai Peninsula. On 8 June 1967, units of the Israeli air force and navy attacked the USS *Liberty* – an intelligence-gathering ship, which was cruising in international waters off the coast of the Sinai Peninsula. Thirty-four Americans were killed. The Israeli government apologised for the tragic mistake and paid $13 million in compensation.

In the 1973 Yom Kippur War (6–24 October), Israel was attacked by Egyptian forces near the Suez Canal and by Syrian forces near the Golan Heights. After recovering from the initial surprise, Israeli forces managed to counter-attack across the Suez Canal and were soon driving towards Cairo itself. The Nixon administration, though crippled by the Watergate scandal, flew over 22,000 tons of supplies to Israel in Operation Nickel Grass. The Soviets resupplied the Arab forces. On 24 October Moscow announced the mobilisation of seven airborne divisions for possible deployment to Egypt. The next day, US armed forces were moved to DEFCON 3 – planes ready to launch in fifteen minutes. Yuri Andropov, KGB chief, declared, 'We are not going to start the Third World War.' Egypt withdrew its request for Soviet troops, and a UN truce was soon agreed to.

American shuttle diplomacy eventually helped to secure the Camp David accord of 1978, which significantly reduced Middle East tensions when a 'land for peace' agreement was hammered out between Egypt and Israel. The Sinai Peninsula was returned to Egypt, and Sadat broke decisively with his former Soviet ally. Billions in US aid soon began flowing to Egypt, as well as to Israel.

During the first Gulf War, Saddam Hussein launched Scud missile attacks on Israel, which killed two and wounded hundreds. He was desperately trying to drive a wedge between coalition forces by prodding a neutral Israel into a military response.

Prior to the start of the 1991 Gulf War, the Israeli government agreed to allow a US Army Patriot unit into Israel – the first time that foreign troops had ever been stationed in that country. And in the end, Israel did stay out of the conflict.

More diplomatic action followed the Gulf War, again with extensive US involvement. In 1994, President Clinton was there when a peace deal between Israel and Jordan was signed, and in 1995, the Oslo II agreement was signed between Israel and the Palestinian National Authority.

In 2006, war broke out in Lebanon between Israel and Hezbollah, and the United States offered Israel extra fuel and munitions.

Today, the search for a complete end to the Arab–Israeli conflict continues, and so does the search for a solution to problems over Iran's nuclear research. In the desert in southwest Israel is located a small US military installation operated by US personnel with hugely powerful radar watching what goes on in the region.

In the context of all the uncertainties about the future in the Middle East, America's partnership with Israel on a wide range of exercises, training, planning, supply, development, intelligence and other military matters remains a central part of US strategy in the region.

Italy

A land forever to be associated with such cultural wonders as Michelangelo, Leonardo da Vinci, and, of course, pizza.

It wasn't long after American independence from Britain that US forces were first in Italian waters and on Italian soil. Perhaps they'd already heard about the art wonders – or indeed the pizza. By 1801, America was at war with the Barbary pirates, and Commodore Edward Preble of the US Navy dropped anchor in Messina, Sicily, to see if he could get any help from King Francis of the Two Sicilies (he wasn't seeing double, that's what the kingdom was called). King Francis happened to be very helpful and gave the commodore access to men, supplies, and port facilities.

During the mid-nineteenth century, American volunteers, a number of whom fought at the Battle of Caserta, helped Garibaldi in his campaign to reunify Italy and establish the foundations of today's modern state. In 1860 Captain Palmer of the USN *Iriquois* even intervened directly and supplied Garibaldi's Thousand with much-needed gunpowder to aid the Redshirts in action against the Bourbon forces in Sicily. Garibaldi, the great Italian patriot, had even lived for a time on Staten Island in New York.

Another early encounter took place amidst a devastating tragedy. On the morning of 28 December 1908, a severe earthquake measuring 7.1 on the Richter scale struck near Messina on the Italian island of Sicily. The quake was followed by tsunamis with waves measuring thirty-nine feet in height.

More than 70,000 people were killed, and over 90 per cent of all buildings in Messina collapsed. Immediately, the word went out, and the US Navy supply ships, USS *Celtic* and USS *Culgoa*, along with other ships from the American Great White Fleet, were diverted from their Mediterranean cruise to provide humanitarian assistance to the Italians.

There were even rougher times ahead for Italy. Another great cataclysm was to strike Europe in 1914. The First World War had arrived, though it didn't arrive until 1915 for Italy. At the start of the war, Italy was technically allied with Austria-Hungary and Germany, but a large portion of what is now northern Italy was under Austrian control. Italy wanted this land, and so didn't join the war on the side of its allies. Instead, it waited and waited, and finally in May 1915, joined the war on the Allied side (that is on the side of the Allies with a big *A*, not on the side of its former allies with a small *a*, who can't have been very pleased at the turn of events).

It was not an easy war for the Italians. As American troops were to find out in the Second World War, fighting in Italy, with its fair bit of mountainous territory, can be a pretty rocky experience. Heavy fighting led to few major gains by the Italians, and in late 1917 the Austro-Hungarians, with German reinforcements, inflicted a devastating defeat on the Italians at Caporetto.

The year 1917 saw even more major developments elsewhere. The United States joined the Allied side in the First World War, and just as American doughboys were soon on their way to France, so they were also soon on their way to fight alongside the Italians. An American regiment (the 332nd Infantry Regiment, 83rd Division, with attached medical and supply units), was sent to the Italian front in July 1918 in response to urgent requests from the Italian government. Ernest Hemingway volunteered for the Red Cross Ambulance Service serving in Italy and was wounded in 1918. The 332nd took part in the pursuit of the retreating enemy after the decisive Allied victory at Vittorio-Veneto in October 1918.

After joining the war on the winning side in the First World War, Italy got it very, very wrong in 1940.

On 10 June Mussolini, witnessing the fall of France to the German blitzkrieg and hoping for his share in the spoils, declared war on the Allies. Then after Pearl Harbor, Hitler declared war

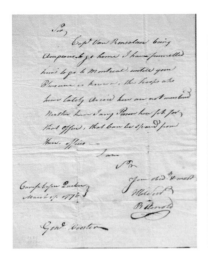

Left: 1. Benedict Arnold letter. Chris Kelly's ancestor, Captain Van Rensselaer, was invading Canada in 1776 under the command of Benedict Arnold. He was 'anxious to go home' to New York. (Photograph by Karim Merie) *Right:* 2. John Paul Jones spiking the guns statue, Whitehaven, UK. John Paul Jones (1747–92) spiked the guns in his raid on Whitehaven in the early morning hours of April 23, 1778. One British collier was burnt. (Author's photograph)

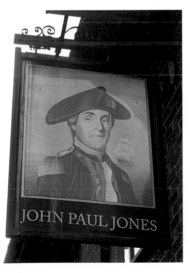

Left: 3. John Paul Jones pub sign, Whitehaven, UK. In 1999, the town of Whitehaven officially pardoned John Paul Jones, 'Father of the US Navy,' for his 1778 raid on their town. (Author's photograph) *Right:* 4. The USS *Constitution* defeated the HMS *Java* on December 29, 1812, off the coast of Brazil. (*Fortunes of War* painting by Geoff Hunt, PPRSMA; photo courtesy of Mark Mirabile and Piranha Productions)

5. USS *Constitution*, Charlestown, MA. The USS *Constitution*, nicknamed 'Old Ironsides', was a 44-gun frigate that won three sea battles against the Royal Navy during the War of 1812. (Photo courtesy of Chris Moran)

6. William Walker plaque, Nashville, TN. William Walker (1824–60), the so-called 'grey-eyed man of destiny', led American invasions of Mexico, Nicaragua and Honduras. (Photo courtesy of Ladonna Parker)

Left: 7. Commodore Matthew Perry statue, Newport, RI. Commodore Matthew Perry (1794–1858) started the process of opening up Japan to the west with two visits to Tokyo Bay in 1853 and 1854. (Photo courtesy of Sam Jernigan.) *Right:* 8. John Monaghan statue, Spokane, WA. Ensign John Monaghan (1873–1899) of the USN was killed on April 1, 1899, in the Battle of Vailele in Samoa. (Photo courtesy of Visit Spokane – Mark Baker)

9. 107th Regiment statue, Central Park, NYC. American doughboys of the American Expeditionary Forces in World War I Regiment. (Author's photograph)

10. Spad S.XIII, American Air Museum, IWM Duxford, UK. Eddie Rickenbacker (1890–1973), the leading American fighter ace of the First World War, scored twenty-six aerial victories. This is a replica of Eddie Rickenbacker's Spad S.XIII. (Photograph by Karim Merie)

Above: 11. Battleship *Texas* BB-35, Battleship *Texas* State Historical Site, Texas Parks & Wildlife Department, La Porte, TX. The *Texas*, the only dreadnought battleship afloat today, was launched in 1912. The ship provided convoy escort in the First World War and shore bombardment at Normandy on June 6, 1944, in the Second World War. (Photo courtesy of James Hooper) *Below left:* 12. Queen Marie of Romania, Goldendale, WA. Queen Marie of Romania (1875–1938), granddaughter of Queen Victoria, was the Soldier Queen of Romania in the First World War. She visited the United States in 1926. (Printed with permission from Maryhill Museum of Art) *Below right:* 13. US Naval Monument, Brest, France. Built to commemorate the service of the USN in the First World War, the monument was destroyed by the Germans on July 4, 1941, and rebuilt in 1958. (Author's photograph)

14. Polar Bear Memorial, White Chapel Cemetery, Troy, MI. The Polar Bear Expedition invaded and occupied parts of Northern Russia from 1918 to 1919. (Photo courtesy of Vicki Aiello)

15. Statue of American Eagle Squadrons, Grosvenor Square, London, UK. This statue commemorates Americans who joined the RAF in the Second World War. (Photograph by Karim Merie)

16. FDR statue, Grosvenor Square, London, UK. Franklin Delano Roosevelt (1882–1945) was president of the United States for most of the Second World War. (Photograph by Karim Merie)

17. USS *Pampanito*, San Francisco Maritime National Park Association, Fisherman's Wharf, San Francisco, CA. The USS *Pampanito* (SS-383), launched in 1943, served in the Pacific. (Author's photograph)

18. Sculpture of Jimmy Doolittle, American Air Museum, IWM Duxford, UK. On April 18 1942, Jimmy Doolittle (1896–1993) led sixteen B-25s in a bombing raid on targets in Japan, from the USS *Hornet*. (Photograph by Karim Merie)

19. North American TB-25J 'Mitchell' bomber, RAF Museum, Hendon, UK. (Photo courtesy of Vincent Driano)

20. Dwight David Eisenhower statue, Grosvenor Square, London, UK. 'Ike' (1890–1969) planned Operation Overlord, the cross-channel invasion of Nazi-occupied Europe, from his offices at 20 Grosvenor Square. It would be the most famous invasion involving Americans of all time. (Author's photograph)

21. Willys MB Jeep, West Point Museum, United States Military Academy. Over six hundred thousand Jeeps were produced by the 'Arsenal of Democracy' in the Second World War. (Author's photograph)

22. P-51 Mustang, RAF Museum, Hendon, UK. The iconic P-51 Mustang could escort Allied bombers all the way to Berlin. (Photo courtesy of Vincent Driano)

23. Tommy Hitchcock's grave, Cambridge–American Cemetery, Cambridgeshire, UK. Tommy Hitchcock joined the Lafayette Escadrille in the First World War, played polo and championed the introduction of Rolls Royce engines into the P-51 Mustang. (Photograph by Karim Merie)

24. Douglas C-47 Skytrain, American Air Museum, IWM Duxford, UK. This Douglas C-47 Skytrain transport plane is painted with the D-Day stripes to try and avoid friendly fire that had plagued the invasion of Sicily in 1943. (Photograph by Karim Merie)

Left: 25. Private John Steele, Ste. Mère-Église, France. Private John Steele (1912–69) of the 82nd Airborne landed on the steeple of the church at Ste. Mère-Église in Normandy on June 6, 1944. (Author's photograph)
Right: 26. Stained glass window of the Virgin Mary and US paratroopers, Church of St. Mary, Ste. Mère-Église, France. (Author's photograph)

Left: 27. George Patton statue, West Point, NY. General George S. Patton Jr. (1885–1945), 'Old Blood and Guts'. (Author's photograph)
Right: 28. Sculpture of General Anthony McAuliffe, Bastogne, Belgium. When asked to surrender by the Germans at the siege of Bastogne in December 1944, General McAuliffe famously replied, 'Nuts.' (Author's photograph)

29. M4 Sherman, Musée Airborne, Ste. Mère-Église, France. Nearly fifty thousand M4A3 Sherman tanks were produced by a variety of American companies during the Second World War. (Author's photograph)

Right: 30. The cliffs of Pointe du Hoc, France. The US Army Rangers scaled these cliffs on 6 June 1944, to take out the German guns that threatened the Allied landing zones. (Author's photograph) *Below left:* 31. *The Spirit of American Youth Rising from the Waves*, Normandy American Cemetery and Memorial, Colleville-sur-Mer, France. (Author's photograph) *Below right:* 32. Statue of Douglas MacArthur, United States Military Academy, West Point. Douglas MacArthur (1880–1964) returned to the Philippines, occupied Japan, and masterminded the landings at Inchon during the Korean War. 'There is no substitute for victory.' (Author's photograph)

Above: 33. Huê, Vietnam. The bullet-riddled walls of the imperial city of Huê bear witness to the site of a major battle between the US Marines and North Vietnamese during the Tet Offensive and the location of a Communist massacre that claimed over three thousand civilian lives in 1968. (Photo courtesy of Bernie Podurgiel.) *Below left:* 34. Major Jack Coughlin (USAF, Ret.), who later flew 'jingle runs' with a C-130 in Vietnam, standing in front of his T-38 Talon trainer. (Photo courtesy of Major Jack Coughlin.) *Below right:* 35. SR-71, American Air Museum, IWM Duxford, UK. The SR-71 'Blackbird' spy plane, introduced in 1964, flew above Mach 3 at over 80,000 feet. (Photograph by Karim Merie)

Left: 36. Statue of Ronald Reagan, Grosvenor Square, London. President Reagan (1911–2004) armed the mujahideen in Afghanistan, armed the Contras in Nicaragua, and authorised Operation Urgent Fury, which invaded the island of Grenada in 1983. (Photograph by Karim Merie) *Right:* 37. Statue of the two Bushes, George W. Bush Library, SMU, Dallas, TX. President George H. W. Bush organised the liberation of Kuwait in 1991, and President George W. Bush ordered invasions of Afghanistan in 2001 and of Iraq and Liberia in 2003. (Photo courtesy of Vincent Driano)

38. A-10 'Warthog,' American Air Museum, IWM Duxford, UK. The A-10 'Warthog' was an effective tank destroyer in both Gulf Wars. (Author's photograph)

Left: 39. American eagle over the US Embassy, Grosvenor Square, London. (Photograph by Karim Merie)

Below: 40. National September 11 Memorial & Museum, New York, NY. Today, the 9/11 memorial in Lower Manhattan is a popular site for enlistment and re-enlistment ceremonies for the US military. (Photograph courtesy of Chance Heath)

on the United States of America, dragging his Italian ally along with him and suddenly (and in spite of Christopher Columbus and pizza), America was at war with Italy.

After northern Africa was finally cleared of Axis forces, it was time to take the fight to mainland Europe. The British favoured a landing in Italy prior to an attack on northern Europe, and after some disagreement America eventually joined the British and other Allied forces in a full-scale invasion of Italy in 1943. Future American president Dwight Eisenhower was the supreme commander.

We're not going to be able to deal in detail in this little book with the full heroism, sacrifice, and ultimate victory of US forces in the Italian campaign, so we'll give just a brief outline here.

It all started on 10 July 1943, with Operation Husky, the invasion of Sicily. The first day of the campaign was also one of the worst when the 504th Parachute Infantry Regiment of Matthew Ridgway's 82nd Airborne Division was decimated by friendly fire. About 1,400 Americans were tragically killed by anti-aircraft batteries on Allied naval vessels. From this painful experience, the Allies learned a valuable lesson. All Allied aircraft participating in the D-Day invasion were painted with black and white stripes prior to the Normandy invasion.

Once ashore, General Patton and British General Montgomery competed in the famous 'Race to Messina' on the other side of the island. To Montgomery's irritation, the indefatigable Patton won, but he didn't have it all his way. He was very nearly court-martialled for slapping a soldier suffering from battle fatigue.

With Sicily under Allied control, it was on to mainland Italy. The Second World War in Italy was a long, gruelling affair in which Americans fought with great tenacity and bravery. For instance, the 442nd Regimental Combat Unit, composed mainly of Japanese-Americans, became the most decorated American military unit in US history winning a staggering 9,486 Purple Hearts. There were times when the possibility of a rapid advance north towards the heart of Europe seemed possible, including when the Germans were initially surprised by the Allied landings at Anzio, but somehow the enemy collapse never came, at least not until right at the end of the war itself.

In spite of the armistice signed by the Italian government and their switching sides to the Allies, the German defence of Italy under the able 'Smiling Albert' Kesselring was stubborn and tenacious. After southern Italy was cleared, the Americans used airbases in Italy to bomb Axis targets, such as the Ploesti oil fields in Romania. George McGovern, the future presidential candidate, piloted his B-24 Liberator bomber on thirty-five missions from San Giovanni Air Base in Apulia.

Rome, Mussolini's former capital, was liberated by American forces on 4 June 1944, an event that didn't last too long in the headlines because of what happened two days later far to the north – D-Day. As Allied armies swept across northern Europe towards the Reich, American and other Allied armies continued their slow, tough advance north through Italy. In fact, fighting was to continue in Italy all the way until 8 May 1945 – VE Day.

Victory in Italy came at a heavy price. There were about 114,000 US casualties in the Italian campaign. Today you will find two American Battle Commission cemeteries in Italy, one in Florence and another near Anzio (Nettuno) where visitors can sit and think about the huge sacrifice made by many young troops.

After the war, the US got briefly involved in border disputes between Italy and Yugoslavia.

Today, America has strong and extensive military links with Italy. Italy joined NATO, and America positioned important military bases in Italy. The US military still maintains about 11,000 service personnel in the land of the Caesars. A little way north of beautiful and historic Venice, Aviano remains a strong USAF base, and the headquarters for the mighty US Sixth Fleet is located at Naples.

Ivory Coast

Ivory Coast is located between Liberia to the west and Ghana to the east and, potentially confusingly, has a flag that looks a bit like the Irish flag.

After the US government turned against the transatlantic slave trade, the area received a certain amount of attention from the US Navy's anti-slaving patrols in the nineteenth century. In 1843, US Marines came ashore in the Ivory Coast region to threaten people after two Americans had been killed.

The area eventually, however, became a French colony (which is why it's also known as Côte d'Ivoire) until independence in 1960, and links with France have remained strong.

In 1997, the USAF used Abidjan in Ivory Coast as a base for Operation Assured Lift into neighbouring Liberia, but soon, sadly, Ivory Coast was going to be in need of peacekeepers itself.

In September 2002, the First Ivoirian Civil War, started as a military uprising, took place in several cities. The government eventually managed to retain control of the main city of Abidjan but lost control of the north of the country to the rebels, including the city of Bouake. In Operation Autumn Return, US C-130s flew into Yamoussoukro, and US Special Forces went into Ivory Coast and worked with French forces, among others, to help rescue Americans and people of some other nationalities, particularly those in Bouake.

UN troops were eventually sent into Ivory Coast with US support to try to stabilise the situation, but violence persisted in the country until a peace accord in 2007.

Once more, a crisis broke out, in 2010, leading to the brief Second Ivoirian Civil War in 2011. French forces again played a major role in resolving the situation.

Recently, the US military has been developing more links with Ivory Coast, with Ivoirian personnel, for instance, taking part with US personnel in 2013 in the counter-piracy exercise Obangame Express 2013 and in Africa Endeavor 2013.

Jamaica

Some armed Americans were active around Jamaica even before the Revolution, though at that stage they were not fighting the British. Thomas Paine of Jamestown, Rhode Island, was a privateer with a commission from Jamaica's British governor, Sir Thomas Lynch. And in 1740, a large contingent of Virginian troops was shipped to Jamaica. But that sort of thing wasn't, of course, to last.

During the Revolutionary War and the War of 1812, US ships targeted assorted ships bound for Jamaica or coming from there. In 1779, the frigates *Providence* and *Queen of France* with the sloop *Ranger* suddenly found themselves in fog and in the middle of a British convoy headed for Jamaica. They managed to capture eleven ships.

In 1873, a ship sailing under the American flag, the *Virginius,* that had been running guns to insurgents in Cuba, picked up another load on Jamaica, only to be pursued and captured in Jamaican waters by a Spanish ship. The Spanish executed some of its crew before a diplomatic deal was finally worked out.

It was during the Second World War, however, that America took most interest in the island militarily. Under the destroyers-for-bases agreement of September 1940, the UK got some old destroyers, and America got access to much British-controlled territory to establish military bases. One of the areas involved was Jamaica.

The US Navy got a naval air station on Little Goat Island and the use of naval facilities at Port Royal. And the USAAF got Vernam Army Airfield. A group of officers and enlisted men known as 'Force Tuna' (great name) arrived there in late 1941 to set things up. Vernam was initially used for anti-submarine flights, but eventually it became a major destination for long-range training flights. It closed in 1949.

Jamaica became independent from Britain in 1962, and in 1972 democratic socialist Michael Manley came to power. His attitude towards Cuba scared some in Washington, and there has been speculation by some that America may have conducted covert attempts to undermine him.

In 1983, Jamaica offered military and political support to the American invasion of Grenada.

In the years since the Second World War, America has had assorted other military links with Jamaica, including training, exercises, exchanges, ship visits and shared humanitarian projects. Jamaica's military connections to the United States and Canada grew as its connections to the UK decreased.

General Colin Powell, who also served as US Secretary of State, is of Jamaican descent, and the District of Columbia National Guard is partnered with Jamaica.

Japan

In 1791, sixty-two years before Matthew Perry's arrival, an American merchant ship reached Japan. The Japanese reported that it belonged to 'American Red Hairs'. Obviously, it would have been unusual if the entire crew of an American ship had had red hair, but presumably to those generally used to jet-black

Japanese hair, red, blond and brown hair must have seemed both exotic and noteworthy.

By the mid-nineteenth century, the race was seriously on among Western nations to open up the East to lucrative trade. Both Commander James Biddle and Captain James Glynn took American ships to Japan in the 1840s, though with very mixed results.

But it was in 1853 that Commodore Matthew Perry (obviously *not* the Matthew Perry who was in *Friends*) sailed into Tokyo Bay with a squadron of four ships. Perry, a native of Newport, Rhode Island, was the younger brother of the impressively middle-named Oliver Hazard Perry (known for his concise report of 'We have met the enemy and they are ours' in the Battle of Lake Erie, War of 1812). Matthew Perry had served in the Mexican–American War and commanded the Africa Squadron. Two of Perry's ships were steamships that belched black smoke; they came to be known to the Japanese, not unreasonably, as the 'Black Ships'.

Perry bore with him a letter from President Millard Fillmore, not exactly now the best known of US presidents, to the Emperor of Japan:

> I have directed Commodore Perry to assure Your Imperial Majesty that I entertain the kindest feelings towards Your Majesty's person and government, and that I have no other object in sending him to Japan but to propose to Your Imperial Majesty that the United States and Japan should live in friendship and have commercial intercourse with each other.

Fillmore went on to request coaling depots based in Japan to serve American ships and a humane response to shipwrecked American mariners in Japanese waters.

Under the Tokugawa Shogunate, Japan had gone through a period of isolation from the rest of the world that lasted over 200 years. Japan was a highly militaristic feudal culture that had opted for near total seclusion (*sakoku*) from foreigners. Japan did not allow foreign visits with the exception of a small Dutch trading enclave near Nagasaki, and the Japanese were, on pain of death, prohibited from leaving as well. Their Samurai used some of the finest swords in the world, but many of their coastal battery guns were extremely outdated.

Perry delivered his letter and said he would return for an answer.

In February 1854, Perry once again arrived in Japan, this time, with ten ships that comprised nearly one quarter of the US Navy at that time. He got what he was after. The Treaty of Kanagawa, signed on 31 March 1854, was negotiated under the guns of the American navy. The treaty represented a capitulation to all of Perry's demands and a humiliation for Japan.

But the battle to open up Japan was not yet entirely won. In 1863, the Emperor issued an order to expel 'barbarians' once again. The mighty Choshu clan of Shimonoseki rushed to obey and started shelling any foreign ship that tried to pass through the crucial Shimonoseki Straits. An American merchant ship, the *Pembroke*, was among those ships targeted. It managed to escape, but, understandably, the crew weren't very happy, and the USS *Wyoming* was sent in to do something about it. The result was the Battle of Shimonoseki Straits in which *Wyoming* exchanged fire with Japanese shore batteries and managed to sink two Japanese ships before withdrawing, having suffered significant damage. It wasn't a defeat for the *Wyoming*, but it wasn't a massive victory either.

It wasn't to be until September 1864 that a multinational Western naval force inflicted a decisive defeat on the Choshu and ensured safety of passage for Western merchant ships.

Japan would now embark on a tumultuous period of radical change and military growth.

The Boshin War was fought between 1868 and 1869 as supporters of the Tokugawa Shogunate battled supporters of the emperor for control of Japan. The United States didn't get officially involved, but there were already plenty of Western weapons and some Western military advisers involved, and the US did send troops to protect American citizens.

The Bakufu ('Tent Government') of warlords led by a Shogun and a titular emperor were eventually replaced by a modern industrial nation state under the rule of the emperor Meiji. The Imperial Japanese Navy was modelled on Britain's Royal Navy, and their army was modelled on the Prussian example. Japan quickly adopted the imperial ambitions that were sweeping the Western world in the nineteenth century, colonising Okinawa, Formosa, and later, Korea.

If there were any doubts about the radical military advances being made by Japan, they were dispelled in the first decade of the twentieth century when, in 1904–05, Japan fought the Russo–Japanese War and destroyed two Russian fleets. President Teddy Roosevelt incidentally picked up a Nobel Prize for himself for helping to secure a peace treaty between Imperial Japan and Tsarist Russia to end the war, the Treaty of Portsmouth.

In the First World War, Japan was on the Allied side, a wise strategic decision, as it turned out, that allowed it to take control of many of the Pacific islands that had previously belonged to the Kaiser's German Empire.

Of course, in the Second World War, it was all to be a very different story. Japan achieved strategic surprise attacking the United States fleet at anchor at Pearl Harbor on 7 December 1941. Some Americans, not realising how advanced Japan's navy and air force had become, made the assumption that German pilots must have been involved. And Japan, in its onslaught in the East, would later launch attacks on American allies, such as the Philippines, and occupy American territory, such as Guam, Wake Island and Alaska.

The American riposte to Pearl Harbor was the spectacular and very daring Doolittle Raid, which took place on 18 April 1942. Sixteen B-25B Mitchell aircraft were launched from the deck of the USS *Hornet* to bomb Tokyo and other Japanese cities before proceeding to China afterwards. The raiders inflicted minimal physical damage, but the psychological impact was enormous as the Japanese felt compelled to initiate the disastrous (for the Japanese) Midway campaign to prevent future American air attacks on their homeland.

As the war progressed, slowly, US forces began to edge closer towards Japan. From 1943 to 1945, the American island-hopping campaign using US naval and marine landings drove closer and closer to the Japanese home islands. From April to June 1945 US forces fought the ferocious Battle of Okinawa, also known as the 'typhoon of steel'. This battle claimed the lives of virtually all 117,000 Japanese defenders, as well as more than a third of the island's total civilian population. Japanese kamikaze strikes resulted in the highest losses ever suffered in a single battle by the US Navy.

On 2 September 1944, US Navy pilot George H. W. Bush was shot down in his Grumman Avenger while flying off the coast of the island of Chichijima. After spending about four hours in a raft, the fortunate future president was rescued by the USS *Finback* submarine.

Advances in the Mariana Islands had put the US airbases within practical reach of the Japanese mainland in late 1944, and the use of incendiary munitions dropped by B-29 Superfortress bombers proved devastating in 1945. Cities such as Kobe, Nagoya, Osaka, Yokohama and Kawasaki were burnt to ashes. Over 100,000 people were killed by the fire-bombing in Tokyo in a single day – more even than the atomic bombs that followed in August.

Americans weren't only attacking Japan from the air. Captain Eugene Fluckey (later Admiral) commanded the USS *Barb*, which sank many Japanese merchant ships in the Second World War. Around 56 per cent of Japanese merchant shipping was sunk by American submarines such as the USS *Pampanito* (now found in San Francisco) during the war, which crippled Japan's ability to feed its population. On 23 July 1945, the USS *Barb* approached Patience Bay near Kashiho, Japan. A cutting-out party was sent ashore by rubber raft; their mission was to mine the tracks on a nearby railway. The team detonated their explosives under a Japanese train and watched as the engine exploded into the air and train cars smashed into each other and toppled off the track.

On 19 February 1945, US Marines landed on Iwo Jima in one of the most famous American invasions of all time. Four marines would soon raise the US flag on Mount Suribachi. The battleship *Texas*, a veteran of the First World War convoys, would provide shore bombardment of Japanese targets. Nearly all 22,000 Japanese defenders would be killed in action on Iwo Jima. Gunnery Sergeant John Basilone of Raritan, New Jersey, a Medal of Honor winner from Guadalcanal, would be killed on Iwo Jima, along with over 6,000 other Americans during the three-month struggle for control of the island. Iwo Jima, today an uninhabited island, was returned to Japanese control in 1968.

In August 1945 the United States dropped atomic bombs on Hiroshima and Nagasaki, devastating the cities, but also avoiding the massive casualties (both Allied and Japanese) that would have occurred in a full-scale Allied invasion of Japan. The Soviets had also, at long last, begun their promised offensive against Manchuria. On 15 August, Emperor Hirohito in a taped radio broadcast admitted, 'The war situation has developed not necessarily to Japan's advantage.' The most destructive war in human history was finally over.

The extensive and detailed plans for an amphibious Allied invasion of Japan would not be needed. Operation Downfall, in which an initial landing on the southern Japanese island of Kyushu (Operation Olympic) was to be followed by a landing on Honshu near Tokyo (Operation Coronet), would never happen.

Instead, on 2 September 1945, the documents confirming Japan's surrender were signed on board the USS *Missouri* in Tokyo Bay. General Douglas MacArthur and Fleet Admiral Chester Nimitz were present beneath Commodore Perry's pennant, which had been flown out from the naval museum in Annapolis. Gunrooms aboard the '*Mighty Mo*' were prepared to fire on the imperial palace in the event of any trickery.

MacArthur presided over the occupation that followed. The Emperor of Japan was the only head of state from the Tripartite Pact who would survive the war. MacArthur, keen to have a strong ally in the region, instead of concentrating on revenge on Japan, focused on alleviating the massive suffering the Japanese people had faced in the latter stages of the war and on the swift reconstruction of Japan and its economy.

US forces remain stationed in Japan to this day, and Japan is one of America's closest allies with numerous and strong military links. Joint exercises are conducted by the US and Japan's Self-Defence Forces with a view to potential regional challenges, such as an unpredictable North Korea.

Jordan

Jordan has traditionally been seen as one of the more pro-Western Arab countries through the long years of the Cold War and the even longer years of the Arab–Israeli conflict. Obviously, times have existed when Jordan and the West have had very different views on a situation, but still the links are long-standing.

America first started giving military aid to Jordan in 1957. In that year, the US also sent forces into the Eastern Mediterranean to show its support for the king of Jordan, Hussein. Hussein was faced with a major political crisis in April 1957, as he dismissed his cabinet, faced large demonstrations, and imposed martial law. The American naval forces sent included two carrier battle groups, a battleship, two cruisers, twenty-four destroyers, the Marine Amphibious Ready Group, and submarines. America certainly wasn't taking it lightly.

And the next year, in 1958, when the king felt threatened by a coup in neighbouring Iraq, the British sent paratroopers and America sent ships again.

In 1970, things got even more tense. Jordan was host to large numbers of Palestinian refugees and PLO fighters. In September, bitter fighting broke out as Hussein launched his Jordanian forces against Palestinian targets. As fighting raged, the Syrians sent forces into Jordan on the side of the Palestinians. US ships and marines were ready to intervene to protect American interests, and the 82nd Airborne Division in Germany was told to prepare to move in and take Amman Airport. However, as the crisis began to subside and a peace deal was finally signed, the intervention was called off. Still, that September and October, USAF C-130 aircraft did fly relief supplies and equipment into Jordan in Operation Fig Hill to help deal with the crisis.

In recent decades, despite occasional disagreements at times, for instance over Iraq, Jordan has become a key US partner in the Middle East, particularly in the search for a peace deal to end completely the Arab–Israeli conflict but also, more recently, for example, in the present crisis in Syria.

America has given huge amounts of military aid to Jordan. A US-Jordanian Joint Military Commission was set up in 1974, and over the years, thousands of Jordanian military personnel have been trained in the United States. US and Jordanian forces regularly work alongside each other in training exercises, and the United States supported the building of the King Abdullah II Centre for Special Operations Training. Jordan has helped to train Iraqi and Afghan government forces and has sent military hospitals and medical personnel to Iraq and Afghanistan.

The Syrian crisis has inevitably focused US attention on Jordan as well, because of its key location next to Syria and because Jordan plays host to large numbers of Syrian refugees. Attempts have been made to play down the US military presence in Jordan during the crisis, but hundreds of troops have been located there, sometimes staying behind after planned exercises, and many of them based near the Syrian border. The troops are there to help prevent any threat to Jordan and to help with refugees, but presumably also to offer the US government some ability to react to future developments in the complex and somewhat unpredictable Syrian crisis. US forces in Jordan have also completed training with some selected Syrian rebels.

Kazakhstan

Kazakhstan is a big country, the ninth largest in the world, in fact. It has a long and interesting history and was the scene of a truly epoch-making event on 12 April 1961.

Perhaps the time America took the most interest in it was during the Cold War when it was part of the Soviet Union. At the time, Kazakhstan was home to some vital Soviet strategic facilities, in particular places like the nuclear weapons site at Semipalatinsk, the ballistic missile range at Sary Shagan, and the space launch area at Baikonur. Yep, it was from Kazakhstan on 12 April 1961, that Yuri Gagarin was launched in *Vostok 1* to become the first man to achieve an orbital spaceflight.

The US wanted photos of all the strategic sites, and U-2s and SR-71s flew over Kazakh territory to get them.

America currently has some strategic interests in independent Kazakhstan, for instance because of oil and its key location in a vital area, and it has signed assorted agreements on military co-operation with the Kazakhs.

A small number of Kazakhs served with coalition forces in Iraq. They have also allowed the US to send flights through their airspace to support operations in Afghanistan. American troops have taken part on Kazakh soil in the Steppe Eagle exercises, and Kazakhstan takes part in America's Caspian Guard Initiative to improve security in the Caspian Sea area.

The Arizona National Guard is partnered with Kazakhstan.

Kenya

Humans have lived in what is now Kenya for millions of years, though Americans have been in the area only comparatively recently!

American privateers and buccaneers did sail the Indian

Ocean in search of plunder in the period before the American Revolution, and not far away, Zanzibar had extensive American trading connections in the early nineteenth century. During the First World War, Americans were caught up in the fighting in this region when some of them joined the 25th (Frontiersmen) Battalion of the Royal Fusiliers in the British Army. The battalion disembarked at Mombasa, the main port of Kenya, in 1915 and was deployed in what is now Tanzania and in Kenya.

During the Second World War, the US set up an air transport base at Nairobi, now the capital of Kenya, though Allied advances in North Africa in 1942 and 1943 eventually reduced its importance.

Kenya gained its independence from Britain in December 1963.

Mombasa has long been a port of call for US naval ships. In 1976, after the Israeli raid on Entebbe in neighbouring Uganda had been launched with Kenyan assistance, the US Navy conducted various manoeuvres to demonstrate US support for Kenya and prevent any Ugandan retaliation, including two US frigates calling in at Mombasa. In 1982 alone, more than 30,000 US sailors made port-of-call stops in Mombasa driving up sales of beer and T-shirts.

And in recent times, Kenya has become a vital area for the US in the fight against Somali piracy and Islamist extremists.

In September 2008, in one of the more lengthy piracy incidents, the MV *Faina*, a Ukrainian merchant ship, was bound for Mombasa. It was seized by Somali pirates. In the hold, thirty-three Russian T-72 tanks and other weaponry were found. The ship was part of an effort by the Kenyan government to supply arms to the militias in South Sudan. US Navy vessels surrounded the ship, and hostage negotiations dragged on for weeks. About four months later, a $3.2 million ransom was paid, and the ship and its crew proceeded to Kenya. Its cargo eventually made its way to South Sudan. In 2009, Captain Phillips's ship, the *Maersk Alabama* finally ended up in Mombasa after his dramatic rescue by the US Navy. The Navy has taken suspected pirates to Mombasa for trial there.

Kenya came to the forefront of the conflict with Islamist extremists in 1998 when the US Embassy in Nairobi was bombed by al-Qaeda killing over 200 people. A similar attack was made in Tanzania at the same time. In response, US military personnel were rushed into Kenya to help deal with the emergency situation.

Camp Simba, where US Navy Seabee engineers have helped to build an airstrip, was established at Manda Bay on the Kenyan coast in 2004. The exact nature of what goes on there is a matter of some debate, but military officials happily accept that Seabees are located there and US military personnel are engaged in work with the Kenyan armed forces and in humanitarian work. Manda Bay is situated not far south of the Somali border, and there is speculation about US Special Forces being stationed there.

Today, a wide variety of links between the US military and the Kenyan military exist, and Kenyan forces have become key partners in the fight against Islamist extremists in Somalia.

In September 2013, a terrorist attack at a mall in Nairobi claimed the lives of over seventy people. The terrorist group al-Shabaab claimed responsibility. US Navy SEALs were later deployed to Somalia in an unsuccessful attempt to capture or kill an al-Shabaab leader.

Kiribati

Kiribati is an island nation in the Pacific consisting of a large number of islands and groups of islands. Before the Second World War, it was an area of major British influence.

The US did, however, have a claim on some of the islands. Yep, and it all started with seabirds. On Enderbury Island, an American company mined guano in the nineteenth century. Under the Guano Islands Act of 1856, it and a number of other islands in the area could be claimed. In 1938, President Franklin D. Roosevelt, thinking they might be in a strategic location, declared Enderbury and nearby Kanton Island under US jurisdiction. The British, though, weren't so keen on the idea, and eventually a compromise was reached where the two islands came under joint jurisdiction.

Then came the war. And then came the Japanese. Some of the more remote islands in what is now Kiribati escaped Japanese invasion. Some of them didn't. The USCGC *Taney* (now in Baltimore's inner harbour) evacuated Enderbury, but the Japanese never came to it. Banaba, or Ocean Island, though, was seized by the Japanese in 1942 and wasn't liberated by US troops until 1945.

With some of the other islands, it was a very different story. One of the major island groups in Kiribati is the Gilbert Islands, and two of the names connected to this group will be familiar to many, Makin and, in particular, Tarawa.

The Japanese took both very early in the war, in December 1941. But in August 1942, 221 US Marines, under the command of Colonel Carlson, landed from submarines on Makin (Butaritari) in an attempt to divert Japanese attention from Guadalcanal and seize intelligence. The raiders dealt with most Japanese resistance on land, though they faced enemy air attacks, and re-embarkation proved a challenge.

In September 1943 US air raids hit both Makin and Tarawa, and then on 20 November US troops stormed ashore on Makin and Tarawa. On Makin, the troops landed on Red Beach and Yellow Beach. Fighting was fierce, but within a few days US troops had taken control. On Tarawa the marines headed for Red Beach 1, Red Beach 2 and Red Beach 3. Heavy and determined Japanese resistance, effective Japanese strongpoints, and problems with boats and reefs meant heavy casualties among the landing force, but eventually the marines managed to get ashore and push inland.

On 21 November, bitter fighting continued as Green Beach was taken and reinforcements landed there. Early in the morning of 23 November, a massive Japanese counter-attack hit US lines but was fought off with artillery support leaving hundreds of Japanese dead. Eventually, after more fighting, the Japanese defenders were split up into pockets and virtually wiped out.

Subsequent operations involved landings on other nearby islands. To add to all the US losses in the actual landings, heavy US casualties were suffered when the aircraft carrier *Liscombe Bay* was torpedoed.

After the battle, assorted US facilities were constructed, including the development of the Japanese airbase on Tarawa, Hawkins Field.

The post-war period saw some US military involvement in the area. For instance, America had a missile-tracking station on Kanton Island at one stage. And in the 1960s, it exploded nuclear bombs on Christmas Island, Kiritimati.

Kiribati became independent in 1979, and the Americans and the British relinquished joint control of Enderbury and Kanton Islands and acknowledged control by Kiribati over some other islands, although the US still has Baker Island and Howland Island and a few other tiny territories.

Kosovo

The US was involved in this area militarily during the Second World War, but it was in the 1990s, of course, that America started taking a bit more military interest in Kosovo. Well, a lot of military interest actually.

Tension between ethnic Albanians and ethnic Serbs had long existed, and in 1997, the Kosovo Liberation Army started a guerrilla war against Serb control of Kosovo. As the guerrilla campaign spread, so did heavy-handed and ruthless measures by Milosevic's forces, leading to the deaths of many civilians as well as guerrillas. After a failed attempt at a ceasefire in late 1998, the Rambouillet Conference was assembled, out of which came the Rambouillet Accords demanding a NATO presence in Kosovo to supervise a peace deal. When Milosevic rejected the accords, the bombing campaign started.

It lasted from 24 March to 11 June, and US aircraft and cruise missiles played a crucial role, hitting targets in Serbia, Kosovo and Montenegro. As time advanced and Milosevic showed no sign of giving up and with the US ground forces of Task Force Hawk building up near Kosovo's border, preparations were also made for the possibility of a ground offensive. In Kosovo itself, Milosevic's forces stepped up a campaign of ethnic cleansing, and the Kosovo Liberation Army, or KLA, attempted to resist. Plenty of people have speculated about assistance by Western Special Forces to the KLA, but it's hard to find out full details of what happened.

Finally on 3 June, Milosevic gave in and agreed to withdraw his forces from Kosovo and allow NATO forces to enter. The United States was allocated control of MNB-East (Multinational Brigade Sector East). On 11 June, a small US advance party of twenty vehicles and fifty-five personnel moved in, and this was rapidly followed by many more US troops, including most of Task Force Hawk, and a contingent from the First Infantry

Division that had been flown from Germany to Macedonia for entry into Kosovo. More US troops were soon to follow, and two initial camp locations would turn into Camp Bondsteel and Camp Monteith.

The NATO forces were welcomed by the ethnic Albanians as liberators, but many ethnic Serbs fled through fear of ethnic Albanian violence in the period during and after NATO's arrival. US forces have been in Kosovo long, long after the departure of Serb forces.

Kosovo declared independence on 17 February 2008, and the US recognised it as an independent state the next day. However, not all countries have recognised Kosovo's independence, so it is not, for instance, a UN member state.

The Iowa National Guard is partnered with Kosovo.

Kuwait

Kuwait is a small oil-rich (very oil-rich) nation on the north-eastern corner of the Persian Gulf that has borders with Iraq and Saudi Arabia. The Al-Sabah family has ruled since 1938. From 1899 until 1961, it was a British protectorate. The United States recognised it as an independent nation in 1961.

Iraq has a long-standing claim to Kuwait and traditionally saw it as part of its territory. In fact, almost as soon as Kuwait was independent, Iraq made threatening moves against it. British troops had to rush in once again until things settled down.

American oil companies established trading links with Kuwait and other Gulf states early on, and after Britain's retreat from empire, the United States eventually took over the British position as the chief protector of Kuwait.

America's first major military action in support of Kuwait took place during the long, bitter Iran–Iraq War. Fearing that revolutionary Iran's influence might spread in the Gulf, Kuwait was, despite Iraq's claims on Kuwait, supportive of the Iraqi war effort. Iran, angered by this as well as Iraqi attacks on its oil industry, started to target oil tankers linked to places it regarded as supportive of Saddam. Kuwait requested American protection for its tankers, and to protect vital oil supplies to the world, the US was happy to oblige. Operation Earnest Will, starting in the summer of 1987, involved re-flagging Kuwaiti ships with the American flag and US Navy escorts through waters where the ships were vulnerable to Iranian attack. The mission came to an end after the war did in the summer of 1988.

However, this is not, of course, the main operation people tend to think about in association with American military operations and Kuwait. Yes, it's that Desert Storm on the horizon.

Saddam Hussein decided to do something about Iraq's long-standing claims to Kuwait and launched his invasion of Kuwait on 2 August 1990. Saddam had, however, seriously miscalculated the reaction to his attack. Only six days later, President George H. W. Bush announced the deployment of US troops to Saudi Arabia to pre-empt further Iraqi aggression. Eventually, over half a million US troops were deployed to the Middle East.

Operation Desert Shield was to be a multi-lateral coalition force deployment with the armed forces of thirty-four different nations. The fall of the Berlin Wall and the end of the Cold War had made multi-lateral action possible. Saddam's invasion of Kuwait was viewed as a direct challenge to the central mandate of the United Nations. Shortly after Saddam's invasion, the UN Security Council, in a series of resolutions, condemned Iraq, issued trade embargoes, demanded an immediate withdrawal from Kuwait and authorised the use of 'all necessary means' to liberate that country. Saddam, however, ignored the UN threats.

An intensive six-week air campaign began on 17 January 1991, targeting vital Iraqi infrastructure and military forces both inside Iraq and in Kuwait itself. Despite firing Scud missiles at Saudi Arabia and Israel in an attempt to drag Israel into the conflict, Iraq had little answer to the onslaught from cruise missiles, stealth aircraft, B-52s, and a wide range of other aircraft. Even before the ground war began, Iraq's ability to resist had been seriously weakened.

The ground assault, Operation Desert Storm, began on 24 February 1991 and lasted only about 100 hours. Much of the actual combat took place in Iraq as a massive allied thrust penetrated Iraqi territory to the west of Kuwait and then swung round towards Kuwait from that direction. The campaign was a complete mismatch. The American main battle tank, the M1 Abrams, destroyed over 2,000 Iraqi tanks without a single Abrams destroyed by enemy fire.

Dire predictions of massive coalition casualties at the hands of the 'elite' Republican Guard in the end proved unfounded. A total of 482 coalition deaths were reported in the war, most of them due to accidents or friendly fire. By contrast, over 25,000 Iraqis were also killed in the course of the campaign, many on the 'highway of death' as they attempted to retreat. Iraq's chemical weapons were never used.

A ceasefire was agreed in April 1991. Coalition forces also agreed to permit Saddam the use of helicopters allegedly for humanitarian purposes. Uprisings against Saddam's regime in Kurdistan and elsewhere, which might have toppled the regime, were brutally repressed by Saddam's helicopter gunships.

The Kuwaiti government and Al-Sabah family were restored to power. The Kingdom of Saudi Arabia largely financed the entire liberation of Kuwait, paying $36 billion out of the $60 billion total cost.

In 1993, Saddam was accused of authorising an assassination attempt on former president George H. W. Bush while he visited Kuwait. Accordingly, in June 1993, President Clinton ordered a cruise missile strike on Baghdad.

When America invaded Iraq in 2003, Kuwait was where most of the invasion force assembled, and when the last US forces left Iraq almost nine years later, they crossed the border into Kuwait, the gate was closed behind them, and US and Kuwaiti forces shook hands and posed for photos.

Kuwait today remains a major non-NATO ally of the United States and America continues to have close military links with the country.

Kyrgyzstan

The name Kyrgyz seems to derive from a word meaning forty, and the sun on the Kyrgyz flag has forty rays. Both are supposed to refer to forty clans that were important in the early history of the region.

Among its other claims to fame (in addition to all the links to the number forty) Kyrgyzstan has the unusual distinction, if distinction is the right word, of having had both Russian and US military bases on its soil at the same time.

America's Manas Air Base, close to the Kyrgyz capital in

Bishkek, opened for business in December 2001, supporting air operations in Afghanistan to the south. Combat aircraft, tankers and transports were all based here, and it became a major transit point for soldiers entering and leaving Afghanistan.

However, the base in the end proved controversial in the area, and American operations at Manas ended in 2014.

The Montana National Guard is partnered with Kyrgyzstan.

Laos

Named in the past as 'The Country of a Million Elephants', Laos is a landlocked nation in South East Asia. That is to say, the Laotians have no ocean.

Laos was a French protectorate from 1893, along with Vietnam and Cambodia. During the Second World War, the Japanese eventually took control, and the United States first got involved militarily against them. In September 1945, the OSS Raven Mission was sent from Kunming to Vientiane to search out Japanese POW camps and gather intelligence on the situation in the area. The mission found 143 internees near Vientiane.

The Kingdom of Laos gained its independence in 1953, but a rough road lay ahead. Civil war broke out almost immediately between the Laotian government, supported by France, and the Communist Pathet Lao, supported by North Vietnam.

As French power in the area came to an end, America stepped in to support the forces opposing the Communists. President Dwight Eisenhower feared that Laos might be one of the falling dominos in South East Asia. His administration provided about $300 million in assistance to the Laotian government.

A complex, and sometimes frankly rather confusing, three-sided battle for power among Laotian Communists, neutralists and rightists would follow, with the United States and its allies intervening in the country alongside Communist powers. It was messy, and despite the fact that at the time the war in Laos got (and still today gets) far less attention than the wars in Vietnam and Cambodia, people were dying.

Laos shares a long border with Vietnam. During the Vietnam War, the Ho Chi Minh Trail ran through Laotian territory. It was by means of this trail that the VC in South Vietnam were re-supplied from the north.

Beginning in 1960, the United States launched a covert war to interdict the Ho Chi Minh Trail. The CIA supported the Hmong people with money, arms and supplies in a war against the Pathet Lao. Visiting US congressional delegations were entertained by CIA officers at the White Rose nightclub in Vientiane.

By April 1961, under the Kennedy administration, about 430 military advisers were operating in Laos.

Two linked wars were basically being fought side by side in Laos, one for control of Laos itself, much of the fighting being focused on the strategic Plain of Jars, and another over the Ho Chi Minh Trail.

CIA officers acted as forward observers for the B-52 strikes that pounded the head of the Ho Chi Minh Trail. American bombing turned Laos into the per-capita most heavily bombed nation on the planet. Unexploded bombs are still being removed from Laos today.

In February 1971, the United States supported an invasion of Laos by about 15,000 ARVN forces with air and artillery support. It wasn't a great success. At least not for the South Vietnamese forces. They encountered five battle-hardened North Vietnamese divisions that routed them, chasing them across the border again.

After both Saigon and Phnom Penh had fallen to the Communists in 1975, later the same year, the Pathet Lao entered Vientiane and took over the country.

After the Communist seizure of power in 1975, the Hmong people who had supported American geopolitical interests were persecuted. Many fled across the Mekong River to Thailand. Some 45,000 may have perished during the journey.

Latvia

Latvia is the middle one of the three Baltic states, with Lithuania to the south and Estonia to the north. The area that now forms the modern state of Latvia had a fairly lively ('lively' in the sense of quite a lot of lives being lost) history during the medieval period, with a lot of jostling for power in the area by Germans, Poles, Russians, Swedes and the locals. The duchy of Courland also had an interesting history, including forming now little-known colonies in the Caribbean and on the African coast. Yep.

Finally, however, by 1795, the whole area had become part of the Russian Empire. And Latvia as a twentieth-century nation struggled to be born in the turmoil that followed the end of the Great War. Finally it declared its independence on 18 November 1918 and Latvian forces ultimately fought both the Germans (Battle of Wenden) and later the Russians.

In the end, US General Sherwood Cheney was a key member of the Allied Commission that organised the removal of German troops from Latvia and Lithuania in 1919.

The US Navy also had forces in Latvian waters during this period to protect US interests and assist with US aid, relief and medical efforts in the area. The American destroyer, the USS *Evans*, under Commander F. H. Sadler, was at Liepaja, Latvia, in July 1919. And in September 1920 American forces unintentionally, and very unfortunately, made a landing. On some Latvian rocks. The USS *Pittsburgh* ran aground near Liepaja, and in Antwerp, the USS *Frederick* had to rapidly disembark members of the US Olympic team it was carrying to the games there and race to Latvia to assist the *Pittsburgh*.

America recognised Latvia on 28 July 1922. The Molotov–Ribbentrop agreement of 1939, however, carved up Europe into spheres of Soviet–Nazi influence. The Baltic states fell into the Soviet sphere and Latvia's fate was sealed. On 17 June 1940, the Red Army invaded Latvia, which offered no resistance. The United States refused to recognise the incorporation of Latvia into the Soviet Union. After Hitler's invasion of the Soviet Union in the summer of 1941, Latvia was occupied by the Nazis. Latvians were drafted into fighting on both sides during the Second World War. Tragically, Latvia's Jewish population of about 75,000 was sent by the Nazis to the concentration camps.

After the war, Latvia was dominated by the Soviet Union. As in the other Baltic states, a local resistance movement, the Forest Brothers, operated for some time against the Soviets, and the CIA made some attempts to assist this process, but in the end, the resistance was crushed.

After the collapse of Communism, Latvia regained its independence from the Soviet Union in 1991.

Since that time, the United States has developed close military links with Latvia. The country joined NATO in 2004 with the other Baltic states. Latvian contingents have fought alongside American troops in Kosovo, Iraq and Afghanistan. American and Latvian troops have trained alongside each other and cooperated on a variety of projects.

After Russia's occupation of the Crimea in 2014 and in the light of ongoing conflict in eastern Ukraine, the US has played a major role in Operation Atlantic Resolve, a programme of multinational exercises and other military activity designed to show, in particular, commitment to the security of the Baltic States and Poland. In 2015, US troops moved through Latvia during Dragoon Ride, a drive along a route through Eastern Europe to demonstrate US commitment to the region.

The Michigan National Guard is partnered with Latvia.

Lebanon

A land with much history and much beauty, and also one that has seen many, many (and add a few more to that) invaders pass through.

The United States first intervened in Lebanon in July 1958, at the request of President Camille Chamoun. Radical Iraqi nationalists had overthrown a monarchy that had received support from Britain. The American-friendly monarchies in Jordan and Saudi Arabia felt threatened. President Dwight Eisenhower responded by ordering three marine battalions of the US Sixth Fleet ashore. Three US aircraft carriers (*Essex*, *Saratoga* and *Wasp*) were deployed off the Lebanese coast. There was no fighting, and no casualties were taken. The marines withdrew four months later.

A brutal, complex, and confusing multi-sided civil war, in which the alliances and enemies changed regularly, tore Lebanon apart from 1975 to 1990. America got sucked into bits of it. The situation was so complex and went on for so long that this can only be a summary of some of the events.

Twice in 1976, the Sixth Fleet went in to evacuate civilians from Lebanon.

The Israeli Defence Force invaded Lebanon in 1982 in an attempt to push the PLO forces away from the Israeli border and end their ability to threaten Israel. After some sharp but short fighting, the Israelis eventually penned much of the PLO's fighting force inside a part of Beirut and laid siege to them there. In the end, a deal was arranged whereby the Palestinian fighters would be evacuated to Tunisia, and President Ronald Reagan sent in hundreds of marines to try to help ensure that the evacuation went smoothly.

By the end of September 1982, with the Palestinians gone, marines were working with the multinational force in Lebanon to try to restore the Lebanese government's control of the chaotic country. On 18 April 1983, suicide bombers blew up the US Embassy in Beirut.

On 19 September 1983, US Navy ships fired 338 rounds in support of the Lebanese army that was trying to defend Souk El Gharb. The next month, on 23 October 1983, a suicide truck-bomb loaded with TNT attacked the US Marine barracks, and 241 US and 58 French servicemen were killed. Then on 4 December 1983, two American aircraft based on the *Hancock* were shot down by Syrian anti-aircraft batteries operating in Lebanon. One pilot was killed, and another, Robert Goodman Jr, was captured and held in a Syrian prison. The Reverend Jesse Jackson subsequently visited Damascus and secured his release from the Assad government.

Reagan ordered the withdrawal of US forces from Lebanon on 7 February 1984. And from 8–14 February, the US Navy fired parting shots at Syrian military positions located in the Bekaa Valley.

On 20 September 1984, a bomb exploded outside the American Embassy annex in East Beirut killing twenty-three people.

In 1985, the carrier *Enterprise* was sent to the Eastern Mediterranean because staff from the US Embassy in Beirut needed to be evacuated to Cyprus by helicopter.

In the late 1980s, the hostage crisis in Lebanon saw US Navy ships sent to the area on a number of occasions.

And in 1989, once again, Americans were evacuated, and US training of the Lebanese military was suspended. In 1990, though, with the end of the civil war, the US ambassador returned, and the US Embassy re-opened in 1991. The same year, America also started selling weapons again to the Lebanese army, and in 1993, America started training them again.

In April 1996, Israel launched Operation Grapes of Wrath

against Hezbollah in Lebanon, and along with France, America co-chaired the Israel–Lebanon Monitoring Group set up to implement the understanding that ended the fighting.

In 2006, US forces were once again headed to Lebanon to evacuate US citizens who wanted to avoid the possibility of being involved in fighting between Hezbollah and Israel. And after the 2006 war, America increased support for the Lebanese armed forces and other internal security forces and, in October 2008, signed a military co-operation agreement that established the US–Lebanese Joint Military Commission. Recent aid has included spares for Huey helicopters to improve the readiness of the Lebanese helicopter fleet, boats and a forty-two-metre coastal security craft for the navy, and for the army, hundreds of Humvees and a wide range of other equipment, including M113 armoured personnel carriers, mortars and anti-tank weapons.

Security concerns about what's going on in Lebanon for a long time focused on the south of the country and the border with Israel. They now have shifted to the north of the country and the border with Syria as the vicious civil war tears apart the neighbouring country and threatens to ignite ethnic and religious tensions in Lebanon.

Lesotho

Lesotho is a small landlocked country and this is going to be a very, very small (also landlocked) chapter. Lesotho is located in southern Africa, or to be more precise, it's located in South Africa, as it is a completely surround enclave within it.

America frankly hasn't had that much military involvement with Lesotho. In 2011, the planning for AFRICOM-sponsored multinational communications exercise Africa Endeavor took place in Maseru, the capital of Lesotho, and members of the Lesotho military took part in Africa Endeavor in Douala, Cameroon, in 2012.

Liberia

Saddam Hussein wasn't the only dictator toppled by President George W. Bush in 2003. Elsewhere in the world and receiving considerably less attention in the West, something else was going on.

Today, few Americans know that much about Liberia. Yet for much of US and Liberian history, Liberia has been a little slice of America in Africa.

Liberia was founded by freed slaves who began returning to Africa in the 1820s under the auspices of the American Colonization Society. The first ship to head there had eighty-six settlers on board and was called the *Mayflower of Liberia*. I think we all get the reference. Monrovia, their capital, was named after the fifth US president, James Monroe. The name Liberia means 'land of the free', and the Liberian flag is similar to the US flag but with one big white star instead of fifty and only eleven stripes instead of thirteen.

For much of its history, Americo-Liberians (Liberians descended from settlers that originally came from America) have played a leading political role. And for much of Liberia's history, the US military has played a leading role there as well.

In fact, the US Navy had played a key role in founding the first Liberian settlement. In 1821, the USS *Crocodile* went looking for suitable land for the colony, and eventually, the US Navy helped to get hold of a stretch of the mainland where the colony would grow.

In November 1843, Matthew Perry (the one later of Japan fame) led another of many US military visits to Liberia as he came ashore with seventy-five sailors and marines in whaleboats at Monrovia in search of information about the murder of two American ship captains. Following that, he then cruised up and down the Liberian coast, showing the US flag to the non-Americo-Liberian locals, landing to talk and accompanied by marines who occasionally had to return fire.

In 1847, Liberia declared independence with a constitution based on the US Constitution, and a first president, Joseph Jenkins Roberts, who'd been born in Norfolk. Norfolk, Virginia that is, nowhere near East Anglia.

Independence did not mean the end of close connections with the United States. Close links with the US Navy, for instance, continued. Monrovia became something of a base for the navy's anti-slaving patrols. Not only did they intercept slavers in the area, but they also brought some of the slaves that they freed to live in Liberia.

However, the process of settling Americans in Liberia in some ways replicated the colonial process where white Europeans created colonies in Africa, and it produced some of the same results. The cultural differences between the Americo-Liberians and the indigenous Africans of the area and the political power of the Americo-Liberians over the indigenous Africans caused friction and conflict.

The US regularly sent naval vessels to Liberia when tensions led to violence. In 1876 tensions between the Liberian government and the Grebo peoples erupted into war, and President Ulysses S. Grant sent the USS *Alaska* to help end the war. Again, in 1910, when there was war between the Liberian government and the Grebo people, President William H. Taft sent the USS *Birmingham*.

In 1912, America took over training the Liberian Frontier Force sending black American officers to take charge.

In 1915, the Liberian government got into yet another war with indigenous people, this time with the Kru, and President Woodrow Wilson sent the USS *Chester* with guns and ammunition for the government.

Liberia eventually declared war on Germany during the First World War a few months after America did.

Liberia, as it turned out, was to play a key role in the American war effort in the Second World War. In 1942, the US signed a Defence Pact with Liberia, under which America would get bases and the vital strategic rubber it needed for its war effort and Liberia would get more infrastructure.

Americans developed the Pan American airbase for transatlantic flights at Roberts Field, and it became a key stop in the air-ferry route that led from Brazil across the Atlantic to Africa and then on to the Middle East and beyond. After the war, it became a major international airport for Liberia. America also developed dock facilities at Monrovia and built roads. Thousands of American military personnel were based in Liberia at the time.

In the decades after the Second World War, American influence on the Liberian army remained strong. In 1951, an American military mission was established in Liberia to help train the Liberian military and in the late 1960s, the Liberian chief of staff was none other than Lieutenant General George T. Washington.

In 1980, however, things changed when Master Sergeant Samuel Doe launched a coup and killed President William Tolbert. Doe was from the Krahn people, and his coup marked the end of 133 years of Americo-Liberian domination of Liberia.

Doe managed to remain friends with the United States through the 1980s because of shared strategic interests, but towards the end of the decade, the Cold War was ending, and inside Liberia, things were starting to fall to pieces. Ahead lay almost a decade and a half of instability and brutal civil war that would tear the old Liberia apart and even suck in neighbouring countries.

The Liberian Civil War of 1989–96 was started by a rebellion led by Charles Taylor against the government of Samuel Doe. This conflict claimed the lives of more than 200,000 Liberians, including Doe, and saw horrific atrocities.

During this war, US forces were sent in a number of times to protect US citizens. In 1990, an assault ship, USS *Saipan*, was sent to Liberia, and US Marines were sent ashore to help evacuate 330 US citizens and others. In 1996, the USS *Guam* was dispatched to assist in the evacuation of forty-nine US citizens and other foreign nationals from the US Embassy in Monrovia.

In September 1996, a peace deal was patched up among assorted militias, and in 1997, Charles Taylor won elections. But the instability did not stop. In September 1998 fighting broke out between fighters loyal to the rebel leader Roosevelt Johnson and some of Taylor's forces. President Clinton again sent troops to Monrovia to protect US citizens from the political instability in Liberia.

In 1999, the civil war resumed, bringing again atrocities and large-scale killing. Finally in 2003, the Special Court for Sierra Leone issued an arrest warrant for Taylor over activities in neighbouring Sierra Leone, and the US Congress also decided to offer a bounty of $2 million for Taylor's arrest. In June, President George W. Bush sent more troops to reinforce the US Embassy in Monrovia, and in August, the UN Security Council authorised the dispatch of a multinational force to Liberia. The US sent in Joint Task Force Liberia, the USS *Iwo Jima*, and the Iwo Jima Amphibious Ready Group with the 26th Marine Expeditionary Unit. On 14 August, marines stormed ashore to capture Roberts International Airport (which saw much US activity during the Second World War) and the Freeport of Monrovia. Nigerian forces were also airlifted into Monrovia.

Charles Taylor was forced into exile where he remains to this day. In 2012, Taylor was convicted of multiple war crimes in The Hague.

Since 2005, the US military has done extensive work in Liberia with the aim of totally reforming and reconstructing the armed forces of Liberia. Recently, the USAF transported Liberian peacekeepers to Mali. And during the recent Ebola outbreak, the US military sent units to Liberia to help in the work of dealing with the outbreak.

The Michigan National Guard is partnered with Liberia.

Libya

It's not going to come as news to many that Americans have been at war in Libya, but not everyone will know what a long history of conflict in the country the US has.

In 1801, Tripoli (now capital of Libya; back then, with its surrounding territory it was a sort of state on its own) became the first nation to declare war on the United States, although obviously (after the Revolution and the failed British attempt to crush it) not the first to make war on it. Yussef Karamanli, Pasha of Tripoli, had his minions chop down the flagpole at the US consulate in Tripoli. Not the most subtle method of expressing your displeasure with another country, but one liable to get noticed.

As covered elsewhere in this book (*see* Algeria, Morocco, *and* Tunisia), America had a bit of a pirate problem at the time – or actually quite a lot of a pirate problem. And America wasn't alone in that. Barbary pirates operating from the North African coast had taken over a million European slaves from the sixteenth to the nineteenth century.

America had tried to solve the problem by paying the Barbary States not to seize its ships and sailors, but finally, Thomas Jefferson had grown weary of paying tribute. Hence the chopped down flagpole. In reply, Jefferson dispatched elements of the tiny US Navy (six ships in total in 1803) to North Africa to fight the First Barbary War.

In one of the first actions of the war, the USS *Enterprise* (with Lieutenant Sterrett in command, not Captain Kirk) defeated a Tripolitan corsair, not very imaginatively named *Tripoli*.

Things didn't go that smoothly for the US early in the war, though. On 31 October 1803, the 36-gun frigate, USS *Philadelphia*, commanded by William Bainbridge, ran aground just off the shore of Tripoli. The frigate and its entire crew of 307 men were captured by the Pasha. He put his first ransom demand for the return of the crew at $1.69 million, which was an enormous amount at the time; in fact it was more than the entire United States' military budget.

US honour was rescued, and the Pasha was prevented from using America's own ship against it, however, by what we would now call a daring commando night raid. On 16 February 1804 Lieutenant Decatur with a small band of marines on board a captured Tripolitan boat crept into the harbour and set light to the *Philadelphia*.

One of the most famous incidents in the history of the US Marine Corps took place in Libya in 1805. William Eaton led a group of eight marines and a party of mercenaries on a 520-mile march through the desert from Alexandria in Egypt to Derna in Libya. It was at the battle of Derna on 27 April 1805 that Eaton led his men against the Pasha's forces in a siege that finally culminated in an assault. Eaton personally led a bayonet charge against a larger foe with Lieutenant Presley O'Bannon by his side. This was the first time the fifteen stars and stripes of the US flag were raised on a foreign shore. It was here that the US Marines famously earned a victory against the Pasha on 'the shores of Tripoli'.

The Pasha of Tripoli was now beginning to feel the heat, and not just because a Libyan summer was approaching. With a US land attack on Tripoli now possible, peace was agreed. After all that, though, Eaton's heroics at Derna were somewhat undercut by a diplomatic deal being done by Tobias Lear who authorised the payment of $60,000 in ransom for the liberation of the *Philadelphia*'s crew.

The Second Barbary War (*see* Algeria) was mainly against Algiers, but in 1815 Decatur was once again in Tripolitan waters, this time using a show of force to secure a favourable deal from the Tripolitans.

In the century and a half after the Second Barbary War, Libya had plenty of dramatic history going on, but not much of it was to do with America. After the Italo-Turkish war of 1911–12, for instance, the Italians took over. Then in 1940, Mussolini attempted, very unwisely and very unsuccessfully, to use Libya as a springboard for an invasion of British-controlled Egypt. His forces had to be rescued by Rommel and the Afrika Korps. But in 1942, British and Commonwealth forces, partially equipped by American Lend-Lease tanks, defeated Rommel's Germans and the Italians at the battle of El Alamein. Axis forces in North Africa surrendered in late 1942.

After the war, Libya came under British and French control for a while, and then it became an independent kingdom.

This may seem in some ways hard to believe, after the recent decades of tension between the United States and Libya, but for a long time towards the end of the Second World War and for many years after, there was a part of Libya that was once a 'little America'. In 1943, US bombers started operating out of a once Italian airfield, then called Mellaha Air Base. In 1945, it became known by the name which many Americans still know, Wheelus. The airbase became a hugely important facility for the American Air Force before the US finally withdrew from the base in 1970.

It was a time when other major changes were also happening in Libya. In 1969, Muammar Gaddafi came onto the international scene, leading a successful coup against King Idris. Gaddafi is one of those characters who, as they say, needs no introduction. Most people will be very well aware of him, so we'll only give some brief examples of America's long history of conflict with a man President Ronald Reagan called the 'mad dog of the Middle East'.

The Gulf of Sidra, claimed by Libya at the time as theirs but regarded by America as largely international waters, was a recurrent source of tension. In an incident on 19 August 1981, a Soviet-built Su-22 fired on US Navy F-14 Tomcats. Two Su-22s were subsequently shot down. In March 1986, US and Libyan aircraft and ships confronted each other in the Gulf of Sidra again, which resulted in the eventual destruction of a number of Libyan patrol craft. And two more Libyan aircraft were shot down over the Gulf of Sidra in 1989.

The 1986 bombing of a Berlin discotheque killed two US servicemen. The US government blamed Gaddafi for the attack, and launched Operation El Dorado Canyon. Eighteen US Air Force F-111 bombers took off from RAF Lakenheath in Suffolk, England, with orders to attack three targets near Tripoli. On

15 April, just ten days after the disco bombing, the bombers were to hit a place called Sidi Bilal where Libyan commandos trained, the military part of Tripoli airport, and the el-Azzizaya barracks.

In 2011, when at first demonstrations and then a rebellion broke out against Gaddafi, the United States and its NATO allies, plus a few other countries, intervened against Gaddafi's forces. This was mainly from the air but some covert activity on the ground took place.

However, the end of Gaddafi did not mean the end of Libya's problems as political, regional and religious conflicts emerged, involving a wide range of army units, militias and armed groups. On 11 September 2012, four Americans, including Ambassador Christopher Stevens, were killed in an attack on the US consulate in Benghazi, Libya.

In October 2013, a commando raid captured Nazih Abdul-Hamed al-Ruqai in Tripoli.

The United States had been for some time trying to help the new Libyan government build a professional army, and in March 2014 small detachments of US troops were sent to Libya to assist with plans for training Libyan soldiers in Bulgaria.

With the central government still struggling to impose its authority on some parts of the country, March 2014 saw US Navy SEALs dispatched to the Mediterranean to seize the oil tanker *Morning Glory* that had loaded oil from a port in Eastern Libya and was outside government control. Sailors from the USS *Stout* then went aboard to help take the tanker to a government-controlled Libyan port.

Chaos and a variety of armed conflicts continue to plague Libya at the time of writing.

Liechtenstein

No, not the pop artist, this Liechtenstein is the country with its capital at Vaduz. It's a tiny European state, sandwiched between Switzerland and Austria, and America hasn't exactly had major military involvement with it, but a few interesting stories are still worth mentioning.

In the First World War, though America wasn't actually at war with Liechtenstein, the Allies did blockade it because it was regarded as being too close both geographically and politically to the other side. A number of men from Liechtenstein volunteered for the Austrian army.

Then, during the Paris Peace Conference in 1919, little Liechtenstein went as far as issuing an ultimatum to the Allied powers. They wanted involvement with the League of Nations negotiations, or they would cut off communication routes. This doesn't at first seem like a massive threat, but at that time, one major route between Paris and Vienna ran through Liechtenstein, so it was a little more serious than it might at first seem. Liechtenstein was in the end considered for League of Nations membership in 1920. And rejected. Some of those opposing its membership raised concerns about its size, how independent it was, and the fact it had no army.

Liechtenstein stayed neutral during the Second World War and escaped the wounds of war, though the Liechtenstein City Palace in Vienna, which is owned by the Liechtenstein royal family, wasn't quite so lucky. It was hit by a falling American bomber during an air raid. American bombers certainly flew on occasion in the vicinity of Liechtenstein and possibly over it.

However, as with Switzerland, Liechtenstein did see a certain amount of espionage activity linked to the American OSS. Some of this was focused on Vaduz, which was seen as a convenient meeting place with comparatively easy access to the large neutral country of Switzerland and to Austria, then part of Hitler's Reich. In 1945, as part of Operation Sunrise, negotiations that led to the surrender of German forces in Italy, it is recorded that OSS representatives were dispatched to Buchs on the Swiss–Liechtenstein border.

In the last days of the war, tiny Liechtenstein saw a certain amount of drama, as hundreds of members of the Russian Liberation Army, which had at times fought alongside the Germans, marched into Liechtenstein and allowed themselves to be interned there, rather than be captured by the Allies and sent to Russia to face Stalin's revenge.

And at almost the same time, US troops occupied territory around the borders of Liechtenstein, including setting up base at Feldkirch, just a couple of miles from the Liechtenstein border. In the chaos of the period, it seems hard to believe that at some stage American troops did not cross the border, even if unintentionally. The Swiss army has demonstrated on more than one occasion how easy it is to get confused about tiny Liechtenstein's borders. In the most recent incident, in 2007, about 170 soldiers managed to wander across the unmarked border and penetrate over a mile into Liechtenstein before they realised their mistake and returned to Swiss soil.

At least one GI did cross into Liechtenstein in 1945, though he did it intentionally because he was visiting his family. Konrad Sele had left Liechtenstein for Los Angeles in 1929. When he returned in 1945 as an American soldier, his native German tongue had fallen somewhat out of use, and his sister had some trouble communicating with him.

Lithuania

Lithuania, with its capital at Vilnius, an ancient and historic city (incidentally the target of Teutonic Knight Crusaders in the fourteenth century) is the most southern of the three Baltic states.

On 16 February 1918, while the First World War was still raging, the Council of Lithuania declared an independent Lithuania. And in the aftermath of the First World War, US Brigadier General Sherwood Cheney, as part of an inter-Allied Commission, helped remove German troops from Lithuania. The United States recognised Lithuania officially in 1922.

America also had a certain amount of involvement in the Klaipeda crisis of 1923. Klaipeda, or in German, Memel, is now a key port in Lithuania, but at the end of the First World War, it had a significant German population, and it had been placed under League of Nations mandate while it was decided who should control it. Lithuania was anxious to secure this vital port, and Lithuanians in the Klaipeda region eventually rebelled and seized control. Lithuanian-Americans assisted this process, and US diplomat Norman Davis eventually chaired a three member international commission that awarded control of Klaipeda to, yes, Lithuania.

On 15 June 1940, the Red Army invaded Lithuania. The *Wehrmacht* would invade and occupy Lithuania from the summer of 1941 until its 'liberation' by the Soviets in 1944. Lithuanians served in both armies in the war, and nearly 200,000 Lithuanian Jews were killed by the Nazis.

From 1944 to 1953, a partisan group called the Forest Brothers fought a bitter guerrilla war in all three Baltic states against their Soviet occupiers. Thousands of Lithuanians were killed, and many more were deported to Siberia. The Forest Brothers received a small amount of covert aid from the CIA as well as MI6 and Swedish intelligence. In 1950, for example, a Lithuanian named Juozas Lukša, who had already fought both Germans and Soviets, was trained by the CIA in West Germany and parachuted by C-47 into Lithuania. He was eventually captured and killed in 1951.

On 11 March 1990, Lithuania became the first republic to break away from the former Soviet Union.

America's closest military links with Lithuania have been in recent years. Lithuania joined NATO in 2004, along with its fellow Baltic states. Lithuanian forces have served alongside American and Western forces in Iraq and Afghanistan. There have been regular visits by the US military and America has offered Lithuania military assistance in a number of different areas, for instance recently advising them on the development of their airpower capabilities.

After Russia's occupation of the Crimea in 2014 and in the light of ongoing conflict in eastern Ukraine, the US has played a major role in Operation Atlantic Resolve, a programme of multinational exercises and other military activity designed to show, in particular, commitment to the security of the Baltic states and Poland. In 2015, US troops who had been training in Lithuania took part in Dragoon Ride, driving along a route through Eastern Europe to demonstrate US commitment to the region.

The Pennsylvania National Guard is partnered with Lithuania.

Luxembourg

Not exactly among the biggest and best-known countries in the world (except in the financial world where this little country is big), but yes, America has invaded it.

The motto of the grand duchy of Luxembourg is, '*Mir wëlle bleiwe wat mir sinn*', or 'We want to remain what we are'. They seem to have done this remarkably well because it's one of those few European micro-states, like Andorra, Monaco, Liechtenstein and San Marino, that has managed to last until the present day without being permanently swallowed up by any of its much larger neighbours.

In the First World War, Luxembourg was occupied by the Germans. With the Germans withdrawing rapidly towards the end of the war, the US 33rd Infantry Division ended up, on 11 November 1918, at Stenay, about twenty-five miles from the Luxembourg border. But it did enter Luxembourg after the war, and, in March 1919, the division headquarters were to be found at Diekirch in Luxembourg.

Hitler invaded tiny neutral Luxembourg in the spring of 1940 as part of his campaign against France.

On 10 September 1944, the US 5th Armored Division liberated Luxembourg City (not surprisingly, the nation's capital) from German control. However, this wasn't exactly the end of the battle. Hitler chose to launch his counter-attack, the Battle of the Bulge, through the northern part of Luxembourg's territory in December 1944, meaning parts of Luxembourg had to be liberated all over again. The area around Wiltz, for instance, saw very heavy fighting. And American forces were in the Diekirch area again. It was the scene, on the night of 18 January 1845, of the famous crossing of the River Sauer by the US 5th Infantry Division.

On 9 December 1945, General George Patton was involved in an automobile accident and eventually died from his injuries. Feeling that it was appropriate for soldiers to rest on the fields where they fell, Patton had insisted his body should not be returned to the United States. He also insisted that his nineteen-year-old military chauffeur should not be punished on account of the accident. General Patton, the commander of US Third Army, is buried amongst over 5,000 other American military personnel in Luxembourg.

Luxembourg today is an active NATO member and long-standing ally of the United States. Mildly interestingly, despite the fact Luxembourg is tiny and only has tiny military forces, NATO's AWACS fleet is registered in Luxembourg.

Macedonia

A country just a little bigger than Vermont, this is a useful fit from an American point of view since Macedonia is partnered with – you guessed it – the Vermont National Guard.

Allied forces did advance into what is now the modern country of Macedonia in the final campaign of the First World War, but US troops were busy elsewhere.

In the Second World War, however, America had more to do with the area militarily. The USAAF bombed assorted targets in the area. For instance, on 18 October 1943 US bombers attacked railway targets in and around Skopje, now Macedonia's capital. On 24 January 1944 B-24s from the Fifteenth Air Force, escorted by P-38 Lightnings, bombed targets in and around Skopje, including the airfield. And America was also flying in supplies and personnel to the partisans then operating in the area. This could be a difficult job. Even apart from the threat from German forces. In late 1944, on one airstrip near Skopje, twenty oxen were needed to pull a C-47 out of a bomb crater.

From 1944 onwards, the area was part of Tito's Communist Yugoslavia, so for a long time, US military links with the area were few and far between. However, on 26 July 1963 an earthquake flattened much of Skopje killing thousands. The USAF rushed to help, flying in whole field hospitals and other emergency supplies.

In 1991, the break-up of Yugoslavia started, and soon Macedonia was to emerge as an independent country. But in a region where several countries were torn apart by war, the new country of Macedonia faced some major challenges. In 1993, President Clinton sent 350 troops to assist the UN Protection Force there, and more US troops arrived in 1994. Camp Able Sentry was established near Skopje Airport. Even though its UN function ceased in 1999, Camp Able Sentry stayed because another international crisis had erupted nearby. When the Kosovo crisis erupted between NATO and Serbia in 1999, Macedonia allowed NATO to conduct some activity from there.

Trouble was about to erupt in Macedonia itself as well. After the Albanian rebellion against Serbia in Kosovo, a rebellion broke out in 2001 among Macedonia's Albanian minority. A compromise was reached a few months later with the Ohrid Agreement, and NATO moved in to enforce the deal first with the Task Force Essential Harvest collecting weapons and then Amber Fox and Allied Harmony. US forces played a part, for instance, in providing air transport.

In recent years, the United States and Macedonian militaries have developed close links, and Macedonia has sent troops to Iraq and Afghanistan.

Madagascar

America's earliest armed connection with Madagascar comes from even before the United States existed.

In the late seventeenth and early eighteenth centuries, Madagascar was a key port of call for assorted American pirates and privateers, including John Halsey and William May, operating in the Indian Ocean. Thomas Tew, a pirate from Rhode Island, had close links to Madagascar and a base there. He is even said to have had a son with a local princess, a son who went on to create a kingdom on the island. American pirate Nathaniel North lost his ship near Sainte-Marie Island off Madagascar when he was cornered by four British warships.

In the nineteenth century, America still took a certain amount of interest in Madagascar, even as assorted other Western powers competed for influence over the island. In the 1860s it signed a trade agreement with Queen Rasoherina, and at one stage, the USS *Juniata* was dispatched from the US Pacific squadron to Madagascar to reconnoitre French moves on the island. In 1884, US Navy Lieutenant Mason A. Shufeldt marched across western Madagascar, across parts nobody from Europe or America had visited, with a small army of locals and soldiers, fighting off assorted attacks until he reached the sea. In 1887, the USS *Alliance* arrived at Madagascar investigating suggestions American-flagged ships had been transporting slaves from East Africa to Madagascar and other islands.

It was the French, though, who ultimately became the Western power dominating the island. This meant that it was Vichy France that had control of the island in 1942 and, as it was strategically located near vital Allied supply routes, this posed a problem for the Allies. The result was the British invasion of Madagascar in that year, Operation Ironclad. America didn't play much of a role in that operation, at least not openly, but it is interesting to note that almost as soon as the invasion was complete and successful, the US sent in people to start shipping graphite from Madagascar to America as a crucial component of the project to eventually create an atomic bomb. The first nuclear chain-reacting pile was built towards the end of 1942 and used 400 tons of graphite. The second was built in the spring of 1943 with the first graphite shipment from Madagascar. Some have even suggested the acquisition of this graphite was at least one of the motives for the invasion in the first place.

In 2007, the USS *Normandy* became the first US Navy ship to visit Madagascar since 1972, and the dock-landing ship USS *Ashland* followed up with another visit the year after. However, in 2009, a change of government that the United States considers a military coup d'état occurred.

Malawi

Malawi's a quite small country in Central Africa with a big, big lake. The lake, called, not surprisingly, Lake Malawi, takes up about a fifth of the country. It had one-party rule from 1966 through to 1994.

Malawi's not been an area of major US military involvement, but it has had a few links.

For instance, Medreach 2011 was an exercise to help the US and Malawian military co-operate on medical and humanitarian matters. America has also built a transit base at Malawi Armed Forces College in Salima that's capable of taking an entire battalion as the US military trains them in peacekeeping technique. The US has trained Malawian peacekeepers for their mission in Ivory Coast, and Malawian peacekeepers have served recently in the Democratic Republic of the Congo and helped defeat the M23 rebel group. In 2014 AFRICOM sponsored the multinational exercise Southern Accord in Malawi.

Malaysia

The amazing land of Malaysia has not been one of the areas where the US has been most involved militarily, but an American diplomat did run part of it for a while.

Claude Lee Moses was appointed Consul General in Brunei in 1864. And at that stage, the sultan of Brunei controlled significantly more territory than he does now, including a big chunk of north Borneo, which C. L. Moses proceeded to lease from him. However, things didn't quite go to plan for Moses on the commercial front, and the sultan leased the lands to someone else. Eventually, after a couple of others taking up the lease, a Briton took control there, and eventually the area became firmly within the British sphere of influence.

During the Second World War when it was occupied by the Japanese, US planes flew many missions against targets connected with the Japanese war machine there. For example, in October 1944, fifteen B-24s mined the inner approaches to Penang. And on 10 March 1945, twenty-four B-29s of the Twentieth Air Force bombed the marshalling yards at Kuala Lumpur, now the capital of Malaysia.

Over the years, the United States has developed extensive links with the Malaysian military, including training and many exchanges, joint exercises, and visits. In June 2013, US Marines and sailors conducted amphibious assault training with Malaysian forces at Batu Beach, Pahang, in Malaysia. The US and Malaysia have co-operated extensively in fighting terrorism, and Malaysia sent a small number of military personnel, including doctors and paramedics, to Afghanistan.

The Maldives

The Maldives has the lowest elevation of any nation on earth, six feet or less above sea level. It's situated south of India and west of Sri Lanka.

American planes used to make regular use of the British airbase on Gan Island and at one stage, after the British temporarily abandoned it in March 1945, the American B-25s that used it occasionally seem to have had it much to themselves. At one time in the 1960s, there was even discussion of the USAF and US Navy making more permanent use of the facilities, but in 1971, America started work on the major base at Diego Garcia a few hundred miles away. The US also had an army air force weather detachment based in the Maldives during the Second World War.

American ships have regularly called in on the Maldives. It's possible some of the colonial-era American pirates and privateers active in the Indian Ocean in the pre-1776 period may have visited here, and certainly the US Navy has been a regular visitor. The USS *Momsen*, the USS *Russell*, the USS *Dubuque* and the USS *Higgins* have all recently visited the Maldives. Obviously a popular venue.

The US has also conducted some training of Maldivian forces and conducted exercises with them. For instance, in 2012 American boots returned to Gan, as US Marines trained with marines of the Maldivian National Defence Force in Exercise Coconut Grove.

Mali

A large, landlocked African county that's been linked to some mighty African empires (Ghana, Malinké and Songhai). Mali has also been a bit in the news in recent years. And, yes, America has been involved.

In the period after 9/11, and as fears began to grow about extremist Islamist activity in the area, US Special Forces started training Malian troops as part of the War on Terror. Special Forces Training Teams from Special Operations Command Europe were at one stage located at Bamako, Gao and Timbuktu helping train Malian troops to protect the country's borders against any attempted incursions.

However, by 2012, despite US assistance with training, the Malian government was facing major problems in the north of the country. Simmering discontent among the Tuaregs there, which had already resulted in conflict, led to the outbreak of fresh rebellion in January 2012 with Tuareg rebels fighting for an independent state they call Azawad. Some of those fighting were Tuaregs who had fought for Gaddafi in Libya and after his death had headed for Mali, battle-hardened and well-armed.

The situation became more complex with extreme Islamist groups, including Ansar Dine and al-Qaeda in the Maghreb, operating increasingly openly and expanding their influence. Then suddenly in March 2012, the crisis became even worse. A coup in Bamako, the capital, led to chaos and the almost total collapse of the Malian army's resistance to the opposing forces in the north. The extremists seized their opportunity and started advancing south taking major cities, like Gao and Timbuktu. In a short time, the Malian government lost control of virtually the entire northern half of the country, and in the following months, as fighting broke out between the Tuareg rebel movement and extreme Islamists, the Islamists took control.

In January 2013, Islamist forces lurched forward and took the town of Konna, only about 400 miles from Bamako. In response, France, formerly the colonial power in the country, rapidly launched a major international intervention to prevent the fall of Bamako and to counter the Islamist assault. The United States played a significant role in this intervention. For instance, America shared intelligence with the French, USAF C-17s flew into Mali hundreds of French troops and hundreds of tons of equipment, the USAF flew in contingents from other countries willing to assist in the international effort and also flew a large number of refuelling missions, with KC-135 Stratotankers of the 100th Air Refuelling Wing. Operating out of RAF Mildenhall in the UK, they aided French fighter aircraft in their sorties supporting French ground troops. Small numbers of US troops have been in the country protecting the US embassy and liaising with French and African forces.

The international effort forced the Islamists to retreat and rapidly pushed them out of large areas and a number of major towns and cities that they had previously held. However, the operation did not totally end conflict and insecurity in parts of Mali.

Malta

Nestling in the Mediterranean, Malta is almost as close to Africa as it is to Europe. Naturally, Malta's people share links with people on the African mainland to the south, yet it has long been linked to Europe and is now part of the EU. The biggest island of the group is, not surprisingly, called Malta. The second largest is called Gozo, which sounds a bit like one of the Marx Brothers but obviously isn't.

Malta has a key strategic location at the centre of the Mediterranean. Look at that map again, and you'll see that it's slap bang in the middle of the sea channel that runs between Sicily and Africa. The only way between the Western Med and the Eastern Med runs past Malta. Good from a trade point of view, bad from a point of view of getting invaded.

Malta has had a long, and often bloody military history,

including involvement in the Punic Wars between Carthage and Rome (sitting where it is between North Africa and Sicily, it could hardly avoid involvement, really), the Great Siege of Malta (not so great for the besieging Ottoman Turks who lost, or even for the defending Knights Hospitaller who won, but at a cost), and a visit from Napoleon (the French took control briefly, and then the Maltese with British help chucked them out).

During the First World War, Valetta, Malta's main city, was something of a base for American subchasers operating in the Mediterranean and escorting convoys in the area.

But it was the Second World War that was to bring one of Malta's most distinguished historical periods, and it's also perhaps the era when Americans have had most to do militarily with this small and beautiful island nation.

Once again, it was Malta's strategic location between Sicily and Africa that put it in the firing line. With the Second World War raging across North Africa and Rommel's eyes fixed on the largely British-controlled Middle East, Malta sat astride some pretty vital supply lines. Also, as it lies only about sixty miles from the Italian island of Sicily but a lot further from Britain, Malta was highly vulnerable to air attack.

The Axis siege of Malta lasted from Mussolini's declaration of war on 10 June 1940, until Italy surrendered and joined the allies in the summer of 1943. During this time, Malta was subjected to the most intense and prolonged bombing of any part of the planet during the Second World War, and the US provided some important assistance to Malta's brave defenders. For instance, in April and again in May 1942, the USS *Wasp* ferried Spitfires and their pilots. Winston Churchill himself rang up the captain of the *Wasp* to thank him.

The SS *Ohio* was an American-built (though English-crewed) ship that was part of the critical convoy codenamed Operation Pedestal and has been called 'the tanker that saved Malta'. Hit by numerous bombs and torpedoes, it barely managed to reach Valletta harbour delivering her precious cargo of aviation fuel. Other American ships, including the SS *Santa Elisa*, also took part, along with their American crews in the campaign to supply Malta.

And flying in the defence of Malta was, among others, one Art Roscoe, a twenty-one-year-old Californian. He had longed to fly but had slight astigmatism in one eye and was turned down by the US military. So instead he joined one of the American Eagle squadrons of the RAF and was trained as a Spitfire pilot in Essex. Transferred to Malta, he became a decorated RAF ace. He was shot down by an ME-109 in October 1942 but managed to survive the crash and the war.

After the siege of Malta lifted in 1943, there was a flood of American troops and officers into Malta. Italy had failed to beat the defenders of Malta; now it was time to strike back at Italy. In June 1943 General Eisenhower, commander-in-chief of Allied Forces North Africa, planned Operation Husky, the invasion of Sicily, from his headquarters in the Lascaris War Rooms, an amazing underground complex in Valetta.

President Franklin D. Roosevelt paid two visits to the plucky island – once in December 1943 and again for the Malta Conference with Churchill in February 1945.

Malta became independent from Britain on 21 September 1964, and the Royal Navy base was closed in 1979. Today, Malta is a member of the European Union. US Navy ships often visit and Maltese military personnel have taken part alongside US military personnel in training exercises.

Marshall Islands

The Marshall Islands are named after British explorer, John Marshall, who turned up there in 1799. The Germans took colonial control of the islands and the people who lived there in 1885, but lost the islands to the Japanese in the First World War when Japan was on the Allied side.

On 1 February 1944, as part of the island-hopping campaign, US troops landed on Kwajalein Atoll in the Marshalls. Their arrival had been preceded by a devastating bombardment from sea and air that included fourteen-inch shells and B-24 Liberators. The result was a pockmarked lunar landscape. One person who saw it suggested it looked as if the whole island had been taken up to 20,000 feet and then dropped. Resistance was, despite this, still sometimes fierce, but within a few days, Kwajalein had been taken.

Other islands were next. Eniwetok Island was invaded on 19 February and had been taken by the twenty-first. Parry Island was captured on 22 February. However, US forces didn't take all the Marshalls at this point. Japanese forces remained in control of Jaluit, Wotje and Maloelap until September 1945. In the areas the US did take in early 1944, however, it rapidly set about building naval and airbases.

After the Second World War, the United States took administrative control of the Marshall Islands as part of the Trust Territory of the Pacific Islands. And parts of the Marshalls were to become even more famous, in particular Bikini and Eniwetok Atolls, with those nuclear explosions.

In 1986, the Marshall Islands became independent under a Compact of Free Association with the United States. Under the compact, the United States is responsible for the defence of the islands and has use of the US Army Kwajalein Atoll missile range. Many Marshallese have volunteered for the US military.

Mauritania

No, not the *Lusitania*'s sister ship (that was the *Mauretania* with an 'e'); Mauritania is the African country situated to the north of Senegal and to the west of Mali.

During the Second World War, America had an airbase in Mauritania. The USAAF Air Transport Command used Atar Airport as a link in various supply routes, particularly in the period after Operation Torch, the American and British invasion of North Africa.

In 1960, the US was the first nation to recognise Mauritania's independence from France, and in more recent times it has had additional, if somewhat limited, military involvement there.

On 8 June 2003, there was a coup attempt in Mauritania, and on 9 June, President George W. Bush announced he had sent about thirty combat-equipped US troops to Mauritania to help protect the embassy in Nouakchott, the capital, and to evacuate American citizens.

The rise of jihadist groups in the region has added to the strategic importance of Mauritania and increased its attractions for anyone interested in counter-terrorism operations and surveillance.

In 2004, US forces were once again at Atar, but this time they were US Special Forces training Mauritanian troops as part of operations against terrorism.

Mauritius

An island nation in the Indian Ocean, Mauritius has some really beautiful places to visit. As a mildly interesting point, the US had a consulate there as early as 1794. A really long way from America in the years before modern transport, but at least the consul could enjoy some lovely views. Not surprising, considering its location, US Navy ships have often called in and continue to do so.

US military aircraft have also visited the island. In January 1980, after a devastating cyclone had hit the island, a USAF C-141 of the 86th Military Airlift Squadron was rushed to Mauritius with emergency supplies for the islanders.

In recent years, the United States has seen Mauritius as a significant partner in its Indian Ocean security policies. So, for instance, in August 2011, sailors from East African coastguards and navies and from the United States could all be found in Mauritius training aboard two Mauritian coast guard vessels, and in January 2015 AFRICOM-sponsored multinational maritime exercise Cutlass Express opened in Le Chaland, Mauritius.

Mauritius claims sovereignty over the Chagos Islands, including Diego Garcia, on which America has a huge military base.

Mexico

Ah, Mexico, a land so closely linked to the United States by history, and by geography. On a significant number of occasions it has probably wished it wasn't quite so closely linked.

After gaining its independence from Spain in 1821, Mexico was a sprawling nation, twice as large as it is today, stretching from its present borders up through the western third of what is now the United States. Mexican administration of these sparsely populated lands was often weak, unstable and vulnerable.

The Comanche had often been allies of the Spanish colonial authorities against the Apaches, and these links had been profitable for the Comanche. The newly established Mexican authorities didn't have the money to keep paying the Comanche, who, under pressure from tribes and settlers from the East, saw opportunity in the weakness of the Mexican authorities. The Comanche launched a long series of raids into Mexican territory in search of livestock and captives. In 1852, they even got as far south as the Mexican state of Jalisco, south of Baja California. And they weren't alone in challenging the recent Mexican nation.

In 1836, the Texas Revolution broke out as Mexican authorities and settlers from the United States struggled for control of the area. Notable during this contest was Mexico's Napoleon, General Antonio de Padua María Severino López de Santa Anna y Pérez de Lebrón, better known as Santa Anna. Born of European descent in Veracruz, he was first a Spanish Nationalist, then a revolutionary, a general, a dictator, and an eleven-time president of Mexico. Quite a CV! He led the siege of the Alamo, attacking and offering no mercy; he also ordered the massacre of Texan prisoners at Goliad. Ultimately, Santa Anna was defeated by Sam Houston at the brief but decisive battle of San Jacinto. The American government and its military did not directly participate in the Texas Revolution, though many of its leaders were American (e.g., Jim Bowie, Davy Crockett, William Travis and Sam Houston).

America played a very minor part in the Pastry War (*not* a Monty Python sketch!) between Mexico and France, which broke out in 1839, but it's worth mentioning here just for the fun of it. Monsieur Remontel, a French pastry cook, claimed that his shop in Mexico had been looted and wrecked. The French government was also pretty unhappy with Mexico over some multi-million-dollar loans, and sent in some warships. A brief war ensued. In the chaos surrounding the war, the US schooner *Woodbury* was sent to protect US ships from Mexican privateers, but it ended up colliding with a French warship and had to put into Veracruz for repairs.

In 1845, just prior to James Polk's inauguration, President John Tyler annexed Texas to form the twenty-eighth state in the Union. And this set the stage for the Mexican–American War of 1846–8.

In 1845, Polk dispatched John Slidell as minister-designate to Mexico City to purchase Mexican territory in the West for the sum of $25 million. He was rebuffed. So Polk, not a man about to take a rebuff for an answer, dispatched Zachary Taylor, a Whig general, with an army of about 3,500 men to Fort Brown, Texas, on the Rio Grande near the Gulf coast.

Polk's order to Taylor of 13 January 1846 indicated that the United States was not intending to go to war with Mexico but, if Mexico declared war or acted with hostility, then operations should not be limited to the defensive. Thus the President of the United States delegated to a field commander the decision as to whether a state of war existed between Mexico and the United States.

The Thornton skirmish was the spark that ignited the powder. On 25 April 1846, a reconnaissance patrol led by Captain Thornton ran into and was defeated by a Mexican force of 2,000 men near Brownsville, Texas.

It might seem surprising, but the Mexican–American War was the costliest war for the United States in terms of percentage of casualties versus participants – 13,768 died out of the 104,556 that served. Many of these casualties were due to sickness and disease as the Americans won nearly every engagement of the war and occupied Mexico City. At the Mexico City National Cemetery, you will find the graves of 750 unknown Americans who perished in the Mexican–American War and are buried in a common grave.

The war, however, was by no means popular with everybody in the US, and, in fact, it produced a vigorous anti-war movement. Henry David Thoreau refused to pay taxes and spent a night in jail over his opposition to the war. The Whig politician Henry Clay, whose son Lieutenant Colonel Henry Clay Jr was killed at the battle of Buena Vista (an American victory), led the political opposition to the war, calling it 'needless, wicked and wrong'. The Illinois congressman Abraham Lincoln would follow his political icon Henry Clay ('my beau ideal of a statesman') in opposition to 'Polk's War'.

Some American soldiers even deserted to the Mexican side and formed the San Patricio, or St Patrick's, battalion. Many of them were later captured and hanged.

Ulysses S. Grant, who served in the Mexican–American War, denounced the war in his memoirs:

For myself, I was bitterly opposed to the measure [annexation of Texas], and regard the war, which resulted, as one of the most unjust ever waged by a stronger against a weaker nation. It was an instance of a republic following the bad example of European monarchies, in not considering justice in their desire to acquire additional territory. Texas was originally a state belonging to the republic of Mexico.

Many future leaders on both sides in the American Civil War served in the Mexican–American War, including Winfield Scott, George Meade, Robert E. Lee, Jefferson Davis and P. T. Beauregard. Brevet Brigadier General Zachary Taylor, known as 'Old Rough and Ready', led American forces to victory over the Mexicans at the battles of Palo Alto and Monterrey. He later used his wartime success to launch a successful bid for the presidency in 1848. Even the legendary founder of American baseball, Abner Doubleday, served in the Mexican–American War with the First Regiment of Artillery. And the victorious storming of the Castle of Chapultepec by US Marines in this war is now commemorated in the 'Marines' Hymn' with the famous reference to the 'Halls of Montezuma'.

The consequences of Polk's War were far-reaching for both Mexico and the United States. The annexation of Texas was confirmed by the Treaty of Guadalupe-Hidalgo, and the region that later formed the states of California, Arizona, Nevada, Utah, New Mexico, and parts of other western states were added to the Union at a cost of $15 million. The disposition of these states as either free or slave-owning would emerge as one of the major contentious issues that led to the outbreak of the American Civil War.

Inspired by the success of the revolution in Texas, William Walker decided to attempt something similar in Baja California and Sonora. In October 1853, he invaded Baja California with forty-five men. The area wasn't exactly hugely populated, so he managed to capture La Paz and declare himself president of the Republic of Lower California. Not content with this, he then expanded his claims by announcing the Republic of Sonora. When the Mexican government did finally react, Walker rapidly had to retreat across the border into the United States. He was tried and somehow acquitted of fighting an illegal war, and he would later go on to launch other wars in other countries in the region (*see* Nicaragua *and* Honduras).

In 1859, the First Cortina War broke out. Mexican folk hero

Juan Nepomuceno Cortina Goseacochea, who championed the cause of the Tejanos or Mexican Texans, ended up occupying Brownsville after a dispute with local law authorities. Assorted clashes in the border area sent Cortina retreating from Brownsville, and US forces crossed the border into Mexico in pursuit of him and his Cortinistas. There were calls from some Americans at this point for a wider invasion of Mexico, but they eventually came to nothing.

In 1860, the US got involved in Mexico, or at least, Mexican waters, yet again. America was supporting the Mexican Liberals against the Mexican Conservatives in a civil war there, and in the Battle of Anton Lizardo, US warships attacked and defeated Conservative ships.

While the war with America had cost Mexico vast amounts of territory, ironically, America's non-intervention in the 1860s very nearly cost Mexico its very existence. Due to American pre-occupation with fighting the American Civil War, the US government was not in a position to enforce the Monroe Doctrine. The French emperor Napoleon III saw the Civil War as an opportunity to expand the French overseas empire and invaded Mexico in 1861, establishing a puppet regime under Archduke Maximilian of Austria. Soon after the Civil War ended, the American government began supplying arms and supplies to the Mexican rebels led by Benito Juarez and eventually even initiated a naval blockade to prevent the French sending reinforcements. The hapless archduke was executed by a Mexican firing squad in 1867. Shortly afterwards his execution was featured in a famous painting by Manet; though even if the archduke had known that would happen, frankly it would probably have been slim comfort to him.

In a somewhat bizarre mini-invasion in November 1866, General Sedgwick crossed the border and seized Matamoros from General Canales and garrisoned it with 100 men. He invaded without orders, and after three days, he was told to withdraw. Once in the United States, he was relieved of command and placed under arrest. His reasons for the invasion are somewhat obscure. Sedgwick claimed he was protecting US citizens, but it's also claimed he was basically there on a debt-collecting mission to force General Canales to pay what he owed to assorted local merchants. Not the most heroic achievement of US arms.

Another slightly bizarre mini-incursion took place in 1870 when the USS *Mohican* was sent in pursuit of the pirate ship steamer *Forward*, culminating in the Battle of Boca Teacapan.

After the expulsion of the French, parts of Mexico remained a somewhat lawless area where cattle thieves and bandits would cross the Rio Grande to raid settlements in Texas and US troops would cross into Mexico in pursuit of them. Porfirio Diaz, who became president in 1876, attempted to modernise Mexico and to police its borders. He also opened up Mexico to foreign investment with Americans taking control of some key assets. Ulysses S. Grant, the reluctant warrior of the Mexican–American War, for instance, became the first president of the Mexican Southern Railroad.

From 1891 through to 1893, Catarino Garza, a Mexican national who had been married (later divorced) to a Texan and lived in Texas, ignited the Garza Revolution. A series of raids were launched from Texas into Coahaila, Mexico. The US Army and, especially, cavalry worked in conjunction with Mexican forces to fight and capture the rebels. Eventually in 1895, Garza was killed while storming a jail in another revolutionary uprising in Colombia.

Then, as if all that wasn't enough, the Mexican Revolution began in 1910 with the deposition of Diaz and resulted in near anarchy in the country.

In September 1913, marines from the transport *Buffalo* briefly landed in Ciaris Estero to rescue US citizens.

President Woodrow Wilson, even though he had denounced the interventionist policies of his Republican predecessors as 'gunboat diplomacy', intervened multiple times in Mexico. In autumn 1913 he is even recorded telling the secretary of the British Ambassador to the United States: 'I am going to teach the South American republics to elect good men!' It was hardly the most anti-interventionist of stances, and Wilson refused to recognise the Huerta regime in Mexico.

After the arrest and brief detention of a party of visiting US Navy seamen in Tampico, Wilson had his pretext. US warships, including the newly commissioned dreadnought *Texas*, were dispatched to shell Veracruz and occupy the port with US Marines. American losses at Veracruz were seventeen killed and sixty-three wounded, while about 126 Mexicans were killed.

Mexican newspapers denounced the American occupation of Veracruz as an 'international crime'.

Wilson intervened again in Mexico in 1916, this time to strike at Pancho Villa, a notorious bandit leader who had launched a series of raids along the US–Mexico border. Brigadier General John Pershing was sent to lead the Punitive Expedition from New Mexico into Chihuahua. Pershing was a tough veteran of Indian wars and the Moro uprising in the Philippines (*see* Philippines), who would later lead the American Expeditionary Forces in the First World War. A young George S. Patton Jr, whose attractive sister Nita was dating the widower Pershing, was detailed to Pershing's staff.

Pancho Villa, as it turned out, proved to be somewhat elusive, but Patton, leading a small patrol, participated in a skirmish at San Miguelito in which three Villistas were killed. When about fifty Villistas approached the hacienda, Patton beat a hasty retreat with the three dead men strapped across his automobile hood. Patton was promoted to first lieutenant.

Among assorted other actions during this chaotic period was the Battle of Ambos Nogales on 27 August 1918. This dispute at a border post at Nogales led to American troops fighting their way into the Mexican border town, and subsequently a permanent border barrier was erected at Nogales.

In the 1930s, President Franklin D. Roosevelt initiated the Good Neighbour Policy, which attempted to normalise links with Mexico and other Latin American nations. This policy bore fruit in the Second World War when Mexico, after Mexican ships were sunk by German U-boats, joined the Allied cause and fought alongside Americans against the Axis from 1942 to 1945. A Mexican expeditionary force even formed an air squadron, often known by its nickname, the Aztec Eagles, that was attached to the 58th Fighter Group of the USAAF, which saw action in Luzon in 1945.

Some military links continued during the period after the Second World War including some Mexican officers receiving US counter-insurgency training.

And, of course, in recent years the United States has been actively helping Mexican police and military forces in their war on the drug cartels. The Merida Initiative for security collaboration between the US and Mexico in the drug war has cost over a billion dollars with mixed results.

Micronesia

The Federated States of Micronesia, its proper title, consists of the states, or island groups, of Yap, Chuuk, Pohnpei and Kosrae.

The islands had a complex experience of European colonialism. The Spanish took full control first. They then sold them to the Germans in the late nineteenth century, who didn't get to enjoy them very long because the Japanese, who were on the Allied side in the First World War, won control and became the colonial power in the islands.

Chuuk is more familiar to many Americans as Truk, its name until 1990. Truk became a massive Japanese naval and airbase, heavily defended with coastal and anti-aircraft artillery. In some senses it could be regarded at the time as Japan's version of Pearl Harbor as it was a strategic target for the US with similar results. On 17 February 1944, in Operation Hailstone, a massive US naval and air assault lasting three days devastated the Japanese base and sank large numbers of Japanese vessels. More US air strikes hit Truk in April, and the area was isolated by US forces.

Finally on 2 September 1945, Lieutenant General Shunsaburo Mugikura, commander of the Thirty-First Army, boarded the USS *Portland*, Admiral Murray's flagship, and signed the surrender of his forces, including almost 40,000 men on Truk.

Yap was bombed on many occasions, and also on 2 September 1945, Lieutenant General Sadae Inoue surrendered his forces on Yap to Brigadier General Ford O. Rogers, island commander on Peleliu.

US forces did, however, take Ulithi Atoll near Yap even before the end of the war. US troops landed there in September 1944 after the Japanese abandoned it, and it became a huge US naval base and staging base for other major operations. As such, it also then became a major target for the Japanese, who launched a number of different attacks on it, including one by manned Kaiten torpedoes and another by kamikaze aircraft.

Kosrae, too, had a Japanese garrison and handed over control to the USS *Wyman* on 8 September 1945.

Pohnpei, or Ponape as it was formerly known, also had a Japanese garrison on it, and US forces occasionally shelled and bombed it. On 11 September 1945, Lieutenant General

Watanabe also boarded the USS *Hyman* to enact the surrender of Ponape, and US troops took control the following day.

After the war, the four island groups became part of the United Nations Trust Territory of the Pacific Islands, administered by the United States. They became independent under a Compact of Free Association with the United States in 1986.

Links between the United States and the Federated States of Micronesia remain strong, and under the Compact of Free Association, the US has defence responsibility for Micronesia. Many Micronesians have volunteered to serve in the US military.

Moldova

Little Moldova is a country in Eastern Europe that's had a frankly complicated history. In the twentieth century, the area was disputed between Romania and Russia with territory changing hands on a regular basis. Finally, in 1990, it became independent.

Moldova is in a sensitive position with Russia, as the Russians have given some assistance to Transnistria, an area on the eastern edge of Moldova, next to Ukraine, that has claimed independence from Moldova.

However, America has had a small amount of military involvement there in recent years. Moldova sent troops to serve in Iraq, and America has trained some of their officers. Moldova is partnered with North Carolina in the State Partnership Program, so National Guard members from North Carolina have been to Moldova for exercises. US Special Forces have trained in Moldova with Moldovan Special Forces.

Moldova has participated in multinational exercises with America, and US military personnel have helped with restoration projects in the country. For example, the US Army Corps of Engineers renovated a fire station in Comrat, Moldova. So, not exactly full-scale US intervention. Nice to have had the fire station renovated though.

Monaco

Monaco is widely known for, among other things, Monte Carlo, motor racing, Grace Kelly and, of course, a lot of rich people.

In 1942, the Italians occupied Monaco, and in 1943, the Germans did. In 1944, US forces arrived to liberate the area. In August mass Allied landings took place in southern France, and in late August, Monaco experienced a number of Allied air raids. Then at the beginning of September, La Turbie and Mont Agel were shelled from the sea, and on 3 September 1944 US paratroopers arrived in Monaco with jeeps and chewing gum. Nice little country, nice little invasion.

Since then, US military forces have occasionally visited. For instance, in November 2012, the amphibious command ship USS *Whitney* visited Monte Carlo to take part in Monaco's National Day celebrations, and sailors from the ship and members of the US Naval Forces Europe Band marched through the streets.

Mongolia

Mongolians, of course, have quite a history as invaders themselves. That Genghis Khan is well-known for his military activities, and in 1241, the empire of his son Ögedei Khan stretched as far as the gates of Vienna. Now that's a big empire.

US forces probably didn't actually reach Mongolia in 1919, but they definitely came pretty close. American troops were deployed in Siberia and northern China, and America had decided to do something useful and get the local railroad running properly. To help achieve this, American railroad professionals, including John F. Stevens and the former Colonel George H. Emerson, both instrumental in the running of the Great Northern Railway, were sent in alongside American troops. The US soon had soldiers installed, among other places, in Harbin in northern China, about 300 miles from the Mongolian border. In the chaos of the period, it's certainly possible that American troops ended up closer to Mongolia at some point, maybe even in it.

Soon after this however, Communists took power in Mongolia, which did little to improve links with the United States. And it wasn't until the end of the 1980s, but really the beginning of the 1990s, that America began to establish closer ties, including minor military links, with Mongolia.

In 1991, the USAF flew emergency medical supplies into Mongolia after the collapse of the Soviet Union, and Mongolia sent small numbers of troops to serve in Iraq and Afghanistan. The US also teamed up with Mongolia to co-sponsor the Khaan Quest series of multinational peacekeeping exercises.

The Alaska National Guard is partnered with Mongolia.

Montenegro

US ships operated in the Adriatic in the First World War, but America's main involvement in Montenegro in that period came at the end of the war.

The 332nd Infantry Regiment had served alongside the Italians. In the period after the armistice, the Second Battalion was sent alongside Italian troops to briefly occupy parts of Montenegro, in particular at the strategic port city of Kotor, where US submarine chasers also ended up at this stage. The American troops, however, reluctantly found themselves in the middle of a confusing political storm (not for the last time in this part of the world) as Italians, Yugoslavs and Montenegrins all competed energetically for control of the area. To add to the international confusion the French got involved as well, and at one stage a French general ordered American troops to suppress a Montenegrin rebellion, the Christmas Rebellion, which had been prompted by a decision to unite Montenegro with Yugoslavia. American troops advanced, but the rebellion basically collapsed before they could get involved, probably much to the relief of the American commander.

Montenegro became part of Yugoslavia, so the next time America got involved militarily in the area was during the Second World War, helping the Yugoslav partisans. US aircraft would fly in supplies to the partisans and take out wounded fighters and civilians. American aircraft also extensively bombed enemy targets in the area, including Podgorica, the capital of Montenegro and a key point on German transport routes.

In 1979, the USAF returned to Podgorica (called Titograd under Tito), this time on a much more friendly mission. A devastating earthquake had hit the area, and US aircraft raced in with over 100 tons of supplies.

However, during the 1999 air campaign against Milosevic, the US had aircraft over Montenegro again, this time with much less humanitarian intent.

Montenegro declared independence in 2006, and since then the US has formed a number of military links with the new country; Montenegro has sent troops to Afghanistan, and has also taken part alongside the US military in assorted exercises.

The Maine National Guard is partnered with Montenegro.

Morocco

Ah, Morocco, the name itself speaks of exotic destinations with fascinating heritages and amazing histories. And the United States military has a place in that history.

We'll come to the invasion part in a bit, but first an interesting diplomacy part because Morocco, after a slightly rocky start, is one of America's longest-standing allies.

Morocco was, in fact, the very first nation in the world to formally recognise an independent United States on 20 December 1777. A treaty of friendship between Morocco and the United States, the longest unbroken agreement in US history, was signed in 1786.

Sounds good. But then came the rocky start, linked to the Barbary pirates. We've dealt with these in a lot more detail in the Algeria and Libya chapters, so we'll just quickly point out here that, at the time the United States came into being, these pirates already had a long history of operating from the North African coast. That wasn't good for US merchant ships, and it wasn't good for US business. In one encounter in 1784, the American ship *Betsey*, carrying salt from Cadiz in south-western Spain and bound for Philadelphia, had been seized by Moroccan pirates and held for a few years. Paying them off didn't work, so America sent in the navy. The Emperor of Morocco at the time was having second thoughts about a treaty with the US but a show of force at Tangier from Commodore Edward Preble with assorted US Navy ships, including *Constitution* and *Nautilus*, persuaded the emperor to renew the treaty in the end.

There was another slight hiccup in America's long friendship with Morocco in 1842. The local US Consul in Tangier, Thomas N. Carr, was unhappy because he had to house and feed two lions given to him by the sultan. Eventually, he was fired by Secretary Webster but then got himself detained by the local lieutenant-governor. Commodore Charles W. Morgan was sent in to rescue the ex-consul, get an apology, and get a twenty-one-gun salute for his flag.

Morocco saw turbulent times later in the nineteenth and early twentieth centuries as European powers battled to control it, with France ending up taking the lion's share (nothing to do with Thomas N. Carr and his pets).

Another minor crisis in the US–Moroccan friendship occurred in 1904. In what has become known as the Perdicaris Affair, an American-born businessman, Ion Perdicaris, was kidnapped and held for ransom by a Moroccan, Ahmed ibn-Muhammed Raisuli, who was seeking money and political influence. Teddy Roosevelt, in turn, sent a naval squadron to Morocco seeking, in the memorable words of Secretary of State, John Hay, 'Perdicaris alive, or Raisuli dead'. The US got Perdicaris alive, and actually, Raisuli got some of his demands.

In 1942, 100 years after Commodore Morgan had turned up on the USS *Fairfield*, Americans were getting ready to invade Morocco seriously. The French authorities in Morocco had stayed loyal to the Vichy regime with its links to Hitler, and Morocco was going to be one of the prime targets of Operation Torch.

Landings were to take place in Algeria and Morocco, and a mighty 35,000-strong task force was sent direct from the United States to invade Morocco, and on 8 November 1942, US troops, under the command of General George 'Blood and Guts' Patton, landed on three sites on the coast.

Despite hopes the Vichy troops would not put up much resistance, there were some fierce clashes. Nevertheless, compared to many later Second World War operations in the Mediterranean, casualties were light, the fighting was brief and the port city of Casablanca, a major target of Torch, eventually fell. About seventy-two hours worth of fighting was sufficient to satisfy the demands of French honour.

Interestingly the classic movie *Casablanca* was actually filmed in 1942 before the US capture of the city but had its world premiere in New York City on 26 November, after it. If the timing of Torch had been different, so might movie history have been.

After the Battle of Casablanca, the red carpet was rolled out for the surrendering French officers who had ruled Morocco. After negotiating the terms of surrender with the French,

Patton, who was fluent in French, told them one last formality had to be dealt with. Worried looks were quickly replaced by smiles as champagne bottles were opened and Patton offered a toast to the renewal of France and America's age-old friendship.

Patton also turned out to be a surprisingly successful diplomat when he served as the putative viceroy of Morocco. He wrote to the Sultan of Morocco assuring him they came as friends, not as conquerors, and did not intend to stay after the war. Patton frequently entertained the Sultan (whom he referred to as Sa Majesté) and escorted him on inspection trips.

Casablanca was transformed into a vast supply depot for the American forces with troops enjoying its pleasures so much that it became known as the Ice Cream Front.

In the period after the Second World War, Morocco gained its independence from France and Spain and became a Cold War ally of the United States. The US maintained strong military links in the area. Nouasseur Air Base near Casablanca was a Strategic Air Command base for most of the 1950s.

America's long tradition of friendly links with Morocco has continued, and Morocco and the United States have, for example, shared many military exercises. However, occasional political differences can still sometimes cause hiccups.

The Utah National Guard is partnered with Morocco.

Mozambique

America has not had a huge amount to do with Mozambique militarily. Indeed, a deliberate decision, after some debate, *not* to intervene there militarily is one of the main events in matters between the US and Mozambique.

American pirates in the pre-1776 period cruised the waters of the Mozambique Channel. Though, to be fair, they were largely interested in the bit of land to the east of the channel, namely Madagascar, than the bit of land to the west, Mozambique.

In the 1960s FRELIMO, the Mozambique Liberation Front, started a guerrilla war attempting to remove Mozambique from Portugal's control. And like other parts of the Portuguese empire, independence was to come to Mozambique after the 1974 leftist military coup in Portugal. By 1975, Mozambique was independent, and FRELIMO was in power in a one-party

Marxist state. Shortly after that, though, a different guerrilla group, RENAMO, or Mozambican National Resistance, emerged, which in turn was dedicated to toppling FRELIMO. RENAMO was anti-Communist, and some in the US Senate argued that the United States should offer it some support. Eventually, however, the US government rejected the idea.

The war between FRELIMO and RENAMO was a long and bitter one and only finally ended in 1992 with the Rome General Peace Accords. The United Nations Operation in Mozambique was sent in to oversee the peace and successfully prepare the way for general elections. Some Americans were involved with this mission, for instance, as helicopter pilots. The Cease-Fire Commission had US members, and the US government provided substantial financial support as well.

Since the war, Mozambique has turned into something of a success story, though in 2014, there was a small amount of renewed fighting.

In recent years, America has had assorted minor military links with Mozambique. For example, a US task force with hundreds of reserve marines among its members, helped Mozambican troops train for peacekeeping operations abroad in Exercise Shared Accord 2010. In 2011, the USS *Samuel B. Roberts* paid a visit to Maputo. The same year, thirty-eight Mozambican soldiers completed a US Navy demining course in Maputo.

Namibia

Namibia has a long Atlantic coastline, but it's located further south than the main area of operations for the United States Africa Squadron's anti-slavery patrols in the nineteenth century.

US Navy ships have occasionally called in more recently.

However, as so often with countries around the world, one decisive point in Namibia's history does involves US military personnel. In the late nineteenth century, Namibia became a German colony. During the First World War Allied troops, mainly from next-door South Africa, invaded and took over Namibia. So South Africa administered the territory under a League of Nations mandate between the wars, and even though after the Second World War the UN eventually revoked South Africa's mandate, the South Africans stayed on. This led to the rise of a guerrilla organisation, SWAPO (South West Africa People's Organisation) fighting for the withdrawal of the South Africans and freedom for Namibia. The whole thing then got tied up with the crisis in next-door Angola because of SWAPO bases there and because of South African intervention in the Angolan Civil War.

Finally, a deal was done with major US involvement to get the Cubans out of Angola and the South Africans out of Namibia, and a UN mission, UNTAG, the not very sexily named UN Transition Assistance Group, was sent in to, well, assist transition to independence. America provided some air transport into Namibia for the initial deployment of the military forces involved. An Australian advance party was flown in March 1989 by USAF C-5 Galaxy from the RAAF (Royal Australian Air Force) base at Learmouth to Diego Garcia and then on to Windhoek, capital of Namibia. And three days later, the advance echelon of the Australian 17 Construction Squadron, another key element of UNTAG, was flown by USAF C-5 Galaxy to Grootfontein in central Namibia.

In recent years, the US military has had assorted links with Namibia. For instance, in 2009, members of the Namibia Defence Force visited Multinational Training Command in Grafenwoehr, Germany to learn how American soldiers and international partners train, and in 2012, HSV *Swift* called in at Walvis Bay, the first time a US Navy ship had visited Namibia since 1999.

Nauru

Appropriately, as the world's smallest republic, Nauru has had an almost equally small involvement by the United States.

This small island country in the massive Pacific Ocean had long been inhabited before Westerners turned up. The Germans took control in the 1880s and then Australian troops took it in the First World War. The Japanese took it in the Second World War, and then in September 1945, the Australians took it back. Finally it became independent and self-governing in the 1960s.

During the Second World War, however, the Japanese presence on the phosphate-rich island and the runway that the Japanese built there were sources of major concern to the United States.

There were fears that the Japanese on Nauru could affect the fighting in the Gilbert Islands (now part of Kiribati).

So from March 1943 to 1945, American aircraft repeatedly bombed Nauru and Japanese attempts to resupply the island. There's a famous photo of a B-24 Liberator over Nauru with smoke and dust and debris rising from the small island below. Inevitably, the bombing campaign came at a price. Japanese troops were killed, but so were some islanders. And US airmen died too. The *Coral Princess*, a B-24 from Makin Airfield that had already flown many combat missions, was hit by anti-aircraft fire over Nauru on 19 June 1944, and exploded. Parts of the wreckage are still to be found on the island.

On 19 November 1943, the US Navy joined in the bombardment as well, with the USS *Saratoga* and USS *Princeton* heavily shelling targets on the island.

Nepal

Nepal's Gurkha soldiers, who have long served British interests and continue to do so, served in the Burma campaign against Japan. Gurkhas also served in the American-led occupation of Japan that followed the Second World War.

The United States first recognised the kingdom of Nepal in 1947.

In 1950, Tibet was invaded and occupied by Communist China. The CIA provided support and training for Tibetan guerrillas based in Nepal from this point until the camps were closed by the Nepalese army in 1974. President Nixon's rapprochement with China ultimately put an end to the covert programme.

Nepalese soldiers have served alongside American forces in Iraq, Haiti and elsewhere. And Nepalese and US military personnel shared in exercises, for instance, in the Pacific Resilience Disaster Response Exercise and Exchange in Kathmandu, Nepal, in September 2013.

Netherlands

Frank Sinatra may never have sung 'New Amsterdam, New Amsterdam', but the US still has a long history with the Dutch.

(Author Chris Kelly's maternal ancestors, the Van Rensselaers, for example, came from the Netherlands to New Amsterdam.)

And in 1780, the Netherlands joined with the French and Spanish governments in supporting the thirteen American colonies in the battle for independence against the British Crown.

The Netherlands managed to stay neutral during the First World War but was not so fortunate in the Second World War when it was bombed, invaded and occupied by the Nazis. A majority of the 140,000 Jews in the Netherlands, including the young Anne Frank, were tragically shipped to Nazi death camps.

US air crews saw extensive action in the skies over the Netherlands, either while attacking targets, like German airbases in the Netherlands, or while heading for or returning from targets in Germany.

After the D-Day landings of June 1944, the Germans began their revenge campaign of launching V-1 and V-2 rockets at London. After the collapse in France, the Germans used the Netherlands as a launching platform for the V-2 rocket campaign. This made the Allies anxious to invade the Netherlands and, perhaps, bring an early end to the war.

On 13 and 14 September 1944, American troops liberated Maastricht, the first Dutch city to be freed from the Nazis. Shortly after, US and British forces launched Operation Market Garden deep into the Netherlands in an attempt to punch a hole through to Germany by taking a number of vital strategic bridges in a row. General Montgomery's idea was to use airborne forces to seize the bridges and then make a heavy armoured thrust through German lines to link up with the American and British paratroopers and glider forces.

The north–south road that ran from Eindhoven to Veghel to Nijmegen to Arnhem was the key to Operation Market Garden. However, fierce German resistance all along this road rapidly led to it being called 'Hell's Highway'.

The US 101st Airborne and 82nd Airborne had significant successes in their missions, though at a price. In particular, a heroic attack by men of the 504th Parachute Infantry Regiment across the River Waal under heavy fire led, after heavy losses, to the capture of the crucial bridge at Nijmegen. Unfortunately, the success of the whole plan still relied on the capture of the bridge at Arnhem, and there serious problems were developing.

A situation created by failure to get sufficient troops to the bridge quickly, communications problems, the unexpected presence of German tanks units in the area, and slow progress against stiff resistance meant that the British and Polish paratroopers that were sent to Arnhem, despite their heroism, could not win. Hopes that Market Garden could end the war by Christmas 1944 ultimately were tragically not fulfilled.

In October 1944 the Timberwolves Division (104th Infantry Division), serving under Montgomery, liberated Zundert, Netherlands, and took control of the Vaart Canal defences. They drove forwards towards the Mark River on 2 November and shortly afterwards reached the Maas River on 5 November.

Sadly, though, after the failure of Market Garden, the Allies were able to free only about a fifth of the country in 1944. In the area still held by the Germans, food supplies ended up being cut drastically due to a number of factors, including deliberate Nazi punitive actions, dislocation caused by war, and a harsh winter that arrived early. These all led to the infamous Hunger Winter of 1944–5 in which something like 16,000 Dutch died of starvation. In 1945, with the war almost at an end, a deal was finally agreed with the German occupation forces to allow the British and Americans to fly food supplies, without being fired upon, to the desperate Dutch. The British had Operation Manna; America had Operation Chowhound, also a great name.

Finally on 5 May 1945, the Germans in the Netherlands surrendered, and 5 May is now celebrated in the Netherlands as Liberation Day.

Today an American cemetery in the Netherlands near Maastricht, liberated by Americans all those decades ago, contains over 8,000 members of the American armed forces, a part of the cost of that liberation.

Since the war, the US has maintained close military links with the Netherlands. The Netherlands became a founding member of NATO in 1949. About 3,000 Dutch soldiers served directly in the US 2nd Division in the Korean War. Dutch contingents have served alongside Americans in Iraq and Afghanistan.

Assorted US military units have been based in the Netherlands. During the Cold War, for example, the US III Corps had a forward headquarters at Tapijnkazerne, also near Maastricht, and for a long time there were major USAF facilities at Soesterberg near Utrecht. The US Army Garrison at Schinnen outside Maastricht, a base for US personnel at the Allied Joint Force Command at nearby Brunssum, is currently the only US Army installation in the country.

We should also make a quick mention here of two overseas territories of the Netherlands, Aruba and Curaçao. America has had military links with both. On Aruba, the US established an airbase at Dakota Field and even helped fight off German submarines attempting to shell the oil refinery during the Second World War and the US army set up coastal guns at Colorado Point. On Curaçao, the US operated anti-submarine patrols from Hato Field, which is now Hato International Airport and still hosts a USAF Forward Operating Base.

New Zealand

The Second World War saw one sort of US invasion in New Zealand.

From mid-1942 to mid-1944, hundreds of thousands of Americans in total were based in New Zealand. The first marines landed at Auckland on 12 June 1942 and two days later marines started landing at Wellington as well. US troops were there to help defend New Zealand but also to use New Zealand as a staging post for operations further north. In the novel *Battle Cry*, much of it based on the author's experiences in the Second World War, Leon Uris tells of the battles fought by a group of marines. It also tells of their two visits to New Zealand, the first time training for Guadalcanal, the second resting and recovering before Tarawa.

Usually links with the locals were friendly, sometimes very friendly. Almost 1,500 New Zealand women married American servicemen. But tensions could arise as well, as in the Battle of Manners Street, on 3 April 1943, when hundreds of Americans and New Zealanders ended up brawling in Wellington.

Gradually, however, as Allied forces began to advance and the fighting moved further away from New Zealand, the number of US troops in New Zealand started to decline. The 43rd Division departed from Auckland in the summer of 1944, and in October, the US naval base there was closed.

But military links remained after the war. In 1951, Australia, New Zealand, and the United States were joined in the ANZUS security pact, and they cooperated in SEATO as well. New Zealand forces served in Korea, and the country even sent troops to Vietnam. In more recent years, New Zealanders have served in the Gulf War as well as in Iraq and Afghanistan. New Zealand has also played an important role in a number of peacekeeping missions. New Zealand's decision to ban nuclear-powered and nuclear-armed warships from its waters did, however, cause tensions, though some recent announcements have suggested closer military ties again.

Nicaragua

Situated just to the north of Panama in Central America, and containing the largest freshwater lake in Central America, Nicaragua occupies a crucial strategic position, and the United States has had a long history of interventions there. A long, long one.

In 1848, gold was found at John Sutter's mill near Sacramento launching the California gold rush. Prospectors wanted to travel from east to west but were frustrated with the difficulties and pace of overland travel through an area where hostile locals controlled much territory. The transcontinental railroad was not completed until 1869, and the Panama Canal did not open until 1914. So, in the meantime, taking a steamship from New York to Nicaragua and crossing over to the Pacific was among the most efficient and safest means of travel.

The American tycoon Cornelius Vanderbilt controlled the highly profitable Accessory Transit Company, which monopolised transportation across the rivers and lakes of Nicaragua. Vanderbilt's steamships would take passengers from New York to Greytown (now San Juan del Norte) on the Atlantic coast and then cross Nicaragua via river, lake, and track arriving at San Juan del Sur on the Pacific coast. Another steamer would then bring these passengers up to San Francisco's Barbary Coast. Handy.

Nicaragua, therefore, occupied a valuable strategic and commercial position (or transit choke point) in the world at that time, and Vanderbilt wasn't the only American interested in it.

William Walker of Nashville, Tennessee, was a doctor, lawyer, journalist and adventurer (quite a full CV) who led a group of American filibusters to Nicaragua in 1856. Sam Houston, an American who had become President of the Republic of Texas, was Walker's inspiration, and in spite of the neutrality acts of 1794 and 1818 that explicitly outlawed such activities, Walker and his filibusters sought to build a Central American empire.

On 11 October 1856, he and his supporters arrived in the paddlewheel steamer *La Virgen* at Granada, Nicaragua's capital. The next day, his forces captured the town and soon after established their own republic of Nicaragua. In June 1856 Walker was elected president of Nicaragua, receiving over 68 per cent of the vote in a four-way race. His government was recognised by President Franklin Pierce and received support from US ambassador John Wheeler. His supporters referred to him as the 'grey-eyed man of destiny'.

Though he was not ideologically pro-slavery, having opposed it while serving as a newspaper editor in New Orleans and San Francisco, Walker was convinced to espouse a pro-slavery policy for Nicaragua.

While Walker may have sullied his reputation with his compromise with slavery, his fatal mistake was in siding with Vanderbilt's commercial rivals, taking away Vanderbilt's transit charter. Vanderbilt dismissed Walker as a mere 'tin sojer boy'.

Many neighbouring Central American states feared Walker's expansionist Nicaraguan republic. Honduras, El Salvador, Guatemala and Costa Rica all received arms, supplies and money from Vanderbilt. The tycoon also worked behind the scenes to undermine Walker's support within the US government. Disease, hunger and desertion plagued Walker's filibuster army, which was soon cut off from outside support in Rivas near the Pacific coast. Of the several thousand Americans who served with Walker in Central America, half are estimated to have died from wounds or disease. Commander Charles Davis, captain of the USS *St Mary's*, finally arrived in February 1857 to negotiate Walker's surrender and to provide evacuation of his remaining filibusters to safety in America.

Indefatigable, Walker returned to Nicaragua seven months later with a second expedition of 270 filibusters aboard the side-wheeler steamer *Fashion* that had sailed from Mobile, Alabama. Walker's second attempt to establish the Republic of

Nicaragua was, however, foiled by Commodore Hiram Paulding of the US Navy who landed a force near Greytown on Nicaragua's gulf coast that compelled Walker's second surrender. Paulding wrote that he considered Walkers' supporters to be 'outlaws who had escaped from the vigilance of the government'.

The Nicaraguan government moved swiftly to restore Vanderbilt's transit charter monopoly.

In 1860, Walker, not a man to be deterred by most things, was killed by a Honduran firing squad while leading a third attempted invasion of Nicaragua (*see* Honduras). That did deter him.

The Walker episode also set the tone for the future of links between the United States and Nicaragua. These would be characterised by American financial investment in Nicaragua, particularly in banana plantations and mining, as well as transportation, and US interventions to safeguard these interests from political instability and violent transitions of power.

Even before Walker, America had sent in the troops. In July 1854, it had already bombarded and destroyed much of Greytown over a variety of grievances. And more, much more was to come. US Navy vessels would land forces on numerous occasions over many American administrations. In 1894, for example, the cruiser *Columbia* landed troops at Bluefields, and in 1898, the gunboat *Alert* landed forces at San Juan del Sur.

And the interventions kept on happening. Major Smedley Butler, who would later become an outspoken critic of US overseas interventions, served in Nicaragua from 1909 to 1912. Rear Admiral William Kimball commanded a US expeditionary squadron of nine American warships that arrived at Corinto on the west coast of Nicaragua in December 1909. US forces fought on behalf of President Adolfo Diaz against rebel forces. The Battle of Coyotepe Hill was the sharpest engagement of the 1912 Nicaraguan expedition. Thirty-seven marines were killed or wounded in the campaign.

In August of 1914, at the same time that the First World War was breaking out in Europe, the United States and Nicaragua negotiated the Bryan–Chamorro Treaty. Nicaragua's independence was to be preserved, sort of, while the United States assumed substantial control over Nicaraguan finances.

In 1925 a civil war broke out. Marines from the USS *Cleveland* were landed in Bluefields yet again to protect American interests.

In 1927, Henry Stimson, who would later become President Franklin D. Roosevelt's Secretary of War, negotiated a peace settlement between the Nicaraguan government and the rebels.

However, a rebel officer named Augusto Sandino had remained sceptical about the Nicaraguan government's position in regard of the United States and led a group of followers, called Sandinistas (sound familiar?) into the mountains to wage a guerrilla campaign. On 16 July 1927 the Battle of Ocotal pitted US Marines and Nicaraguan National Guard units against the Sandinistas. One marine and 300 Sandinistas were killed. Sandino starting using a depiction of a rebel decapitating a US Marine with a machete on his official seal. So, neither hugely subtle nor diplomatic.

Finally, President Hoover ordered the withdrawal of US Marines, which took place in January 1933. The year 1936 marked the beginning of the Somoza dynasty (Anastasio Somoza Garcia and, after his 1956 assassination, his sons) that was to rule Nicaragua until 1979. The United States assisted the Somoza regime in training the Nicaraguan National Guard, and links with America remained strong. President Franklin D. Roosevelt said of Somoza, 'He may be an SOB, but he's our SOB'. On 8 December 1941, following the Pearl Harbor attack, Nicaragua joined the Allies in declaring war on Japan and Germany. Nicaragua did not contribute troops, though it did receive some Lend-Lease aid, and airbases were constructed in Corinto.

In the 1970s, however, a civil war erupted in Nicaragua pitting the Somoza regime against rebel forces that included, yep, the Sandinistas. At least 25,000 people were killed in the fighting and repression, including ABC reporter Bill Stewart, executed by the Nicaraguan National Guard, before President Jimmy Carter cut off US military support to the Somoza government, leading to its collapse. In 1979, Sandinista leader Daniel Ortega formed a provisional government, and in 1984, elections confirmed him in power.

However, the Sandinistas were developing increasing links with Cuba and other Communist countries. In spite of congressional opposition, the Reagan administration responded to the growing crisis in Central America by funnelling support to the Contras, or Counter-Revolutionaries, and the neighbouring Honduran government. In defiance of international law, in April 1984 the CIA arranged the mining of Nicaraguan waters near the port of Corinto on the Pacific coast. Colonel Ollie North's 'neat idea' to pay for illegal arms shipments to the Contras with Iranian funds led to the Iran–Contra scandal that disrupted much of President Reagan's second term. A guerrilla resistance movement also sprang up in Miskito territories.

Many Nicaraguans also fled into neighbouring countries creating a refugee crisis throughout the region. In March 1986 Sandinista forces invaded neighbouring Honduras in pursuit of Contra forces who opposed the Sandinista regime.

Finally, after years of bitter conflict, in February 1989, the Tesoro Beach Accords brought regional peace to Central America. The Contra forces agreed to disband, and Nicaragua agreed to hold free elections. Over 30,000 lives were lost in the Sandinista–Contra conflict (or Nicaraguan Revolution).

On 25 February 1990, certified free and fair elections in Nicaragua drove the Sandinistas from office. However, in 2006, Daniel Ortega, leader of the Sandinistas, was returned to power in elections, and he is still president of Nicaragua.

The United States has left a complicated, ambivalent legacy in its long and tangled history of interventions in Nicaragua. Nicaraguans today celebrate 14 September as one of their national days in commemoration of a Nicaraguan victory over General Walker's Yankee *filibusteros* at the San Jacinto ranch.

However, that is not the entire picture. In 2004, a contingent of Nicaraguan troops served alongside US troops in the American-led coalition's invasion of Iraq, and the US military has been involved in humanitarian projects in Nicaragua.

The Wisconsin National Guard is partnered with Nicaragua, and part of this programme has included the Wisconsin Military Engagement Team's missions to Nicaragua.

Niger

Niger is the middle of the three big states in northern central Africa. Mali is situated to the west, and Chad is to the east.

Since the rise of al-Qaeda-linked jihadis in the region, Niger has become a highly strategic location. Before French-led intervention, extreme Islamists had taken control of half of Mali and were threatening the south. Boko Haram (means 'Western education is sinful') has been a major threat in Nigeria to the south, and the chaotic situation in Libya to the north has left the southern region of that country often only weakly controlled by the government in distant Tripoli.

It's hardly surprising, therefore, that the US has been taking an increased military interest in the country recently. AFRICOM recommended placing unarmed, remotely piloted aircraft in Niger and in February 2013 President Obama announced that the last of 100 US military specialists had been sent to Niger in support of intelligence gathering and sharing operations in the region. Not surprising, they're mostly air force specialists, and they're based in the capital Niamey.

Niger saw a couple of serious terrorist attacks within its borders in 2013, including one on a vital uranium ore mine at Artit and one on military barracks at Agadez. The Niger foreign minister said in September 2013 that he would welcome the deployment of armed drones in the country.

The United States in 2014 also held regional military manoeuvres in Niger, called Operation Flintlock, and has been assisting the Nigerien military with assorted other support as well, such as supplying them with a couple of new planes and some trucks through US security co-operation programs.

Nigeria

US military forces first came into contact with the area during the US Navy's anti-slaving operations in the region in the nineteenth century.

During the Second World War, America used Kano Airport in Nigeria and Maiduguri and Lagos as links on air-ferry routes across Africa.

During the long and bitter Biafra War, America was deeply involved in the humanitarian airlift to take food and supplies to starving civilians, supplying also a number of C-97 US Air National Guard transport aircraft and pilots. Among those who volunteered for the often dangerous missions was August Martin, a former Tuskegee airman who was killed in a plane crash.

The US and Nigerian governments haven't always been best of friends. For instance, in 1993, the United States imposed sanctions on Nigeria over human rights and other concerns.

However, in recent years, the United States has been getting along much better with the Nigerian government, and a variety of military links have developed. In 2003, Nigerian forces took part alongside US forces in operations in Liberia to oust Charles Taylor and restore stability. Nigerian peacekeepers have also played a significant role in a number of conflict-hit areas, including Darfur and Mali. The US Air Force has helped to fly Nigerian peacekeepers and the US military has helped train them. Nigerian forces have also taken part in assorted exercises alongside US forces.

The rise of the extremist Islamist organisation Boko Haram in Nigeria has been a major concern for the US military, and AFRICOM has been partnering with Nigerian forces to counter Boko Haram's attacks. In 2014, after the abduction of hundreds of girls by Boko Haram, America sent military personnel and aircraft to assist with finding and rescuing the girls.

The California National Guard is partnered with Nigeria.

North Korea

Ah North Korea, a land that has given many Americans many sleepless nights. America's first contact with what is now North Korea was frankly not a happy one. In 1866, an American ship, the SS *General Sherman*, arrived off Korea and then proceeded to sail upriver to Pyongyang, now the capital of North Korea, in an attempt to start Western trade with Koreans. The Koreans were wary of Western traders, and a dispute arose that led to violence and the eventual burning of the SS *General Sherman*. Not a great start.

America's next major visit to North Korea was going to prove pretty tough as well. (To avoid too much repetition in this book, the beginning of the Korean War until the first liberation of Seoul will be covered in the South Korea chapter.) After the liberation of Seoul by UN forces on 26 September 1950, the United Nations forces faced a strategic dilemma. Would they advance north of the thirty-eighth parallel and end the regime there, or would they stop at the line that originally divided North and South Korea?

Two considerations – the discovery by the UN command that thousands of civilians in South Korea had been killed by the Communists between June and September 1950 and the comparatively swift collapse of the North Korean army after Inchon – were seized upon by those arguing in favour of crossing the thirty-eighth parallel. In the end, both the UN command and the Truman administration opted for regime change.

As a result, United Nations forces swept north of the thirty-eighth parallel. On 19 October, Pyongyang was captured. Bob Hope even gave a USO performance for the troops in the North Korean capital.

United Nations forces were advancing towards the Chinese border and Kim Il Sung's northern regime was in a state of near total collapse when suddenly the situation changed, and changed entirely.

Mao, mindful that North Korea had recently been the jumping-off point for the Japanese invasion of Manchuria in the 1930s, decided to intervene in Korea on a huge scale. In late October 1950 massive Chinese formations began to cross the Yalu River into North Korea. In the end, over 1.3 million Chinese would fight in the war.

The Chinese forces had years of experience in battling the Japanese and the Chinese Nationalists. They employed human-wave tactics and specialised in night attack to avoid UN superiority in the air. The autumn also saw the first MiG-15s deployed in the country in support of the North Koreans and Chinese, challenging UN dominance of the skies.

Among Mao's forces were recently surrendered Nationalist Chinese. This later complicated the negotiations over prisoner exchanges as many who had fought on the Communist side had no desire to be repatriated to North Korea or the People's Republic.

The Chinese intervention was a hammer blow to the UN forces. During the Chosin Reservoir campaign of December 1950, the commander of 1st Marine Division, O. P. Smith, famously remarked, 'Gentlemen, we are not retreating. We are merely advancing in another direction.'

The UN retreat continued through the bleak winter of 1950, and the Chinese tidal wave swept all in its path. Pyongyang was recaptured on 5 December 1950, and Seoul itself was evacuated by UN troops on 4 January 1951. In desperation at the situation, Douglas MacArthur began to support drastic measures to stem the Chinese tide, including bombing the Yalu bridges across which the Chinese supply lines flowed, and even considering the use of atomic weapons. On 5 April 1951, MacArthur released a letter criticising the Truman administration's policy of limited war. In response, President Harry Truman, who never cared much for 'Dugout Doug', charged the supreme commander with blatant insubordination.

Before MacArthur's final removal, however, the Chinese onslaught had already been slowed and then halted. The Eighth Army under Matthew Ridgway, the commander of the 82nd Airborne in Operation Market Garden (*see* Netherlands) began to push north again, and on 5 March 1951, Seoul changed hands for the third time as his forces advanced towards the thirty-eighth parallel. Nevertheless, a grinding war still lay ahead with no apparent end in sight.

Out of over 1,319,000 Americans who served during the three years of the 'forgotten war' in Korea, about 36,000 were killed – comparable to the 58,000 claimed by Vietnam over ten years. Over a million Koreans from the north, south, and all ideologies, including many civilians, were also killed in the war. Truman's ambition for a third presidential term was also a casualty of the war.

With a simple five-word speech, 'I shall go to Korea', Dwight Eisenhower was catapulted to electoral victory in November 1952. As president-elect, America's most distinguished soldier visited Korea later that month. Mark Clark, a West Point classmate of Eisenhower's, tried to argue that the war was winnable, but Eisenhower was determined to gain a truce. He told Clark, 'I have a mandate from the people to stop this fighting.'

The Eisenhower administration launched a high-stakes poker game designed to resume the stalled peace talks at Panmunjom. A tactical nuclear device, designed to be used by artillery, was tried out in January 1953. In May of that year, Allen Dulles, the Secretary of State, visited Prime Minister Nehru of India and asked that a warning be conveyed to the Chinese: if a truce were not agreed to, bombing north of the Yalu would commence. The talks resumed and made rapid progress.

Finally, the Korean War ended with an armistice signed on 27 July 1953, which basically restored the antebellum status quo. But the truce has not been an unbroken one. Regular incidents have occurred, including in 1968 when North Koreans boarded and captured the USS *Pueblo*. The *Pueblo* remains today the only US Navy vessel in enemy hands.

And today, it is Kim Jong-un, the grandson of Kim Il Sung from the Korean War, who presides over secretive North Korea and keeps the rest of the world guessing about what he's going to do next.

Norway

Leif Ericson, who was of Norwegian descent, may have launched the first European incursion into North America sometime around the year AD 1000. America returned the favour nearly a thousand years later during the Second World War.

The Nazis invaded Norway in April 1940 and occupied it for the remainder of the war in Europe. King Haakon VII of Norway fled with a government in exile to England. In Norway, with German support, Vidkun Quisling formed a collaborationist government.

Not surprisingly, since America wasn't actually in the war at the time, it didn't have anything much to do with the fighting in Norway in 1940. However, on 21 April 1940, Captain Robert Moffat Losey, serving as US military attaché in Norway, was killed by Luftwaffe bombs while trying to ensure the safe evacuation of American diplomats to neutral Sweden.

After the launch of Operation Barbarossa, the Nazi invasion of the Soviet Union, the Axis occupation of Norway became a particular thorn in the Allies' side as Norwegian air and sea bases were used to prey on the arctic convoys that were bringing Lend-Lease supplies to the Soviet Union. Film star Douglas Fairbanks Jr was a naval lieutenant aboard the USS *Wichita* in the summer of 1942 and witnessed the disastrous PQ 17 convoy that was almost wiped out by German attacks. Plenty of supplies did, however, get through on convoys.

In addition, the German presence in Norway helped assure the transportation of vital Swedish iron ore for use in building the *Wehrmacht* war machine. Consequently, Churchill repeatedly advocated Operation Anvil, a projected Allied invasion of Norway, to address these concerns. Eisenhower and others in the Allied staff, however, believed that Operation Anvil would be a distraction from the cross-channel invasion of France through Normandy; they prevailed in Allied strategy sessions.

US planes did, however, conduct assorted air operations over occupied Norway. For example, American aircrews were part of the campaign to prevent a Nazi atomic bomb. The Germans were attempting to make heavy water for their nascent nuclear programme at a hydroelectric plant in Vermork, Norway. In 1943, this plant was hit by a 143-plane raid of USAAF B-17s that did extensive damage.

But not all US operations in Norway during the Second World War were to be in the air. On 24 March 1945 a squadron of B-24 Liberators launched Operation Rype (Norwegian for 'grouse') dropping a team of specially trained OSS forces near Jarlsbad in central Norway. The thirty-six-man group immediately linked up with Norwegian resistance forces. The 99th Infantry Battalion, who were proficient skiers and demolition experts, managed to destroy the Tangen bridge near Jorstad. On 12 May 1945, they took over Steinkjer from German forces. Major William Colby, who was later appointed head of the CIA by President Nixon, was the leader of the OSS team in Norway.

On 10 June 1945, the 99th Battalion would form the guard of honour for Crown Prince Olaf's triumphant parade through Trondheim.

Norway was a founding member of NATO in 1949. Norway's strategic location on the northern approaches to the Soviet Union made it an important area for bases for the USAF and US Navy during the Cold War.

America still has strong military links with Norway. For example, the USAF's 501st Combat Support Wing remains based in Stavanger to this day. The Norwegians sent troops to fight in Afghanistan, and Norwegian jets played a major role in the operations in Libya in 2011.

Oman

One of the many interesting facts about Oman is how long America has had links with the country.

We tend to think of US interest in the Gulf and Arabian peninsula as a comparatively recent phenomenon, but actually as early as 1833 the US signed a Treaty of Friendship and Navigation with Muscat (the capital of Oman) when diplomat Edmund Roberts turned up on the USS *Peacock*. At the time, the Sultan of Oman also ruled Zanzibar (see Tanzania) and was interested in America as a possible counterbalance to the expansion of British influence.

As the nineteenth century wore on, however, British influence did increase in Muscat. And it was during the Second World War that the United States started to take a renewed interest in the country. For instance, America requested and received permission for USAAF planes to use facilities in the country.

British influence in Oman remained strong for a considerable time after the Second World War (and the countries still have strong links), but in 1980 America signed an agreement on US access to assorted Omani military facilities, airbases and naval bases, and America then started work on the facilities there.

One of the main airbases the US has used in Oman is Thumrait Air Base. US aircraft, for instance, operated out of Thumrait during Operations Desert Shield and Desert Storm, and US refuelling aircraft have used the base as well.

Omani troops served with the Gulf War coalition during Desert Storm, and Oman has become a partner valued by the US in fighting terrorism.

Pakistan

One of the shortest and most dramatic American invasions in US history took place in Pakistan in 2011.

Pakistan occupies a strategically significant location, and the US first got militarily involved with the area in the Second World War precisely because of its location. US aircraft that had been ferried across from Africa and the Middle East needed to pass through it so they could reach airbases in India and China. It was also a location where supplies could be landed from the sea. So among other facilities, America established a major presence at the airport at Karachi, Pakistan's major city and major port.

In 1947, as the British Raj came to an end, Muslim-majority Pakistan and East Pakistan (now Bangladesh) were separated from India.

As Cold War tensions developed, Pakistan's conservative

military elite and strong Muslim identity were increasingly seen by the United States as a bulwark against Communism. In 1954, the United States signed an arms agreement with Pakistan. Pakistan shared concern about the encroachments of the nearby Soviet Union. The United States sought assurances that the weapons would not be used against India, with which Pakistan had long-standing disputes.

Pakistan granted the United States the right to build an airbase at Budaber, near Peshawar. U-2 spy planes operated from there, and a major NSA listening post was developed. On 1 May 1960, Francis Gary Powers, flying a U-2 surveillance plane at 70,000 feet over the Soviet Union, was shot down; his plane, originally headed for Norway, had taken off from Budaber.

In 1959, METO (Middle East Treaty Organisation) was formed allying the United States with Pakistan, Iran and Turkey. Pakistan was a founding member of the South East Asia Treaty Organisation in 1954 but withdrew in 1973, precipitated by what it perceived as insufficient support for its conflict with India over Bangladesh.

In one of those little-known links, Sardar, the horse Pakistan gave to Jackie Kennedy, was the riderless horse used at JFK's funeral in 1963.

In 1965, America suspended military assistance to Pakistan (as well as India) during that year's war between the two countries, and arms sales weren't started again until 1975.

Prior to his historic trip to China, President Nixon, had however, come to regard Pakistan as 'a valuable channel to China', and he developed something of a personal friendship with President Yahya. In spite of the evidence of massive human rights violations, the United States supported Pakistan in its efforts to retain its hold on East Pakistan. In 1971, however, East Pakistan separated from West Pakistan and became the independent nation of Bangladesh. During the crisis, Nixon deployed the carrier *Enterprise* into the Bay of Bengal.

After the Soviet Union invaded neighbouring Afghanistan in December 1979, Pakistan became a major conduit of arms supplies to the mujahideen resistance. In 1981, the United States agreed to a $3.2 billion military and economic assistance programme to Pakistan.

Many Americans tend to think of the mujahideen struggle

against the Soviets in Afghanistan as 'Charlie Wilson's War'. Wilson was a Texas congressman who lobbied for arms shipments to the mujahideen that were funnelled through Pakistan's intelligence service, the ISI. But the conflict could also be considered 'Zia-ul-Haq's (the President of Pakistan) War', 'William Casey's (the head of the CIA) War', or even 'Ronald Reagan's War'. Prior to becoming president, Reagan had said, 'My idea of American policy towards the Soviet Union is simple: We win and they lose.'

In order to avoid US casualties and create deniability, billions of dollars worth of support were funnelled through Pakistan's ISI. The Saudis matched the American financial contribution.

After Zia-ul-Haq met Reagan on a visit to Washington, the president noted in his diary that the two leaders got along well, that Zia-ul-Haq had given his word Pakistan wasn't building a nuclear bomb, and that the Pakistanis were dedicated to helping Afghanistan and stopping what the Soviets were up to. And the Soviets were indeed stopped in Afghanistan, though at a terrible cost to the Afghan people and at the cost of giving a boost to jihadi radicalism.

Close ties between the CIA and the ISI dissolved in the 1990s as the United States lost interest in Afghanistan after the Soviet withdrawal. On other levels, too, the implosion of the Soviet Union seemed to make Pakistan a less important American ally, and the nuclear question was about to re-emerge big time.

In 1990 America again suspended military assistance to Pakistan over concerns about Pakistan's nuclear programme. In May 1998 India demonstrated its nuclear capability by exploding nuclear bombs underground and in response Pakistan did the same.

However, the US was about to focus on the region again even more intently and for reasons even more compelling than the Pakistani and Indian nuclear weapons programmes.

As warlords fought for control of Afghanistan after the Soviet withdrawal and the eventual collapse of the Afghan regime they had supported, the 1990s saw the rise in Afghanistan of the Taliban, an organisation with strong links across the border in Pakistan, and alongside the Taliban was rising another new force.

On 20 August 1998, after the embassy bombings in Kenya and Tanzania, President Clinton launched a cruise missile strike on Osama bin Laden's camp at Khost in eastern Afghanistan.

Bin Laden managed to evacuate the camp prior to the arrival of about seventy missiles, which killed around twenty people.

General Mahmud Ahmed, the head of the Pakistani ISI, happened to be in Washington at the time of the 9/11 terrorist attacks. Summoned to a meeting the next day with Richard Armitage, the Deputy Secretary of State, Ahmed pledged his country's unwavering support to the new War on Terror, despite the fact that Pakistan had been one of only three countries to recognise the Taliban regime in Afghanistan.

The Pakistani government did, indeed, prove useful in the fight against terror, and the United States supplied extensive financial assistance. In 2004, with Afghanistan now the US government's priority, not Pakistan's nuclear weapons, President George W. Bush declared Pakistan a major non-NATO ally. However, as fighting increased in Afghanistan, US concerns about Taliban links inside Pakistan grew, particularly those in the border areas of the country which were only very loosely controlled by Pakistan's central government. The use of drones to attack targets began.

During the 2008 election campaign, Senator Obama staked out a surprisingly aggressive position: 'If we have actionable intelligence about high-value targets and President Musharraf won't act, we will.' After being elected president, Obama would have an opportunity to follow through on those words.

The use of drones to attack targets within Pakistan increased dramatically and became a regular occurrence creating in many senses a new form of war involving new opportunities but also new risks. But in 2011, the biggest target of all in the War on Terror was about to present itself, and it wouldn't be a drone that was sent in.

On 1 May 2011 four US helicopters flew from Jalalabad in Afghanistan to Abbottabad, Pakistan, on a mission aimed at Osama bin Laden. In spite of the crash of one stealth Black Hawk into the compound, Operation Neptune Spear was a near total success. Two Black Hawk helicopters carried US Navy SEALs to Bin Ladens's secret compound. Two CH-47s carried extra fuel and additional forces. The SEALs relayed the code signal 'Geronimo' back to the White House confirming that Osama bin Laden had been positively identified. Bin Laden, three other males and one female were killed; there were no SEAL casualties.

The intelligence gathering phase of this mission had required about ten years, with several 'enhanced interrogation' sessions along the way. The action phase of this invasion of Pakistan and the subsequent withdrawal lasted about four hours. No Pakistani military or civilians were killed in the raid.

Bin Laden's body was identified with DNA methods and transported to the USS *Carl Vinson*. The burial was at sea in the north Arabian Ocean. Soon after the mission and its success were announced a crowd thronged around the White House chanting 'USA, USA ...'

One of the MC-130E Combat Talon I planes that had been used when President Carter ordered the disastrous Operation Eagle Claw to free American hostages in Iran was used to ferry SEAL Team Six to Kentucky for a congratulatory visit with President Obama. Navy SEAL Team Six received a Presidential Unit Citation – the highest unit award in the US military. President Obama credited the 'countless intelligence and counter-terrorism professionals' who had laboured for over a decade in three US administrations to achieve this result.

But the death of Bin Laden did not mean the end of the drone war in Pakistan. In October 2011 Secretary of State Hillary Clinton, on a visit to Islamabad, warned Pakistan that the United States would continue to take unilateral action against terrorists, and drone strikes continued.

Currently Pakistan's problems with the Taliban are unresolved. The Pakistani government was attempting to hold negotiations with the Pakistani Taliban, and subsequently a lull occurred in drone strikes. However, since then US drone strikes in Pakistan have been resumed by the Obama administration.

Palau

The name of one of the Palau Islands in the Pacific will be more familiar to many than others: Peleliu.

In the nineteenth century, the Spanish were in colonial control of the Palau Islands and the people who lived there until they sold the islands to Germany in 1899. The Japanese, who were on the Allied side in the First World War, received control over the islands in the temporary peace that followed.

On 15 September 1944, after underwater demolition

teams had tackled beach obstructions, and after bombing and bombardment of Peleliu, the 1st Marine Division stormed ashore. The initial landings faced heavy resistance, but the marines battled forward and, by the end of the day, held a beachhead. On the next day, they advanced further and managed to capture the airfield on Peleliu. Bitter fighting for Japanese fortifications on 'The Point' followed, and US forces faced a number of desperate Japanese counter-attacks. But even though the fighting had already been tough so far, the worst was yet to come. The American forces had to try to take a ridge running along the island, one that the Japanese had heavily fortified. Bitter fighting followed on Bloody Nose Ridge, and the Japanese tried to reinforce their troops by sea at night. By 26 September, the Japanese defenders were finally surrounded, but the fighting continued. In late September and increasingly in October, troops from the 81st Division took up the burden of the fighting. It wasn't until November that fighting ceased. American forces suffered huge casualties, but the Japanese lost even more.

Meanwhile on 17 September the 81st Division landed on nearby Angaur Island. Other nearby islands, including Ngesebus Island, were also captured by US forces.

The end of the bitter battle for Peleliu and nearby islands did not, however, mean the end of the war in the Palau Islands. Some of them, notably Koror and Babeldoab (or Babelthuap), remained occupied by the Japanese, and more intermittent action, particularly bombing raids against them, took place.

After the war the Palau Islands were under US control as part of the Trust Territory of the Pacific Islands. In 1994 after an extended dispute over the Compact of Free Association with the United States, both parties signed it, and Palau became independent, and the United States took responsibility for the defence of Palau.

Many Palauan citizens have volunteered for service in the US military. The US Navy visits, and US military and Palauan security forces have trained alongside each other.

Panama

Panama is known for being a place the US has taken a bit of interest in. Well a lot of interest actually. A big lot.

John Quincy Adams, America's sixth president, recognised the strategic importance of Panama in the 1820s and even helped to set up an isthmian canal company. Though a lot of time was yet to pass and a lot of Frenchmen were going to be disappointed before a Panama Canal was finally built.

However, even without a canal, people were using the isthmus to travel between the Atlantic and Pacific Oceans. With the finding of gold in California, many Americans crossed overland through Panama on their roundabout route way to and from the gold fields (*see* Nicaragua).

As an indication of America's major interest in the strategic isthmus, in 1846 the Mallarino–Bidlack Treaty was signed with Colombia, which was then the national power in Panama. In 1847, almost as soon as the ink on the treaty was dry, New York businessmen started the Panama Railroad Company. The Panama Railway, financed by Americans, was opened in 1855.

Already, by 1856, US troops were being deployed in Panama. In that year, the Watermelon War broke out, though it was really more of a Watermelon Riot, which was triggered by an intoxicated American railroad traveller who took a slice of watermelon from a Panamanian fruit merchant and refused payment. Fifteen Americans were killed in Panama City, and America sent in troops to restore order and protect American citizens. Quite an expensive slice of watermelon in the end.

In 1860, the USS *Saint Mary's* sent sailors and marines ashore in order to protect the Panama Railway from insurgents. US troops were deployed yet again in 1865, this time to protect Americans during a revolution. In 1873, more of the same really, as local groups clashed and American troops moved in.

And all the while people had been thinking about the possibility of a canal between the Atlantic and the Pacific. After the American Civil War, the United States tried twice (1867 and 1884) to build a canal through Nicaragua. In 1880, Frenchman Ferdinand de Lesseps, who had tackled the Suez Canal, began building a Panama Canal. By 1889, however, the venture was out of money, and construction stopped with the canal incomplete.

Meanwhile, in 1885 Pedro Prestan led a revolt in Panama, which formed part of Colombia at the time. The rebels burned the American consulate in Colón and destroyed considerable property. A force of six US Navy warships and the full East Coast complement of US Marines (about 2,000) were dispatched to Panama where the Colombians requested their intervention against the rebels. A derby-wearing Prestan was hanged in front of a large crowd.

In 1901 America sent in troops once again to keep transport flowing and protect American property, and it was about now that America also began a serious push to build Panama its canal. Soon after, the US government began to think it would be easier to build such a canal through an independent Panama, rather than continuing to deal with the Colombian government.

Soon after that, in 1903 when Panama helpfully revolted against Colombia, this time the United States, led by Teddy Roosevelt, unsurprisingly sided with the Panamanian rebels. Roosevelt dispatched two US Navy ships (*Nashville* and *Dixie*) in support of the rebels. A battalion of marines commanded by Major John Lejenue landed at Colón. A bribe of $8,000 was paid to the Colombian commander to hasten his exit from Panama. The US government recognised the new Panamanian nation and negotiated a treaty to control the Canal Zone. The treaty gave the United States extensive rights in the Canal Zone that extended about five miles on either side of the canal and some rights in Panama outside the Canal Zone and was, perhaps inevitably, to be a source of a certain amount of tension between Panama and the United States in the years ahead.

And the years ahead were also to see more deployments of US troops. For instance, in 1918, US Marines were sent to Chiriqui Province to quell local disturbances. In 1925, US troops were used, at the request of the Panamanian government, to disperse a mob of rent rioters.

The outbreak of the Second World War in 1939 and rising tensions around the world only increased the strategic importance of the canal. Matters were complicated by the fact that, for the early part of the war, Panama was ruled by the Fascist-leaning Arias. However, he was handily toppled in October 1941, before Pearl Harbor. After the Japanese attack on Pearl Harbor, fears of subversion or a Japanese naval strike intensified. Consequently the US organised a deal with the Panamanian government to allow it to occupy additional sites in order to defend the canal if necessary.

In 1977, the Torrijos–Carter Treaty was signed that provided for the return of the Panama Canal Zone to Panama in 1999. That, however, obviously isn't quite the end of this chapter.

In 1983, Manuel Noriega, a cocaine kingpin, became President of Panama. He had also been the CIA's man in Panama from the 1960s until 1988 when he was indicted in Florida. Presidents Reagan and George H. W. Bush had tried to dislodge him by covert means and failed. It would take an invasion to remove this former American friend from power in Panama.

On 16 December 1989, an off-duty US Marine was shot and killed at a Panamanian Defence Forces roadblock. A line had been crossed.

In December 1989, only a month after the Berlin Wall fell, President George H. W. Bush launched the not very subtly named Operation Just Cause to drive Manuel Noriega from power. A force of 25,000 troops overwhelmed Noriega's Panamanian Defence Force. Twenty-three Americans were killed in the fighting. The Panamanian strongman sought refuge in the Vatican embassy where US soldiers blasted him with rock 'n' roll hits, such as 'The End' by the Doors, 'Welcome to the Jungle' by Guns 'n' Roses, and 'All I Want Is You' by U2, among others. Noriega was extradited to Miami where he was convicted of drug trafficking, racketeering and money laundering.

In more recent years, the US has maintained assorted military links with Panama, for instance taking part in joint exercises. US warships still travel through the Panama Canal.

The Missouri National Guard is partnered with Panama.

Papua New Guinea

Papua New Guinea is the eastern half of the enormous island of New Guinea, just north of Australia, plus some additional islands. Errol Flynn, before his discovery by Hollywood, lived on the island for five years between the world wars, trying to make his fortune raising tobacco and mining.

The western half of New Guinea is now part of Indonesia but used to be Dutch East Guinea. Papua New Guinea also has a colonial past. North of the island's central mountains used to be German New Guinea, while south of it was Papua controlled by Australia. In the First World War, the Australians invaded and occupied German New Guinea so that all the east of the island was under Australian administration. Its principal islands, which used to be called the very Germanic New Pomerania and

New Mecklenburg are now, the very much less Germanic New Britain and New Ireland.

The area was to see a lot more action in the Second World War. In January 1942, less than two months after the attack on Pearl Harbor, Japanese troops took Rabaul, the capital of former German New Guinea, and landed at Buna on the north coast. One of their ultimate targets was Port Moresby on the southern coast of the island, just a few hundred miles across the sea from Australia. In the Battle of the Coral Sea, the American Navy prevented a Japanese attempt to take Port Moresby from the sea, so the Japanese decided to take it by land instead. They advanced over the Kokoda Trail through the mountains of the Owen Stanley Range towards Port Moresby. Bitter fighting followed as Australians fought desperately to prevent their homeland from falling to the advancing Japanese. Finally, the Japanese were forced to retreat, and a combined Australian and American offensive was launched against some of the Japanese bases in the north of the island. The fighting was intense, and casualties were heavy. The US 32nd Infantry Division had a particularly rough time, and the 41st Infantry Division suffered as well. Eventually, it was an Allied victory, and Buna was captured, but many Japanese still remained in the area.

The Japanese lost again in the Battle of Milne Bay in September 1942 when they launched an attack on an Australian base there. And in March 1943, in the Battle of the Bismarck Sea, the US Navy did severe damage to a Japanese attempt to bring thousands of reinforcements to their base at Lae.

In April 1943 Magic (US decryption of Japanese wartime codes) revealed that Admiral Yamamoto would be flying from Rabaul to Bougainville over New Guinea. On 18 April 1943, American P-38 Lightning aircraft from Henderson Field in the Solomons were ordered to intercept and shoot down his aircraft. His charred corpse was later found in the jungle near Buin showing evidence of being hit by 50-calibre bullets. His body was returned to Japan and given a state funeral on 5 June 1943. Operation Vengeance marked the first time that a US president authorised an assassination in wartime. Both President Roosevelt and the Japanese admiral were alumni of Harvard University.

Douglas MacArthur was focused on the Philippines, but before he could return there, he had to smash Japanese resistance in key places like Lae. The push for Lae began. On 30 June, the

First Battalion of the 162nd Infantry landed at and captured Nassau Bay, forty miles from Lae. As American forces advanced along the coast, Australian forces advanced from Wau in a pincer movement.

On 5 September, ninety-six C-47s, with 200 fighters and bombers escorting them, ferried the US 503rd Parachute Regiment to the Nadzab airfield near Lae. They rapidly took the airfield, and Australian troops were soon flown into it. By mid-September 1943, the town had fallen to Allied forces.

In December 1943, US troops landed on the island of New Britain. More landings on islands and New Guinea itself followed, and on 22 April 1944, the US I Corps landed in Hollandia on the western side of the island. MacArthur now had a platform from which to launch his liberation of the Philippines. However, pockets of Japanese resistance in the jungles of New Guinea and on assorted smaller islands lasted until the war's conclusion.

Papua New Guinea gained its independence in 1975.

In recent decades, Papua New Guinea has faced a mix of challenges, including the fighting on Bougainville in the 1990s. The United States had some minor involvement in the Bougainville crisis, including certifying the collection of arms on Bougainville.

The US military has also had some recent minor links with the country. US forces, through PACOM, have given some training to the Papua New Guinea Defence Force and have held small-scale exercises there.

Paraguay

Paraguay, with its capital at Asunción, is about the size of California. Spanish is a major language, but over 90 per cent of people speak and understand the local language, Guarani.

In 1855, the USS *Water Witch*, a steam-powered side-wheel gunboat captained by Thomas Jefferson Page of Virginia, was cruising along the coast of Paraguay. His mission was to chart the course of the Rio de la Plata. The US ship was fired upon by guns in a Paraguayan coastal fort in what was labelled an 'unprovoked, unwarrantable and dastardly attack'. One crewmember, the helmsman (Samuel Chaney), was killed. Unsurprisingly America wasn't happy about this. In 1858, the

Paraguayan expedition, made up of nineteen US naval ships, arrived at Asunción to demand an apology from the Paraguayan government. This was received, compensation was paid and a bilateral commercial treaty was negotiated.

In 1886, Elisabeth Nietzsche, the sister of the philosopher, helped to found a 'racially pure' colony in Paraguay, which was called Nueva Germania. The colony was a failure, but German influence in Paraguay persisted. Paraguay formed the first Nazi party in South America in 1932, which was the last to dissolve in 1946. However, as the Second World War progressed, Paraguay gradually became closer to the Allies. A US Military Aviation Mission and US Army Mission were established there in 1943. Paraguay eventually joined the United States in the Allied cause, though only three months prior to VE Day.

The dictator Alfredo Stroessner, whose father was originally from Bavaria, was president of Paraguay from 1954 to 1989. He already had links with the US military having graduated from a general staff course at Fort Leavenworth, and in 1953, he was invited to tour assorted military facilities in the United States. After he took power in a coup, his regime received over $100 million in US government support. The United States assisted with counter-insurgency training and supplied trucks, planes, artillery and small arms. Stroessner enjoyed close links with President Johnson and even offered to send Paraguayan troops to Vietnam. In 1968, he went on a formal visit to Washington.

The Carter era, however, saw Washington distancing itself from Stroessner, and in the 1980s, the US ambassador was several times threatened with expulsion over criticism of press censorship. Finally, Stroessner was toppled in a coup in 1989. In 1996, the United States helped prevent another military coup in Paraguay.

In recent years, US troops have taken part alongside Paraguay in both bilateral and multilateral exercises, and the presence of US troops for exercises inside Paraguay in 2005 led to speculation about the possible creation of a US base there.

The Massachusetts National Guard is partnered with Paraguay.

Peru

Peru, the land of (among many other things obviously) the Incas, and home to the amazing city of Machu Picchu.

The US had a little bit of involvement with Peru early on, but not that much. In 1813, an American frigate captured a Peruvian privateer off Chile, and in the same year, the same US ship helped recapture another American ship off Callao in Peru.

In 1835 and 1836, US Marines landed on several occasions in Peru to protect US lives and property in Callao and Lima during revolutionary conflict there.

Interestingly, the French had quite a lot of military influence in Peru at the end of the nineteenth century and in the early twentieth century, but after the First World War, America began to take more of a serious interest. For instance, in the 1920s, the US Navy helped to construct a naval academy in Peru.

During the Second World War, links expanded. America sent Lend-Lease equipment to Peru, and a US military mission began operations there. The US even operated an airbase at Talara, Peru, from 1942 to 1944 (and used the base after that until 1947 for communications training). Peru declared war on the Axis powers late in the war.

After the Second World War, the Cold War was a factor throughout South America, and an American Military Assistance Advisory Group organised a programme of military aid to help keep Peru closer to the United States than to the Communist powers. In 1965, when guerrilla groups emerged in mountainous territory, US aid and advisers helped the Peruvians rapidly crush them. The Tuna War (*see* Ecuador) also caused tensions with neighbouring states.

In the 1970s, by contrast, with a left-wing government in power, significant amounts of Soviet military assistance flowed in.

In the 1980s with the rise of the Shining Path (Sendero Luminoso) and the beginning in Peru of the war against illegal narcotics, US military links with Peru were reinvigorated. In September 1989, President George H. W. Bush sent US Special Forces to Peru to help train government troops for operations against illegal drug producers and traffickers. The United States also dispatched AWACS and Orion planes to fly over significant parts of Peru and established two radar stations in Peru to track aircraft used in connection with illicit drugs. Political disagreements between US and Peruvian governments, however, sometimes affected such programs.

The battle against illicit narcotics has continued to be a focus for the United States in Peru, and the US and Peruvian militaries have regularly co-operated on activities, such as training and exercises.

The West Virginia National Guard is partnered with Peru.

Philippines

The name of the Philippines is derived from King Philip II of Spain (the one with the Armada), and the Spanish did indeed control the country for hundreds of years. Then America came along.

Early on the morning of 1 May 1898, Admiral George Dewey turned to his captain and said, 'You may fire when you are ready, Gridley.' The US Navy sent the Spanish navy's Asian fleet to the shallow bottom of Manila Bay that day in the Spanish–American War.

A rebel who had fought the Spanish for Philippine independence from Spain, Emilio Aguinaldo, was brought by the Americans from Hong Kong back to the Philippines in an attempt to enlist the help of the Philippines' freedom fighters against Spain. US and Filipino forces fought side by side against the Spanish, and on 12 June 1898, they proclaimed Filipino independence. It was not to last.

By the peace deal that ended the Spanish–American War, the Spanish handed control of the Philippines not to the Filipinos but to the United States.

After a period of increasing tension between US forces and Filipino forces, the situation erupted into outright war.

In the initial phase of the war, the Filipinos attempted to fight US forces in a conventional war. However, it rapidly became apparent that it was a hugely unequal fight, and the Filipino forces dispersed in an attempt to wage a guerrilla war that required over 120,000 US soldiers to tackle it over years. There were 4,324 US casualties in the war, most on account of disease. More than 20,000 Filipino fighters were killed, and perhaps as many as 200,000 civilians died through violence, disease or starvation. This war was brutal, featuring American machine guns, heavy artillery and naval bombardments against Filipino troops, some of them armed with little more than spears and bolo knives. This war also saw the first use of waterboarding by American troops.

The Americans decisively won the Philippine–American War in the space of three years with a combination of extensive force, guile and some enemy disarray. Major General Arthur MacArthur, a US Civil War veteran, helped implement the 'pacification' of the islands, earning him much hostility among the Filipinos. (His son, Douglas MacArthur, would eventually somewhat make up for what his father had done in the islands.)

In 1935, under the Tydings–McDuffie Act, the Philippines became a self-governing commonwealth with future full independence from the United States envisaged.

However, Japanese bombers began hitting airbases in the Philippines on 8 December 1941 and immediately destroyed half the American air forces on the ground. An invasion followed later that month, and the Americans fell back to the island fortress of Corregidor. Over 100,000 Americans were made prisoners of the Japanese for the duration of the war while MacArthur (the son) escaped via PT boat to Australia vowing, 'I shall return'. Many Americans and their Filipino allies were killed in the Bataan Death March.

The Japanese occupiers compelled a Filipino puppet government to declare war on the United States.

In October 1944, MacArthur made good on his promise wading ashore with a force of 160,000 US troops at Leyte. In spite of opposition from the US Navy, which preferred a more direct island-hopping strategy, MacArthur had secured the support of President Roosevelt for his return to the Philippines. Manila was almost completely destroyed in the battle with 60 per cent of the housing demolished by bombing, shelling or fire.

After the surrender of Japanese General Yamashita, however, problems persisted in the Philippines. On 4 July 1946, the independent Philippine Republic was proclaimed, but American influence was still strong. The Huks, who had resisted the Japanese, turned their attention against the Philippine government.

Major General Edward Lansdale, a former Madison Avenue professional who had worked with the OSS in the Second World War, helped lead a successful counter-insurgency against guerrillas in the Philippines during the Cold War.

In 1989, US fighter planes helped the Aquino government defeat a coup attempt.

For decades, the Philippines were home to large numbers

of US service personnel. Many Filipinos also served in the US military. Clark Air Base and the US naval facilities at Subic Bay were particularly important US bases. Both closed in 1992, but America still has military links with the Philippines. Under the 1999 Visiting Forces Agreement, US military personnel on a rotational basis have assisted the Philippines military in developing their expertise, among other things, for the fight against Islamist rebels.

The Guam and Hawaii National Guards are partnered with the Philippines.

Poland

Poland may be a long distance from the United States but the two countries have close links.

Tadeusz Kosciuszko (1746–1817) fought for America's independence from Britain in the American Revolution and then went on to fight for his homeland's independence from Russia. He directed the fortification of West Point and rose to become a brigadier general in the Continental Army. A statue of Kosciuszko stands atop the US Military Academy at West Point today.

Another Pole, Casimir Pulaski (1745–1779), also rose to the rank of brigadier general in the Continental Army and fought against both the Russians in Poland and the British in America. At the battle of Brandywine on 11 September 1777, he even helped save General George Washington from near-certain capture. Pulaski died from wounds received at the Battle of Savannah. For his efforts and for his bravery, he has often been called the 'father of the American cavalry'.

Kosciuszko, Pulaski, and the other Poles who fought on America's side in the Revolution, were major factors in giving Poland a good reputation in the United States. In November 1830 the Poles rose against up against Russia, with plenty of support from the United States. A young soldier in the US Army wrote this letter to his commanding officer in 1831:

> Having no longer any ties which can bind me to my native country – no prospects – nor any friends – I intend by the first opportunity to proceed to Paris with the view of obtaining, thro'

the interest of the Marquis de La Fayette, an appointment (if possible) in the Polish Army. In the event of the interference of France in behalf of Poland this may easily be effected – at all events it will be my only feasible plan of procedure.

The author of this letter was Edgar Allan Poe (who, in the end, never did make it to the fight in Poland).

However, a Georgia native, Dr Paul Fitzsimmons, did join the Polish army in the 1830–31 war against Russia where he served as a field surgeon.

It was all in vain, though. Russian forces crushed the Poles, and despite further armed resistance and continued sympathy in the United States, it would take until 1918 for an independent Poland once again to emerge. That Poland was able to do so, and received international recognition, was to a certain extent due to President Woodrow Wilson who championed the cause of the Poles. His thirteenth point (of his famous Fourteen) specified an independent Polish state.

In the turbulent period after the First World War, US forces played an occasional minor role in Poland. The USS *Pittsburgh*'s first visit to Estonia ended prematurely when US Navy Secretary Daniels instead sent it to Danzig, now the Polish port of Gdansk, to protect US citizens there. The efforts of Tadeusz Kosciuszko in the American Revolution against Britain were still being appreciated. American volunteer pilots, including Cedric E. Fauntleroy, joined the 7th Air Escadrille to fight the Russians in the Polish–Soviet War, and in reference to Kosciuszko, the squadron became known as the Kosciuszko Squadron.

However, when Hitler invaded Poland on 1 September 1939, followed by Stalin's invasion from the east on 18 September, the United States, not yet a part of the Second World War, remained a neutral observer.

For Poland, the war was a tragedy of almost unimaginable proportions. Suffering six years of war and occupation from 1939 to 1945, Poland lost over six million people in the Second World War, representing over 16 per cent of its total population in 1939.

Once America was in the war, it did make some efforts to help the Polish resistance. The OSS supplied arms and equipment from August until October of 1944 in support of the Warsaw revolt, and the USAAF dropped some supplies from the air. But the revolt was doomed. Stalin ordered a pause in the advance of the Red Army to allow the Nazis to crush the rebellion, thus eradicating a source of potential opposition to Stalin's plans for Communist domination of post-war Poland.

American planes also attacked German targets in what is now Poland. For instance, on two occasions, B-17s attacked a Focke-Wulf plant at what is now Malbork in Poland, and the USAAF bombed Stettin, which is, after border changes, now Szczecin in Poland.

The Cold War years saw assorted US covert operations inside Poland, including a fiasco when the CIA attempted to aid the Freedom and Independence Movement, known as WIN, in the early 1950s.

When the Solidarity trade union was formed in 1980, it received strong support from the American government. President Ronald Reagan, a former union leader himself (of the Screen Actors Guild), developed a strong personal friendship with both Lech Wałesa and the Polish pope, John Paul II.

Since the collapse of Communism in 1989, strong bilateral military links have formed between Poland and the United States. Poland joined NATO in 1999, and Poland sent large contingents to the wars in Iraq and Afghanistan. Today, the US even has a small permanent military presence stationed on Polish soil at Lask Air Base, although there has also been much arguing over US plans for a missile defence system based on Polish soil.

After Russia's occupation of the Crimea in 2014 and in light of ongoing conflict in eastern Ukraine, the US has played a major role in Operation Atlantic Resolve, a programme of multinational exercises and other military activity designed to show, in particular, commitment to the security of the Baltic states and Poland. In 2015, US troops moved through Poland while taking part in the Dragoon Ride, a drive along a route through Eastern Europe to demonstrate US commitment to the region.

The Illinois National Guard is partnered with Poland.

Portugal

Portugal has a long history of exploring the world, and at one stage, it had a major empire too.

Obviously US Navy ships have sailed the waters off Portugal and sometimes fought in them. On one occasion, in February 1815, the US frigate *Constitution* captured the British ship *Susannah* off Lisbon.

Over the centuries, American Navy ships have frequently called in at Portuguese ports. For instance, in 1904, four US battleships, USS *Alabama*, USS *Kearsarge*, USS *Maine* and USS *Iowa* paid a special visit to Lisbon to mark the entrance of the *infante* (Prince of Portugal) into Portuguese naval school.

In the First World War, Portugal, like the United States, was neutral at first but later joined the Allies in fighting the Central Powers. Portuguese troops arrived at the Western Front in 1917, the same year as the American Expeditionary Forces.

In the Second World War, despite being a long-standing British ally, Portugal remained neutral. Consequently, Lisbon became a hotbed for espionage intrigue during the war. The Japanese alone are said to have had 200 agents based in the city. 'Wild Bill' Donovan set up OSS stations in Lisbon, and the OSS in Portugal managed to infiltrate the Japanese embassy.

But America's closest military involvement with Portugal during the Second World War, and indeed after it, wasn't on the mainland of Portugal but on the Azores, strategically located Portuguese islands in the Atlantic.

In May 1941, prior to the Pearl Harbor attack, President Roosevelt had ordered the War Department to create War Plan Gray, a plan for a US invasion of the Azores. The president feared that the Germans might try to take control of these Atlantic islands to attack Allied shipping. In the end, it was never implemented.

By 1943, however, Portugal had granted the US basing rights in the Azores. Over 2,000 US planes stopped at Lajes Airbase over the course of the war. And US Naval blimps flew ASW air patrols in neighbouring waters from Port Lyautey during the war. Meanwhile in the seas off the Azores, the US Navy was hunting U-boats too.

Portugal became a founding member of NATO in 1949 and remains one today. There are various links between the US military and the Portuguese military, including joint exercises, aviation training, many port visits and assorted agreements. Portugal sent national guards to Iraq for a time and troops to Afghanistan.

Lajes Airbase, though it has recently been downsized, remains home to the 65th Air Base Wing to this day.

Qatar

The country of Qatar is now one of the wealthiest in the world. It was part of a British sphere of influence until 1971.

With the decline of British influence in Qatar, US influence increased. The United States opened an embassy in Doha in 1973. US interest in Qatar was inevitably boosted by the fall of America's ally, the Shah of Iran in 1979 and the conflict with Saddam over Kuwait.

The war to liberate Kuwait was a key milestone in the developing friendship between the United States and Qatar. For instance, Qatar sent troops to join the coalition forces, with a battalion involved in the fighting at Khafji, and it helped in other senses as well, including hosting US aircraft and their crews.

After the 1991 Gulf War, many US bases in Saudi Arabia were repositioned to Qatar. Qatar is the high-tech home to US Central Command (CENTCOM). The strategy for Operation Iraqi Freedom and Operation Enduring Freedom (Afghanistan) was formulated largely from Qatar.

The United States operates major facilities in Qatar at Camp As Sayliyah and Al Udeid Air Base.

On 15 October 2007, a Patriot missile based in Qatar was accidently fired in a training exercise. The missile landed in the backyard of the Qatari Minister of Defence. Oops! Fortunately, no one was injured.

Forces from Qatar joined the United States and NATO in 2011 in operations to remove Gaddafi from power in Libya.

In 2013, America signed a new Defence Cooperation agreement to continue joint training and exercises with Qatar, such as Exercise Eagle Resolve 13, which was conducted at various locations in Qatar, Bahrain and the UAE in April and May 2013.

Republic of the Congo

This one is the other Congo country, distinct from the Democratic Republic of the Congo (formerly called Zaire; *see*

Democratic Republic of the Congo). The Republic of Congo's capital is Brazzaville.

It used to be a French colony. Because it was one of the earliest French territories to support the Free French instead of the pro-German Vichy French government in France, after the 1940 German invasion of France, Brazzaville was, from 1940–43, interestingly, a sort of capital of the Free French.

The US has had less military involvement with this Congo than with the other Congo. However, it has had just a little.

In 1993, a USAF C-5 Galaxy flew into Brazzaville with heavy equipment for Belgian paratroopers preparing for a possible rescue mission in next-door Zaire, and in March 1997, US troops were sent to Brazzaville in preparation for an evacuation from Zaire.

Then, in June 1997 when fighting broke out in Brazzaville itself, the USAF flew in with a team of communications and security experts and flew out with civilians, thirty of whom were Americans, and a dog. The operations commander reported later that nobody had asked the nationality of the dog.

Romania

In Romania you can find Transylvania (as well as many other things obviously), the legendary home of vampires and actual birthplace of Vlad Dracul, who had the not very PR-friendly nickname Vlad the Impaler.

During the First World War Romania initially remained neutral but later, influenced by Queen Marie, joined the Allied side. As a result, most of Romania ended up being occupied by enemy troops in the ensuing conflict. However, Queen Marie, with the assistance of her friend, the American dance pioneer Loie Fuller, got hold of a major American loan that helped the Romanians to resist.

When the Russian Revolution eventually took Russia out of the war, Romania found it could not fight on alone, and it was forced to seek peace with the enemy. It only re-entered the war (on the Allied side) on 10 November, a day before the armistice. Better late than never.

After the Allied victory, Romania received some compensation for all its suffering. Thanks largely once again to the energetic efforts of Queen Marie, Romania acquired large tracts of territory that had previously been part of the Austro-Hungarian and Russian Empires.

In 1939, Romania again initially tried to remain neutral. Marshal Antonescu, however, led a fascist coup in 1940, and this time Romania ended up on the German side. Bad choice. Romanian forces participated in Operation Barbarossa, the invasion of the Soviet Union in 1941, and Romanian oil fields were a vital strategic resource to the Axis.

On 5 June 1942, the US Congress unanimously authorised a declaration of war against Romania and it wasn't long before the US was targeting Romania militarily. USAAF B-24 bombers based in Egypt began bombing the Ploesti oil fields in 1942, and Bucharest was bombed beginning in April 1944.

Romania, however, was not going to hang on for ultimate defeat and devastating destruction as Germany did. On 23 August 1944, with Soviet tanks streaming towards Bucharest, King Michael of Romania, in co-ordination with Romanian opposition politicians and Communists, staged a successful coup, switched sides and declared war on Germany.

The OSS staged Operation Bughouse a week later arriving in Bucharest to assess damage to the Ploesti refineries and to gather intelligence. Two former college professors managed to locate forty intact mailbags full of German military documents at a Luftwaffe headquarters. Even more important, OSS members also helped to retrieve some 1,350 downed Allied airmen in Romania.

The Romanian volte-face did not, however, prevent the Red Army from moving into Romania. At first, OSS agents were able to hand out free cigarettes to Russian soldiers in exchange for information, but the Soviets soon forced the American teams out of the country.

In 1946, a newly formed CIA attempted to help form an underground resistance to the Soviet occupiers. The former Romanian foreign minister and other colleagues were smuggled out of Romania to Austria. Soviet intelligence services, however, immediately cracked down on the covert operations.

Hundreds of thousands of Romanians were imprisoned during the Communist era. President Nicolae Ceauşescu attempted to steer a more independent course for Romania within the Warsaw Pact, and even condemned the Soviet crackdown in

Prague in 1968. Because of that, and despite the brutality of his regime, Ceauşescu was at times popular with some Western governments.

In November 1989, free passage was allowed through the Berlin Wall, and its demolition started almost immediately. In December 1989, the Romanian revolution erupted. On Christmas Day 1989, Ceauşescu and his wife, Elena, were executed by firing squad. And a few days later, two C-130s flew into Bucharest bringing medical supplies to help those wounded in the fighting.

Since the revolution, close military links have developed between the United States and Romania. All four US service branches have conducted exercises within Romania. Romania has been a NATO member since 2004. The Romanian contingent deployed to Iraq was among the last to leave that country and Romania sent troops to Afghanistan. The US has an anti-missile base now under construction in southern Romania.

The Alabama National Guard is partnered with Romania.

Russia

Those who lived through the Cold War are so used to the image of the Soviet Union as a heavily defended superpower, bristling with nukes, and probably prepared to use them if ever invaded, that the idea America has ever invaded Russia can seem hard to believe, and yet it has.

During the Crimean War, many Americans sympathised with Russia in its battle against Britain, France and Turkey, and Americans even sent some minor assistance to the Russians.

Occasional contacts between the US Navy and Russia continued throughout the nineteenth and early twentieth centuries. A diplomatic squabble saw the USS *Prometheus* arrive in Kronstadt, St Petersburg's port, in 1809 to calm the situation down. On the other hand, in 1866, the US sent the monitor USS *Miantonomoh* (rather slowly) as far as Kronstadt to thank the Russians for supporting the Union side during the American Civil War and to congratulate Tsar Alexander II (who emancipated the serfs) on luckily escaping a recent assassination attempt.

During the war of 1877–78 between Russia and Turkey, America supplied the Russians with naval ships and weapons.

President Teddy Roosevelt helped to broker a peace between Russia and Japan with the Treaty of Portsmouth that ended the Russo–Japanese War of 1904–05. Roosevelt even won a Nobel Prize for his efforts.

However, in the period leading up to the First World War, tensions were rising between the Russians and the US over anti-Semitic actions in Russia.

There wasn't to be much crossover between Russia and the United States during the First World War. By the time America entered the war in April 1917, the tsar had already abdicated, and Russia was in the grip of revolution. Nevertheless, the US did manage to send some war material and loans to Russia. After Lenin signed the Treaty of Brest–Litovsk, dropping out of the Triple Entente and making peace with the Kaiser's Germany, some of Russia's former allies felt betrayed. Some of them felt inclined to do something about it. Winston Churchill spoke about trying to 'strangle the Bolshevik baby in its cradle'.

The American president wasn't entirely happy about the situation either. In 1918, Woodrow Wilson ordered American forces to form part of the Allied North Russia Expeditionary Force that was being readied to support the White forces that were battling the Bolshevik Red forces in Russia. American sailors first landed in Murmansk from the USS *Olympia* on 8 June 1918.

Wilson had, for one of the few times in US history, granted authority to allow American troops to serve under foreign leadership. In November 1918, just as the war in Europe was coming to a close, British Major General Edmund Ironside took over command of the force, what became known as the Polar Bear Expedition – great name, but not, as it was to turn out, such a great success. In his diary, Ironside expressed doubts about his mission comparing the advance into Russia to sticking your hand into a huge sticky pudding. And certainly things were going to get very sticky for the Polar Bear Expedition.

After initial success, stiffening Bolshevik resistance rapidly put the intervention forces in an increasingly desperate situation. Throughout the bitter Russian winter of 1918, General Ironside had to order his forces to retreat into a smaller and smaller area. Ultimately they would be fighting just to survive.

Nevertheless, as in almost all wars, there were occasional brief, happier interludes. Godfrey Anderson was a Michigan farm boy who served in the 337th Field Hospital Unit in the Polar Bear Expedition. He describes a Christmas dinner in Shenkursk that featured fricassee of rabbit and a chocolate layer cake. A balalaika orchestra and a dozen or so Russian girls were invited to attend and dance with the troops. On occasions, fraternisation could lead to more; Private Joseph Chinzi of the 339th Supply Company married a Russian bride in Archangel.

A further 8,000 American soldiers were sent to Vladivostok in the east, along with a variety of other Allied troops, including Japanese. US General Graves had more modest, and perhaps more realistic, ambitions than some of the other Allied generals in Siberia, and American troops there ended up protecting the Trans-Siberian railroad from Bolshevik raids. Nevertheless, the intervention in Siberia proved ultimately as pointless as the intervention in northern Russia, as chaos and conspiracy weakened the White Forces and the Red Forces advanced.

Wilson feared that the presence of American troops in Russia after the First World War had ended could impede settlement of the Versailles Peace Treaty, in which he had sought the creation of a League of Nations. The war to end all wars was finished. The Americans wanted all their boys to come home, and there was a growing feeling in the United States that the Russian intervention was a disaster that had failed to achieve anything very positive. Eventually, the US did pull its forces out.

Today, although you can find a polar bear sculpture in a Detroit cemetery, the Allied North Russia Expedition is largely forgotten in the United States. The motto of the US 339th regiment, however, is in Cyrillic and means 'the bayonet decides'.

Obviously, after all this, things weren't going to be hugely friendly between Russia and the United States, and as late as 1959, on a visit to the United States, Nikita Khrushchev decided he needed to bring up the subject.

Finally, though, in 1933, the US recognised the Soviet Union. And, of course, there are few things to make you feel better about a former enemy than finding yourself fighting a new enemy with your former enemy on your side, especially in a fight on the scale of a world war.

On 22 June 1941, as Adolf Hitler launched his Panzers into the Soviet Union, Russia suddenly found itself at war with Germany. President Franklin D. Roosevelt, already sympathetic to the Allied cause, started the process of aiding Russia. Then shortly after 7 December 1941, Hitler declared war on America, and it suddenly found itself allied with Russia, and the process of providing aid to Russia accelerated. Lend-Lease supplies, including thousands of aircraft and tanks and hundreds of thousands of trucks and even thirteen million pairs of boots, were sent to Russia. This played a vital role in helping the Red Army destroy the German army on the Eastern Front.

There was occasional co-operation on the combat front as well. In Operation Frantic, US bombers based in Britain and Italy used Soviet airbases to land and refuel after bombing missions. (Since the Soviet airbases involved were in what is now Ukraine, we'll deal with this further in that chapter.)

As the Second World War ended and the Cold War began, friendly military co-operation came to an end. In the decades after 1945, there were to be assorted US operations in and over Russian territory and in Russian waters, but such covert activities are largely beyond the remit of this book. We'll just mention here Gary Powers, shot down in his U-2 near Sverdlovsk in Russia on 1 May 1960. The SR-71 Blackbird spy plane, which could fly at speeds over Mach 3.0 at 80,000 feet, was a significant improvement over the U-2.

Since the end of the Cold War, relations have at times been more friendly between the Russians and the US. On 9 May 2010, for instance, a friendly invasion by American troops occurred in Russia. The 2nd Battalion of the 18th Infantry Regiment and a naval band participated in the Victory Day parade in Moscow to mark the sixty-fifth anniversary of the end of the Second World War.

The crisis over Crimea and eastern Ukraine has, however, recently caused major problems between Russia and the United States.

Rwanda

Most will be aware of part of Rwanda's history, the very worst part of it. The genocide of 1994 is one of the most shocking and horrifying events of the post-war era.

In recent years the US has had a little military involvement in this small central African nation, for example, helping with training for peacekeeping.

Fortunately, Rwanda has been for some time in a situation where it can send peacekeepers to other countries, rather than other countries being required to send peacekeepers to Rwanda. America has trained Rwandan peacekeepers that were headed for Darfur as part of UNAMID, the United Nations Mission in Darfur, and helped with transport flying supplies for the Rwandan peacekeepers from Kigali, the capital of Rwanda, to Darfur.

Samoa

The Samoan Islands in the South Pacific are divided into two groups, each a separate political entity, American Samoa and the Independent State of Samoa, or more commonly, just Samoa. Until 1997, Samoa was called Western Samoa, a term some still use. It can all get slightly confusing.

You won't be surprised to know that America does have strong connections with American Samoa, but it has actually also had quite a lot of military involvement with the Independent State of Samoa.

It started early and it started pretty violently. As early as February 1841, marines from the USS *Peacock* landed on the island of Upolu and burned three villages there after the death of an American sailor. But it was later in the nineteenth century that the US managed to get even more seriously involved.

In 1888, the First Samoan Civil War was raging with local factions fighting each other. Western powers, including America, played a role as well. Since America had an interest in and interests on the islands, marines were sent ashore to Apia to protect American lives and property. Things were already tense between the US and the Germans (one of the other Western powers involved) when shelling had damaged American-owned property, and in 1889, the US could potentially have ended up in armed conflict with Germany long before the First World War. The Germans had sent warships, SMS *Adler*, SMS *Olga* and SMS *Eber* to Apia harbour, and America had replied with USS *Nipsic*, USS *Vandalia* and USS *Trenton*. The British, the third Western power involved, had sent HMS *Calliope*. The German and US ships were in a tense stand-off for months until finally the weather decided matters. A devastating cyclone hit on 15 March, sinking four of the US and German ships and forcing the remaining two onto the beach. Only HMS *Calliope* was left afloat. By the time it was all over, nobody could really be bothered any more to fight, and frankly they didn't have anything much left to fight with even if they could have been bothered.

However, that was not to be the end of the nineteenth-century superpower dispute over Samoa. By 1899, fighting between local factions was raging once again, with the United States and Britain throwing their (considerable) weight behind Prince Tanu and with the Germans supporting his opponent, Mata'afa Iosefo. British and US naval forces, including the USS *Philadelphia*, shelled Apia in March 1899, and then US and British marines and sailors along with Tanu's followers pursued Mata'afa Iosefo's forces. What followed was the Battle of Vailele, in which the American, British and Tanu's forces were ambushed by large numbers of attackers.

The American commander and three other Americans were killed (including Ensign John Monaghan, a graduate of Gonzaga University and the US Naval Academy who was later commemorated with a statue in Spokane, Washington), and the attacking party had to withdraw. Shortly afterwards, a peace deal was reached, which split Samoa into German and American areas while Britain received territory elsewhere. The American part became American Samoa, and the German portion was captured by New Zealand forces at the beginning of the First World War, long before America entered the war.

During the Second World War, in addition to having forces in American Samoa, the US had marines based in the other part of Samoa, as well as building an airfield and seaplane base there. The country became independent as Western Samoa in 1962.

In 2013, the amphibious dock-landing USS *Pearl Harbor* visited Apia for Pacific Partnership 2013.

San Marino

A tiny country of just twenty-four square miles, San Marino is well-known for its stamps, but it also has a fascinating history and America has played a part (a fairly small part, but still a part) in that.

To protect itself, San Marino has its own Crossbowman Corps, and even today, the San Marino Crossbow Confederation continues this proud tradition.

The nineteenth century saw a few interesting minor historical links between San Marino and the United States. In 1849, on one of Garibaldi's early (and unsuccessful) forays into Italy, the Italian patriot found himself forced to retreat with his men into Sammarinese (yes, that's the adjective) territory to avoid the pursuing Austrian forces. Commanding a rearguard operation against the enemy was Colonel Hugh Forbes. He was an Englishman, but he was later to play a very significant part in US history when he was recruited as a military expert by one John Brown, keen to fight slavery in the South.

Not long after, in 1861, San Marino wrote to Abraham Lincoln offering him honorary Sammarinese citizenship. Lincoln, in May 1861, with a few other minor distractions on his mind at the time, like the start of the American Civil War, still took the time to write warmly to San Marino to accept the offer and to comment on the two countries' shared experience of being republics.

However, it's the twentieth century that brought US forces to San Marino. Just a bit. The country remained neutral in the Second World War. However, the major Italian port and communications hub of Rimini is situated just a few miles to the north-east of San Marino, and targets there were repeatedly attacked by Allied bombers. Since many of them were coming from bases in Algeria or Tunisia, it seems likely that US bomber crews must on some occasions have flown through Sammarinese airspace, even if unintentionally. Then on 26 June 1944, in a tragic accident, Allied bombers accidentally bombed San Marino.

As Allied forces advanced north through Italy, the land war grew gradually closer to San Marino's borders. With British and Commonwealth forces poised to take Rimini in Operation Olive, in early September, German forces moved into San Marino. The subsequent battle for San Marino was short but sharp, and by 21 September, Allied forces were mopping up the last German soldiers in San Marino. That same day, the first American soldiers also entered San Marino. Alfred Connor Bowman, an American officer, was there to help ensure that the people of San Marino were fed during the coming winter. He rapidly brought thirteen trucks loaded with supplies into the small country. It seems appropriate that the first American that came to liberated San Marino, the land of the crossbowman, was a Bowman himself.

São Tomé and Príncipe

São Tomé and Príncipe is a country that consists basically of two big islands and some little ones. The two big islands (which are not surprisingly, São Tomé and, yep, Príncipe) are situated in the Gulf of Guinea, sort of south of Nigeria and west of Gabon.

Príncipe, or Prince's Island, as Americans tended to know it then, was a key point on the US Africa Squadron's patrol routes when the US government finally ordered its navy to act against the transatlantic slave trade. Prince's Island regularly appears in accounts of the Africa Squadron's operations, and São Tomé (or St Thomas) also sometimes gets a mention. On 29 September 1857 the USS *Cumberland* spotted a suspicious-looking ship, the *Pearl*, off the coast of São Tomé. It was battle stations on the *Cumberland*, and Lieutenant Greene boarded the *Pearl*, only to let her go when he found her papers in order. Slight anti-climax. The Africa Squadron hadn't freed any slaves that time, but, to be fair, it wasn't always so unlucky.

Rather more recently, the US Navy has helped the São Tomé and Príncipe Coast Guard install a new surface surveillance system, and the crew of the USCG Cutter *Dallas* have helped train coast guard personnel from São Tomé and Príncipe.

Saudi Arabia

Saudi Arabia has, of course, long been a focus of American interest in the Middle East.

The United States began diplomatic relations with Saudi Arabia in 1933. That same year, the California Arabian Standard Oil Company (later ARAMCO) was formed to develop Saudi oil resources.

During the Second World War, Saudi Arabia remained technically neutral but also supplied Allied forces with masses of critical petroleum products.

Mussolini's Italy joined the Axis side in 1940, and on 19 October of that year, four Italian bombers (Regia Aeronautica) took off from the island of Rhodes to attack Middle East oil facilities. The Italian bomber pilots bombed oil refineries in Saudi Arabia and Bahrain and then flew on to airfields in Italian East Africa (Eritrea) – the longest bombing run in aviation history at the time and one that exposed Saudi Arabia's military vulnerability.

The Second World War saw the real beginning of US military involvement with Saudi Arabia. For instance, the Saudi kingdom allowed America to operate an air transport facility at Jeddah as part of a network that stretched across Africa and the Middle East and permitted the construction of a US airfield near Dhahran.

In 1945, President Franklin D. Roosevelt, on his way back from the Yalta Conference, travelled on the USS *Quincy* to the Great Bitter Lake on the Suez Canal. He was there to meet three important regional leaders – Emperor Haile Selassie of Ethiopia, King Farouk of Egypt and King Abdul Aziz ibn Saud of Saudi Arabia. The American military would protect the Saudi kingdom, while their oil would help fuel the tanks, planes and ships of the US military. The broad outlines of America's pact with Saudi Arabia, despite profound differences between the two nations, have now lasted seventy years through many tumultuous times.

During their discussions, the Saudi king warned President Roosevelt that the Arabs would fight if the Jewish settlements in the British-controlled Palestine Mandate were expanded. Thus, the creation of Israel in 1948 with American support put strains on US links with Saudi Arabia, particularly during the Arab–Israeli Wars of the Cold War era.

However, America and Saudi Arabia still had shared interests. For instance, during the Yemen Civil War, the royalist and conservative Saudi Arabia clashed with Nasser's Communist-supported revolutionary Egypt, and each ended up supporting a different side in the war. President Kennedy threw US support behind the Saudis. USAF planes were mobilised to deter Nasser's Egypt from further action against Saudi Arabia.

Relations between the United States and Saudi Arabia reached a low point after the 1973 Arab–Israeli War, but eventually the relationship stabilised again. The Iranian Revolution created a new power feared by both Saudi Arabia and the United States, and in the 1980s America and Saudi Arabia found themselves jointly immersed in arming the Afghan mujahideen and helping them fight the Soviets in Afghanistan and helping the Afghan regime they supported.

During the Iran–Iraq War, Saudi Arabia backed Iraq. On 5 June 1984, a US AWACS plane detected an Iranian fighter approaching Saudi's offshore oil facilities in the Gulf. Saudi aircraft intercepted the Iranian plane and shot it down.

However, when America really went to war in Saudi Arabia, it wasn't Iran that was the problem. Instead it was, of course, Iraq. In August 1990 Saddam Hussein's Iraqi Army invaded Kuwait and threatened Saudi Arabia (*see* Kuwait). President George H. W. Bush led an international coalition that responded with Operation Desert Shield. In January 1991, Saddam Hussein ordered Iraqi forces to attack across the Saudi border. Saudi and Qatari troops, aided by US Marines, artillery and airpower, fought the Battle of Khafji. The Iraqi forces were repulsed at a cost of twenty-six American lives and eighteen Saudi lives.

American airpower based in Saudi played a decisive role in the First Gulf War. A-10 Warthogs, championed by the maverick USAF Colonel John Boyd, flew missions from Saudi bases destroying over 900 Iraqi tanks.

In the course of the war, over half a million US troops were deployed to Saudi Arabia. Many stayed after Iraq was expelled from Kuwait in Operation Desert Storm. Thousands of US troops stayed on to help enforce the no-fly zone over neighbouring Iraq in Operation Southern Watch. The Saudi king and government supported the American alliance, but many in the Arab streets were troubled. To some, of course, this represented an American occupation of the Muslim holy land and was one of the grievances behind Osama bin Laden's attack on 9/11. Indeed, fifteen of the nineteen hijackers in the 9/11 attack, along with their mastermind, were Saudi nationals.

Attacks on US personnel took place in Saudi territory too. For instance, in 1996, a huge truck bomb destroyed part of the Khobar Towers complex and killed nineteen US servicemen. And in 2004, the US consulate in Jeddah was attacked.

The USAF operated Prince Sultan Air Force Base from 1990 until 2003.

Most American military personnel left Saudi Arabia in 2003.

Small numbers are still based there, some of them apparently connected with the campaign of drone strikes in Yemen.

Saudi Arabia remains a significant ally of the United States. The two countries share interests in oil and nervousness about Iran. Military links continue to be strong. The United States has been actively training Saudi defence forces from 1953 to the present, and the Saudi military has purchased large quantities of weaponry and military equipment from American manufacturers, including aircraft, armoured vehicles and air defence weapons.

Senegal

In the fourteenth to sixteenth centuries, Senegal was home to the Jolof Empire.

Its location on West Africa's coast meant it was involved in the slave trade, and the US Navy's anti-slavery squadron patrolled the seas off Senegal in the nineteenth century. Gorée, in Senegal, was a significant slaving port, and in 2013, President Obama paid an emotional visit to the island.

The area eventually became a French colony, and when America entered the Second World War it was under Vichy French control. However, Operation Torch, the Allied invasion of Morocco and Algeria, changed all that. The Free French took control of the area, and America was free to fly planes there. This was important as the transatlantic route for ferrying cargo and aircraft to the Middle East had been forced to use a more southern route, but with the Allies in control of Senegal, a shorter route could now be used. US forces first used an existing French airbase at Eknes Field, but then in 1944, they opened Mallard Field, which became the international airport of Dakar, Senegal's capital.

Senegal became independent from France in 1960, and in the decades since then, the US has had some minor military involvement with the country.

Among recent measures within Senegal, the US military has trained Senegalese troops for peacekeeping missions under its Africa Contingency Operations Training and Assistance programme, and the United States has recently been upgrading the peacekeeping operations training centre at Dodji in Senegal.

American troops have participated in exercises in Senegal; for example, in 2013 US Marines conducted amphibious landings in Senegal.

The Vermont National Guard is partnered with Senegal.

Serbia

Many will be aware that the United States bombed Serbia when Milosevic was in power there, but America actually has a long and much less well-known history of involvement with Serbia in wartime.

In 1941 the Germans invaded Yugoslavia which at that time included Serbia (among others) and occupied the country. In reaction to that, two resistance movements emerged in Yugoslavia to fight the Germans – the Royalist Chetniks under General Mihailović and the Communist Partisans under Tito.

America was involved with helping both groups in Serbia sending supplies and OSS teams to help them. Colonel Richard Weil Jr was sent to Tito's headquarters to assess him. Weil decided that Tito was both nationalist and Communist but more nationalist than Communist and emerged with a letter of greeting to President Franklin D. Roosevelt. Both Partisans and Chetniks helped save American airmen shot down over Serbia, and in a major success, hundreds of airmen were successfully airlifted out in US planes from an airstrip at the Chetnik headquarters at Pranjani in 1944. Many US aircraft in the air over Serbia during the war were destined for crucial targets elsewhere, such as the oil fields at Ploesti in Romania, but they also hit targets within Serbia. Targets in Belgrade, for instance, were bombed heavily on a number of occasions.

Partisans and Chetniks not only fought the Germans, however; they also fought each other. This was of less concern to the British and American governments than fighting the Germans. In the end, the British government decided that Tito's Partisans were more effective in their attacks on the Germans. The British therefore committed themselves to the Partisans and abandoned Mihailović and the Chetniks. The American government was less clearly decided about the matter but went along with their key allies in the end. After the war, Mihailović was accused of treason by the new Communist government and shot. President Harry Truman posthumously awarded him the Legion of Merit for saving American airmen.

American airmen were in action again over Serbia not that long ago. After an ultimatum to Milosevic over Kosovo was rejected (*see* Kosovo), NATO's bombing campaign commenced on 24 March 1999. US aircraft and cruise missiles played a key role attacking many sites in Serbia, including many in Belgrade. In the end, on 3 June Milosevic agreed to withdraw his forces from Kosovo and allow NATO troops in.

The conflict in Serbia witnessed the first substantial use of Predator drones by the CIA to monitor Serbian troop movements; this also allowed President Clinton a live feed in the White House. Since the conflict about Kosovo, the US and Serbia have now re-established some military links.

The Ohio National Guard is partnered with Serbia.

Seychelles

An island nation with some stunningly beautiful scenery, Prince William and Kate Middleton spent their honeymoon in the Seychelles. America has had US military personnel visiting and based there as well.

The US Air Force built a tracking station on Mahé in 1963. It only finally closed down in 1996.

In 1976 the Seychelles became fully independent from Britain, and then in 1977 the socialist France-Albert René came to power in Seychelles. Assorted alleged attempts to topple René followed. It's hard to know what the United States and the CIA may have known about any of these plans. In 1993, multi-party elections were held, which the involved parties and international observers accepted as free and fair. René was declared the victor, and went on to hold on to power in elections in 1998 and 2001.

The US Navy has been a regular visitor to the Seychelles in recent years. The USS *Bainbridge* and the USS *Carter Hall* both visited in 2013, and the Seychelles Coast Guard has trained with US Navy personnel.

The United States has flown drones from bases in the Seychelles intermittently since 2009.

Sierra Leone

Yes, the mountain range, or 'sierra', of the lion.

It was the British in the late eighteenth century who started a settlement on the African coast for various groups of people, including freed slaves (some of them loyalists from America fleeing the American Revolution). So, it was effectively a British (and somewhat American) version of Liberia. Or, since the settlement in Sierra Leone started before the one in Liberia, Liberia is the American version of what was happening in Sierra Leone.

The US Navy's anti-slaving patrols operated in the vicinity in the nineteenth century. Eventually, the whole area became a British colony until independence in 1961.

By 1991, with a vicious civil war raging in neighbouring Liberia, a group called the Revolutionary United Front (RUF) launched their own rebellion in Sierra Leone. A decade of war and instability followed.

In 1992, after a coup, President Clinton sent in US planes to rescue Americans and others. In Operation Silver Anvil, US Special Forces flew into Sierra Leone and evacuated hundreds of people.

After another coup in 1997, the RUF and those who'd mounted the coup took Freetown, the capital of Sierra Leone. This time, Clinton sent in the USS *Kearsarge* Amphibious Ready Group, which evacuated thousands of Americans and others, and troops from ECOMOG went in to recapture Freetown for the government.

The Lomé Peace Accord was signed in 1999 but it didn't stop the war, and in 2000 the RUF were once again advancing on Freetown. Once again, international forces went in to resist them. This time Clinton sent in a navy patrol craft to be ready to help evacuate Americans and a C-17 aircraft to fly supplies to the international forces.

Finally, decisive action by British troops defeated the RUF, and the war was officially declared finished in January 2002.

In recent years, America has developed more links with Sierra Leone's military. For instance, in 2013, a US-trained battalion deployed to Somalia as part of AMISOM, the African Union Mission in Somalia.

Singapore

The US already had a consulate in Singapore in 1836, long before it became the independent country it is today.

Of course, for much of the nineteenth and twentieth centuries, this great city was controlled by Britain, and its loss to the Japanese on 15 February 1942 was almost the same kind of shock to Britons as the attack on Pearl Harbor was to Americans.

The recapture of Singapore was inevitably more of a British priority than an American one, but American planes did take part in bombing and mining targets in and around Singapore. In one attack on 1 February 1945, eighty-eight Superfortresses, each carrying at least four 1,000 lb bombs, were in the air over Singapore. Sixty-seven of these bombed the primary target, the Admiralty IX Floating Dry Dock at the navy yard, damaging it severely and setting light to a large ship inside it. The remaining twenty-one B-29s bombed a different part of the naval base causing extensive destruction. One B-29 was lost to Japanese fighters and another was badly damaged.

In recent years, America has developed close military links with Singapore. American and Singaporean troops conduct an annual bilateral military exercise, and Singaporean troops served in Afghanistan. American naval and air units have made use of Sembawang base, and a logistical support group for the US Seventh Fleet is based at Sembawang. This happens to be the same base those B-29s were bombing on that February day during the Second World War. The US Navy also makes use of Singapore's newer naval base at Changi, and the USAF has made extensive use of Paya Lebar Air Base, which is home to the air operations of the 497th Combat Training Squadron.

Slovakia

Yep, this is the other half of what used to be Czechoslovakia.

As covered in the chapter on the Czech Republic, Americans played a significant role in the establishment of an independent Czechoslovakia after the First World War. American volunteers joined Czechoslovak units that fought alongside the Allies in the war and helped gain sympathy for the cause of Czechoslovakia.

President Woodrow Wilson's support for granting autonomy to the people who had previously been part of the Austro-Hungarian Empire was crucial as well.

In 1993, at the same time as Yugoslavia was in the process of tearing itself apart to the south, the state of Czechoslovakia split peacefully into its two constituent parts, a Czech state and a Slovak state. Peacefully, but not without controversy – the decision to split the country was made without a referendum in Slovakia.

However, this was not the first time since the formation of Czechoslovakia that Slovakia had been separated from the Czech part of the country. After the debacle of the Munich Agreement in 1938, in March 1939, the Slovak Republic declared independence, and on the next day the Germans occupied the rest of Czechoslovakia. The government of the new Slovak Republic was, however, very much under German influence and became an ally of Germany, sending troops to fight alongside the Germans in their invasions of Poland and the Soviet Union. On 13 December 1941 (two days after Germany), Slovakia declared war on the United States.

As the US bombing campaign across Europe got going, facilities inside the Slovak Republic that were important for the Axis war effort made the list of targets. In one mission, on 16 June 1944, American bombers attacked the Apollo Oil Refinery in Bratislava.

Soon, Americans were also to be involved in fighting on the ground in Slovakia.

As the Red Army pushed west in 1944, local resistance to the Germans and their collaborators increased. On 29 August 1944 the Slovak National Uprising began as Slovak troops and partisans tried to liberate their country. Early September saw a number of successes for the rebels, and the US and the Soviet Union tried to send help. Later in September, America sent in an OSS team to liaise with the rebels and on 17 October B-17s with a fighter escort landed at Tri Duby airbase to offload supplies and more OSS men and pick up escaped American aircrew.

However, the Soviet advance in the east stalled, and vicious German counter-attacks in October eventually largely crushed the rebels.

A tragic fate awaited the OSS members. They headed for the mountains and were awaiting an OSS supply drop on Christmas

Day when they were betrayed and captured by the Germans. Only two Americans escaped to the Russian lines. Others were taken to Mauthausen Concentration Camp, brutally tortured, and then executed.

On 4 April 1945, the Red Army entered Bratislava, and post-war Czechoslovakia became part of the Soviet sphere of influence.

During the 1968 Soviet invasion of Czechoslovakian territory, the United States, pre-occupied with the Vietnam War, did not intervene. Americans did, however, cheer on the Czechoslovak hockey team in its famous victory over the Soviets at the 1968 Winter Olympics in Grenoble, France.

Slovakia joined NATO in 2004. Slovakia criticised the United States over its 2003 invasion of Iraq but sent troops to Afghanistan as part of the Allied coalition. And in recent years, the US and Slovak military have teamed up to conduct assorted training operations and exercises.

The Indiana National Guard is partnered with Slovakia.

Slovenia

Slovenia, with its capital of Ljubljana, contains the northernmost point of what used to be Yugoslavia and has Italy to its west, Austria to its north, Hungary to its east, and Croatia to its south.

During the First World War, Slovenia was all part of the Austro-Hungarian Empire, but the war would change that. For much of the war, Italians had faced the Austro-Hungarians in the area of the River Isonzo, and some vicious fighting had already taken place in the region of what is now the Slovenian frontier. One of the battles, a huge disaster for the Italians, took place in 1917 near Caporetto, the Italian name for the Slovenian town of Kobarid. Caporetto features in *Farewell to Arms* by Hemingway, who served as an ambulance driver on the Italian front and was wounded by mortar fire.

In October 1918, American troops of the 332nd Infantry Regiment were part of the Vittorio-Veneto Offensive and, in the last days of the war, found themselves advancing eastwards towards what is now the Slovenian–Italian border. By the time the Austro-Hungarian Empire disintegrated, Slovenia had already broken away to become part of the state of Slovenes, Croats and Serbs, which later joined with Serbia and other territory, and eventually all became Yugoslavia. But in the chaotic period after the armistice, before the Allied powers had decided exactly how the Austro-Hungarian empire should be split up and what new states and new borders should be internationally recognised, American forces were either in Slovenia or certainly very close to it, near Gorizia and at Rijeka. So there or thereabouts.

Something curiously similar, in fact, was also to happen at the end of the Second World War. The war had seen assorted US activity over and in Slovenia. For instance, on 9 March 1945, American bombers with fighter escorts bombed the marshalling yard in the Slovenian capital, Ljubljana. And on the ground, the OSS carried out vital activity. In November 1943, an OSS team was parachuted into partisan-held territory near Ljubljana. Its primary objective was that, in 1944 and the vital period around D-Day, it could report on German troop movements up from the Balkans.

However, in the last weeks of the war, US ground forces once again found themselves advancing on the Italian front towards Slovenia; this time they went right into what is now the country. Unlike in 1918, where Italy had been a victorious Allied power and Slovenia had been part of the defeated Austro-Hungarian power, Italy had abandoned Germany in 1943 after being invaded by the Allies, whereas Tito's Yugoslav partisans had fought for a long time on the victorious Allied side. But once again, the border between Italy and its neighbour was being disputed. While the details were (once again) being worked out, the entire border region was split in two by the Morgan Line, which left a portion of what's now Slovenia under American and British administration. The line was supposed to ease potential tension, but it did not succeed entirely. US reinforcements had to be rushed to the area, and at one stage two US planes were shot down.

In 1991, Slovenia became independent, and a very short war followed before the action moved to the much longer and more devastating wars in Croatia and Bosnia. Since then, assorted military links between the United States and Slovenia have developed. Slovenia became a member of NATO in 2004 and sent troops to Afghanistan.

The Colorado National Guard is partnered with Slovenia.

Solomon Islands

Although a lot of people will not be hugely familiar with the Solomon Islands, a lot will recognise the name of at least one of the islands. It's one of the biggest names in American military history – Guadalcanal.

Different islands within the nation have different histories. Britain ended up being the main Western colonial power in the history of the Solomons, but on its Sikaiana Atoll, some inhabitants reckon they have been American since the nineteenth century. According to one view, Sikaiana is part of the Malaita Province of the Solomon Islands. But Hawaii was offered sovereignty over Sikaiana in 1856 and to some extent accepted it. Some, therefore, argue that when Hawaii became part of the United States, so did Sikaiana. However, the United States doesn't accept this. Interesting.

Soon after Pearl Harbor, Japanese forces occupied some of the Solomon Islands as part of an eventual plan to interdict shipping lanes from the United States to the eastern coast of Australia. Something had to be done about it, and a start had to be made on recovering territory from the Japanese. In the summer of 1942, it was.

The marines stormed ashore on 7 August 1942. After fierce fighting, they took Tulagi and some other small islands. On Guadalcanal, they encountered little opposition at first and soon took control of the island's vital airfield, which US forces would call Henderson Field. However, things were soon going to change.

The fighting raged at sea, in the air, and on the land.

At sea, ferocious battles took place near Savo Island, and the waters around it and Guadalcanal are known as 'Ironbottom Sound', due to the number of ships and sailors that are entombed beneath its waves. US Navy and cruise ships in the area still observe silence while cruising these waters. Japanese and US carrier forces also clashed in the Battle of the Eastern Solomons.

In the air, Japanese fighters and bombers flying from Rabaul clashed with US aircraft based at Henderson. The Cactus Air Force, commanded by Admiral John McCain Sr, was the name given to the mainly marine aviators who defended the airspace over Guadalcanal with obsolete Wildcat fighters.

On land, fighting raged on Guadalcanal as the Japanese

began to bring in reinforcements in an attempt to retake the island. The so-called Tokyo Express saw Japanese troops rushed to the island on fast warships, and on occasions, US and Japanese warships clashed as the Japanese tried to land troops and supplies and to bombard US positions on Guadalcanal.

Ferocious battles followed as the Japanese desperately tried to retake the airfield and American forces desperately tried to stop them. Eventually, however, the Japanese command concluded that it was going to be impossible to retake the island and it would be necessary to evacuate what remained of their forces on the island.

By the time the Japanese finally withdrew from Guadalcanal in February 1943, ending a bitter campaign fought in a sometimes difficult environment, more than 7,000 Americans and 21,000 Japanese were dead.

After the Japanese withdrawal, the US developed extensive air, sea and land facilities in the area.

The P-38 Lightning fighters that shot down Yamamoto in April 1943 (*see* Papua New Guinea) were based on Henderson Field.

In August 1943, a certain John F. Kennedy's motor torpedo boat, PT-109, was cut in half by a Japanese destroyer, and members of the crew had to hide on assorted islands in the Solomons until they could be saved in an epic rescue with the help of brave Solomon Islanders. Part of PT-109 was finally located in the waters of the Solomon Islands in 2002.

All in all, the Solomons saw large numbers of US troops, equipment and infrastructure during the war, and strong links were established.

After the war, British colonial administration resumed, but the capital was transferred from Tulagi to Honiara because of US military infrastructure there. The Solomon Islands became independent in 1978.

Starting in 1998, assorted internal conflicts and disputes erupted, sometimes turning violent, and resulted in the deployment in the Solomon Islands of an international force led by Australia and New Zealand in 2003.

The US has had a little recent military involvement with the Solomon Islands. It has provided training to the Solomon Islands Border Protection Force and carried out small-scale exercises with it.

Somalia

A land that has, sadly, been through plenty of troubled periods recently, and is still going through them.

America's first major involvement in Somalia happened in the context of the Cold War. In 1977, war broke out in the area as Somali dictator Siad Barre attempted to reclaim territory occupied by ethnic Somalis in the Ogaden and seize other bits of land. At the time, both he and the Ethiopian government were linked to the Soviet Union. The Somalis made big advances at first, but eventually, the Soviet Union and Cuba decided to support Ethiopia in the war, not Somalia, and their intervention in the conflict eventually helped the Ethiopians repel Barre's forces. Looking round for a new sponsor, Barre picked – you guessed it – the United States.

However, during the 1980s, assorted militias and guerrillas, some of them clan-based, sprang up to challenge Barre's dictatorial rule. By 1990, the Somali economy was in deep crisis, and in 1991, Barre's government was toppled. The total collapse of Somalia was about to start, and the US was about to get dragged deeply into the area.

For a start, it wanted to get its diplomats out. On 1 January 1991, the attempt to topple Barre turned into a confused and chaotic battle for control of Mogadishu. The US launched Operation Eastern Exit, quite aptly named since it pretty much involved an exit eastwards. Marines, SEALs and CH-53 and C-46 helicopters successfully rescued US diplomats and diplomats from other nations and took them to US Navy ships waiting offshore.

So the US was out of Somalia, but not for long it wasn't. Pretty soon it would return. As Somalia collapsed into violent chaos, people began to starve, and UN relief operations in the country were at risk. The United Nations Security Council decided the disaster in Somalia represented a threat to international peace and in late 1992 American troops entered Somalia as part of Operation Restore Hope. On 9 December, marines from USS *Tripoli*, USS *Juneau* and USS *Rushmore* hit the beach at Mogadishu while other marines took the airport and port. US forces also went on to occupy other targets in Somalia, including the important port of Kismayo.

Ultimately, Operation Restore Hope did, in fact, restore a bit of hope ... for a while, and the security and food situation in

Somalia improved greatly. By May 1993, the US was beginning to withdraw some forces.

However, in June of that year, things took a big turn for the worse as the forces of militia leader Mohammed Farrah Aidid attacked Pakistani UN troops and killed twenty-four of them. The UN Security Council consequently demanded Aidid be stopped, and US forces went in to do exactly that. The scene was set for Black Hawk Down.

In early October 1993, eighteen Americans were killed in an ill-fated attempt to capture leaders of Aidid's militia in Mogadishu. Helicopters were shot down, and American and UN rescue forces battled to reach the crash sites to rescue any Americans still alive (as depicted in the movie). However, many more Somalis were also killed. A few days after the carnage, President Clinton announced that American troops would withdraw from Somalia no later than 31 March 1994. In fact, they were gone by 3 March.

But this wasn't to be the end of US involvement in Somalia. Far from it. For a start, there were other international and UN forces still in Somalia, and when they finally withdrew in March 1995, the US sent in troops to help get them out safely.

And then 9/11 took place, and what happened at the Twin Towers would change what happened in Somalia as well.

Among the forces competing for control of Somalia, Islamists started playing a more major role, and by 2006, the Islamic Courts Union (ICU) had taken control of much of Southern Somalia. However, the US, along with Ethiopia, the African Union, and much of the international community, were giving support to the Transitional Federal Government (TFG) against the ICU, and in December 2006, TFG and Ethiopian forces entered Mogadishu driving the ICU out.

In January 2007, ICU forces found themselves trapped in Ras Kamboni, a Somali town near the Kenyan border, between Kenyan army forces to the south and TFG and Ethiopian forces advancing from the north. Though the details of exactly what happened still remain controversial, at least one American AC-130 gunship was involved in operations in and around Ras Kamboni against Islamist targets.

In addition to clan militias and the ICU, however, the US was also getting involved with another opponent in Somalia and, more importantly, off Somalia's shores. By about 2008, Somali piracy was becoming a major problem, and American forces became deeply involved in the international effort to combat it.

In 2009, Somali pirates captured the US-flagged *Maersk Alabama* – the first American vessel to be captured by pirates in some 200 years. Captain Richard Philips, of Underhill, Vermont, was held hostage as the pirates attempted to sail a boat back to Somalia. The US acted decisively deploying the USS *Bainbridge* and two other ships in the rescue of Captain Philips from the clutches of the Somali pirates. He was rescued after US Navy SEALs shot three of the pirates and captured one.

But the war against jihadis in Somalia goes on as well. In recent years, al-Shabaab has emerged as the leading Islamist force in Somalia. Even though a combination of Somali government forces and the Kenyan army have dealt it heavy blows, it is still a powerful force and has increasingly developed international links with al-Qaeda and other jihadi groups.

On 5 October 2013, US Navy SEAL Team Six launched a raid into Barawe on the Somali coast south of Mogadishu. They were trying to capture or kill Abdulkadir Mohamed Abdulkadir, a senior al-Shabaab leader. After an intense firefight, concerned about high potential civilian casualties, the SEALs eventually withdrew, their covert mission uncompleted. Drone strikes have also been reported targeting al-Shabaab, and in 2014, it was reported US military advisers had been sent in.

South Africa

In 1863 the *Alabama*, a Confederate commerce raider, stopped in Cape Town to resupply. The steamship was led by Captain Semmes, a Marylander who had served in the US Navy during the Mexican–American war. Its visit inspired the Afrikaans song 'Daar kom die Alibama'.

A few hundred Americans did fight on the side of the Boers in the Second Anglo–Boer War. One of them, John A. Hassell, who had served with the Vryheid Commando and been twice wounded, went on to form an entire American volunteer unit. Some Americans also fought on the British side in the Boer War.

South Africa fought on the same side as America in both world wars, and during the Second World War, as well, Wonderboom

Airport at Pretoria in South Africa was the terminus for a US air-ferry route across Africa.

During the Korean War, the US supplied the South African Air Force's 2nd Squadron first with P-51 Mustangs and then with F-86 Sabres, and it gave their pilots conversion training in Japan.

In the years since the collapse of apartheid and the development of South Africa as a full democracy and important African power, a range of military links have been established. For instance, in 2000, three Pave Hawk helicopters operated from Hoedspruit Air Force Base in South Africa, helping with flood relief efforts in next-door Mozambique. In 2009, ships from the *Theodore Roosevelt* Carrier Strike Group paid a visit to Cape Town to boost links. Operation Shared Accord 2013, a bilateral US military and South African Defence Forces exercise in South Africa, involved more than 4,000 troops and included airborne operations, as well as a humanitarian aid project.

The New York National Guard is partnered with South Africa.

South Korea

South Korea is a major long-term focus of course, of the US military. And the focusing started surprisingly early.

In the period from the end of the Second World War until the liberation of Kuwait in 1991, one of the most decisive strategic moves made by the US military was the landing at Inchon during the Korean War. However, what a lot of people don't know is that America had already made a landing near Inchon almost eighty years earlier in its first intervention in Korea, one in which nine Medals of Honor were won for outstanding bravery.

In 1853, the same year that Commodore Matthew Perry first called on Japan, in a rather less well-known visit the USS *South America* arrived for a brief stop at Pusan in what is now South Korea. Just as Japan opened up after Perry's visit, America was hoping Korea now would do the same. However, the Koreans were wary, not entirely surprisingly, after they'd seen what Western involvement had been doing to China. It wasn't going to be easy.

In 1871, a US naval force of five ships, plus US Marines arrived off Inchon. It was sent to open up Korea for trade, and also to try to find out what had happened to the SS *General*

Sherman (*see* North Korea). This was an American ship that had disappeared on a previous attempt to start Western trade with Korea and had, unknown to the US naval force, been destroyed in a conflict with the locals.

At first, the situation seemed peaceful, but then as matters proceeded, the American force was fired upon. The Americans returned fire, and when no explanation or apology was forthcoming, they attacked the Korean forts on Ganghwa Island. The fighting was bitter, but in the end, they won the battle decisively and destroyed a number of the forts. What they did not win, again not entirely surprisingly, was the trade deal they had hoped for. The US had to wait until 1882 for that.

In 1888, American troops arrived in Seoul to protect American citizens during civil disturbances.

After the First Sino–Japanese War of 1894–95 (during which American troops were sent to Seoul to protect American diplomats and citizens), Korea was removed from the Chinese sphere of influence. But then after the Russo–Japanese war of 1904–05 (during which, again, American marines were sent to protect American diplomats in Seoul), Korea came under Japanese dominance, and it basically became a Japanese colony by 1910.

In August 1945, Soviet forces advanced deep into northern Korea smashing aside Japanese resistance, and when Japan surrendered on 15 August, Korea, like Germany, was divided into different zones of occupation. Korea was split along the famous thirty-eighth parallel.

In September 1945, another American landing party arrived at Inchon but they were there, peacefully this time, to supervise the Japanese surrender. As the Cold War set in, though, just as with Germany, the division of Korea became increasingly solid and long-term. A corrupt right-wing government led by Syngman Rhee soon led the new government of the Republic of Korea while a Communist government supported by Stalin prevailed in the north.

Kim Il Sung had sounded out Stalin and Mao for support in a Moscow meeting in the spring of 1950. Mao would support Kim with the return of ethnic Korean soldiers who had been fighting the Nationalists in China. Stalin supported the North Koreans with weapons and supplies. At 4.00 a.m. on the morning of 25 June 1950, a deafening artillery barrage broke out. The North Korean Army, equipped with T-34 tanks, began advancing south of the thirty-eighth parallel. The North supported their advance with an air force of some 200 Yak-9 fighters providing close air support.

The North Koreans had achieved total strategic surprise just as the Japanese had at Pearl Harbor. The OSS had been disbanded by Harry Truman after the Second World War, and the CIA was too small and focused on Europe to identify the North Korean threat.

Memories of the 'betrayal at Munich' were fresh in the minds of many Americans, and Truman was determined not to repeat the mistakes of the 1930s (*see* Czech Republic). Due to a Soviet boycott of the Security Council, the United Nations voted unanimously to 'furnish such assistance to the Republic of Korea as may be necessary to repel the armed attack and to restore peace and security in the area'. Fifteen other nations would join the United States in contributing troops to defend South Korea.

Even from the start of the conflict, a divide appeared between the Truman administration, between those who believed they were fighting a limited war, or wanted 'police action' to protect South Korea from aggression, and their supreme American commander, Douglas MacArthur, who believed that the battle raging on the Korean peninsula was the opening round in a struggle to eradicate Communism from the region.

Seoul and a large part of South Korea were rapidly captured by the North Koreans, and harsh measures were taken against those perceived by the North Koreans to be a threat. By August 1950 US and Republic of Korea forces were driven into the Pusan pocket of south-eastern Korea.

One of the few areas of UN success was in the skies where UN forces took on and ultimately triumphed over the North Korean air force allowing UN air forces to concentrate on attacking North Korean ground forces and supply routes instead.

Something dramatic had to be done, and MacArthur was about to do it with the Inchon Landings. He advocated the landings, in spite of strenuous opposition from many in the US military.

The US Marines, however, would soon deliver all that MacArthur had promised. On 15 September 1950 the US 1st Marine Division landed at Inchon, and North Korean resistance immediately began to crumble. On 26 September Seoul was liberated, and soon thereafter the strongman Syngman Rhee was re-established amid much fanfare.

On 15 October 1950, President Truman met General

MacArthur on Wake Island to bask in the glow of Inchon's military success. The war situation would soon change, however, dramatically. To avoid repetition in this book, the rest of the war, the story of American participation in the advance into North Korea, of the subsequent Chinese intervention that pushed Western forces some distance south of the thirty-eighth parallel again, and of the see-saw struggle after that can be found in the North Korea chapter.

An uneasy peace, with a significant number of violations, has reigned between North and South Korea since an armistice was signed on 27 July 1953. At the time of writing, over 28,000 US military troops remain stationed on the south side of the de-militarised zone (DMZ). Their main function is not so much to defend South Korean territory but to be a tripwire where American casualties resulting from a North Korean incursion would trigger a deeper military commitment from the United States.

South Korea has remained a steadfast ally of the United States, and a wide variety of long-standing military links exist. South Korea was one of the few countries to send ground troops in support of US efforts in the Vietnam War.

South Sudan

When it split from the rest of Sudan in 2011, South Sudan became both Africa's and the world's newest country. It hasn't had an easy life so far, though, with tribal violence and renewed border conflict with Sudan causing major problems for the new state.

During the long years of war between the main southern rebel group, the Sudan People's Liberation Army (SPLA) and the Sudanese government in Khartoum, the American government showed some signs of support for the SPLA. The United States at the time was strongly opposed to the Khartoum government on other matters, but it remains unclear exactly what kind of aid it may have supplied the SPLA. In November 1999, for instance, the Clinton administration approved a policy of sending food aid to the SPLA, but in the face of opposition from, among others, some people within the State Department, it then cancelled the policy.

America played a key role in supporting the 2005 peace deal

with Sudan that eventually led to the creation of South Sudan, and it has had a military team based at Nzara in South Sudan to help the authorities deal with the notorious Lord's Resistance Army.

Heavy fighting, however, broke out between two factions in South Sudan in December 2013. Two USAF C-130s flew into Juba and evacuated 120 people, including diplomats and US citizens. When trying to evacuate US citizens from the town of Bor, scene of some of the worst violence, three US military personnel were wounded.

Spain

With Spain at the very western end of Europe (along with Portugal, of course) and the Spanish a major naval power for much of their history, it's hardly surprising that they played such a big role in the European exploration and settlement of both North and South America. The British, of course, were not far behind them, and with a long history of hostility between the two countries, there was bound to be trouble.

So interestingly, among the first Americans fighting in Spanish regions is one dating from before the American Revolution who was actually fighting on behalf of Britain. In 1704, with Britain at war with the Spanish (or at least some of them since there were Spanish on both sides), John Halsey, a privateer born in Boston, arrived in the Canary Islands not for a holiday but to attack assorted Spanish ships.

After all the wars between Spain and Britain, Spain was only too delighted when America rebelled against English rule, and the Spanish crown accordingly supplied the rebel colonies with food, ammunition and intelligence during the American Revolution. King Charles III of Spain even sent livestock to George Washington's farm at Mount Vernon. Very friendly.

However, on 21 October 1805 Admiral Horatio Nelson led the Royal Navy to one of the most decisive victories in its history off the coast of Spain at the Battle of Trafalgar. Twenty-two Americans served aboard Nelson's flagship, the *Victory*, with many more throughout his fleet. A percentage of these were, no doubt, pressed men, forced to serve in the fleet. Serve though they did with honour, and they shared in the victor's prize money, as was their right.

In 1815 Americans again ventured into Spanish waters when, during the Second Barbary War, Commodore Stephen Decatur scored naval victories over Barbary pirates based in Algiers at Cape Gata and Cape Palos off the coast of Spain.

But things were starting to get distinctly less friendly between the United States and Spain. In 1818, Andrew Jackson led a successful invasion of Florida and the Spanish ceded Florida to the United States in 1821.

Then in 1898, the United States, led by President William McKinley, got into a full-scale war against Spain. In the Spanish–American War, however, despite occasional plans for the US to do things like attack the Canary Islands (again), in the end there was no actual fighting in Spain. Loads of fighting happened elsewhere, particularly in Cuba and the Philippines, but nothing much going on in Spain itself.

In 1936, the Spanish Civil War, as sort of a pre-game warm up for the Second World War, broke out. It's a fascinating and important war and deserves to be better known. When General Franco mounted a right-wing military coup against the left-wing Spanish government, foreign volunteers flooded in from across the world to defend the Republic, and among them were plenty of Americans. The Soviet Union supported the Republic. Hitler and Mussolini supported Franco.

The best-known American unit sent to aid the floundering Republic was the Abraham Lincoln Brigade, or Battalion, many of its volunteers being members of the Communist Party United States, but there was also a George Washington Battalion, later amalgamated with the Abraham Lincoln unit. The fighting was ferocious, and Americans were right in the thick of it in bitter struggles, like the Battle of Jarama and the Brunete and Aragon offensives, with horrifying casualty rates to match. Something like 800 of the approximately 2,800 Americans who served in the Spanish Civil War were killed. One, Oliver Law, was a US Army veteran, a Chicago taxicab driver, and a Communist party member; during the Spanish Civil War, he became the first African American officer to lead an American military unit. Many US veterans of the Spanish Civil War would go on to serve in the OSS during the Second World War.

Ernest Hemingway and the woman who would later become his third wife, Martha Gellhorn, went to Spain to report on the war. Robert Capa, a friend of Hemingway's, took his famous dying soldier photograph in the Spanish Civil War.

Even Errol Flynn, a naturalised American citizen, went to Spain as a war correspondent. The Loyalist side attempted to recruit Errol to their side in the conflict and gave him a machine gun, but he decided that killing people for politics in somebody else's war wasn't really his cup of tea.

Not all US military involvement with the chaos created by the Spanish Civil War was unofficial. On one occasion in August 1936 the destroyer USS *Kane* was sent to Bilbao in Spain to rescue American citizens. On the way into Bilbao, a three-engine monoplane dropped bombs within a hundred yards, and the ship's crew had to open fire three times to drive it away. *Kane* then joined up with US Navy Squadron 40-T under the command of Arthur P. Fairfield, which during its time in the area rescued hundreds of Americans and others from the war.

Franco eventually led the Nationalists to victory in the bitter civil war. Spain, however, officially remained neutral during the Second World War, even though it did send the so-called Blue Division to fight alongside the Germans in Russia, and German U-boats were able to utilise the 'neutral' ports of Spain to resupply. Amidst fears that Franco might still join the Axis the OSS made contact with the remnants of the Republican underground and exiled Spanish government to explore the possibility of subverting Franco's regime, but nothing much came of it.

Today Spain is a constitutional monarchy, and a member of NATO and the EU.

The US has major bases in Spain. Rota, once a sleepy fishing village near Cadiz, has served as a US naval base from 1953 to the present. It is referred to as the 'Gateway to the Med' for the US Sixth Fleet and other NATO forces, not entirely surprisingly, since it's very close to the straits that lead from the Atlantic to the Mediterranean. The USAF also maintains Morón Air Base in Andalusia.

Sri Lanka

A beautiful island but in recent decades it has suffered a long-running civil war in the north of the island that only finally ended in May 2009.

In the Second World War, the Allied South East Asia Command headquarters were based from April 1944 at Kandy in Ceylon (as Sri Lanka was then called), and US forces made use of both naval and air facilities on the island. The RAF airfield at China Bay in Ceylon was the base for one of the USAAF's most spectacular raids of the whole war. On the night of 10 August 1944 thirty-one B-29s of the 58th Very Heavy Bombardment Wing assembled at China Bay and took off on a vital mission to bomb an oil refinery in distant Palembang, Sumatra, and sow mines in a river there. When they completed the mission and returned to China Bay, with the loss of one B-29 that ran out of fuel, they had completed the longest non-stop mission by USAAF combat aircraft in the Second World War. An OSS Maritime Unit based in Ceylon also launched infiltrations of Japanese-occupied Sumatra.

The Japanese launched air raids against Ceylon causing the loss of many lives, but there was no land action during the war there. However, the classic war movie, *Bridge on the River Kwai*, winner of seven Academy awards, including Best Picture, was filmed in Ceylon, even though the events shown were supposed to be taking place in Thailand.

Ceylon became independent from Britain in 1948, and there have been limited US military connections with Sri Lanka since then. For instance, the US Navy has been a regular visitor to Sri Lankan ports in recent decades, in particular Colombo, the capital of Sri Lanka. And sometimes, the American Navy has gone for purposes other than official visits and exercises. In 1957, when devastating floods hit the island, President Dwight Eisenhower sent the aircraft carrier *Princeton* with twenty helicopters on board, a seaplane tender, and two destroyers to help relief the effort. After the 2004 tsunami, the US military provided US Marines from the 9th Marine Expeditionary Support Battalion and sailors from the 7th Seabee Battalion providing engineering support on the island.

Some reports suggest recent US Special Forces links to Sri Lanka.

St Kitts and Nevis

St Kitts is a sort of abbreviation of St Christopher, a former name for the island and still sometimes used. America hasn't exactly had that much military involvement with the Caribbean islands of St Kitts and Nevis, but it has had just a bit.

When the US was at war with Britain, American privateers captured assorted British ships in the area, or at least tried to.

And it wasn't just the British whom America fought in the area. In 1799, during the Quasi-War with France, the US frigate *Constellation* clashed with the French 40-gun frigate *L'Insurgente* in a battle fought off Nevis and, after a bitter fight, eventually captured the French ship. In July 1800 the US schooner *Enterprise* also enterprisingly captured a French privateer off Nevis. In October 1800 the US frigate *Merrimack* captured the French privateer brig *Phoenix* off St Kitts. However, since then, US military personnel have visited the islands on a much more friendly basis.

In recent years, personnel from St Kitts and Nevis have taken part alongside US personnel in exercises such as Tradewinds 2011.

St Lucia

A beautiful Caribbean island now visited by many American tourists, St Lucia has not had a huge involvement with America militarily.

In the colonial period, the island changed hands several times between the French (they even imported guillotines to the island, though obviously they brought some less sharp-edged examples of French culture as well) and British, and eventually it ended up as a British colony.

Armed Americans, however, did occasionally pay some attention to the area during the period. In 1814, for example, Captain Boyle on board the armed brig *Chasseur* came within range of the guns on St Lucia in its attempt to take the transport ship *Lord Eldon*. Not only that but he then proceeded to hoist the Stars and Stripes.

However, the period when the US was most actively involved with the island militarily was the Second World War. As part of the destroyers-for-bases deal, America was given access, among other locations, to sites on St Lucia, and airfield preparation began in early 1941. Beane Field, or Beane Air Force Base, was used by the US Air Force for transport aircraft and for flying anti-U-boat patrols in the surrounding seas. There was also a naval air station at Gros Islet Bay.

The closure of the two airbases was not entirely the end of US forces in St Lucia, however. For example, the US maintained a missile-tracking facility in St Lucia.

St Lucia became independent from Britain in 1979. In 1983, St Lucia offered military and political support to the invasion of Grenada. Since then, the US has developed assorted other links with St Lucia on the security front, including giving some training to the coastguard and the Special Services Unit and taking part together in exercises. In May 2013 Exercise Tradewinds 2013 saw the US Coast Guard Cutter *Oak* involved in a live fire exercise off the coast of St Lucia.

St Vincent and the Grenadines

American ships were in action in the waters around St Vincent and the Grenadines during America's early conflicts with Britain. During the War of 1812 the US privateer *Chasseur* under the famous Captain Thomas Boyle caused so many problems to the merchants of St Vincent by effectively blockading the Caribbean island that they reputedly demanded the Royal Navy's Admiral Durham do something about it. The British frigate *Barossa* was eventually sent.

Since then, US ships have visited the islands on a more helpful basis. On one occasion, in May and June 1902, after a volcanic eruption, the USS *Dixie* was put to work transporting emergency supplies to Martinique and St Vincent.

St Vincent and the Grenadines supported the American invasion of Grenada in 1983, and in recent years the US military has worked with personnel from the islands in assorted humanitarian projects and training exercises. In 2012 the United States donated patrol boats and communications systems to the islands to help the fight against transnational organised crime.

Sudan

A lot of people will know about Sudan because of the tragedy in Darfur, but it's a country with an interesting history and America has played a small part in that.

Charles Chaillé-Long (mentioned in the Egypt chapter), was

an American soldier from Maryland who had already fought in the Union Army at Gettysburg. In 1874, after the war in Egypt, he found himself in Khartoum (now the Sudanese capital), appointed as second in command of an Egyptian army to a Brit, General Charles Gordon. As if the situation wasn't confusing enough from a nationality point of view, Gordon's nickname was 'Chinese' Gordon because of his previous military activities in China.

However, it was in the Second World War that America first had serious state military involvement in the Sudan. A number of airbases there became crucial in US transport and air-ferrying links from the Atlantic, across Africa, to the Middle East and beyond. America had personnel based at El Geneina, El Fasher and Khartoum, and even though they were a long distance from the frontlines then, it could still be dangerous (crashes by American aircraft are recorded at all three bases).

Sudan has not had an easy time in the years since gaining independence in 1956. In particular, two civil wars and the conflict in Darfur have killed many thousands and done enormous damage to the country's people and economy. America went through a comparatively brief period in the 1980s of supplying equipment to the Sudanese military, but that stopped after a military coup in 1989.

However, in 1993 the US government designated Sudan as a state sponsor of terrorism, and in August 1998, after the bombings of the US embassies in Kenya and Tanzania that month, President Clinton ordered cruise missile strikes on targets in Afghanistan and on the Al-Shifa factory in Sudan.

America was involved in the 2005 peace agreement that led to the end of the north–south wars and the creation of an independent South Sudan in 2011. The US military has also been involved in efforts to end the Darfur crisis. Since 2004, they have spent a lot of time and effort airlifting thousands of peacekeepers and their equipment to and from Darfur and a lot of time and effort training and equipping those forces.

Suriname

Suriname is situated on the north-eastern coast of South America with Brazil to its south, Guyana to its west, and

French Guiana to its east. With both Guyana and French Guiana in the area, it's not surprising that Suriname often used to be called Dutch Guiana (though that entity did include other areas).

Interestingly, in 1667, in a peace deal ending a war between England and the Dutch, the English kept New Amsterdam that they'd taken from the Dutch while the Dutch kept a bit of the territory that they'd taken from the English. The English had called it Willoughby Land. The Dutch renamed it Suriname. If history had been different, it might have been Willoughby Land with a seat at the UN. Interesting thought.

Suriname became independent from Holland only in 1973 (and plenty of Dutch is still spoken there), so you might think the US had never sent troops into the country. If so, then you'd be wrong. In 1940, the Netherlands fell to the Nazis. The bauxite mines in Suriname were strategically vital, then supplying more than 60 per cent of the needs of the US aluminium industry. So in late November 1941, with war in the Pacific just a few days distant, US forces moved into Suriname with the agreement of the Dutch government in exile.

At the same time, America also established an airbase at Zandery (now Zanderij) Airport, twenty-eight miles south of the capital, Paramaribo. This then became a major link in the chain of airbases sending Lend-Lease supplies and aircraft across the Atlantic. US planes also flew some anti-submarine missions from the base during the war, and the US Navy was involved in trying to counter the U-boat threat in the waters off Suriname.

The US could again have become involved militarily with independent Suriname in the early 1980s as well. Dési Bouterse seized power in Suriname in 1980 in a military coup. Some in Washington feared that Bouterse would become a major Cuban ally, and discussions in CIA circles took place about the possibility of mounting armed action to remove him.

Suriname has seen a variety of political conflicts, controversies and governments in the period since then. The United States has, on occasions, attempted to put pressure on Suriname's rulers, but it has also supplied training to Surinamese forces. Currently, Dési Bouterse is once again president.

The South Dakota National Guard is partnered with Suriname.

Swaziland

Swaziland is a small southern African country with which, frankly, the US hasn't had much military involvement at all

However, in recent years, AFRICOM has been involved in efforts to help improve Swaziland's military medical capabilities. For instance, in 2009 AFRICOM and the Umbutfo Swaziland Defence Force conducted a two-week medical exercise, Medflag 09. And again in 2013, US military healthcare personnel visited Swaziland to observe and assess.

Sweden

Sweden, the land of Vikings, ABBA and Gustavus Adolphus, one of the best-known generals of the Thirty Years' War that devastated large parts of Europe in the seventeenth century.

During the American Revolution, many Swedes volunteered to fight on the patriot side against Great Britain. Swedish Count Axel von Fersen served as an interpreter between George Washington and the French General Rochambeau. Count von Fersen was also present at the battle of Yorktown and became a founding member of the Society of the Cincinnati.

Even greater links between Sweden and the United States were still to come. Interestingly, something like one third of the total Swedish population emigrated to North America between 1820 and 1930. Sherwood 'Shakey' Johnson, for example, was one of a huge number of Americans of Swedish descent. He served in the US Navy during the Second World War and founded Shakey's, the pizza restaurant chain, in his hometown of Sacramento, California. He had learned about pizza while cruising on a US Navy ship that called on Italian ports during the war.

In the Second World War, Sweden supplied iron ore to Germany, which helped build the Nazi war machine.

The US didn't actually attack Sweden. However, it wasn't long after the entry of the United States into the war that American service personnel ended up there.

American bombers that had been so badly damaged that they could not reach their bases in Britain preferred to land in neutral Sweden rather than in German-held territory. Having landed in

Sweden, the planes and crews were supposed to be held for the war's duration, but a secret repatriation programme returned some to Allied territory.

Eventually, US ground troops arrived in Sweden as well. On 24 March 1945, near the close of the war in Europe, the OSS launched Operation Rype to infiltrate a battalion of skiing demolition agents into Norway (*see* Norway). A squadron of eight B-24 Liberators was flown from Scotland, but one went off course and dropped its agents by parachute in Sweden. With help from the Swedish, the crew eventually rejoined their unit of thirty-six men in Norway.

The OSS battalion, commanded by Major William Colby (future head of the CIA), attacked infrastructure targets in Norway. On one occasion, after blowing up a bridge in Norway, they were spotted by Luftwaffe aircraft and pursued by *Wehrmacht* forces. According to Colby's account, they skied non-stop over two days for forty miles and across the border into neutral Sweden. There they found Sugartop Hill where they rested and dined on elk.

As the war progressed, neutral Sweden gave more evidence of it not always being as neutral as sometimes thought. Starting in 1943, the Swedish authorities started training Danes and Norwegians as paramilitary units to take over in Denmark and Norway after a German surrender or withdrawal. These units were officially described as police, but these Danish police included an air unit equipped with Swedish SAAB fighter-bombers, which are rather heavier weaponry than what is used by the average police force. In early 1944 British and Swedish weapons were smuggled through Sweden to the Danish resistance as part of an extensive programme. Thousands of pistols and millions of rounds of ammunition went into Denmark this way. In 1945 American planes flew supplies from the Swedish capital of Stockholm to some of these Norwegian 'police' in liberated northern Norway to help maintain order there.

After the war, Colby returned to Stockholm where he was the CIA station chief in the 1950s. There he worked on Operation Gladio, which sought to create stay-behind cadres that would resist Soviet occupiers in the event of a successful Russian invasion of Sweden.

More recently, Sweden has a contingent of about 500 troops serving in Afghanistan alongside NATO members. The Swedish air force was also involved with the NATO-led action in Libya in 2011, sending eight fighter jets to the Mediterranean. Sweden is also a key participant in the Baltic Operations series of maritime exercises hosted in the Baltic by the US Navy.

Switzerland

Mountainous, picturesque Switzerland has a long history of neutrality. So has America ever attacked any fondue-eating, yoghurt-slurping and chocolate-devouring Swiss (or indeed any Swiss who don't like fondue, yoghurt or chocolate)? Well, not intentionally, but unintentionally, yes.

During both world wars, Switzerland remained neutral. In the First World War, despite one or two Allied plans to invade Switzerland, or at least invade enemy territory through Switzerland, America didn't really have that much to do with the country militarily, apart from a bit of inevitable espionage.

With its strategic location at the heart of Europe, Switzerland became famous (along with the fondue, clocks and knives) for spies during both world wars. There can be few more famous American spymasters than Allen Dulles, and he spent time in Switzerland during both wars. In the First World War, he operated out of Berne and ran spies in Austria-Hungary, the Balkans and Eastern Europe. Also, one night he apparently hung up the phone after a conversation with a Russian revolutionary. The revolutionary was about to leave Switzerland and was desperate to speak to an American diplomat. That revolutionary turned out to be Lenin; his destination was Russia, the Bolshevik Revolution and plans for the development of Communism that would give American spies sleepless nights for many decades afterwards.

In the Second World War, Switzerland once again became a hotbed of espionage activity while the war raged all around the country. And once again, Allen Dulles appeared on the scene, this time heading up the OSS there. Germany was now his focus, and Dulles worked with many Germans who were anti-Hitler. While in Switzerland, he managed to gather intelligence on the Me 262 jet and the German rocket programs. He also helped the Italians change sides.

Stalin, not exactly a fan of capitalists anyway, denounced

the Swiss as 'swine' and urged US forces to attack from France. America didn't. Well, as mentioned above, not intentionally anyway.

The air war over Europe was wide-ranging, vicious and often chaotic, fought by crews with, by today's standards, very limited navigational technology. Some mistakes were inevitable. In September 1944, for instance, US pilots invaded Swiss airspace sometimes as many as thirty times a day. In another example, a squadron of US P-47s shot up a train headed from Zurich to Basel assuming it was German. In one of the most tragic incidents, Americans inadvertently bombed the Swiss town of Schaffhausen, killing some civilians. To be fair, Swiss airspace was also violated by the Luftwaffe hundreds of times in the course of the war. After the war, the US government paid compensation to the Swiss.

Sometimes, however, Switzerland became the intended destination of American aircraft. A number of Allied bomber crews, their planes too damaged to return home, preferred to avoid becoming POWs and landed deliberately in neutral Switzerland where their planes and crews would be impounded for the duration of the war.

Syria

Syria is an ancient land with a remarkable history, and its capital, Damascus, has been (and continues to be) the centre of it. On visiting Syria in 1867, Mark Twain wrote about the Syrian capital:

> To Damascus, years are only moments, decades are only flirting trifles of time. She measures time, not by days and months and years, but by the empires she has seen rise, and prosper and crumble to ruin. She is a type of immortality.
> Near immortal she may be, but she is suffering today.

It has been alleged that the CIA attempted to mount coups inside Syria, including a plan for one in 1957. America also clashed with the Syrians in Lebanon when the US had forces there.

During the Gulf War, however, Syria was on the same side

as the US against Saddam. But that rapprochement was not to last for long.

Already by 2002, then Undersecretary of State John R. Bolton was grouping Syria alongside the original 'axis of evil'. And after the invasion of Iraq, clashes occurred near the Syrian border as the insurgency developed there and the Syrians started to assist local insurgents against US forces. In 2004, a bitter battle took place between US forces and insurgents at Husaybah near the border. On 26 October 2008 US helicopters and commandos were reported to have crossed the border into Syria to attack a purported al-Qaeda target in a village a few miles inside Syria.

During the current Syrian crisis, America has sent support to the Syrian opposition and given training to some Syrian rebels. In 2013 preparations were being made to bomb Assad's forces after the use of poison gas but after the wars in Iraq, Afghanistan and Libya there was little appetite among many in the west for involving western combat forces in another Middle Eastern war. In September of 2014, however, following the beheading of two American journalists, the United States and some allies began launching air strikes against Islamic State targets located in Syria. President Obama announced, 'We will degrade and ultimately destroy the terrorist group known as ISIL.'

In May 2015, US special forces launched a raid into eastern Syria killed a number of Islamic State fighters, including a prominent Islamic State figure called Abu Sayyaf.

Tajikistan

Tajikistan hasn't exactly been destination *numero uno* for US forces. If US forces have met native Tajiks, it has tended to be in Afghanistan where they make up a significant portion of the population.

Tajikistan was part of the Soviet Union for a long time, up until gaining independence in 1992, so obviously it was basically off limits to the US military, except for things like spy flights at that stage. A strong Russian military presence continues in Tajikistan to this day.

After Tajikistan's independence, things got very messy with a bloody civil war raging until 1997. In October 1992, a USAF

C-141 Starlifter flew into Tajikistan to evacuate Americans and other nationals.

In the same period, the situation was pretty bad in Afghanistan to the south with civil war and the rise of the Taliban and al-Qaeda there.

As America started operations in Afghanistan after 9/11, the Tajiks offered the US permission to use their airspace. America accepted, and US forces sometimes refuelled in Dushanbe. America has also supplied equipment and training for Tajik counter-narcotics and counter-terrorism operations. But there are also suggestions that US Special Forces have been involved in some skirmishes inside Tajikistan.

Defence Secretary Donald Rumsfeld visited Tajikistan in 2001 in hopes of negotiating an American airbase in Tajikistan. Instead, in the end, the US government decided to concentrate on the airbase in Manus, Kyrgyzstan. The US government helped to pay for a bridge in Tajikistan as a goodwill gesture – more long-lasting than flowers or a box of chocolates.

The Virginia National Guard is partnered with Tajikistan.

Tanzania

Tanzania is a country that includes the fascinating island of Zanzibar. In fact, the name Tanzania comes, in part, from Zanzibar, because like the country itself, the name Tanzania is a combination of Tanganyika and Zanzibar.

Zanzibar has long been a major trading centre and port, and America took quite an early interest in it. In fact, a very, very early interest. Zanzibar was actually one place in Africa where, in the early nineteenth century, the US had more influence than the British, the French, or the Portuguese.

Zanzibar sent America vast quantities of ivory and animal skins, and America sent Zanzibar cotton and guns. The sultan signed a Treaty of Amity and Commerce with the US, and in 1837, America sent him a US consul, Richard Waters, four years before the first British consul and seven years before the first French consul. And in 1838, the USS *John Adams* dropped into Zanzibar for a visit. In 1844, the USS *Constitution* called in on its round-the-world cruise.

One thing the sultan may have hoped for from the United States was some protection from British efforts to close down the slave trade. Indeed, not every US diplomat in Zanzibar was hugely keen on stopping the slave trade. But as time passed and attitudes in the United States changed, so eventually did those among US diplomats in Zanzibar. The USS *Yantic* arrived at Zanzibar in January 1873 as part of efforts to pressure the sultan to abolish slavery.

By the 1880s the Germans were busy constructing their colony of German East Africa on the mainland. And with the arrival of the First World War a few decades later, the British got busy demolishing it, or at least occupying it. One unit involved in the little-known, but often rather vicious, war in East Africa during the First World War was the 25th (Frontiersmen) Battalion of the Royal Fusiliers. It was formed in 1915 from a fairly varied assortment of volunteers, including a famous hunter who'd hunted in Africa with Teddy Roosevelt in 1909 and, allegedly, a number of American cowboys.

A big chunk of what had been German East Africa became a British colony, and in 1961 gained independence as Tanganyika. In 1964, a revolution in Zanzibar forced the sultan to flee. The day after the revolution started, the USS *Manley* raced in to rescue American citizens, only to be met by armed revolutionaries because no prior permission had been granted. After a tense stand-off and assorted negotiations, however, eventually the *Manley* was allowed to carry out its mission.

Tanganyika and Zanzibar united to form Tanzania the same year.

Under long-term ruler Julius Nyerere, Tanzania became very friendly with Communist China, which, with the Cold War still going, tended to mean that US military involvement with Tanzania was pretty minimal.

In 1998, terrorists bombed the US Embassy in Dar es Salaam, Tanzania, and US military and security personnel were rushed to Tanzania to help deal with the aftermath of the attack and to help boost security.

In recent years, US military personnel have trained with members of the Tanzanian military, for instance on a military police exercise in 2011 and on a programme to develop expertise in international peacekeeping. Recent news on Tanzanian troops serving with the UN mission that defeated the rebel M23 group show that it can be a tough mission. A number were killed and wounded while serving there.

Thailand

A monarchy that prides itself on never having been conquered by a foreign invader, Thailand, or Siam as it was formerly called, was the first Asian country to establish diplomatic links with the United States in 1833 when the USS *Peacock* arrived in the Gulf of Siam.

Following that, Townsend Harris of New York was the consul to Siam who negotiated the Harris Treaty in 1856.

Thailand was on the Allied side in the First World War, but in the Second World War, the country faced a much more challenging situation. Hours after the attack on Pearl Harbor, Japanese troops began moving into Thailand. After a brief period of fighting, Premier Pibun decided to order the Thai army to offer no further resistance. As a result, Japanese troops moved through Thailand to invade British-controlled Burma with their sights ultimately set on India.

Soon Thailand had agreed to an alliance with Imperial Japan. On 25 January 1942 Thailand declared war on the United States. There were, however, many Thais who sympathised with the Allied cause. The Thai ambassador to Washington, Seni Pramoj, refused to deliver the declaration to the American government. Instead, he helped to start the Free Thai movement.

As early as April 1942 the OSS began working with Thai dissidents to subvert the Pibun government. Efforts were also made to rescue downed Allied airmen from the Japanese and return them to China.

After the Japanese naval defeat at the Battle of Midway, seaborne efforts to supply Japanese ground forces in Burma became problematic. The Japanese responded by using thousands of Allied prisoners and Asians to construct a railway line 258 miles long to link Kanchanaburi to the Japanese base camp in Thanbyuzayat in Burma. This was the infamous 'Railway of Death' depicted in the classic film, *Bridge on the River Kwai*.

From 1942 onwards, American aircraft also launched a large number of bombing raids on targets within Thailand. For instance, on 5 June 1944, the very first combat mission of the epic B-29 Superfortress was a raid aimed at vital railway yards in Bangkok.

Finally, pro-Japanese Premier Pibun was ousted from office in July 1944 by a coup led by forces that secretly began to take a more pro-Allied line. In January 1945 two OSS majors landed by seaplane in Thailand bringing with them gifts for Premier Pridi from President Franklin D. Roosevelt and 'Wild Bill' Donovan, the former head of the OSS – two gold cigarette lighters. Ultimately, however, Japan surrendered before the Allies could launch the planned invasion of Thailand.

In 1946, the current king of Thailand, who is the world's longest reigning monarch, came to the throne. Bhumibol Adulyadej was born in 1927 in Cambridge, Massachusetts, when his father was studying at Harvard.

In 1953, 'Wild Bill' Donovan, was appointed ambassador to Thailand by President Dwight Eisenhower in the 1950s. Eisenhower wanted someone experienced in intelligence operations in charge in Thailand to provide a launching pad for American covert operations to thwart Communist expansion in South East Asia.

In the post-war period, as the Cold War heated up and with the French fighting in Vietnam, Thailand became an increasingly close US ally.

Thai troops fought alongside American forces in the Korean War, and in 1955, Thailand was a founding member of SEATO, an alliance of non-Communist countries with its headquarters in Bangkok.

In May 1962, with the Soviets having decided to arm the Pathet Lao in nearby Laos, the US sent the 3rd Marine Expeditionary Brigade to Thailand as a show of force. It withdrew after a couple of months.

During the Vietnam War, the alliance became even deeper. Thailand was one of the few countries to send troops to fight alongside US forces. And America has made extensive use of Thai naval bases and particularly airbases, with the USAF, for instance, flying a high percentage of air strikes against North Vietnam from Thailand. Bangkok was also used as a popular 'R and R' stop for the American military. The fictional Sherlock Holmes of Thailand, John Burdett's Sonchai Jitpleecheep, is the son of an American Vietnam veteran and a Thai prostitute.

Thailand has been designated a major US non-NATO ally. Thailand sent hundreds of troops to help America in Iraq, and the Thai and US forces regularly share exercises. For example, the US military has made regular use of U-Tapao airfield as a refuelling stop to support operations in Iraq and Afghanistan.

The Washington National Guard is partnered with Thailand.

Timor-Leste (East Timor)

One of the world's newest countries and located just to the north of Australia, Timor-Leste came into being as an internationally recognised independent nation in 2002.

Before 1974, Timor-Leste had been a Portuguese colony. Portugal remained neutral in the Second World War but in December 1941, after Pearl Harbor, Allied forces in West Timor feared a Japanese invasion. Thinking that an enemy landing in Timor-Leste would outflank them, the Allies occupied Portuguese Timor-Leste. The expected Japanese invasion wasn't far away; in February 1942, the Japanese landed in both West Timor and Timor-Leste.

A bitter battle ensued lasting a year, until the last Allied units were forced to evacuate the island, and even then, local forces continued to resist the Japanese. Most of the Allied forces involved were British, Australian and Dutch (West Timor was part of a Dutch colony and would become part of independent Indonesia), but the US did have some involvement in the battle. The last Allied ground troops were evacuated from Timor-Leste by the American submarine USS *Gudgeon* on 10 February 1943. And in the air, American aircraft flew bombing missions against Japanese targets in Timor-Leste, including in and around the capital, Dili, both before the Allied withdrawal and after.

After the Second World War, the Portuguese once more took control of Timor-Leste, until in 1974 a leftist military coup overthrew the government in Portugal, and the days of the Portuguese empire started coming to an end. In 1975, after the Portuguese withdrew, Indonesia invaded Timor-Leste in an attempt to unify it with West Timor, which was already part of Indonesia. What ensued was a long battle for freedom by Timor-Leste guerrillas, which came to an end only in 1999. As the Indonesian forces finally withdrew, the International Force for Timor-Leste, INTERFET, moved into the politically and militarily tense area to establish security. America took part in INTERFET, for instance, providing aircraft and helicopter transport and sending in the USS *Mobile Bay*, USS *Belleau Wood* and the USS *Peleliu* and a number of troops on the ground.

Today the US military has assorted links with Timor-Leste, including involvement with some civilian projects and exercises with the Timor-Leste Defence Forces (TLDF). In October 2012,

US Marines took part with TLDF units in Exercise Crocodilo 2012.

Togo

Togo is a long, thin country sandwiched between Ghana to the west and Benin to the east.

A town in south-eastern Togo, now called Aného, used to be called Little Popo. It was the first capital of Togo when the country was a German colony, and before that, it was a big slave market. Consequently, it received a certain amount of attention from the US Africa Squadron when it started trying to combat the transatlantic slave trade. In 1848, Captain William C. Bolton took USS *Jamestown* and USS *Boxer* for a cruise along the coast there, and he had Little Popo on his list of potential places to investigate.

The French took control of what is now Togo in the First World War. It remained a French colony until 1960, and thereafter it was an area of significant French influence, under its long-term leader General Gnassingbé Eyadéma, who had himself served in the French army in the Indochina and Algeria wars.

In recent years, though, the US has had some minor links with the Togolese military. The US has been involved in Togo with training for multinational peace-support operations. Togo has supplied hundreds of troops to the French-led effort in Mali, to which the US has also given political and logistical support.

Tonga

Tonga is located east of Australia and north-east of New Zealand, though its name means 'south', understandable since for its Polynesian inhabitants it's the southernmost bit of central Polynesia. After British Captain Cook visited it, Tonga rather sweetly became known to the British as the Friendly Islands, Cook presumably being unaware that some of the locals were allegedly arguing over who should attack him.

America did take some interest in Tonga in the nineteenth century. In 1886 the USS *Mohican* turned up there, and on 2 October, in Nuku'alofa, the US signed a Treaty of Amity, Commerce and Navigation with the Kingdom of Tonga. The treaty allowed US warships to use Tongan harbours as coaling stations. When the local prime minister was toppled in a coup in 1890, he asked for US intervention. The US, however, refused. Tonga was soon to pass firmly into the British sphere of influence, and in 1920, Britain terminated the agreement 'on behalf of the King of Tonga'.

With the Second World War, though, the US military returned to Tonga in force. Tonga declared war on Japan shortly after the attack on Pearl Harbor, and in 1942, US forces arrived in Tonga to help the tiny Tongan Defence Force resist any Japanese attack and to prepare bases to assist in the general Pacific war effort. US forces gave it the codename 'Bleacher'.

Tonga became fully independent from Britain in 1970, and since then, the US has developed assorted military links with Tonga. It has supplied training to Tongan military personnel, and Tongan forces have served in Iraq and Afghanistan.

Trinidad and Tobago

During the Revolutionary War and the War of 1812, American ships targeted assorted ships sailing from Trinidad and Tobago. For instance, in 1777, the American privateer, the *Oliver Cromwell* allegedly raided the coast of Tobago near Fort Milford, apparently without much success. The American privateer *Jack's Favorite* (although presumably not Trinidad's favourite) returned to New York in July 1812 having captured the schooner *Rebecca*, which was taking sugar and molasses from Trinidad to Halifax. And in February 1814, the US frigate *Constitution* captured a number of ships off Trinidad.

During the Second World War, the US took a major military interest in the islands. Under the destroyers-for-bases deal, Trinidad became the home of a number of US bases. America got a naval air station and a naval operating base. Perhaps most important, the US got a couple of big airbases, Waller Field and Edinburgh Field. Waller Field served two major purposes. Aircraft employed on anti-submarine operations were based there, and Waller was a key point on the transatlantic air transport and air-ferry route connecting the United States to the Middle East and European combat zones on the other side of the ocean. President Franklin D. Roosevelt passed through Waller en route to the Casablanca Conference in 1943. The air transport and ferry function, in fact, became so significant and demanded so much space that Edinburgh Field, later named Carlsen Field, took over responsibility for most of the anti-submarine operations. US blimps were based on Trinidad as well. Both bases closed soon after the war, but that wasn't the end of US military personnel there. For example, America built a missile-tracking site at Macqueripe Bay, Chaguaramas, on Trinidad during the Cold War.

Trinidad and Tobago became independent from Britain in 1962. In the period since, the US has had assorted training and exercise links with Trinidad and Tobago. For example, in 2011 Trinidad and Tobago hosted the multinational disaster response exercise Allied Humanitarian Forces 2011 in co-operation with US SOUTHCOM. Trinidad and Tobago's fast patrol craft *Chaconia* took part along with US Coast Guardsmen in a simulated counter-drug operation during Tradewinds 2013.

The Delaware National Guard is partnered with Trinidad and Tobago.

Tunisia

Cato the Elder famously said, '*Carthago delenda est*' – 'Carthage must be destroyed!' The mighty ancient city of Carthage was located in what is now Tunisia, not far from the current capital, Tunis. And Carthage eventually was destroyed by the Romans after three bitter wars, which featured, among other things, Hannibal and his elephants. Cato might have been slightly disappointed to know, however, that after his death, Carthage rose from the ashes and became one of the largest and richest cities of the Roman Empire.

As with other North African countries (*see* Algeria *and* Libya), parts of what is now Tunisia fell under the sway of the Barbary pirates. And as with other North African countries, America had to find a way of dealing with this fact. The US approach to the Barbary States incorporated a carrot and stick approach, or more accurately carrot and then stick, since America started out paying the pirates of Tunis to leave its ships alone, and then to free its sailors when they didn't leave its ships alone, and then it ended up threatening them in order for them to leave its ships alone.

Thus, President Thomas Jefferson sent warships to Tunis, and in February 1803 Commodore Richard Morris arrived with three frigates. As soon as he disembarked from his ship, he was arrested by Bey Hamouda of Tunis who demanded payment of $22,000. Commodore Morris, from a wealthy Vermont family, agreed to pay the tribute. So not a huge success for US arms.

By contrast, in 1815, during the Second Barbary War, Stephen Decatur with a large American squadron stopped in Tunis to demand $46,000 in compensation for an American ship that had been captured the previous year. The Bey of Tunis agreed to pay, and Decatur later boasted to the Secretary of the Navy that the terms of settlement had been 'dictated at the mouths of our cannon'. Much more of a success. At least from the US point of view, obviously.

Tunisia was incorporated into the French Empire later in the nineteenth century.

But by late 1942, it was the Allies who were about to invade it. Operation Torch was launched on 8 November with US and British landings in Vichy French-controlled Morocco and Algeria in an attempt to attack Rommel's Afrika Korps from behind. In response to these landings, however, the Germans rushed men and tanks into Tunisia to try to hold it against US and British forces advancing from the west, and American troops were in for something of a shock.

In February 1943 two veteran panzer divisions attacked the inexperienced American forces at Sidi-Bou-Zid and Kasserine Pass pushing rapidly forward against them.

However, the situation was soon to change dramatically. Supreme Commander (and future president) Dwight Eisenhower dismissed General Lloyd Fredendall and put General George 'Blood and Guts' Patton in command of II Corps in Tunisia. With fresh leadership, there was an almost immediate improvement in morale. On 16 March, Patton, not a man usually in love with the subtle approach, told his staff, 'Gentlemen, tomorrow we attack. If we are not victorious, let no one come back alive.'

On 3 April, Patton held a meeting in Gafsa with Air Marshal Sir Arthur Tedder to demand that his soldiers receive better air cover; during the talks, they were interrupted by three Focke Wulf fighters that strafed the streets and headquarters. Tedder, dusting himself off, enquired how the Germans had managed to achieve this, to which Patton famously replied, 'I'll be damned if I know, but if I could find the sonsabitches who flew those planes, I'd mail each one a medal.'

With new leadership and growing experience, American performance rapidly improved. With vastly superior Allied numbers being brought to bear on the Axis forces, trapped and short of supplies in Tunisia, the battle there was going to end only one way. Von Arnim surrendered on 12 May 1943, and over 250,000 others surrendered as well, about the same number as surrendered at Stalingrad, though the Soviet victory at Stalingrad seems to have received rather better press over the decades and remains much better known today.

The Allies now had a secure platform from which they could invade Italy and drive Mussolini out of the war. Churchill commented in his memoirs that one continent had, at that point, been redeemed. President Franklin D. Roosevelt visited Tunis on 20 November 1943. The president inspected the ruins of Carthage before flying off to meet Churchill in Cairo.

The Allies suffered just over 76,000 casualties in the Tunisian campaign, of which over 18,000 were Americans. Today at Carthage, where Romans and Carthaginians clashed over 2,000 years ago, a visitor will also find a cemetery with the names of 3,724 Americans who fell in battle in North Africa.

In 1956, the United States was one of the first major powers in the world to recognise the independence of Tunisia from France.

Americans brought war of an interplanetary nature to Tunisia again when George Lucas filmed parts of *Star Wars Episode IV: A New Hope* in the Tunisian desert. *Star Wars* would return to film parts of episodes I and II in Tunisia as well.

Since the Jasmine Spring swept aside President Ben Ali's repressive government in January 2011, the United States has supplied hundreds of millions of dollars in aid. In August 2014, it was announced that over the next year, the US would give the Tunisian military about $60 million in aid.

The Wyoming National Guard is partnered with Tunisia.

Turkey

Considering how far Turkey is from the United States it's again somewhat surprising how soon it is in the history of the US that Americans got involved there. A Turkish–American trade treaty was signed in 1830 and Americans helped start the process of modernising the Turkish navy, operating the Imperial Naval Arsenal on the Haliç. Two Americans, Charles Ross and Forster Rhodes, served as naval advisers to the sultan.

In 1849 however, the US Navy intervened in Smyrna (now Izmir) when an American was detained there. And in 1856, the Navy returned to Smyrna for what has to be one of their more unusual missions. Jefferson Davis wanted to form an experimental United States Army Camel Corps for service in territory recently acquired from Mexico. So the USS *Supply* was sent to Smyrna to get camels, which it did, and took them to Indianola, Texas. Though, obviously in the end the United States Army Camel Corps did not become one of the more major units of the US military.

In 1912 the First Balkan War broke out, which removed most of what remained of Ottoman territory in Europe. And towards the end of that year, American troops were put on duty guarding the American legation in Istanbul.

Meanwhile, one North American deeply involved in the Balkan Wars was Rear Admiral Bucknam who continued the tradition of American links with the Ottoman navy – by heading it, in fact. Ransford D. Bucknam was born in Canada but had been working in America and, according to some sources, became an American citizen. He had arrived from Philadelphia on board a gunboat built for the Turks and stayed on to captain it for them. During the First Balkan War, he engineered a sortie through the Dardanelles by a Turkish cruiser, which sank a number of Greek ships and shelled coastal fortifications. He died in 1915.

In the First World War, the Ottoman Empire was allied to the Central Powers. The United States, led by President Woodrow Wilson, declared war on the Ottoman Empire in April 1917, shortly after the American declaration against Germany. US forces were not deployed against Turkey, although the American reporter Lowell Thomas did manage to boost his career by promoting Lawrence of Arabia's campaign against the Turks in the Middle East.

American marines did, however, land in Turkey shortly after the war. In 1919, during the Greek occupation of the city, marines from the USS *Arizona* were sent to guard the US consulate in Istanbul. And again in 1922, troops were landed in Smyrna (Izmir) to protect US citizens and property.

Actually, America could have ended up running part of Turkey after the First World War because there was even discussion among the Allies about forming an American mandate in the area.

In 1923, Kemal Atatürk became the first president of the Republic of Turkey. He is widely regarded as the founder of the modern secular Turkish state.

Turkey remained neutral during most of the Second World War, and consequently, Istanbul became a hotbed of espionage intrigue. The OSS maintained an important base in neutral Istanbul as Axis and Allied espionage and diplomatic services all plotted to bring Turkey over to their side in the war. The question of Turkish chrome shipments to Germany was also vital with Germany wanting them to continue and the Allies keen to stop them. In the end, Turkey joined the Allied side in February 1945 and became a founding member of the United Nations.

The Turkish ambassador to the United States, Mehmet Munir Ertegun, died suddenly in Washington DC, near the war's end. A naval task force built around the USS *Missouri* was charged with returning the ashes of the ambassador to his home country. US authorities wished to send a message to Stalin to deter any aggressive moves against Turkey. The battleship was received with great pomp and circumstance by the Turks.

Mutual fear of the Soviet Union brought Turkey and the United States into a close partnership after the war, and that was reflected in extensive military links that have remained, with occasional hiccups, to the present. What follows will, therefore, be only a summary of some of the key elements in those links.

During the Korean War, a Turkish brigade served on the peninsula alongside American forces.

Turkey joined the NATO alliance in 1952 at the same time as Greece and a formal defence treaty with the US followed in 1959. The Jupiter missiles, which may have been Khrushchev's strategic target in the first place, were removed from Turkey after the Cuban missile crisis in 1962.

The US military has made use of a range of facilities in Turkey. The most important is Incirlik Air Base, first used by the United States in 1951. It has long been a major US base and remains the home of the USAF 39th Air Wing with about 5,000 personnel. It was a key base for operations during the crisis in

Lebanon to the south of Turkey in 1958 (*see* Lebanon). The US Navy has made use of the major Turkish naval base at Aksaz. Turkey is also home to some key NATO headquarters.

Links between Turkey and the United States were strained in the 1970s due to the conflict in Cyprus and subsequent arms boycotts authorised by the US Congress, but gradually recovered. During the Gulf War, sorties were flown from Incirlik into Iraq. After the Gulf War, the base played a central role in efforts to help the Kurds in northern Iraq and in enforcing the no-fly zone over northern Iraq. In 2001, it again played a crucial role in facilitating air operations in Afghanistan. And 2001 was a big year for Incirlik in another sense; after *Ocean's Eleven's* premiere in Los Angeles, George Clooney, Matt Damon, Andy Garcia, Brad Pitt and Julia Roberts, with director Steven Soderbergh, visited the base.

In 2003, the Turkish parliament, with grave concerns over the future of the Kurds, denied use of Turkish territory for the Allied campaign against Saddam's Iraq. Links between the United States and Turkey experienced something of a brief chill.

A battery of Patriot missiles is currently deployed in Turkey to defend against possible attacks from Syria, and Turkey and the United States have co-operated to help the Syrian opposition in its attempts to force Assad out of power in Syria. A flood of refugees has streamed across the border into Turkey fleeing the Syrian Civil War.

Turkish troops have also served in Afghanistan. Turkey has received billions of dollars of military aid from the United States, and its military has made use of a lot of American-designed equipment. Turkish forces regularly take part in military exercises alongside US personnel.

Turkmenistan

Turkmenistan's capital, Ashgabat, is a sister city of Albuquerque, New Mexico.

One of the Doolittle crews from the daring 1942 raid on Japan eventually ended up in Ashgabat, then a Soviet city, after they had landed in the east of the USSR. They tried to persuade the Soviet authorities to let them go but, in the end after many months, gave up. Instead, they bribed a local smuggler to take them across the border to Iran, where they then contacted a British consul who arranged to get them across the border to British-controlled territory in what is now Pakistan.

During the Soviet era, some surveillance flights operated over Turkmenistan. For instance on 10 September 1957 a US flight that set off from Adana in Turkey flew over the Caspian coastline city that was then called Krasnovodsk and is now Türkmenbasy in independent Turkmenistan.

Post-independence links seem to have been mainly small scale. At one stage the US gave the Turkmenistani border guards one or two patrol boats to help build a navy.

Turkmenistan has a policy of positive neutrality but has allowed humanitarian overflights and ground transport to deliver humanitarian aid in the Afghan crisis and refuelling privileges for humanitarian flights.

Tuvalu

An island nation located in the Pacific, Tuvalu lies between Hawaii and Australia.

Americans happen to have been some of the earliest Western visitors to the islands and to the people who lived there. In 1841 the United States Exploring Expedition under Charles Wilkes called in. However, Germany and Britain were the main Western powers competing for control of the area, and in the end, the British won control of Tuvalu.

During the Second World War, Tuvalu was just a little beyond the reach of the Japanese. Even though they occupied nearby islands, including Nauru to its north-west, the Pacific being a big, big place made 'nearby' too far.

Still, America did send men and military equipment to Tuvalu to defend it from Japanese attack and use it as a base for operations against the enemy. Patrol torpedo boats (PTs) were based there, as well as an airfield and a seaplane ramp. On 20 April 1943 B-24 Liberators from Funafuti bombed Nauru. In response, the Japanese bombed Funafuti and did so again on a number of other occasions. The Funafuti airfield became the location for the headquarters of the USAAF VII Bomber Command. Tuvalu also became a staging post for operations as US forces began to push westwards onto Japanese-held islands, and as the war moved west, inevitably Tuvalu's strategic significance became less.

Tuvalu became independent from Britain in 1978, and in 1979, America recognised Tuvalu's possession of a number of islands it had previously claimed.

The Funafuti airfield is now Funafuti International Airport.

Today the US has only minor military contact with Tuvalu.

Uganda

American soldier and explorer Charles Chaillé-Long was sent to Uganda by the Egyptians on a political mission in the late nineteenth century.

In 1976, the infamous Idi Amin was in power, and the daring Israeli raid on Entebbe to free the hostages took place on the day of the US bicentennial celebration. Following that, the USS *Ranger* Carrier Battle Group (CVBG) was ordered to move into position to prevent any attempts by the Ugandan military to take revenge on Kenya for enabling the Israeli aircraft to access Uganda. And again the year after, when Amin placed restrictions on Americans in Uganda, another carrier battle group, this time the *Enterprise* CVBG was positioned off the Kenyan coast until Amin lifted travel restrictions.

Amin was forced from power in 1979, and in 1986, Yoweri Museveni became president.

Military training that the US was giving to the Uganda People's Defence Force was cut off in 2000 because of Ugandan activities in the neighbouring Democratic Republic of the Congo, but some links were restarted in 2003.

Uganda has faced some major challenges during its history, and one of those has been the Lord's Resistance Army (LRA).

Beginning in 1986, the brutal, rebel LRA started operations in the north and east of Uganda frequently murdering and kidnapping civilians and causing huge numbers to flee. The war against the LRA has dragged on and on, though the LRA has been steadily ground down and forced into smaller and smaller areas.

In May 2010, President Obama signed into law the Lord's Resistance Disarmament and Northern Uganda Recovery Act. As a consequence, US Special Forces have deployed to Entebbe, near Uganda's capital, Kampala, to train Ugandan forces and assist them in the hunt for the Lord's Resistance Army, and in particular, for its leader, Joseph Kony, accused of multiple crimes. In March 2014, US Special Forces with US aircraft were again dispatched to assist in the hunt.

The US military has also developed other links with the Ugandan military, whose most important role is in Somalia. Uganda has had thousands of troops fighting extreme Islamists in Somalia, and a significant number have been killed or wounded.

The US has given considerable assistance to Uganda with its peacekeeping role.

Ukraine

A country that's been in the news a bit recently – well, a lot. Ukraine's location among assorted competing power blocs ensured significant chunks of its territory were devastated in both world wars and the local conflicts that sprang out of them. And generally, Ukraine's history in the twentieth century includes plenty of tragedy. So far, the twenty-first century has been pretty difficult for the country as well.

The first time America focused on a military crisis in Ukraine was during the Crimean War in the 1850s. Though the war was fought in a number of places, the prime area of battle was the Crimea in the south of Ukraine (then part of the Russian Empire) where British, French and Turkish forces landed in an attempt to take the key Russian port of Sebastopol. Much of the US public, interestingly, in fact sympathised with the Russians. Some Americans even asked the Russians about the possibility of the Americans acting as privateers, and in Kentucky, 300 riflemen volunteered to fight alongside the Russians. Okay, nothing ultimately came of either of those ideas, but thirty-five American doctors did actually volunteer to go to Russia, and the majority of them actually worked in the Crimea. Captain George B. McLellan, later a general on the Union side in the American Civil War, also led a US military delegation to Russia to study the fighting.

Americans were involved again in the area during the bitter fighting at the end of the First World War. In particular, the

American volunteer pilots of the Kosciuszko Squadron (*see* Poland) played a significant part in the fighting against Soviet forces on territory that is now part of Ukraine, for instance, in the defence of what was then called Lwów. Between the wars, Lwów was Polish but is now Lviv in Ukraine.

During the Second World War, a lot more American flyers arrived in Ukraine, but this time they were there on a more official basis. Under Operation Frantic, Stalin allowed the US Air Force to establish three bases in Ukraine, at Poltava Airfield, Myrhorod Airfield and Pyriatyn Airfield, with the aim of enabling US bombers to reach targets deeper inside Nazi-held territory than they had previously been able to. The operation was, however, somewhat marred by suspicion from some Soviet authorities, and Allied advances elsewhere reduced the value of the basic plan, but still, it's a fascinating example of US–Soviet co-operation during the Second World War.

Such military co-operation was, of course, soon to come to an end as the war drew to a close and the Cold War started. And with the start of the Cold War, once again, some US eyes were focused on the possibility of involvement in Ukraine.

In the period after the Second World War, some in the CIA wanted to use Ukrainian nationalists against the Soviets. So, starting in 1949, the CIA began training Ukrainians and then parachuting them into Ukraine. The first team were sent over in a C-47 on 5 September 1949, and they landed in the dark near Lviv. Unfortunately for the CIA and its Ukrainians, the Soviets captured most of the Ukrainians that were sent in, sometimes forcing them to send fake messages to the CIA requesting more personnel and supplies be sent. After five years, the CIA finally gave up on the operation.

Various other Cold War covert and surveillance operations in and over Ukraine were to follow, and then in the aftermath of the collapse of the USSR, American planes returned openly to Ukraine. In October 1991 US Air Force aircraft airlifted 146 tons of medical and relief supplies into the capital, Kiev.

The United States has since developed a number of military links with the Ukrainian military. It has given training to Ukrainian personnel, and the Ukrainian military has joined in assorted exercises alongside US forces. US Navy ships have visited Ukraine, and Ukraine has helped with operations in Kosovo, Iraq and Afghanistan. In 2008, the United States implemented the US–Ukraine Charter on Strategic Partnership. The California National Guard is partnered with Ukraine.

In February 2014, in a conflict that started over whether Ukraine should be closer to the EU and America or closer to Russia, mass demonstrations in Ukraine forced President Yanukovych out of power after he accepted a Russian deal. During the confused situation that then developed, extra US Marines were sent to Kiev to help guard the US Embassy there. Subsequently, Russian troops took control of Crimea, and pro-Russian fighters became active in parts of eastern Ukraine. In response, among other actions, the United States sought to reassure countries in the region that felt threatened. For instance, it sent F-15s to Lithuania and US troops to take part in exercises in neighbouring countries, while at the same time launching a diplomatic campaign against the Russian move. In 2015, US troops arrived in Ukraine to start training some Ukrainian forces.

United Arab Emirates

British influence was strong in the Persian Gulf area for a long time (and to a certain extent still remains strong), so American military links with the United Arab Emirates (UAE) prior to the 1980s and 1990s were somewhat limited.

However, during the Second World War, the USAAF did use the RAF base at Sharjah on air transport routes.

America became more closely involved with the UAE during the Tanker War element of the Iran–Iraq War and during the Gulf War to liberate Kuwait. And the US has established military links on the ground, in the air and at sea. For example, the UAE has bought huge amounts of US military equipment. It has worked closely with the United States on counter-terrorism and sent personnel to help liberate Kuwait and to serve in Afghanistan. The UAE participates with CENTCOM in exercises such as Eagle Resolve.

US aircraft have operated out of a number of bases in the UAE. For example, US A-10 Thunderbolt aircraft operated out of Sharjah Airport during Operations Desert Shield and Desert Storm, and the US has had aircraft based at Al Dhafra. Aircraft from the base have aided US operations in both Iraq and Afghanistan.

Jebel Ali has port facilities that have been very useful to the US Navy.

United Kingdom

After two world wars, America has a long record of fighting alongside Britain, and today the UK is one of its firmest allies. But that doesn't mean America hasn't fought Britain in the past. It, of course, had, most notably during the American Revolution and the War of 1812. And even though most of the fighting took place in or around North America, not all of it did.

In fact, pretty much as soon as Americans had declared independence from Britain, some of them set off to invade it. In April 1778, Captain John Paul Jones, the founding father of the American Navy, and the crew of the *Ranger*, an 18-gun sloop, arrived in Britain and, unlike many Americans today, they weren't there to visit Westminster Abbey or have a taste of fish and chips.

Jones selected the English fishing village of Whitehaven on the Irish Sea as his target; Whitehaven was Britain's third busiest seaport at that time. He would attempt to destroy its shipping and to kidnap the Earl of Selkirk. The harbour of Whitehaven was protected by two small forts. In the early hours of 23 April 1778, Jones and about forty volunteers from his crew scaled the fortress wall. They kicked in the door of the guardhouse. The sleeping guards surrendered without a shot. Jones's men proceeded to spike about thirty-six guns of the battery with nails driven into the cannon's touchholes. About half of his crew then broke into a local tavern and proceeded to get drunk. This caused a commotion and roused the local townspeople. Jones beat a hasty retreat and set fire to a merchant ship, a collier (that's a coal ship and nothing to do with Lassie) named *Thompson*.

Soon after, the *Ranger* sailed about twenty miles to enter the bay off St Mary's Isle. Jones took about a dozen men armed with cutlasses and muskets to a Georgian manor house owned by the Fourth Earl of Selkirk. Jones soon discovered that the earl was not in residence and was therefore unavailable to be kidnapped. Instead, Jones demanded the silver plate be delivered up. The loot was hauled back to the *Ranger*. Shortly after, the 18-gun

Ranger fought and captured the 20-gun *Drake* of the Royal Navy in an action that Jones described as 'warm, close and obstinate' – a description that sounds more like some marriages than a sea battle.

Jones's raid on Whitehaven had succeeded in bringing the American Revolution 'home to their own doors', as he put it. The English press was, not surprisingly, incensed. They had no wish whatsoever to have the American Revolution home to their doors. The *London Public Advertiser* asked, 'When such ravages are committed all along the coast, by one small privateer, what credit must it reflect on the First Lord of the Admiralty?' Not very much, was the clearly implied answer.

No one was killed or even injured in the Whitehaven raid, but insurance rates doubled. The Whitehaven raid lasted about two and a half hours and was an even shorter invasion than the assassination of Osama bin Laden in Pakistan in 2011. Jones later had second thoughts about the silver he stole from the Earl of Selkirk and returned most of the loot.

In 1797, in pretty much the last major hostile invasion of British soil, an Irish-American, Colonel William Tate, led *La Légion Noire* ashore near Fishguard in Wales as part of revolutionary France's attempt to attack Britain. It wasn't a huge success for Tate, or his troops, or revolutionary France. In fact, it wasn't really a success at all. Three days after landing, they surrendered.

The United States would fight its last war with Britain in the War of 1812, which, in fact, ran from 1812 to 1815. Canada was invaded, the American Navy won its first major laurels, the White House was burned by the British, and Andrew Jackson led the Americans to victory at the Battle of New Orleans. There were assorted actions at sea, and US Navy sailors, like the crew of the USS *President* under Commodore Rodgers, once again cruised British waters, but there was to be nothing quite like the Whitehaven invasion of 1778.

The next American invasions of Britain were to be much friendlier all round. This little book isn't the place to cover in full depth the well-documented close friendship and military partnership that developed between the United States and the UK after the nineteenth century, playing a key role in winning two world wars. Instead, we'll just touch on a few stories from those years.

In December 1910, President William Taft sent twenty-six battleships of the Atlantic fleet to visit Portsmouth. Admiral William Sims of the US Navy gave a prophetic speech at London's Guildhall, 'There is a strong blood-tie between our two peoples ... If the time ever comes when the British Empire is seriously menaced by an external enemy, it is my opinion that you may count upon every man, every dollar, and every drop of blood of your kindred across the seas.'

The First World War was the first war in which Americans joined the British and fought alongside as allies. Many doughboys were transported through Britain on their way to the Western Front.

But it was in the Second World War that the friendship between the British and Americans became particularly close. Even prior to the attack on Pearl Harbor on 7 December 1941, many Americans volunteered to serve with the British forces in the war against Hitler. The American Eagle squadrons, made up of American pilots, served with distinction in the Battle of Britain in 1940. And on the home front, expatriate bankers, teachers and others formed the 1st American Squadron of the Home Guard, ready to battle Hitler's panzers if they ever landed in Britain.

Meanwhile CBS correspondent Edward R. Murrow delivered live broadcast reports from London during the blitz that stimulated great sympathy for the besieged British people.

After the Japanese attack, there was a flood of American military personnel to Britain as the US prepared to fight Nazi tyranny. Brave people from all the US services went to Britain to battle for victory over Hitler. US troops were immediately dispatched to help garrison Northern Ireland.

Brave US Navy crews defied the U-boats and escorted vital convoys across the Atlantic to ports in the UK, like Liverpool, Southampton and Plymouth. The critical battle of the North Atlantic could not have been won without the assistance of the US Navy.

The USAAF used Britain as an unsinkable aircraft carrier from which to bomb Nazi Germany. Many thousands of American aircrew flew from Britain to face the perils of Luftwaffe fighters, anti-aircraft fire, and in general, flying long distances with, by today's standards, unsophisticated equipment. Among them was Jimmy Stewart, drafted by the US Army in 1940 and the first major American movie actor to serve in the war. He piloted over twenty combat missions in a B-24, bombing Axis targets while stationed at two RAF bases in Norfolk (Tibenham and Old Buckenham). He won two Distinguished Flying Crosses and the Croix de Guerre.

Dwight Eisenhower became the supreme Allied commander and planned for the invasion of occupied France from his offices at 20 Grosvenor Square in London. You can find a statue of Ike adorning Grosvenor Square today.

Like their counterparts stationed in other English-speaking countries during the war, the American soldiers in Britain squeezed in some fun. Famously 'overpaid, oversexed, and over here', the young American soldiers, armed with Coca-Cola, chocolate, cigarettes and nylon stockings, often proved very attractive. There were an estimated 70,000 GI brides and 9,000 out-of-wedlock war babies born as a result of this friendly (very friendly) invasion.

And then there was D-Day. It was in Britain that the American contingent for Operation Overlord assembled and from Britain that they bravely landed on 6 June 1944 in one of the most dramatic military operations ever.

But all this bravery came at a heavy price. Visit the American Memorial Chapel in St Paul's Cathedral, and you will find the Roll of Honour, which lists over 28,000 American dead from the Second World War who served in Britain. A page from this book is turned every day. The American Battle Monuments Commission maintains two cemeteries in England, located in Brookwood and Cambridge.

On 12 August 1944, Lieutenant Joseph Kennedy Jr, the son of Ambassador Kennedy and older brother to JFK, was killed in Operation Aphrodite when the bomb being towed by his modified B-24 Liberator exploded shortly after takeoff. He is memorialised on the Wall of the Missing at the Cambridge American Cemetery.

Two months before D-Day, Tommy Hitchcock was killed while flying an experimental P-51 Mustang. Hitchcock, an accomplished polo player and former member of the Lafayette Escadrille in the First World War, had championed the introduction of Rolls Royce engines into the iconic American fighter enabling it to escort bombers all the way to Berlin. He is buried at the Cambridge American Cemetery.

In 1949, Britain became a founding member of NATO, and America's long military partnership with Britain continues to this day. There are still US military bases in Britain. In 1999, the town of Whitehaven in Cumbria officially pardoned John Paul Jones and the Freedom of the Harbour was granted to the US Navy. In 2003, the USS *Leyte Gulf*, a missile cruiser, paid a friendly visit to Whitehaven.

The latest major IRA campaign, the Provisional IRA Campaign, lasted from 1969 until the last ceasefire in 1997 and was mainly fought in Northern Ireland with occasional campaigns on the UK mainland. Support from some Americans, particularly financial, was a significant factor in assisting Irish Republican activity during this period.

Although the British Empire is gone, Britain still controls small territories (British Overseas Territories) around the world, and the US has had major involvement with a few of them. For instance, with the Turks and Caicos Islands, American loyalists fleeing after the Revolution settled on the Caicos Islands.

And what about Bermuda? Famous for shorts and that triangle, this British Overseas Territory is a site of assorted US military bases. And what about another British territory, the Falkland Islands, scene of Argentinian and British invasions in 1982 and everlasting controversy? Yep, America has invaded them as well. Briefly. In 1831, after three American ships had been seized in a dispute over seal hunting and fishing, the USS *Lexington* descended on the Falklands, seized seven prisoners, and charged them with piracy.

Uruguay

America recognised Uruguayan independence in 1836, but things didn't always run smoothly in Uruguay's early decades, and, yes, soon the United States was sending in the marines.

In November 1855, the US sloop *Germantown* landed marines in Montevideo to protect US property and interests while somebody was attempting a revolution. In January 1858, it was a similar situation, only this time it was the US frigate *St Lawrence* landing the men. Ten years later, in February 1868, the US was going in again, this time with six US warships landing marines and seamen in Montevideo.

In the late nineteenth century and early twentieth century, Uruguay had military links with a number of different countries, for instance, buying warships from, among others, Britain, Germany and Italy.

Relations between the United States and Uruguay, however, got a little friendlier during the First World War. Uruguay didn't actually declare war on Germany, but it did break off links with the Germans in October 1917, one of only a few South American countries that did. It then proceeded to lease to the United States Emergency Fleet Corporation eight German vessels it had seized for use during the war, which must have made the Germans even more cross.

Things lapsed a little between the wars, but US military influence in the country began to rise again, as in some other South American countries during the Second World War. Uruguay did not actually declare war on the Axis Powers until 1945, but it had already given some assistance to the Allies, including in the matter of convoys. In 1944 the US even got involved in a local dispute, despite having a few other military commitments at the time. The cruiser USS *Memphis* and the destroyer USS *Somers*, plus Vice Admiral Jonas H. Ingram, arrived in Montevideo to express US support for Uruguay in a tense situation that had developed with Argentina. And later in 1944, America sent Lend-Lease arms to Uruguay.

During the Cold War period, the United States was concerned about the activities of left-wing groups in Uruguay, and the full extent of US attempts to aid in crushing these is still a matter of much controversy. The 1960s saw the rise of the Tupamaro left-wing urban guerrillas and ruthless police attempts to combat them. This was followed from 1973 on by a military government that took its campaign against left-wings groups even further by committing a range of major human rights abuses.

In recent years, although the US hasn't been deeply militarily involved in Uruguay, it has provided military assistance to the Uruguayan military with equipment and training.

The Connecticut National Guard is partnered with Uruguay.

Uzbekistan

The second biggest city in Uzbekistan is Samarkand, home of the mighty conqueror Timur, or Tamerlane. He was no slouch at invading, leading invasions of China, Russia and India.

Uzbekistan has recently become of interest to the United States because of matters like energy sources and narcotics, and because, of course, of Afghanistan.

Between 2001 and 2005, US forces were present at Karshi-Khanabad Air Base, which acted as a major US support base for operations in Afghanistan. Eventually, however, US comments on Uzbek human rights matters led to a rift, and the Uzbeks forced the closure of the base.

Nevertheless bilateral agreements were signed with the Uzbeks in 2012, and since then the Mississippi National Guard has been partnered with Uzbekistan.

Vanuatu

Vanuatu used to be called the New Hebrides during the colonial period, at least by part of the colonial administration. The islands had a rather unusual colonial arrangement. They were ruled by both Britain and France in a condominium. Yep. With two different administrations. So they were also known as the Nouvelles-Hébrides.

This could have caused a major problem after the German invasion of France in 1940, because the new Vichy authorities wanted the French administration on the Nouvelles-Hébrides to comply with their pro-German policies at a time when the British authorities on the New Hebrides were committed to fighting them. Fortunately for all concerned, the French administration on the Nouvelles-Hébrides instead declared for the Free French.

The New Hebrides/Nouvelles-Hébrides were conveniently located for a number of key sites like Guadalcanal, so in 1942 US forces turned up and built various airstrips, a seaplane base and assorted support facilities on the island of Espiritu Santo. In July 1942, B-17s flying from there attacked the Japanese trying to complete the airfield on Guadalcanal.

Another bomber base was added in 1943, and America built a major sea base there as well. Huge numbers of Americans passed through the island during the war. Consequently the Japanese would attack the island occasionally by sea or by air.

The US also built airstrips and a naval operating base on nearby Efate Island.

Vanuatu became independent and took its new, single name in 1980.

In recent years, the US military has had minor involvement with Vanuatu. Training links exist. And as part of Pacific Partnership 2011 to help with assorted humanitarian projects and actions, the amphibious transport dock ship USS *Cleveland* was the first US Navy vessel to visit Vanuatu since the period of the Second World War bases.

Vatican City

Vatican City, a small enclave within Rome that is home to the pope and the central administration of the Catholic Church, is an actual state. It's not a member of the UN, but it does have observer status there.

And, yes, US forces have sort of invaded the Vatican. America has obviously never been at war with the Vatican, and during the Italian campaign, as President Franklin D. Roosevelt himself emphasised, Allied airmen had been specifically informed of the borders of the Vatican City and instructed to make sure none of their bombs fell within its borders. However, the pope owns a variety of sites in Italy, which are outside the borders of the Vatican City but have extraterritorial status. Some of these were a lot closer to the action than the Vatican itself. The pope specifically complained about Allied bombs falling in the vicinity of the papal summer residence at Castel Gandolfo and killing refugees there.

When American troops of the Fifth Army liberated Rome in June 1944, some of them ventured into the Vatican.

From the Italian surrender in 1943 until the liberation of Rome on 4 June 1944 the Vatican was under siege by the Nazis. Some Nazi leaders even considered kidnapping Pope Pius XII. To the immense relief of the pope and his Swiss Guard the last German soldiers fled Rome on the evening of 4 June.

In the early morning of 4 June 1944 Swiss Guards spotted a scout car with a large white star on St Peter's Square – a technical violation of Vatican neutrality in the conflict. A gendarme from the Swiss Guards politely requested that the American soldiers of the Fifth Army withdraw across their side of a white line that marked the border between Rome and Vatican City. Captain Carlo Fehr of the US Army, who had previously served as a member of the Swiss Guard, was among the first Americans to visit the Vatican; he helped to calm the situation between the Americans and the Swiss Guard with gifts of chocolate.

Just over a week after the capture of Rome, on 12 June, after a number of instances of armed Allied vehicles entering St Peter's Square inside the Vatican City, barricades had to be installed across the end of the Bernini colonnade to prevent any further such occurrences. If it was any kind of invasion, though, it was an entirely friendly one. On 12 June for instance, the pope is said to have received fifteen hundred Allied troops.

Venezuela

In 1812, in the Battle of La Guaira (outside the Venezuelan port of, yes, La Guaira), the *Saratoga* under Captain Charles W. Wooster defeated the British ship *Rachel*. Although having said that, subsequently, HMS *Fawn* turned up and recaptured *Rachel*, so it wasn't exactly America's greatest ever victory.

The great Venezuelan Crisis of 1902–03 was precipitated by Cipriano Castro's default on its debts to European creditors. The European creditors weren't happy at all, and the German and British navies collaborated to blockade Venezuelan ports. The Kaiser's warships also sank Venezuelan gunboats and fired on her coastal forts.

Initially, some American officials expressed sympathy for the European actions. Vice President Theodore Roosevelt even said, 'If any South American country misbehaves toward any European country, let the European country spank it.'

After William McKinley's assassination, however, Roosevelt was sworn in as president on 14 September 1901, and in his new capacity he began to see the Venezuelan debt crisis in a very different light. The rise of Imperial Germany was seen as a potential threat to US interests.

Roosevelt began to champion the longstanding Monroe Doctrine, but he went much further by introducing the Roosevelt Corollary. This insisted not only that European nations should stay out of the Western hemisphere but also that the United States had a right to intervene in Central and South America to protect lives and property. Roosevelt famously said, 'Speak softly and carry a big stick'. The US Navy was Roosevelt's biggest stick.

Consequently, in 1903, Teddy Roosevelt sent US naval forces under the command of Admiral Dewey from their Caribbean base in Puerto Rico towards the coast of Venezuela. The crisis was eventually resolved when the European nations changed their approach and the matter was referred for arbitration at the international court at The Hague. The court ruled in favour of preferred rights for the European powers.

Venezuela remained neutral for most of the Second World War, though it did supply oil to the Allies and did declare war on Germany in February 1945. Venezuela also received Lend-Lease from the United States.

In January 1958, America got a bit nervous about the situation in Venezuela, during a period of violence in Caracas. Marines were sent on board the USS *Des Moines* to the waters off Venezuela to be ready to launch an evacuation if necessary. But it never actually happened.

In May 1958, Vice President Nixon's motorcade was attacked by a crowd as it was travelling from the airport to Caracas. Assorted troops and vessels were put in place to be ready to intervene if necessary, but they weren't needed, and Nixon left Venezuela a couple of days later.

At times, Venezuela received substantial amounts of US military assistance, but the arrival of Hugo Chavez as president was going to change that situation. A lot. Chavez served as president of Venezuela from 1999 until he died in 2013. Chavez aligned himself with Iran and was a fierce critic of the US. After 9/11, Chavez expressed his disapproval of the global War on Terror and repeatedly accused the United States of plotting to launch a coup or invasion of his country.

Terrible floods hit Venezuela at the end of 1999, and over 100 US troops rushed to help relief efforts, but when the United States prepared to send two vessels with military engineers and equipment to help, Chavez objected, saying he didn't want US troops in the country.

Vietnam

The American military's experience of Vietnam didn't even start that well.

In 1832, Edmund Roberts, a US diplomat on board the USS

Peacock arrived in Da Nang Bay in an attempt to a negotiate a trade deal with the emperor in Huê but much talking at cross-purposes achieved little. In April 1836, Roberts returned, and the process was pretty much repeated, though it did not exactly help negotiations that Roberts was extremely ill at the time and died soon afterwards.

And things weren't about to get much better. In 1845, the USS *Constitution* arrived at Da Nang. Some dispute exists about whether much actual firing took place, but Captain John Percival, believing a French bishop's life to be in danger, landed with marines to investigate and then took hostage local VIPs and seized a number of ships before finally releasing them and departing.

Increasingly through the nineteenth century, though, it was France that became the colonial power in what is now Vietnam. And by contrast, after those initial difficulties, the United States eventually began to become something of an inspiration for those in the area wanting freedom.

In 1919, a young Ho Chi Minh, or Nguyen Ai Quoc as he was then known, was working as a busboy at the Hotel Ritz in Paris. Inspired by President Woodrow Wilson's vision of a world in which people would be granted freedom and self-determination, wrote a letter to try to interest the American delegation in his vision of greater freedom for the 'Annamite people'. A note still exists from an American official acknowledging receipt of his letter, but it is now impossible to tell who may have seen it. Certainly little, if anything, seems to have been done about it.

In 1940 France was conquered by Hitler and replaced with a Vichy government. Japan immediately seized on French weakness to expand their empire. On 23 September 1940 the Japanese occupied the northern portion of Indochina. By July 1941 Imperial Japanese forces would occupy the whole of Indochina. President Franklin D. Roosevelt demanded that Japan withdraw from China and Indochina; Japan responded with the attack on Pearl Harbor. On 10 December 1941, Japanese warplanes based on airbases in Indochina would sink the Royal Navy's battleships *Prince of Wales* and *Repulse* opening the door to the Japanese conquest of Singapore.

The Japanese occupation had devastating consequences for the Vietnamese people. In 1945 alone, a famine swept through Japanese-occupied Indochina, killing an estimated two million people – more than *all* the combat deaths on *all* sides in America's ten-year-long Vietnam War.

During the Second World War, America was supporting the cause of the Vietnamese. President Roosevelt believed that French colonial rule in Indochina was 'rotten to the core'. He even told Stalin at a 1943 conference that after a century of French rule in Indochina, the inhabitants were worse off than before.

Near the end of the Second World War, an OSS team, code-named 'Deer', parachuted into northern Vietnam to make contact with Ho Chi Minh and aid him in his struggle against the Japanese. The US supplied arms, and a Deer team member, Henry Prunier of Worcester, Massachusetts, even instructed Vo Nguyen Giap on how to throw grenades. US involvement with Vietnam has not been short of irony.

On 2 September 1945, American P-38s even flew above Hanoi that day in apparent celebration as Ho Chi Minh declared Vietnam's independence from France. He quoted words very familiar to Americans: 'All men are created equal. They are endowed by their creator with certain unalienable Rights; among these are Life, Liberty and the pursuit of Happiness ...'

Ho Chi Minh went on to list a set of grievances with the French colonial administration that very much paralleled the colonists' objections to George III. Ho Chi Minh sought more OSS assistance and American recognition.

Despite all that, Ho Chi Minh was not George Washington. He was an ardent revolutionary and a dedicated Communist who looked to Moscow and Beijing for support.

In 1923, Ho Chi Minh had begun studying at the Stalin School in Moscow, which was also known as the Communist University of the Toilers of the East. He also became a disciple of Mao's theory of guerrilla insurgency. During what the Vietnamese call the American War, the Soviet Union would supply billions of dollars' worth of military equipment and around 3,000 military advisers and technicians for the radar and surface-to-air missile batteries. The Vietnamese would refer to the Russians as 'Americans without dollars'. From 1965 to 1970, more than 300,000 Chinese troops would assist with air defence, construction and military training. North Vietnamese air force pilots would also receive training in the People's Republic of China.

The Soviet Union officially recognised Ho Chi Minh's government in February 1950. On receipt of this news, Dean Acheson, President Harry Truman's Secretary of State, declared that this should remove any illusion that Ho Chi Minh was primarily a nationalist.

For four years beginning in 1950 the United States would provide massive amounts of money to finance the French effort to maintain its control of Indochina. In 1954, though, the French were lured into battle at Dien Bien Phu, which one French official compared to a chamber pot (*vase de nuit*), with the beleaguered French at the bottom and the Viet Minh shooting from the rim above. The desperate French requested American air support. President Eisenhower sent ten planes and 200 mechanics – about half of what they had asked for.

When the Joint Chiefs of Staff recommended the use of atomic weapons to aid the French forces trapped at Dien Bien Phu, Eisenhower dismissed them out of hand. Nor would he sanction an escalation of conventional US ground forces in Vietnam.

However, things were about to change. President Kennedy did not share Eisenhower's compunctions about the use of ground forces in Vietnam. At his inaugural address in 1961 Kennedy declared, 'Let every nation know, whether it wishes us well or ill, that we shall pay any price, bear any burden, meet any hardship, support any friend, oppose any foe to assure the survival and the success of liberty'. Few in the audience that day recognised that the price paid in South East Asia would be so very high. The number of US military advisers based in South Vietnam soared during JFK's administration from 800 in 1961 to over 16,000 by the end of 1963.

President Johnson almost immediately began to escalate US involvement in Vietnam. On 2 August 1964, the USS *Maddox* came under attack by North Vietnamese torpedo boats in the Gulf of Tonkin. The *Maddox*, which had been gathering intelligence at the time, sank one torpedo boat and was unharmed. Just a few days later, the US Congress passed the Tonkin Gulf Resolution that gave broad discretionary war powers to Johnson's administration.

From 1964 to 1968, Johnson dramatically escalated the US military presence deploying over 500,000 troops in Vietnam. American bombers struck North Vietnam while American ground forces fought a counter-insurgency against the Viet Cong in South Vietnam. General William Westmoreland was in command, but Johnson was in the driving seat. Johnson, who with his team loved to micromanage the war, famously said, 'Those boys can't hit an outhouse without my permission.'

In spite of the bombing and declaration of free-fire zones, the Viet Cong guerrilla war throughout South Vietnam continued while supplies flowed down the 600 mile length of the Ho Chi Minh trail, which snaked through Cambodia and Laos.

In January 1968, the North Vietnamese and the Viet Cong launched the Tet Offensive during the holiday, which marked the Vietnamese Lunar New Year. 84,000 troops launched simultaneous attacks across the country. The American Embassy compound in Saigon was penetrated by a squad of VC commandos. US forces and their allies repulsed the attacks and launched punishing counter-attacks, which claimed many enemy lives. The US Marines, for example, prevailed in the Battle of Huê.

On 1 February, the execution of a VC prisoner by the South Vietnamese national police chief, Nguyen Ngoc Loan, was captured on film. The prisoner had recently killed one of Loan's best friends, but the footage and the black-and-white photograph was another propaganda victory for Hanoi.

In spite of Tet being a US military victory, it was also a shattering political defeat for the Johnson administration. In a historic departure, the ubiquity of television sets and the introduction of colour television had brought the violence of Vietnam into most American homes with devastating political repercussions. The CBS news anchor Walter Cronkite declared that the United States was 'mired in stalemate'.

In March 1968 Westmoreland was relieved of command and replaced by Creighton Abrams.

On 16 March 1968 Lieutenant William Calley ordered the slaughter of over 100 unarmed women and children at My Lai. That same year, the Communists massacred civilians at Hue killing over 3,000 people and receiving far less media attention than My Lai. On 31 March, Johnson stunned Americans with the announcement that he would halt the bombing campaign and suspend his own re-election bid.

In November 1968, Richard Nixon, promising peace with honour in Vietnam and an end to the draft, was elected president. Nixon accelerated the process of 'Vietnamization'

– turning greater operational responsibility over to the South Vietnamese army (ARVN). Nixon also recognised that the rate of US soldiers killed per year (peaking at 16,899 in 1968) was politically unsustainable. Nixon expanded the war in Cambodia and Laos to interdict supplies along the Ho Chi Minh Trail (*see* Cambodia *and* Laos), but he also began significant drawdowns in US forces deployed in Vietnam.

Some time between Tet and the final US withdrawal of forces in 1973, the US military very nearly reached its breaking point. There was a pronounced breakdown in morale and discipline. The number of reported 'fragging' incidents (soldiers murdering fellow soldiers and especially officers, often with fragmentation grenades) peaked in 1971 at a rate of 333 per year. In 1969, about 4,500 sailors in the US Navy were discharged for drug use – thirty times more than in 1965.

On 4 May 1970, national guardsmen in Ohio fired on anti-war protestors at Kent State University killing four students. The anti-war movement exploded across the country.

(Captain Jack Coughlin, a friend of Chris Kelly's, is a retired USAF C-130 pilot who flew 'jingle runs' from Taiwan to Saigon in the 1970s. On a jingle run, his plane would be loaded with three wooden pallets; each pallet contained ten million dollars in stacks of twenty-dollar bills. This was how the US helped to fund the South Vietnamese government. Similar tactics would be employed much later in Afghanistan and Iraq.)

In December of 1972, Nixon launched a 'Christmas Bombing' offensive that shattered North Vietnamese anti-aircraft defences and may have forced Hanoi to reopen negotiations at the stalled Paris peace talks.

In 1973, Nixon made good on his pledge to end the draft, and the United States transitioned to an all-volunteer military. On 29 March of that year, the last US troops were withdrawn from the Republic of Vietnam. Also that year, the Watergate scandal ended with Nixon's historic resignation from the presidency. The scandal paralysed the US government and made air support for Thieu's Saigon government an impossibility.

On 30 April 1975, Saigon finally fell as Operation Frequent Wind evacuated hundreds of Americans and just over 4,000 Vietnamese to safety aboard US ships offshore. A much-anticipated bloodbath did not occur, but thousands were sent into re-education camps while many more attempted to flee Vietnam by boat. Tens of thousands of 'boat people' died of exposure while attempting to flee Vietnam.

Today the names of 58,193 Americans who died while serving in Vietnam line the wall of the Vietnam Veterans memorial in Washington DC. America's own casualty totals, however, were dwarfed by those of the Vietnamese people. Over 200,000 ARVN, about 1.1 million Communist troops (Viet Cong and People's Army of Vietnam), and about 2 million Vietnamese civilians were killed, all told about 3.3 million Vietnamese.

After the war was over, both sides claimed that it had been a noble effort. President Ronald Reagan, when dedicating the Vietnam memorial in Washington DC, said, 'We remember the devotion and gallantry with which all of them ennobled their nation as they became champions of a noble cause.' General Giap said in the 1990s that, for his side, the war had been a noble sacrifice.

The Vietnam War left a devastating legacy of loss and injury both in the United States and in Vietnam, but in recent years, some links between the US military and Vietnam have restarted.

In 2003, the USS *Vandegrift*, a guided missile frigate, paid the first US Navy visit to Ho Chi Minh City (formerly Saigon) since 1975. A new era in links between America and Vietnam began that has included, for instance, humanitarian visits by US military personnel to Vietnam.

Yemen

Some US military personnel had already become acquainted with the area during the Second World War when the American Air Force used the RAF base at Khormaksar in Yemen on air-ferry and transport routes.

During the 1960s, the US had some peripheral military involvement in the area often involving US Navy ships being in the vicinity to keep an eye on conflict in the country and be ready to evacuate Americans if necessary. In 1994, six USAF planes did evacuate hundreds of Americans and others from Yemen during yet another period of civil war.

However, with the appearance of al-Qaeda, America started taking a serious military interest in Yemen. US involvement became so extensive there over the years that we can only give details here of a selection of recent incidents.

In 1999, al-Qaeda planned an attack on a US Navy destroyer, *The Sullivans*, named after four Irish-American brothers who died on a ship in the Second World War. They planned to place a boat laden with explosives alongside. Their plans were foiled when the boat sank.

The USS *Cole*, a guided missile destroyer, was anchored in Aden's harbour in Yemen on 12 October 2000. A fibreglass fishing boat pulled up alongside and detonated killing seventeen and wounding more. In November 2002, a man suspected of involvement with the bombing, was killed by a missile fired at his Toyota Land Cruiser.

After the US Embassy in Yemen was attacked on 17 September 2008, by Islamic terrorists and sixteen people were killed, General David Petraeus dramatically expanded the US presence in the country.

Actions were taken against suspected al-Qaeda activity with cruise missiles and bombs delivered by jump jets. On 17 December 2009 several Tomahawk cruise missiles armed with cluster bombs hit a desert camp in Abyan. There were several civilian casualties.

On 15 January 2010, an air strike killed at least five al-Qaeda members in the mountains of northern Yemen. In May 2010, a missile strike killed Jaber al-Shabwani, who was the deputy governor of Ma'rib Province.

In May 2011, the United States again authorised armed drones over Yemen that flew from bases in Djibouti and Ethiopia. Since the beginning of 2011, one source reckons at least eighty drone strikes have taken place. In December of 2013, the Yemeni Parliament, concerned about exactly who was being killed by all the strikes and under what circumstances, passed a non-binding motion to ban drone strikes from its territory.

In 2015, with civil war raging in Yemen, Saudi Arabia and some other Arab countries launched air raids against Houthi rebels in Yemen. The US expressed some support when the Saudis launched their campaign.

Zambia

An American scout and warrior, Frederick Russell Burnham, was one of the earliest Westerners to ride into what is now the

African nation of Zambia, and in the process, he helped create the industry that is still a main part of Zambia's economy. Admittedly he was an American working for Britons at the time he rode into what is now Zambia, but he was still an American.

Frederick Russell Burnham had, to put it mildly, an unusual career. He was born on a Sioux reservation and experienced the Old West, getting sucked into the Pleasant Valley War and working as a tracker for the US military before heading for Africa. There, he got involved in the British drive into the African interior, seeing service in the First and Second Matabele Wars. Somewhere in the middle of it all, he was sent on an exploration mission into Zambian territory. While there, he saw locals wearing copper jewellery and evidence of copper deposits. The copper industry would later become massive in Zambia. Burnham went on to the Klondike Gold Rush, the Second Boer War, and to teach some of his tracking and scouting methods to Robert Baden-Powell, the founder of the world scouting movement.

After Zambia became independent from Britain in 1964, Kenneth Kaunda was president from 1964 all the way through to 1991. Under Kaunda, Zambia eventually became a one-party state, and Kaunda adhered to a broadly left political stance. In terms of Cold War positioning, he became a leading member of the Non-Aligned Movement. As such, it was unlikely that Zambia under Kaunda was ever going to have major links with the US military.

However, in recent years, America has had a bit more military involvement with Zambia. For instance, Zambia hosted Africa Endeavor 2013, AFRICOM's annual communications exercise, and the US has assisted the Zambian military with training for international peacekeeping missions.

Zimbabwe

The British took colonial control of what is now Zimbabwe in the late nineteenth century, and until 1965, what was then called South Rhodesia (and eventually just Rhodesia) was administered by Britain. However, in 1965, the white minority inside Rhodesia, who basically controlled the country, made a unilateral declaration of independence from Britain with the intention of avoiding majority democratic rule.

Britain rejected the declaration and asked the UN to impose sanctions on the Rhodesian government, which it did, but Britain took no military action against the country. The US government supported the UK government's position and maintained the same approach as a bitter guerrilla war broke out and two organisations, ZAPU (Zimbabwe African People's Union) and Mugabe's ZANU (Zimbabwe African National Union), that received support from other African countries and from Communist bloc countries attempted to oust the Rhodesian government.

Some American individuals did, however, travel to Rhodesia to join the Rhodesian armed forces fighting the guerrillas, and some of them died there.

In 1976, Governor Ronald Reagan announced that if he were ever elected president he would consider sending a limited number of American troops to Rhodesia to help implement a peace deal. In 1977, the US government (but not under Reagan at that time) did help Britain come up with the Anglo–American proposals to end the conflict. This eventually led to the Lancaster House peace agreement, the end of the war and the international recognition of an independent Zimbabwe. A force from Britain was sent to supervise the ceasefire, and four American Air Force planes, a C-5 Galaxy and C-141 Starlifters, flew into Zimbabwe as part of the airlift to establish the mission.

However, early American hopes of close links with the new nation eventually faded, as the United States accused Mugabe of authoritarianism and human rights abuses. Consequently, any recent military links with Zimbabwe have been of an extremely minor nature.

For instance, in June 2012, eleven African defence attachés visited AFRICOM's headquarters in Stuttgart to find out more about how AFRICOM operates. One of those defence attachés was Zimbabwean.

Conclusion

So there you have it. America has invaded, bombed or fought in not far short of half the countries of the world (countries, apart from the USA itself, that are members of the UN) and been militarily involved with all of them except Andorra, Bhutan and Liechtenstein. That's quite a track record. A track record that has involved a lot of deaths both of Americans and others, a lot of victories, a lot of defeats, and that has involved both glory and shame, honour and dishonour.

Whatever you think of America, it's an amazing country with an amazing history. Over the centuries it has come to occupy a unique place in world history. It is a country that has changed the world we live in and continues to change it, sometimes for the better, sometimes for the worse.

Nobody can predict the future either of the United States of America or of the world but of one thing we can all be pretty sure. And that is that if another edition of this book is published in a few years' time, some of the chapters will need to be significantly updated.

Appendix and Maps

From author Chris Kelly

I have in my possession a letter that is dated 17 March 1776 and was written on behalf of another ancestor of mine, Stephen Van Rensselaer. The letter was a gift from my grandmother, Georgina Van Rensselaer, of Bedford, New York. James Van Rensselaer was, at the time, a captain in the American army invading Canada. He was a leader of the New York colonial militia who fought in the American Revolution and evidently longed to go home. The letter is signed simply 'B. Arnold'.

This is the full text:

Sir [General Wooster],
Captain Van Rensselaer being anxious to go home I have permitted him to go to Montreal, until your pleasure is known. The troops who have lately arrived here are not mustered. Neither have I any person here fit for that office, that can be spared from their office.
I am your obedient servant,
B. Arnold
Camp before Quebec
March 17, 1776

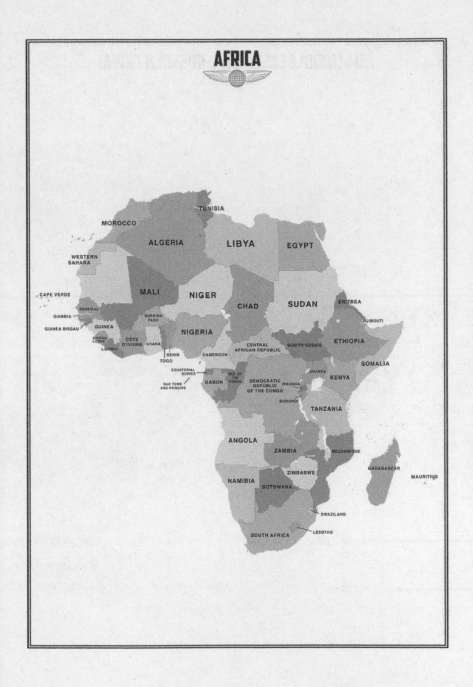

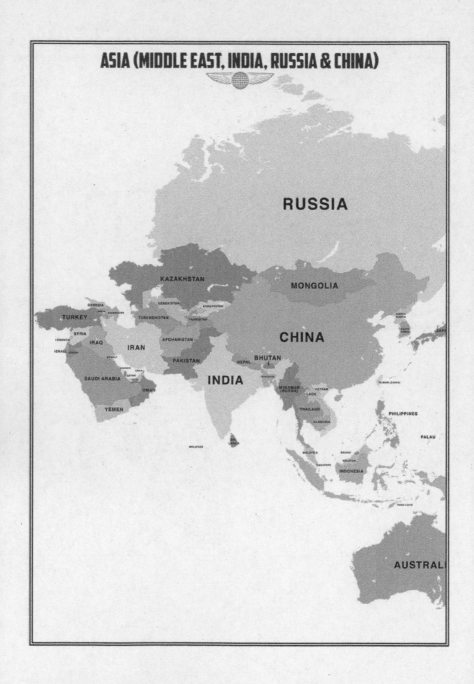

ASIA (MIDDLE EAST, INDIA, RUSSIA & CHINA)

RUSSIA

KAZAKHSTAN

MONGOLIA

GEORGIA
TURKEY
UZBEKISTAN
KYRGYZSTAN
AZERBAIJAN
TURKMENISTAN
TAJIKISTAN
SYRIA
LEBANON
AFGHANISTAN
ISRAEL JORDAN
IRAQ
IRAN
NORTH KOREA
JAPAN
SOUTH KOREA
CHINA
BAHRAIN
KUWAIT
PAKISTAN
NEPAL
BHUTAN
QATAR
SAUDI ARABIA
INDIA
TAIWAN (CHINA)
OMAN
MYANMAR (BURMA)
VIETNAM
LAOS
YEMEN
THAILAND
PHILIPPINES
CAMBODIA
PALAU
MALDIVES
SRI LANKA
MALAYSIA
BRUNEI
SINGAPORE
MALAYSIA
INDONESIA
TIMOR-LESTE

AUSTRALIA

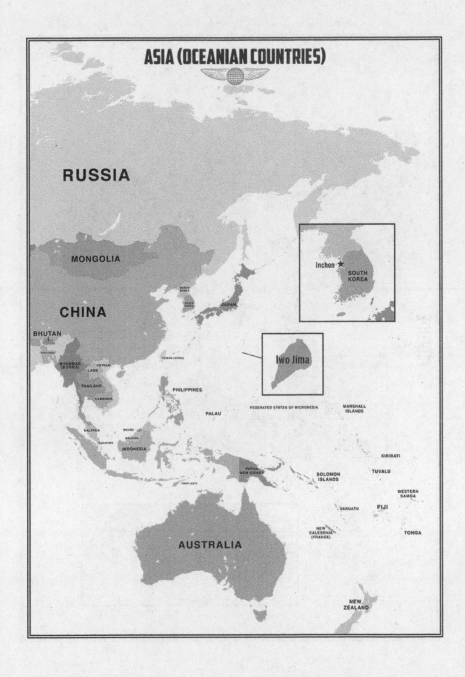

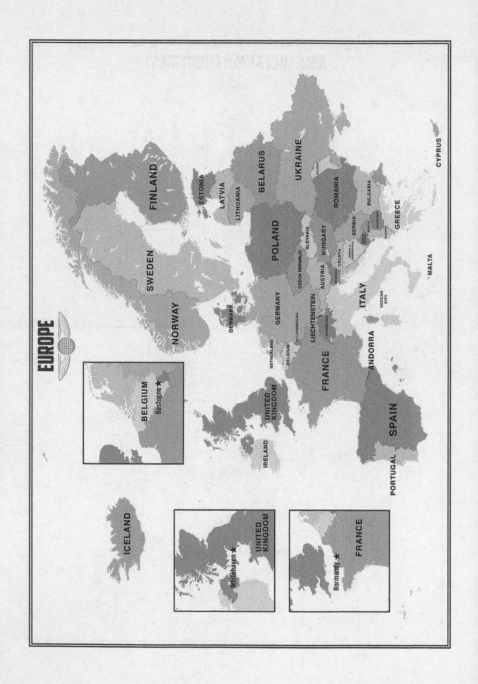

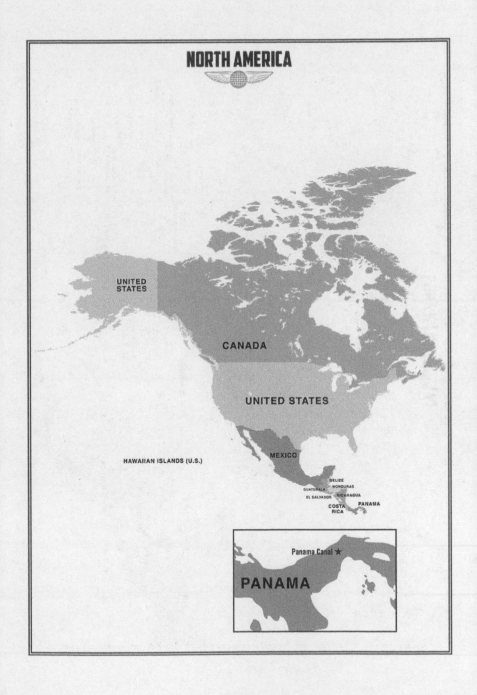

NORTH AMERICA

UNITED
STATES

CANADA

UNITED STATES

HAWAIIAN ISLANDS (U.S.)

MEXICO

BELIZE
GUATEMALA   HONDURAS
EL SALVADOR   NICARAGUA
COSTA   PANAMA
RICA

Panama Canal ★

PANAMA

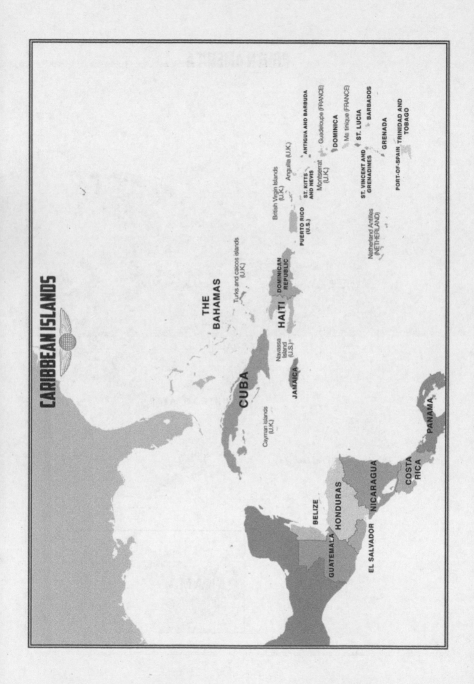

Defining whether a country has been invaded, bombed or fought in by America can be somewhat subjective. For instance, should the replacement of British occupation troops in Iceland by American troops be defined as an invasion? Should an accidental incursion be defined as an invasion? And obviously US use of Special Forces represents a particular problem in this context. In some instances it is hard to be certain whether they were present or not, and even where it is certain they were present, it can be hard to know whether their role was genuinely restricted to training or involved actual combat.

Country	Invaded, Bombed, or Fought In	Military Involvement
Afghanistan	Yes	Yes
Albania	Yes	Yes
Algeria	Yes	Yes
Andorra	No	No
Angola	No	Yes
Antigua and Barbuda	No	Yes
Argentina	No	Yes
Armenia	No	Yes
Australia	No	Yes
Austria	Yes	Yes
Azerbaijan	No	Yes
The Bahamas	Yes	Yes
Bahrain	No	Yes
Bangladesh	No	Yes
Barbados	No	Yes
Belarus	No	Yes
Belgium	Yes	Yes
Belize	No	Yes
Benin	No	Yes

Country	Invaded, Bombed, or Fought In	Military Involvement
Bhutan	No	No
Bolivia	No	Yes
Bosnia and Herzegovina	Yes	Yes
Botswana	No	Yes
Brazil	Yes	Yes
Brunei	Yes	Yes
Bulgaria	Yes	Yes
Burkina Faso	No	Yes
Burma	Yes	Yes
Burundi	No	Yes
Cambodia	Yes	Yes
Cameroon	No	Yes
Canada	Yes	Yes
Cape Verde	No	Yes
Central African Republic	No	Yes
Chad	No	Yes
Chile	No	Yes
China	Yes	Yes
Colombia	Yes	Yes
Comoros	Yes	Yes
Costa Rica	Yes	Yes
Croatia	Yes	Yes
Cuba	Yes	Yes
Cyprus	No	Yes
Czech Republic	Yes	Yes
Democratic Republic of the Congo	No	Yes
Denmark	Yes	Yes

Country	Invaded, Bombed, or Fought In	Military Involvement
Djibouti	No	Yes
Dominica	No	Yes
Dominican Republic	Yes	Yes
Ecuador	No	Yes
Egypt	Yes	Yes
El Salvador	No	Yes
Equatorial Guinea	No	Yes
Eritrea	No	Yes
Estonia	No	Yes
Ethiopia	No	Yes
Fiji	No	Yes
Finland	No	Yes
France	Yes	Yes
Gabon	No	Yes
The Gambia	No	Yes
Georgia	No	Yes
Germany	Yes	Yes
Ghana	No	Yes
Greece	Yes	Yes
Grenada	Yes	Yes
Guatemala	Yes	Yes
Guinea	No	Yes
Guinea-Bissau	No	Yes
Guyana	No	Yes
Haiti	Yes	Yes
Honduras	Yes	Yes
Hungary	Yes	Yes

Country	Invaded, Bombed, or Fought In	Military Involvement
Iceland	No	Yes
India	No	Yes
Indonesia	Yes	Yes
Iran	Yes	Yes
Iraq	Yes	Yes
Ireland	Yes	Yes
Israel	No	Yes
Italy	Yes	Yes
Ivory Coast	Yes	Yes
Jamaica	No	Yes
Japan	Yes	Yes
Jordan	No	Yes
Kazakhstan	No	Yes
Kenya	No	Yes
Kiribati	Yes	Yes
Kosovo	Yes	Yes
Kuwait	Yes	Yes
Kyrgyzstan	No	Yes
Laos	Yes	Yes
Latvia	No	Yes
Lebanon	Yes	Yes
Lesotho	No	Yes
Liberia	Yes	Yes
Libya	Yes	Yes
Liechtenstein	No	No
Lithuania	No	Yes
Luxembourg	Yes	Yes

Country	Invaded, Bombed, or Fought In	Military Involvement
Macedonia	Yes	Yes
Madagascar	No	Yes
Malawi	No	Yes
Malaysia	Yes	Yes
The Maldives	No	Yes
Mali	No	Yes
Malta	No	Yes
The Marshall Islands	Yes	Yes
Mauritania	No	Yes
Mauritius	No	Yes
Mexico	Yes	Yes
Micronesia	Yes	Yes
Moldova	No	Yes
Monaco	Yes	Yes
Mongolia	No	Yes
Montenegro	Yes	Yes
Morocco	Yes	Yes
Mozambique	No	Yes
Namibia	No	Yes
Nauru	Yes	Yes
Nepal	No	Yes
Netherlands	Yes	Yes
New Zealand	No	Yes
Nicaragua	Yes	Yes
Niger	No	Yes
Nigeria	No	Yes
North Korea	Yes	Yes

Country	Invaded, Bombed, or Fought In	Military Involvement
Norway	Yes	Yes
Oman	No	Yes
Pakistan	Yes	Yes
Palau	Yes	Yes
Panama	Yes	Yes
Papua New Guinea	Yes	Yes
Paraguay	Yes	Yes
Peru	No	Yes
Philippines	Yes	Yes
Poland	Yes	Yes
Portugal	No	Yes
Qatar	No	Yes
Republic of the Congo	No	Yes
Romania	Yes	Yes
Russia	Yes	Yes
Rwanda	No	Yes
Samoa	Yes	Yes
San Marino	Yes	Yes
São Tomé and Príncipe	No	Yes
Saudi Arabia	No	Yes
Senegal	No	Yes
Serbia	Yes	Yes
Seychelles	No	Yes
Sierra Leone	No	Yes
Singapore	Yes	Yes
Slovakia	Yes	Yes
Slovenia	Yes	Yes

Country	Invaded, Bombed, or Fought In	Military Involvement
Solomon Islands	Yes	Yes
Somalia	Yes	Yes
South Africa	No	Yes
South Korea	Yes	Yes
South Sudan	No	Yes
Spain	No	Yes
Sri Lanka	No	Yes
St Kitts and Nevis	No	Yes
St Lucia	No	Yes
St Vincent and the Grenadines	No	Yes
Sudan	Yes	Yes
Suriname	No	Yes
Swaziland	No	Yes
Sweden	No	Yes
Switzerland	No	Yes
Syria	Yes	Yes
Tajikistan	No	Yes
Tanzania	No	Yes
Thailand	Yes	Yes
Timor-Leste	Yes	Yes
Togo	No	Yes
Tonga	No	Yes
Trinidad and Tobago	No	Yes
Tunisia	Yes	Yes
Turkey	No	Yes
Turkmenistan	No	Yes
Tuvalu	No	Yes

Country	Invaded, Bombed, or Fought In	Military Involvement
Uganda	No	Yes
Ukraine	No	Yes
United Arab Emirates	No	Yes
United Kingdom	Yes	Yes
Uruguay	No	Yes
Uzbekistan	No	Yes
Vanuatu	No	Yes
Vatican City	No	Yes
Venezuela	No	Yes
Vietnam	Yes	Yes
Yemen	Yes	Yes
Zambia	No	Yes
Zimbabwe	No	Yes
Subtotal invasions/military involvement	84	191
Subtotal no invasions/military involvement	110	3
Total countries	194	

About the Authors

Christopher Kelly is the former Chairman of Chyron Corporation and a retired television executive. He has had a lifelong passion for military history, and many of his family have fought in previous American wars including one, Stephen Van Rensselaer of New York, who led an ill-fated invasion of Canada. He is a graduate of the University of California at Berkeley.

Stuart Laycock has a degree from Cambridge University. He has worked in advertising, marketing and TV. Stuart has authored or co-authored a number of history books in the UK, including *All the Countries We've Ever Invaded and the Few We Never Got Round To*.